A.P. Giddy

New World of Knowledge

New World of Knowledge

Science and Invention

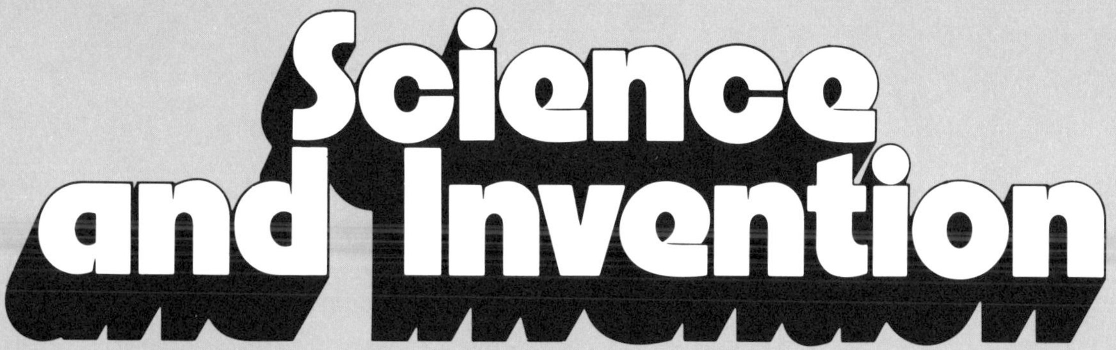

Compiled and edited by Kenneth Bailey

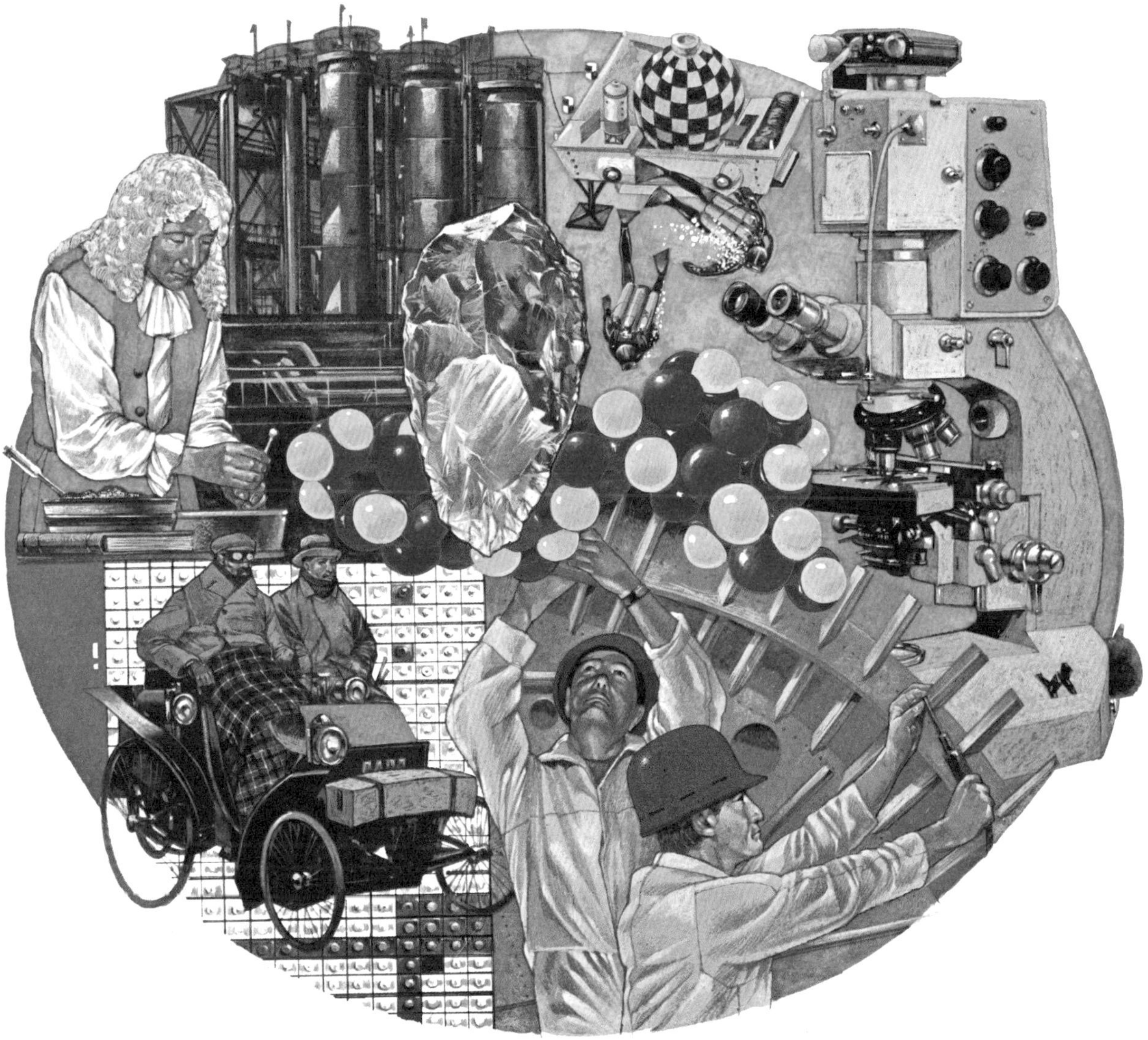

Collins

Glasgow and London

Written by David Roberts

Designed by Richard Hook

Illustrated by Fred Anderson, Max Ansell, C. J. Ashford, Gordon Davies, Ronald Embleton, The Garden Studio, Harry Green, Peter Griffin, Nicolas Hall, Halligan and Raby, Trevor Holder, Richard Hook, Angus McBride, David Nash, Peter North, Kenneth Ody, Edward Osmond, Bill Robertshaw, Richard Sherrington, Gwen Simpson, John Smith, George Thompson

First published 1974

Published by William Collins Sons and Company Limited, Glasgow and London

Printed in Great Britain

ISBN 0 00 106163 1

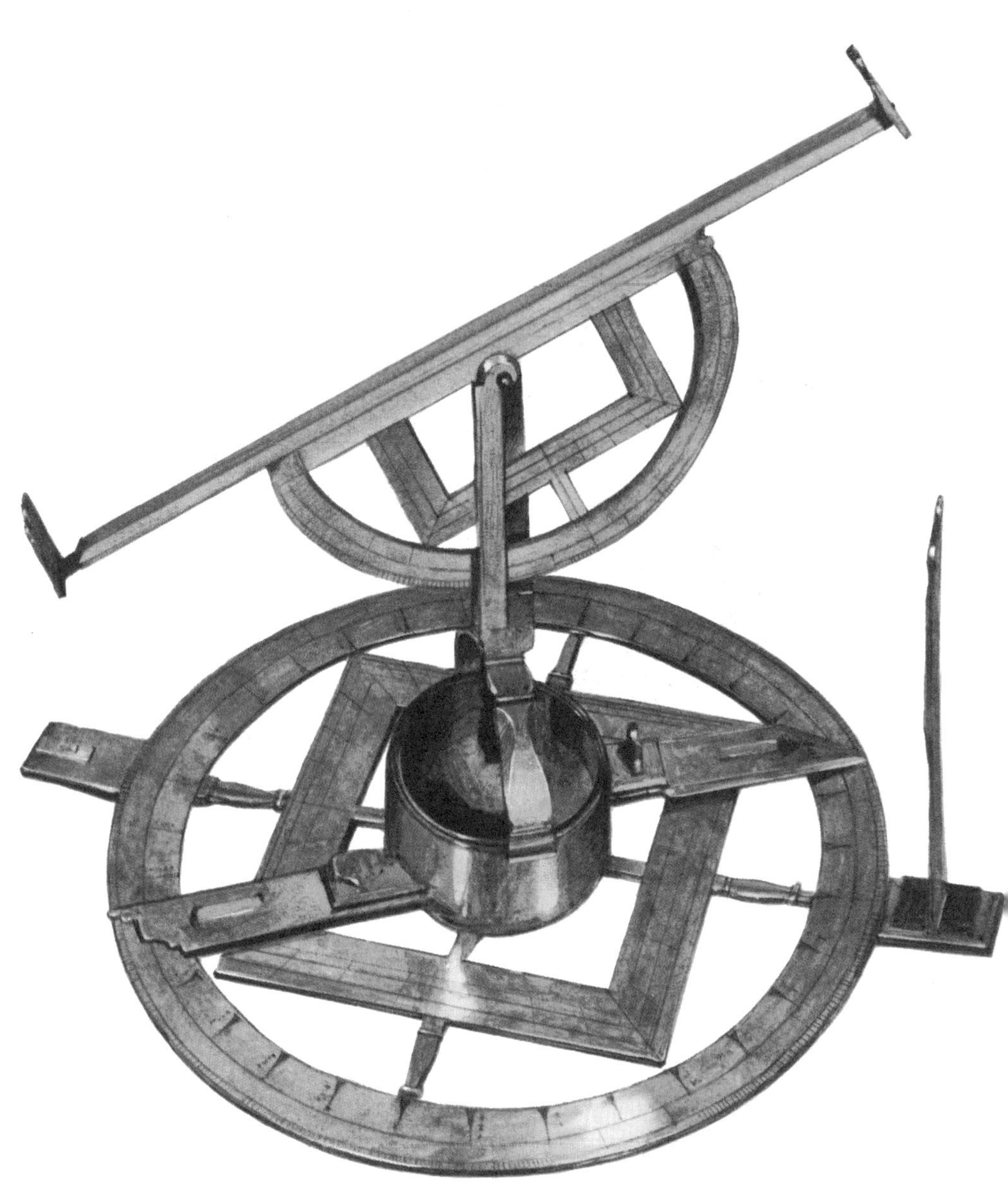

Contents

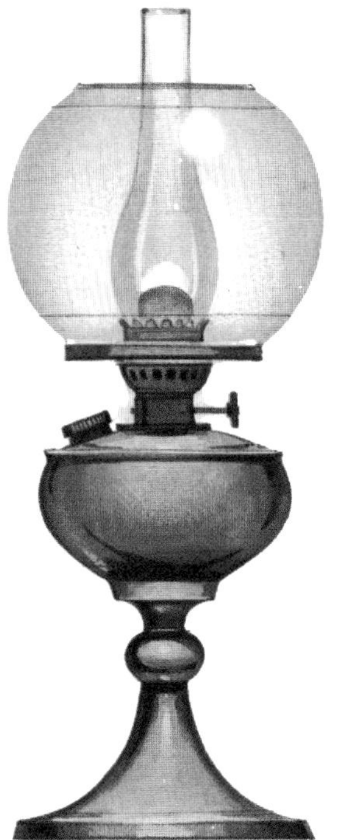

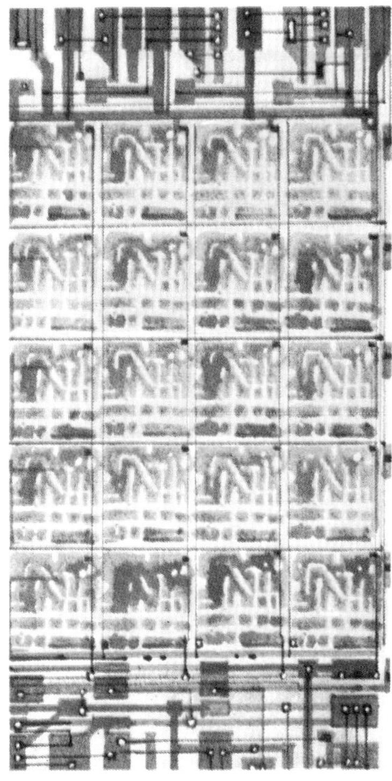

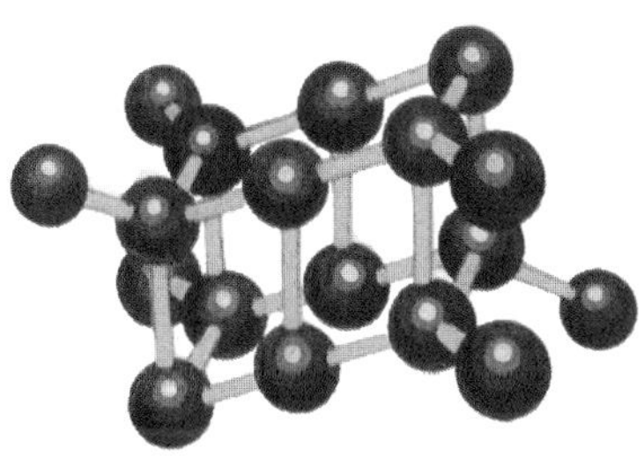

ARMY

The Growth of Unde

The most important ability that distinguishes man from the other animals is his inventiveness, a combination of the skill of hand and brain. During the millions of years of evolution, animals have developed parts of their bodies to perform remarkable tasks. Birds use their beaks not only to gather food, but to construct finely engineered nests. Beavers use their chisel-sharp teeth to fell and trim trees for the building of their lodges. Within their own bodies, spiders manufacture silk for their webs. But these are specialised skills, peculiar to the species. The hand that man inherited from his tree-dwelling ancestors is adapted not only to perform the most intricate tasks, but to construct tools to make those tasks easier. After use, a tool can be discarded and a different one taken up for the next job. The ability to manufacture different tools for different purposes has made man the most adaptable of creatures.

Man the Inventor

This ability suggests a greater brain power than other animals possess. In a primitive sense, some animals do make use of tools. Some birds use twigs to poke out insects from the crevices in tree bark. Wild chimpanzees have been observed shaping grass blades and stems to look for termites in ant hills. A captive chimpanzee called Sultan discovered how to chew a point in one stick and insert it into the end cavity of a length of bamboo, thus making a longer pole for reaching bananas hung beyond his reach. But such abilities require a comparatively simple thinking process. The materials, the stick and the length of bamboo, are to hand. The reward, the banana, is in sight. The problem can be solved on the spot.

True inventiveness requires the ability to visualise future circumstances based on experience and memory, to devise a plan to deal with those circumstances and to construct tools to carry out the plan. Man's inventive genius could not have made progress without imagination and the power to communicate with others of his kind.

If one is naked and shivering with the cold and yet sees a furry animal apparently oblivious to wind and rain, it requires some imagination to conceive the idea of robbing the animal of its fur and wrapping it around oneself. Yet one man can do it, one man can be the sole inventor of fur clothing.

But to take the fibres of the animal's fur and spin them between the fingers into a yarn, to change its form entirely, then to invent a way of knotting the yarn, to make knitting needles to aid in the knotting process, to construct a garment from the knitting requires considerable imagination. To invent other machines to harness the power to operate the knitting machine, all this has required the imagination of many men. Without each man's ability to communicate his progress to the next, the long process could never have been achieved. The invention of language helped men to pass on their ideas and discuss them. The invention of writing made it possible to record ideas and preserve them for future generations. The invention of printing made these records available to everyone.

World-wide communication was not always available. The earliest inventions were conceived over and over again, quite independently in scattered

standing

and isolated communities. Progress at first was extremely slow, though it gathered momentum faster in some areas than others.

New Ideas

Prehistoric man was eager to adopt new ideas that would make his harsh life easier. As he followed the migrations of the great herds of animals, he would meet other men with better tools and weapons. Where he settled down to farm the land in certain areas, he would not lose his curiosity about his neighbours. In time, when the most progressive and inventive people were able to produce more of some things than they needed for their own use, they would try to exchange them for other things they lacked. Trade routes were established. Envy of its prosperity would impel one tribe to invade the territory of another, and then the invaders would often adopt what was most useful in the culture of the defeated people. Throughout his history, man has been on the move and his various cultures have mingled.

With the end of the last Ice Age, about ten thousand years ago, the melting ice raised the level of the sea so that certain land masses were cut off from others and communication between them became difficult. The whole of North and South America was cut off from Asia by the Bering Strait. When the continent was 're-discovered' by explorers in the 14th and 15th centuries, some people were found to be still living in the Stone Age, others had reached the stage of an ancient Egyptian culture, yet nowhere had the wheel or the alphabet been invented. Similarly backward people were found in Australasia and the islands of the Pacific. Even today, pockets of Stone Age people are being discovered in remote jungle areas, although few can hope to escape the influence of the western world.

Man has emerged from the darkness of his primitive life into the light of continual discovery. In the beginning he constructed simple tools, materials and instruments to help him hunt for food, build a home and make clothes. As time went by, his ambition spurred on his inventiveness, and so fire, the wheel, the ship, the steam pump and the jet engine were discovered. This chart traces the principal milestones of man's scientific achievement. So long as man exists his story of discovery will no doubt continue into the future.

Throughout Asia, India, Europe and Northern Africa, however, communication was more or less constantly maintained. It was in these areas that man advanced most rapidly and was most inventive. This advance and the prosperity it brought, eased the burden of providing the necessities of food and warmth. Some men could specialise. The craftsman and the artist appeared, as did the specialist inventor. Some men could use their imagination to ponder on the nature of the universe they inhabited. Some used it to fill in the gaps in their knowledge with myths, allegories and just plain guesswork.

Study and Experiment

We must all study the past to a certain extent in order to understand the present. The scientist must study the past and verify the facts by experiment. He must then correct the mistakes of his predecessors. With his new knowledge and the latest tools, he must then use his imagination to advance into the future.

This first part of our story traces the early development of technology, that is invention and the use of tools, instruments and machinery. It reaches the point when the first rules of a modern scientific method of experimentation were laid down, and when civilised man first began to understand the patterns of the universe and the forces that move it.

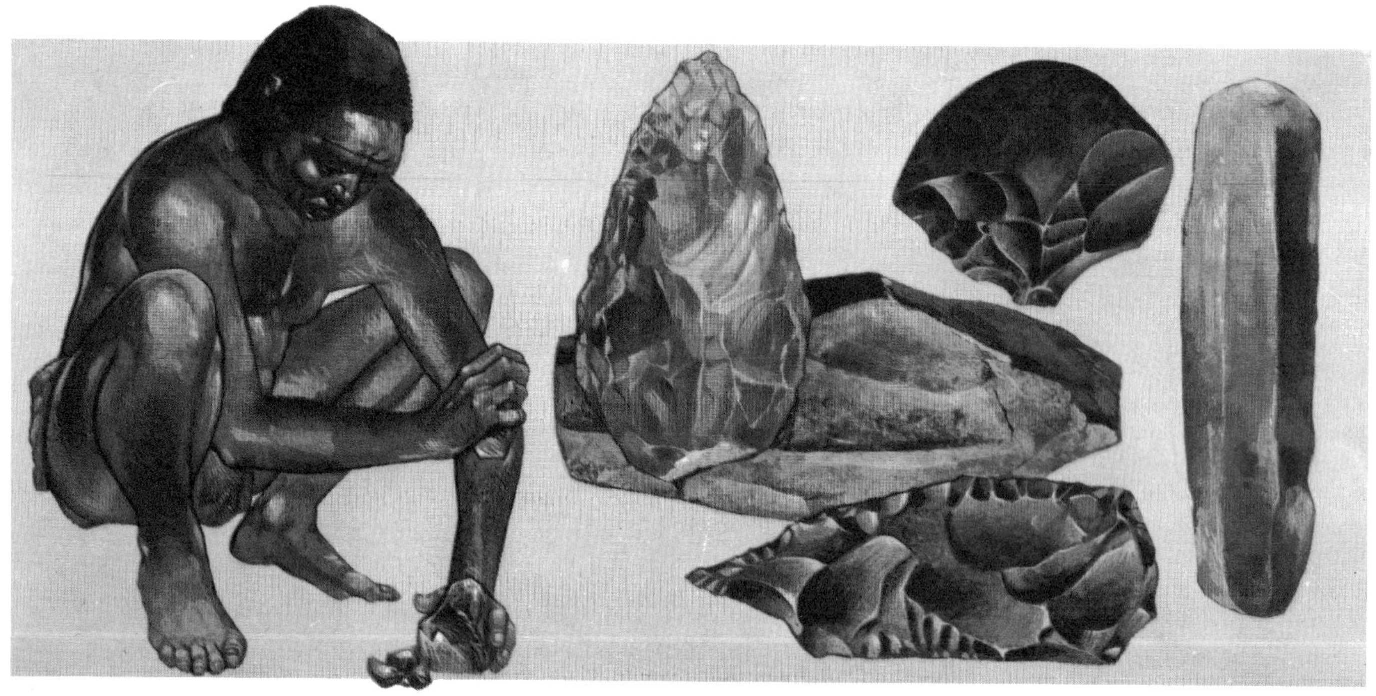

The Toolmakers

Early man began to shape his future as he learned to make hand-tools (above) by chipping flakes from flint-stones. The bow drill (below) was used to bore holes and to produce fire through friction.

At the time of writing, the oldest, undoubtedly manufactured tools are those found in 1969 by Richard Leakey at East Rudolf in northern Kenya. They have been dated by modern scientific methods as being two million six hundred thousand years old. They are the type known as pebble-tools. A more or less smoothly-rounded pebble has flakes knocked off in two directions to make a sharp edge. Such an edge can be used for cutting, chopping and scraping.

The creature who made such tools was unlike any human being living in the world today. He was about 1·2 metres (4 feet) tall, the height of a modern pygmy, but his skull was shaped more like an ape's. He had a body somewhat like a man's, however, and walked or ran on his hind legs, leaving his hands free to carry tools, spears or clubs. Living in a warm climate, he wore no clothes and seems not to have used fire. His diet of small animals and perhaps roots and berries was eaten raw. His stone tools were used for cutting up his meat and splitting the bones to get at the tasty marrow within. He and his like have been extinct for about a million years. Because he used tools of his own manufacture, he has been named Handy Man.

The Development of Man

The long and slow process of evolution does not develop a species in one descending line. Frequently, there are side branches which die out because, for one reason or another, they have not become sufficiently adapted for survival. Alongside the doomed Handy Man, there developed a taller creature with a much larger brain and more pliant and adaptable hands. His face remained rather ape-like with a thick ridge of bone over the eyes, a wide, flat nose and large, almost chinless jaw. This creature is known as Erect Man and is the inventor of the hand-axe.

The Hand-axe

For hundreds of thousands of years, the hand-axe was the universal tool. Though Erect Man appears to have originated in Africa, his descendants moved into Europe and Asia, taking the hand-axe with them. Its use spread over one-fifth of the world's land surface.

To make a hand-axe, a lump of stone, usually flint or quartzite, was chipped into a roughly almond shape with a point at one end and sharp wedges on either side of the point. The end opposite the point was rounded for holding in the hand. With this tool, our ancestors could stab and chop, cut and scrape. With the passing of hundreds of thousands of years, it was refined into a work of art.

At first, the stone to be made into a tool was held in the hand or against the knee and flakes knocked off it by striking with another stone. Some show signs of a third stone being used on the ground as an anvil. Later, it was

discovered that more accurate flaking could be achieved by striking the tool-stone with a stick or cylindrical piece of bone. Later still, a wood or bone punch was used, either struck with a hammer-stone, or simply by pressing down on the punch with the tool-maker's weight. Very fine flakes could be removed by this method, known as pressure-flaking.

How do we know all this? There are two ways of finding out about our prehistoric ancestors. One is by examining the stone tools they left behind and by trying out different methods of copying them. The other is by observing the primitive people who have been discovered in isolated parts of the modern world. This latter method must be treated with caution, since there were many stages in our evolution before Erect Man developed the brain and general characteristics of the most primitive modern man.

Peking Man

From a time before the appearance of Erect Man until about ten thousand years ago, the earth went through a series of changes in climate called the Ice Ages. There were four of these Ice Ages, each lasting tens of thousands of years, when the north polar ice advanced into Europe and Asia. In caves near the village of Choukoutien, south-west of Peking, teeth, skulls and other bones of about forty specimens of Erect Man have been discovered. With them were their stone tools and the bones of animals, some charred with fire. All these discoveries were found to date back to the end of the second Ice Age, about 350,000 years ago.

Fire became man's most precious possession, giving heat, light and protection from wild animals.

Peking Man was not as advanced as his African cousin in the manufacture of hand-axes. But he seems to have overcome the fear most wild animals have for fire, and learned how to produce it. This and his choice of a cave to lie in was presumably brought about by the severity of the winters so far north at that period. Animal bones found with him indicate that Peking Man was an accomplished hunter. No doubt his mastery of fire helped him. Flaming torches could be used to drive his prey into traps or over precipices, and fire would be a defence against carnivores (flesh-eating animals).

To discover how fire was first made, we can study only the methods used by primitive people in modern times. A pointed stick rubbed to and fro in a groove in a flat piece of wood will produce sufficient heat from the friction to set fire to the dust which in turn ignites the kindling. A wooden stick revolved in a hole in another piece of wood has the same effect. At some time, it was discovered that the stick could have a bowstring wrapped around it and the bow worked to and fro to turn the stick. Thus the first lathe was invented. Flint struck against a lump of iron ore found in its natural state will produce a spark, an early method still in use today. Once obtained, fire is treated as a precious thing by primitive people, smouldering tinder being carried about from camp site to camp site.

With the mastery of fire-making, cooking would follow, most probably as an accidental discovery. Ape-like man, like his modern descendant, did not have the long, flesh-tearing teeth of other carnivores. He would find his meat easier to chew after baking or roasting. Cooking meat destroys much of the salt content without which no animal can live. Our ancestors must have observed vegetarian animals at a salt-lick and followed their example. Obtaining salt has always been an important feature in the survival of man throughout his long history and marks the beginning of the study of chemistry.

The Uses of Fire

Erect Man, and perhaps Handy Man before him, must have used the wooden spear. Fire would soon be found useful

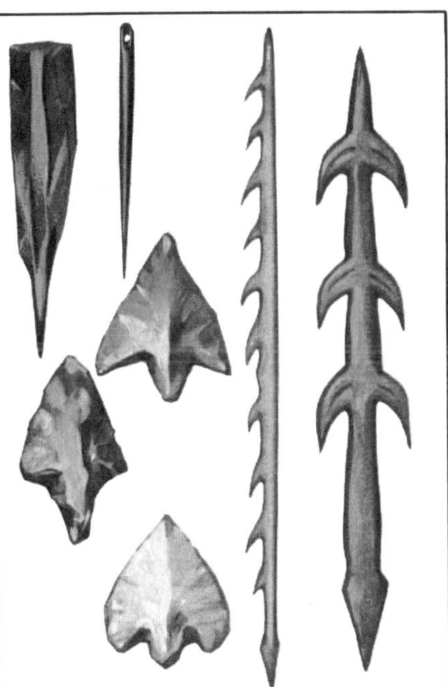

Man the hunter produced specialised weapons and tools. Pictured are bone needles, flint arrow- and spear-heads and bone harpoons (above) and (below) hand-axes, one with a bone handle.

Hunters used spear-throwers to give extra speed to the flight of weapons.

in shaping and hardening the point. It would also be used to shatter stone for the tool industry. If a rock is heated and then cold water is dashed on it, internal pressures are set up which break up the rock. The first use and manufacture of stone tools qualifies Handy Man to be our earliest known ancestor and the first inventor. Erect Man's use of fire sets the human race on its long battle for mastery of the forces of nature and makes him the first scientist.

The bolas—three stones linked by cords—was used to bring down wild animals by entangling their legs.

Neanderthal Man

The evolution of early man is not easy to follow, since there was, to begin with, no burial of the dead. What fossilised remains have been found are few and fragmentary. In Europe and Asia, the Ice Ages interrupted the migratory movements of the animal herds which the hunters followed. Some isolated species of man no doubt failed to adapt and died out. In 1856, remains of a more successful creature were discovered in a cave in Neanderthal near Dusseldorf, Germany, though the workmen who found them damaged them badly. In 1907, a whole skeleton was found buried with flint implements and food in a cave on the banks of the River Soudoire in the French district of La-Chapelle-aux-Saints. This second find confirmed the existence of a species of early man later discovered to be widespread during the last Ice Age. The fact that they buried their dead with provisions for a life in an afterworld indicates a great leap forward in imaginative power.

Neanderthal Man, as this creature has been called, practised a new method of making tools. One side of a stone was first prepared to the required shape, and then a large flake knocked off which needed little more work on it to produce the finished tool. Further flakes could be struck from the original stone so that several tools could be made from it. This marked a considerable advance in the planning and economic production of the stone-tool industry. The old type of hand-axe, the flakes from which were usually discarded, was superseded.

Decorated implements—the beginnings of art.

Neanderthal Man used fire regularly and is thought to have worn fur clothing. He used wooden spears and may have been the first to fit flint points to them. He had a brain case as large as modern man's. There was a prominent ridge of bone across his brow, and his powerful lower jaw had very little chin. His head, which was large in proportion to the size of his body, was set low on the shoulders so that he could not easily lift his head to look up. His natural stance was with knees bent forward, and his long arms would hang down like an ape's. His

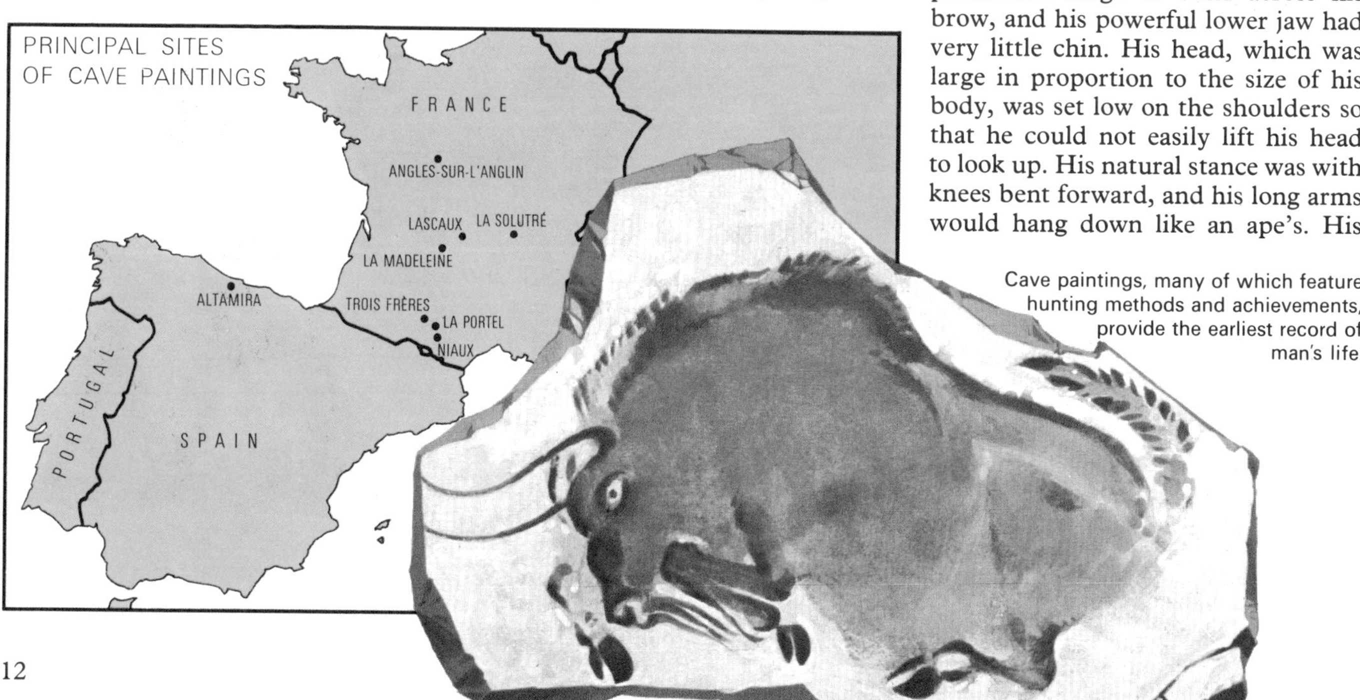

Cave paintings, many of which feature hunting methods and achievements, provide the earliest record of man's life.

or antler for the first time. Tiny blades called microliths became possible. These were used to top spears and arrows. When set in a row along a wooden stick, they formed the barbs of a harpoon or the teeth of a saw. Associated with the arrival of Modern Man in Europe are stones made perfectly spherical. Man must have discovered this to be a shape that could be thrown with greater accuracy when used as a missile. These stones gave power to his weapons with the use of a spear-thrower, a bow, a blowpipe or a sling. Man hunted reindeer, bison, horses and, in the far north, woolly mammoth.

Best of all, from our point of view, man made works of art, carvings in the round and engravings on rock walls, and later, paintings in the darkest recesses of caves where no light could reach to fade the colours. These are the first records of life in man's distant past. They show us the hunting methods employed and the huts built in the summer camps. Remains have been found of more permanent winter quarters which were pits dug in the ground and roofed with wood and turf or stone.

From his graves, his camp sites and the centres of a flint industry, we know that man had fish-hooks and net-making needles, so he must have been able to spin twine from plant fibres. We know that he could join lengths of wood together and bind arrow and spear heads on to wooden hafts. We know he had needles for sewing together fur clothing and leather containers. We know that he could model expertly in clay and make earth colours into paint. From the cave paintings, we know that he decorated himself with feathered head-dresses and made necklaces of perforated shells, boring through quite hard material. There is one painting of a man on skis, and others indicate that he must also have made use of sledges. Primitive lamps with wicks floating in animal fats or seed-oil gave him light to execute the cave paintings.

The Making of Boats

From the descendants of Modern Man who became isolated and continued their way of life even into modern times, we know how he probably constructed his boats. Where logs were plentiful, these could be hollowed out by fire and stone adzes to make dugout canoes. In marshy districts, reeds would be tied into bundles and joined to make rafts. Wooden frames would be wrapped in skins and made watertight with tar, like the age-old Welsh coracle and the Eskimo umiak.

Since the African ape-like man who had first thought of using a sharp stone for skinning and cutting his meat, perhaps five million years had passed. Slowly Modern Man evolved, the first animal to speed the rate of its own progress by the power of imagination. He was the first creature to dream of a life after death, to believe in magic, to invent language. So much did he delight in the skill of his hands that he added decoration to craft and invented art. He was set on the long road of ingenious invention and scientific discovery that was to bend nature to his will and fashion his own environment.

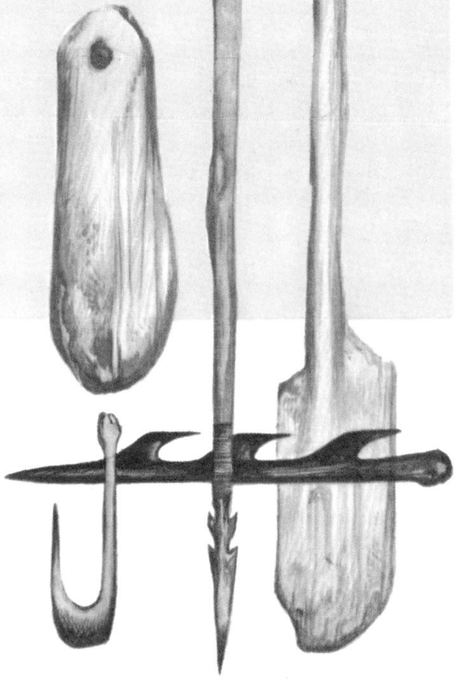

In his search for fish from dugout canoes early man was well equipped with floats, hooks, spears and paddle.

run must have been a sort of loping trot.

Contemporary with Neanderthal Man, but appearing first probably in Central Asia, was *Homo sapiens* or Modern Man. He began to replace Neanderthal Man in Europe about the end of the last Ice Age. During the 40,000 years of his spread across the world the different races we know today developed. Everywhere he survived where his forerunners became extinct, no doubt because of his superior inventiveness.

Blade-tools

A whole new range of tools was developed, produced by the use of a hammer-stone and a wooden or bone punch. This method produced long narrow flakes of stone known to archaeologists as blade-tools. With these, man learned to work in wood, and where that was scarce, to use bone

The Farmers

At the end of the last Ice Age, ten thousand years ago, no one had achieved a more sophisticated way of life than the most primitive people living in the world today. The growth of civilisation and its progress was slow. New inventions and discoveries did not spring into being overnight, any more than they do nowadays. But now we have all those years of accumulated knowledge and the elaborate machinery and instruments they have given us. Ancient Man had to move forward by a painfully slow series of trials and errors and happy accidents. Where conditions were favourable, early progress was made and continued steadily. The spread of ideas and their adaptation to harsher conditions was so gradual that northern Europe, for instance, was four thousand years behind the Near East, which has been called the cradle of civilisation.

Development of Farming

What began it all was the invention of farming, and before that could happen, the right situation had to prevail. Hunters of animal meat had long gathered other food on their wanderings, such things as edible roots, corn-grain and fruit. In order to make grain more pleasant to eat, ways were found to grind it into flour for baking into unleavened bread. Corn was ground between a flat stone and a smooth rock, and so the quern was invented. Stone blades already existed for cutting the corn and, from them, the first sickles were developed. As the grain was ripe for harvesting only at one time of the year, pits were dug in the ground for storing it. A basketwork of straw was devised to line the pits. Such grain-stores would need to be protected, so settled communities developed alongside them. The first villages are older than the first farms. Villages would naturally be found at oases, such as Jericho, where man employed primitive methods of irrigation in an attempt to improve the water supply.

It so happened that the areas where the wild wheat and wild barley flourished were the homes of the wild ancestors of goats and sheep. Settlers would capture the young animals and keep them in stockades to fatten for food. Such a close association with wild corn would teach people that the part they ate was the seed from which new plants could spring. Soon cornfields would be planted where wild corn had never grown before. Where the best seed was planted in the most fertile soil, the best crop would be obtained. With the selection of seed, preparation of the ground and improvement of the crop, the science of agriculture had begun. Weeds would be seen to choke the growth of the young plants, and to clean the land the first hoes were invented. The heaviest of these, dragged by manpower, could be called the first plough. More land would be cleared of trees, and the first mixed arable and animal farms were created.

In India and the Far East, millet was the principal crop of the first farmers. Rice, which requires more labour and therefore better community organisation, was not cultivated until about 2000 B.C. in India, from where it spread into China. In America, maize was cultivated to the point where it cannot pollinate itself without human assistance, and thus can be described as an invention of man.

Spinning and Weaving

Oil-producing plants, such as olives, sesame, the castor-oil plant and flax were grown for food as a substitute for animal fats, and to provide oil for lamps. Flax was found to contain

The early farmers in Mesopotamia and Egypt used bone sickles with flint blades (above) and hand ploughs (left).

Ancient art forms illustrate man's progress. The Greek vase shows olive gatherers; the Egyptian model (left) depicts animal power harnessed to assist ploughing.

very strong fibres that could be spun together to make yarn. The weaving of this into cloth was no doubt a development from early basket and mat making. The early hunters had used twine for many purposes, wool having long been an alternative to vegetable fibre. With their domesticated sheep and goats to provide wool, and their understanding of the cultivation of flax, the early farmers were ideally placed to develop a spinning and weaving industry.

Spinning had begun between the fingers, but now the distaff, spindle and whorl were invented. The rough fibres are attached to the distaff and a length drawn out to fasten on to the spindle which is weighted by the stone, clay or bone whorl. The whorl keeps the spindle rotating as more fibre is drawn out from the distaff. As the length of yarn grows it is wound on to the spindle.

A loom is any sort of apparatus that can stretch out the threads of the warp for the threads of the weft to be woven through them. The first looms were laid out flat on the ground as depicted on a pottery dish from Egypt dating back to 4400 B.C. Vertical looms, which were much more convenient for the weaver, who could sit in front of them, came later. Such looms had weights of stone or clay pierced with holes to keep the warp threads taut, and many of these weights have been found at ancient sites. The oldest known example of woven textile dates back to 6500 B.C. and is made of wool fibre. Vegetable fibres such as flax need to be soaked, beaten, scraped and combed before spinning. Therefore, the discovery of all these processes and the production of linen flax probably came later.

Working with Stone

The early farming communities with their new skills still used stone as the basic material for their tools. But they had learned how to drill it for the fitting of wooden handles, and how to polish it to achieve a fine, long-lasting cutting edge. The search for the best stone for the purpose led to a wide trade and to the mining of flint to satisfy it. Flint miners sank shafts into chalk hills and dug horizontal tunnels from them. Often their only tools were picks made from antlers and shovels from deers' shoulder-blades. Modern experiments have been made with such tools. Antler-picks were found not to break, though some points splintered and all became worn down with use. Shoulder-blade shovels were found to be no use for actual digging, but quite efficient for shovelling up loose chalk for loading into baskets and drawing up the main shaft to the surface. Alongside the flint mines developed a stone-axe industry from which tools were carried along trade routes covering hundreds of miles.

The early farmers who began to grow corn, peas and beans needed containers that would stand heat to cook their food. The new skills of polishing stone produced stone vessels, but these involved considerable labour. It was inevitable that pottery would be invented. The woman who built a fire on clay soil would find it baked hard when the ashes were raked away. Baskets and leather bags would suggest the shape to be given to the clay to make a vessel. At first, the shape would be achieved by starting with a coil of soft clay which could then be smoothed by hand. To make the pot waterproof, a slip of finer clay was added and polished with a pebble to close up all the pores. Bigger pots would be made in two halves to avoid sagging with their own weight during the drying process. The slip method could then be used to fix the two halves together.

Firing pottery was first done on the ordinary domestic hearth. Later, the firing was done in a sealed oven of earth which excluded the air and kept the fire smouldering and the heat in for several days. Eventually, the kiln was invented, a brick-built oven with a perforated clay floor through which the heat could reach the pots. Fire and flue provided indirect heat so that smuts and soot would not disfigure the pots. In early kilns, temperatures of 800°C were possible, creating chemical changes in the clay which makes it stronger and less porous. It was rare in those times for temperatures to be reached that would vitrify the clay and give it the glaze of modern pottery.

By selecting the best seeds and preparing the soil the early farmer improved his crop. In this way wild corn (left) became sturdier, with heavier ears (right).

The use of animal wool in spinning and weaving may have developed from the discovery that vegetable fibres could be spun together to form a yarn.

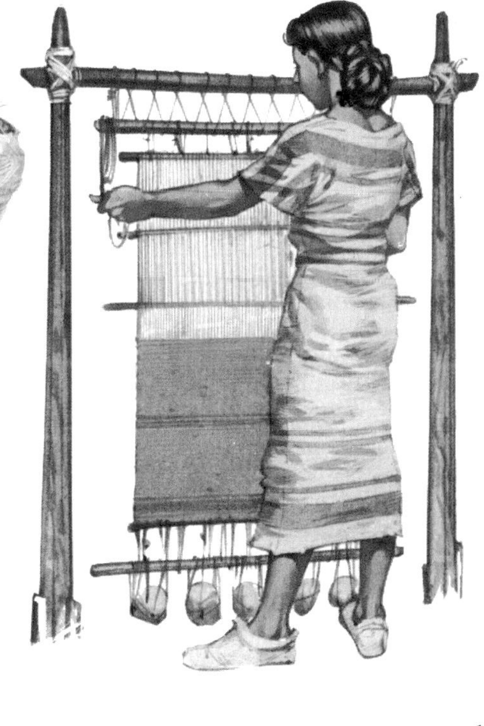

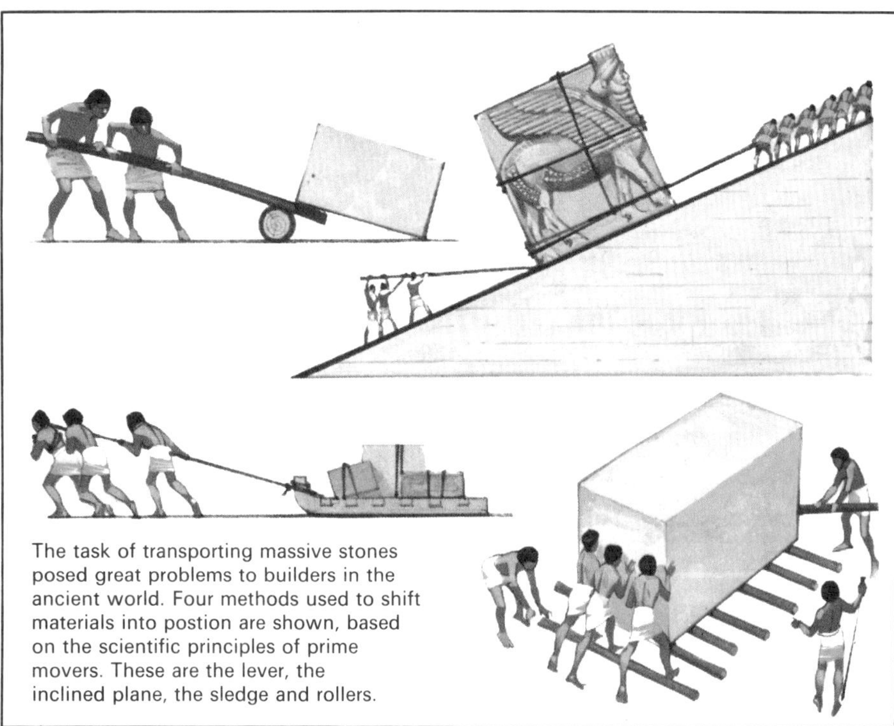

The task of transporting massive stones posed great problems to builders in the ancient world. Four methods used to shift materials into postion are shown, based on the scientific principles of prime movers. These are the lever, the inclined plane, the sledge and rollers.

The Potter's Wheel

The potter's wheel was not invented until about 3000 B.C., though there are signs on earlier Chinese pottery that a turntable was used to make the hand-shaping easier. The first wheels were mounted on a pivot which fitted into the socket of a stone. The bigger the wheel, the faster it could be spun, but the more difficult it became for the potter to reach the pot he was shaping. It seems to have taken a thousand years before another larger wheel was mounted below the first which could be turned by the potter's foot or by his assistant with the aid of an endless belt.

The invention of the potter's wheel and the wheeled sledge seem to have come about at the same time. The earliest known sketch of a sledge mounted on four solid wheels dates back to about 3500 B.C. Such wheels were cut from three planks which were clamped together with a pair of cross-struts. It is not known whether the axles turned with the wheels, though they still do on some primitive farm carts in India.

Building Materials

It has been said that the village or small town developed before farming, usually close to a place where there was a year-round supply of water. In the Near East, where there was a shortage of trees for timber, houses were built of sun-dried brick. Clay was softened with water and chopped straw or dung trodden into it. The bricks were shaped in wooden moulds open at the top and bottom, usually two bricks to each mould. These were left in the sun to dry, being turned over from time to time. They were joined together in the building with a thinner mixture of clay for mortar, and the inner walls plastered with the same material. Furniture was often built in, including benches, hearths, store-places and clay basins set in the floor of trodden mud. With the coming of pottery and the invention of the kiln, fired bricks were used, at first as roof tiles or flooring where water-proofing was important.

From the first, such towns were fortified. Jericho had town walls built of stone and at least one solid stone tower with a stairway inside it leading from a passage. In front of the tower, there was a ditch cut wide and deep into the solid limestone. At Catal Huyuk in Turkey, a town covering fourteen hectares (32 acres) was flourishing by 6800 B.C. The rooms were entered through holes in the flat roofs—reached by ladders which could be drawn up when an enemy attacked.

The Craftsman

The success of the early farmers in supplying themselves with a surplus of food freed many of them to specialise in such crafts as tool-making, pottery and building. It also collected them together in one place in sufficient numbers to organise works of massive proportions and labour. All along the Mediterranean coast to the Atlantic seaboard, they have left memorials to their ingenuity and their religious attitudes. Their tombs and sanctuaries illustrate how well they understood the principles of mechanics. Architecturally, they advanced no further than the lintel or crossbeam balanced on two uprights, the principle on which the Greek temples were built. But they achieved structures on a giant scale.

The raising of standing stones weighing many tons must have involved great labour. Such stones were

Pottery is one of the oldest crafts, brought about chiefly by man's experiments with wet, pliable clay in search of storage containers and drinking vessels. These examples show (from top to bottom) a painted jar from the Near East (c. 5000 B.C.). a cosmetic jar from the Indus Valley, an Iranian tumbler (c. 3500 B.C.) and two vessels (19th century B.C.) from Cappadocia in Asia Minor.

probably cut from the quarry by driving in wooden wedges which were afterwards wetted so that they expanded and split the stone along the grain. Rollers were used to drag the dressed stones to the place of erection. There, inclined ramps of earth were built which sloped gradually to a steep drop. The stones were dragged up the slope and tipped over the drop into pitholes dug to receive them. Once two standing stones had been placed in position, their lintel stone could be dragged up the ramp and levered into position across them. The carpenter's mortice and tenon joint was often used, with the tenon protruding from the top of the standing stones and fitting into mortice holes cut into the lintel. The principles of leverage must have been fully understood by the craftsmen before the erection of such a building could be considered.

Burial of the Dead

Tombs were built with roofed-in stone passages and chambers also made on the lintel principle and then covered over with earth. Such are the long barrows found throughout western Europe. The earliest burials were in caves, and the barrows seem to be constructed to simulate caves where they did not occur naturally. Early religious observance was connected with the ground beneath men's feet and the returning of the dead to the earth. To the farmer, however, the seasons, sunlight and rain were important. Men began to look up towards the heavenly bodies. Cremation of the dead and the burning of sacrifices which sent their smoke upwards became common practice. The passage of the sun, high in summer and low in winter, had both a practical and a religious significance. Some modern scientists believe that the standing stone rings are observatories and mathematical instruments for determining the seasons of the year, and for estimating the time to sow and the time to reap.

The anthropologist's study of the primitive societies of the world may tell us much about the domestic life of our ancient forebears. The mathematician's study of the work of the great megalith builders may tell us how man first plotted the movements of the universe and began to think of this earth's place within it.

The invention of the wheel was one of the greatest steps forward taken by man along the path of discovery. The wheel was an essential factor in the development of transport. Its use at different times in history is illustrated by the Sumerian cart (top), Egyptian chariot, Celtic chariot and 19th-century stagecoach.

The Metalworkers

The largest ancient sculpture in copper found in western Asia is this relief from the Temple of the Cow-goddess near Ur.

Sumer

The early farmers knew very little about conservation of the soil. They had not discovered the advantages of a rotation of crops or the use of a fertiliser. Their hoes and the first man-powered plough could not go very deep into the surface soil, which eventually became exhausted. They had continually to break new ground and search for new grazing for their sheep and cattle. Farming began in the high plateau regions of the Near and Middle East where there was sufficient rainfall and the climate was right for wild wheat and barley to flourish, and where the new strains could be cultivated.

Valley Farmers

A different situation prevailed in the valleys of the great rivers such as the Tigris and Euphrates in Mesopotamia and the Nile in Egypt. Here, soil nutrients were carried down by the current and spread over the land during the season of floods. So much silt was brought down by the twin rivers of the Tigris and Euphrates, that areas beneath the waters of the Persian Gulf were raised higher and higher, until patches of dry land appeared. On these, farmers settled to till the most fertile soil that had yet been cultivated.

The valley farmers met with new difficulties. There was very little rainfall in Sumer, as the people called their new land between the twin rivers. This meant that land away from the rivers was too dry for farming. Much of the land affected by the flooding every year remained too marshy. There was too little water in some places, too much in others. The Sumerians found the answer to their problem in irrigation, the draining of areas of too much water and the channelling of water to dry areas.

Irrigation Systems

The flooding of the Tigris and the Euphrates is dangerous and unpredictable. The Tigris rises first, but the Euphrates carries twice as much water and recedes more quickly. The floods end at the beginning of the hot season, so that the water dries up too soon. The irrigation system that was eventually devised was elaborate and required immense labour. The lower valleys were intersected by a series of large canals. The most famous of these was the Nahrwan, 122 metres (400 feet) wide and perhaps as much as 320 kilometres (200 miles) long. From them, the water passed into feeder-canals, and then into irrigation ditches. Finally, trickles of water could be directed into individual plots of land.

To maintain a regular flow through such a system, the level of water in the main canals had to be slightly higher than the surrounding land. The flow had to be controlled so that it would not run too fast and wear away the banks, or too slowly so that the channels would silt up. Great brick barrages and weirs were built. Brick walls and reed matting were used to strengthen the banks. The whole system was a vast undertaking.

Of course, it was not created all at once. But so fertile was the soil of Sumer and so productive each new area brought under cultivation that there was always enough to feed the vast army of workers continuously employed on extending and maintaining the irrigation system. All this required strong leaders to plan the operation and direct the workers, and centres of administration from which the leaders could operate.

The Sumerians were the first people to build permanent cities with a properly organised civil government. Since the word civilisation means the art of living in cities, it can be claimed that the Sumerians formed the first civilised communities. They were

The Sumerians built some of the first family houses. This reconstruction of a house at Ur (c. 2220 B.C.) is based on excavations.

based on the food surplus created and on the religious attitude of the time. Each city had its own personal god with his own temple at the city centre. Food surpluses were brought to the temple as offerings to the god, and the priests who controlled the temples became both the first bureaucracy and the first leisured class. Freed from the business of producing their own food, and rich enough to employ assistants to carry out the more routine administrative duties, the priests could devote themselves to planning improvements to the area controlled by their own particular god. The farmers and the irrigation workers continued to live in the country. But in cities such as Kish, and Nippur, Ur and Lagash, the specialised traders and craftsmen, the potters, the builders and the metalworkers gathered together.

Working with Metals

It is not known how or where the first working of metals began. Copper and gold occur in a more or less pure form and are soft enough to be hammered into shape without heat. Though hammering hardens the metal, copper and gold in their pure form are too soft to have much more than a decorative value. Bronze, an alloy of copper and tin, is much harder, and its wide use for axes and other tools, as well as spearheads and swordblades, gives the name Bronze Age to this period of man's scientific development. Iron, which does occur naturally on earth in the form of meteorites from outer space, was much too scarce to have a widespread use until methods of ore smelting were mastered, a discovery attributed to the Hittites around 1200 B.C.

Ores are metals in chemical combination with other elements. Malachite, a green carbonate of copper, seems a likely candidate for having been the first ore to be smelted to extract the metal. Malachite occurs fairly widely in the Middle East, and from about 5000 B.C. was used as a pigment, especially as a cosmetic for painting the lower eyelid. A little malachite dropped into a fiercely burning wood fire would produce a bead of copper. Such a chance discovery would lead to experiments in smelting other ores. Since copper ores and oxides of tin occur naturally together, the accidental smelting of a mixture of the two would produce a form of bronze. The superior hardness and durability of this metal would

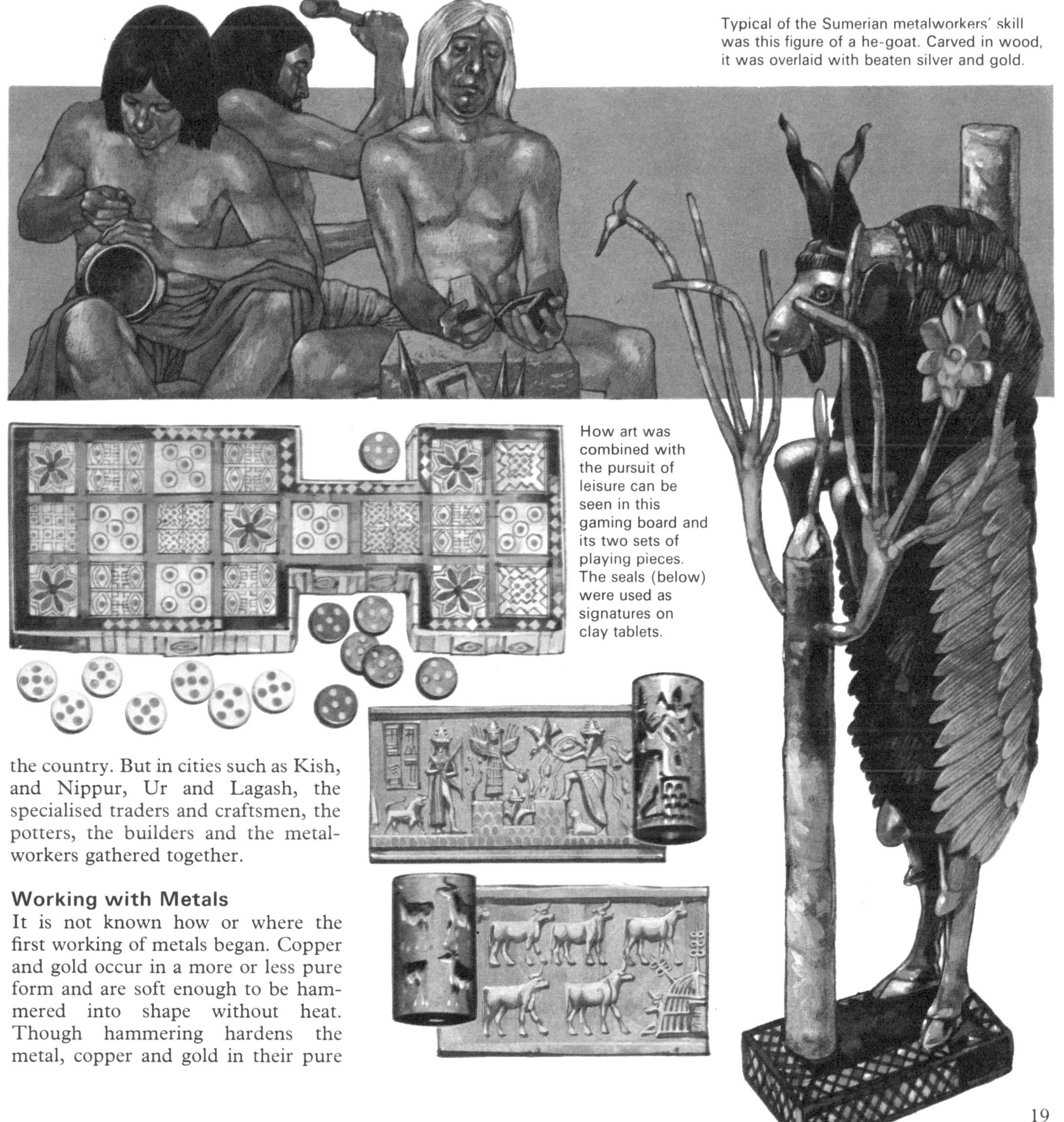

Typical of the Sumerian metalworkers' skill was this figure of a he-goat. Carved in wood, it was overlaid with beaten silver and gold.

How art was combined with the pursuit of leisure can be seen in this gaming board and its two sets of playing pieces. The seals (below) were used as signatures on clay tablets.

soon be discovered, and an ideal balance of about 90% copper to 10% tin eventually became the most widespread metal alloy in use. Yet it remained expensive, and stone tools continued in use throughout the Bronze Age. Only with the beginning of the Iron Age, and the smelting of iron ore, were cheap metal tools available to everyone.

Discoveries in the royal cemetery of Ur in Sumer show that by 2500 B.C. all but half a dozen of the metalworking processes used nowadays were well understood. Yet Sumer had no metal ores, no flint for stone tools and no building stone. Apart from the palm tree there was no timber. All the raw materials needed by Sumerian craftsmen had to be imported. Timber came from the mountains of the north-east. Stone and copper came from the Persian Gulf. The ancient name for the Euphrates river was the Urudu or copper river, indicating how the ore was delivered to the cities of Sumer. Silver and lead came from the Taurus mountains of Turkey, tin from as far north as Europe, and semi-precious stones from Afghanistan.

Pupils at a Sumerian school learn to read and write under the watchful eye of their tutors.

Early Ploughs

All this trade was made possible by the wealth created by the fertile soil of the river valleys and the irrigation system that had brought it under cultivation. The Sumerian farmer improved his productivity by his inventiveness. The ox-drawn plough appeared. The hoe had been designed for manpower, the yoke to ease the burden for women. Now the pole at the front of the plough was lengthened and yoked between a pair of oxen. Handles were fitted at the back so that the point could be driven deeper into the ground, and the soil more thoroughly broken up. The seed drill, a light ox-drawn plough that dug a furrow into which seed was fed through a funnel, was invented. In later years, this useful machine was forgotten and had to be 're-invented' in England by Jethro Tull in the late 18th century A.D. The ass, long a beast of burden, was harnessed for the first time to a wheeled cart. Honey bees were persuaded to make their homes in straw skeps so that the production of honey, the universal sweetener of the times, could be industrialised.

Sumerian Invention

In the cities the craftsmen of Sumer, as well as mastering the arts of metalwork, discovered the salt-glazing of pottery and ornaments. They glazed beads with soda and even made solid glass objects. From the quern, they developed the pestle and mortar, and they invented the sieve. They made the first lime kilns for expelling carbon dioxide from limestone or chalk, to produce lime for plastering their walls. They built houses of two or three storeys with kitchens, lavatories, workrooms, servants' quarters, guest and living rooms, with wooden balconies at each level and staircases overlooking an inner courtyard. They constructed harbours and quays for loading and unloading their cargo ships. They built huge temples for their city gods, like the Ziggurat at Ur, home of the moon-god Nanna. They have left us the earliest known map of a city, inscribed on a clay tablet.

This clay tablet (c. 3500 B.C.) bears picture symbols which became cuneiform writing.

The Art of Writing

All this required an administrative organisation of a high order. The Sumerians had to establish a civil service to collect the tribute due to the god and to keep records of what had been received. They had to invent writing. To begin with they used pictures. For instance, a picture of a cow's head with a number of dots beside it would indicate that that number of cattle had been collected. As time went on, the pictures developed into mere symbols, stamped in the clay with the end of a wedge-shaped reed. This developed into the characteristic wedge-shaped or cuneiform writing of Sumer. Later still, the symbols stood for sounds of individual syllables, just as our word 'pantry' might be written with the symbol for a pan and the symbol for a tree. In Sumerian, there were about 600 such symbols to learn. Scribes had to wait for another couple of thousand years before the Phoenicians developed the first modern alphabet of only 22 consonants. Yet Sumerians not only kept records, but invented literature

The Sumerians were keen musicians. This silver lyre (c. 2600 B.C.) is reconstructed from remains found at Ur.

by writing down their own myths and legends, such as the first story of a great flood and the building of an ark by Ziusudra, the Sumerian Noah.

Arithmetic was invented in Sumer. Though we count in tens and hundreds, the Sumerians counted in sixties. From them we get the division of our hours and minutes into sixties, and the method of dividing a circle into six times 60 or 360 degrees. They measured lengths in cubits, and had a system of weights. They worked out a calendar, based on the phases of the moon, so that the year was divided into twelve months with some odd days left over. The moon has four quarters into which the month was divided giving us the origin of our seven-day week. The creation of a calendar gave the priest-scientists an interest in the stars. Theirs was the first recorded study of astronomy. The Sumerians were fond of music. They made trumpets, horns and flutes, harps and lyres, timbrels, clappers and drums. They founded the first boys' schools, run by teacher-priests.

The Akkadians

The very success of the Sumerian city civilisation brought about their downfall. Semites, nomadic tribes who were the ancestors of the modern Arabs and Jews, began to settle in an area north of Sumer which they called Akkadia. The Sumerians had never formed themselves into a nation. Each city maintained its own army, and city warred against city. Eventually, weakened perhaps by too much good living, the Sumerian cities fell one by one to attacks from the Akkadians, until all of Sumer became subject to them about 2400 B.C.

The Akkadians were a more backward people than the Sumerians, but they soon adopted the technologies of their new subjects. Under their leader Sargon, they carved out the first empire, which stretched from the Persian Gulf to the shores of the Mediterranean. About 1750 B.C. a later Semitic Emperor, Hammurabi, succeeded to control of this empire which henceforward became known as Babylonia.

The advances made by the Sumerians were not all lost. In fact, the conquered people civilised the conquerors who took to living in cities. Babylon, with its canals, its fine buildings and its famous hanging gardens, became one of the greatest cities of its age.

The Sumerians had a system of weights and studied mathematics and astronomy.

Working the shaduf—part of the irrigation system.

Egypt

The situation in the enclosed valley of the Nile was different from the open plain between the Tigris and the Euphrates. The creation of the great civilisation of ancient Egypt happened more slowly but it lasted longer. The Egyptians were somewhat behind the Sumerians in technological progress, but they did something the Sumerians never managed. They created the first nation.

The 1,200 kilometres (750 miles) between the Mediterranean Sea in the north and the first cataract on the Nile at Aswan is naturally divided into two distinct regions. In the north, the river for its last hundred miles or so fans out into a number of tributaries which create the marshy delta known as Lower Egypt. South of this, the river flows between high cliffs with a narrow strip of fertile land between them known as Upper Egypt. Every year the river floods, spreading a rich silt over this narrow strip.

The first farmers who settled along the banks of the Nile from about 8000 B.C. fled from the floods each season and returned to plant their crops when the waters had subsided. But like the people of Sumer, they slowly began to control the floods by digging irrigation ditches. Little by little villages were established and quarrels broke out between one village and the next about land boundaries and water rights. Slowly, the stronger villages subdued their weaker neighbours, forming themselves into districts or nomes as they were called. Eventually, the nomes were welded into two kingdoms of Upper and Lower Egypt. At last, a king of Upper Egypt, whose name was probably Narmer, conquered the northern kingdom about 3100 B.C. King Narmer built his capital of this, the world's first nation, at Memphis on the border between the two kingdoms.

Ancient Wonders

Though there were intermediate periods of internal strife and foreign conquest, for nearly 3,000 years ancient Egypt flourished under 30 dynasties of its pharaohs. Protected on either side by mountains and desert, and in the north by the sea, they lived for much of this time in comparative peace. They were able to create some of the greatest wonders of the ancient world. By a combination of the dry climate, which preserved even their writing on paper, and their habit of burying with their dead some of their richest and most beautiful possessions as well as ordinary everyday things, we know a great deal about them. From what the Egyptians left behind, we know they brought the civilisation begun in Sumer to a high peak, and that they did so by being both a proud and practical people.

They had a pride in their own nation and in the pharaoh who ruled it as a god. As a divinity, the pharaoh needed to be served on all sides by lesser mortals: men could rise to great heights in his service. Perhaps for this reason, ancient Egypt has given us the first famous scientist known to history. His name was Imhotep, and he was architect, doctor, priest, magician, author and personal adviser to his master, King Zoser. It was these two who devised the first large structure built entirely of natural stone, the step pyramid at Saqqara.

The Pyramids

Early Egyptian rulers were buried in tombs with flat roofs and sloping sides called mastabas. They were built of bricks made from sun-dried mud. The step pyramid at Saqqara was really six mastabas built one on top of the other. It was made of small blocks of stone laid like bricks, but it was enormous. The whole edifice stood about 60 metres (200 feet) high. It contained underground chambers, and outside were courts and temples with stone columns carved with plant designs, ceilings made to look like wooden logs and walls with an engraved pattern like the reed matting used in ordinary houses.

What Zoser and Imhotep started in

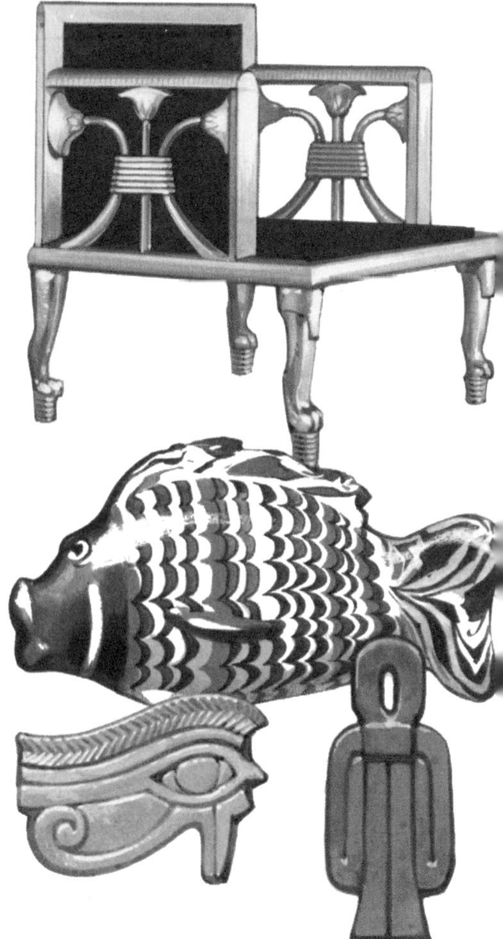

Part of a wall painting from the tomb of Rekhmara at Thebes, which shows Egyptian craftsmen at work. They were highly skilled in the making of pottery, furniture, glassware and jewellery; some examples of their work are shown below.

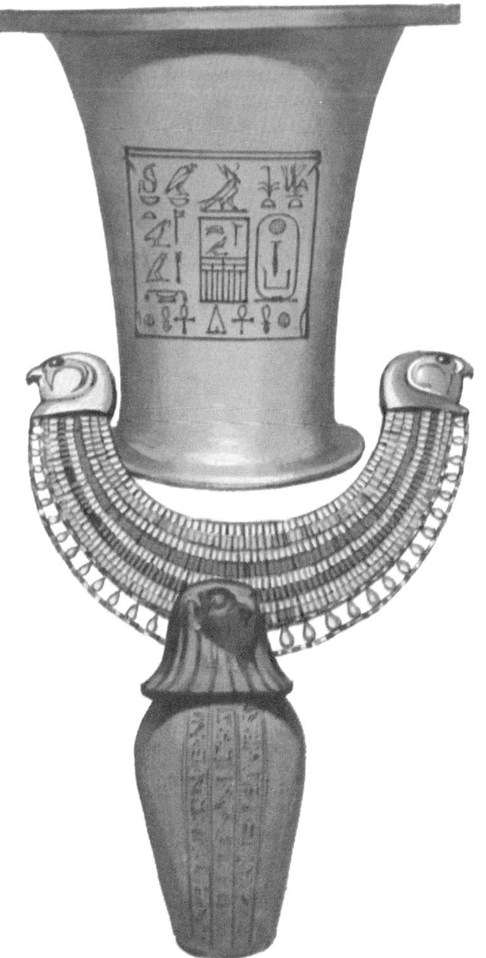

the 27th century B.C., other pharaohs and their architects copied and improved upon. The great age of pyramid building lasted about 400 years. The pyramid of the pharaoh Cheops contained more than two million stone blocks, most of them weighing about $2\frac{1}{2}$ tons, and it was built with the aid of stone and copper tools, without the use of either draught animals or the wheel. Such building was the wonder of people who came later to gaze at it, and modern engineers have worked out how it might have been accomplished.

The stone used was mostly limestone but some granite, a very hard material to work, was included. Special hardstone hammers were needed to chip slots for the wooden wedges which expanded on wetting and split the rock. Considerable skill would be needed in the placing of the wedges to extract the right size and shape of block, which would then need careful measurement and trimming to ensure that all the blocks were of a uniform size. Then the blocks were levered on rollers and dragged on sledges to the river bank where barges waited to carry them to the building site.

The Nile was the great highway linking the cities and villages of Egypt. The prevailing wind came from the north, blowing against the direction of the current of water. It is possible that here man made his first use of wind power by fitting his oared boats with sails. Certainly the earliest known picture of a boat with a sail is on an Egyptian pot dating from 3200 B.C. Sailing barges on the Nile could drift downstream with the current and use wind power to aid the oarsmen on the upstream journey.

Architects and Engineers

While the stone was being quarried and transported to the building site, surveyors were at work preparing the foundations. A square was marked on the top of a rocky prominence and ramps cut in the hillside leading to it. A perfectly flat base was needed, and this was probably achieved by building waterfilled trenches round all four sides. Strings, stretched across from trench to trench and attached to sticks with their lower points just touching the water level, would then give the basic guidelines from which all measurements could be taken.

As the pyramid rose higher, ramps were built up along the sides, each taking the length of three sides to reach the top. There could be four ramps altogether, three for the stones to be dragged up and one for the workmen to descend. These were not slaves but free workers willing to join in the task during the seasons between seed-time and harvest, for their keep and for the glory of their pharaoh. Messages on some of the blocks from the 'Vigorous Gang' or the 'Enduring Gang' indicate their cheerful pride in their own achievement.

The interior of the Cheops pyramid was a testament to its designers' confidence in their own engineering skill. Two shafts leading to burial chambers, one underground beneath the pyramid, were dug, but both these were abandoned. The final burial chamber was constructed higher within the pyramid above the first two. A long gallery led from the entrance passage to the burial chamber itself which had six roofs, one above the other, to take the weight of stone above it. The gallery was built on the slope with three huge stones wedged halfway up it. After the burial these three blocks could be released to slide back into the entrance passage to seal it. Grooves can be seen in the gallery walls where beams were placed to take ropes for the raising of the sealing blocks into position. An escape tunnel was provided for the men who performed this final act, as also were ventilation tunnels, all of which would be sealed from the outside.

Painting and Sculpture

What the early pyramid builders learned about surveying, engineering and the working of stone was passed on to their descendants, who created some of the most beautiful buildings ever erected. The Egyptians became masters in the delicate carving of stone, from the smallest detail to the lofty colonnades of carved columns and lintels. Eventually, they produced massive portraiture in stone. The head of the Sphinx, carved out of the solid rock, is still the largest portrait sculpture in the world. Their painters added brilliant colour to the sculpture and painted vivid murals of the life of the times. The designers were sensitive to the pattern of light and shade cast by their buildings. They invented the clerestory, an upper row of windows placed above a half-roof and providing extra interior light.

Furniture and Textiles

In other crafts, the Egyptian artisans excelled. The design and structure of their furniture, particularly beds and chairs, are followed to this day. In fact, the art of woodworking as we understand it began in Egypt around 4000 B.C. They were skilled at inlay work, veneering and the application of gold leaf. Some of the earliest known examples of textiles date from Egypt in 5000 B.C. and include mats, basketry and primitive fabrics. Their skill developed until their linen became some of the finest ever produced, with woven-in patterns and colours of great elaboration. Wool was considered by them unclean. They had a method of treating leather called tawing, which involved the application of alum sometimes mixed with salt, producing a stiff white leather softened by pulling over a curved frame.

Around 1500 B.C. they produced the earliest known glass vessels. By 1350 B.C. Egyptian glass factories were famous, and they understood the use of added mineral salts to colour the glass. They learned how to hammer metal sheets into the most delicate and exact shapes and of even thickness

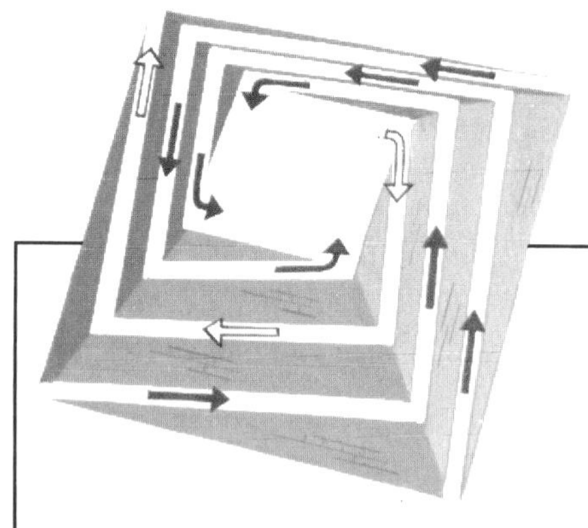

The most striking achievement of the Egyptian architect is the Great Pyramid at Giza, which still stands as witness to the superhuman effort of the massive labour force that built it. Erected to house the body of the pharaoh Cheops (c. 2650 B.C.), no one knows exactly how it was constructed. This scene and the plan above illustrate one theory which suggests the use of four ramps. Stones were hauled up three of these and the workers returned down the other.

so that the detail was reproduced on both sides. There is part still remaining of a beaten copper portrait of a pharaoh of 2300 B.C. which was originally fitted over a wooden frame. They made filigree ornaments from wire which was at first cut in a narrow strip from a circular disc. By 2500 B.C., however, they knew how to draw wire by passing molten metal through a die. They brought cloisonné, which is filigree filled with enamel, to perfection.

The Nilometer

They invented the nilometer to keep a constant observation on the level of the river. They invented sluices to regulate the flow of water, and the shaduf, a counterbalanced lever with a bucket on one side for lifting water to a higher level. They discovered the artesian well, from which water is forced from a deep borehole by its own pressure. They had the earliest known balances with a pivoted beam and standard weights. From 1450 B.C., they had shadow clocks, water clocks and sand clocks, the three kinds of time measurement that were not superseded until the invention of mechanical clocks in the 13th century A.D. Though the priests continued to use the moon-phase calendar of Sumer, in about 3500 B.C. they devised the first 365-day calendar for practical secular purposes. The earliest perfectly preserved war chariots were found in Egypt. Though the use of the horse and the spoked wheel were introduced to them about 1800 B.C., no doubt by enemy armies, the Egyptian wheelwrights and harnessmakers later produced some of the finest work of ancient times.

One invention that originated in ancient Egypt and remained their monopoly for several thousand years

The first celebrated scientist in history was Imhotep, chancellor, physician and architect to King Zoser. Imhotep's name in Egyptian hieroglyphs is seen above. He lived during the Third Dynasty (c. 2686–c. 2613 B.C.) and invented the technique of building with hewn stone and erected the first great building of this type—the Step Pyramid at Saqqara. His genius was not limited to architecture. He was revered as a sage and had a reputation for his great wisdom and learning. It was for his achievements as a physician—he was said to have miraculous healing powers—that he was declared a god of medicine shortly after his death.

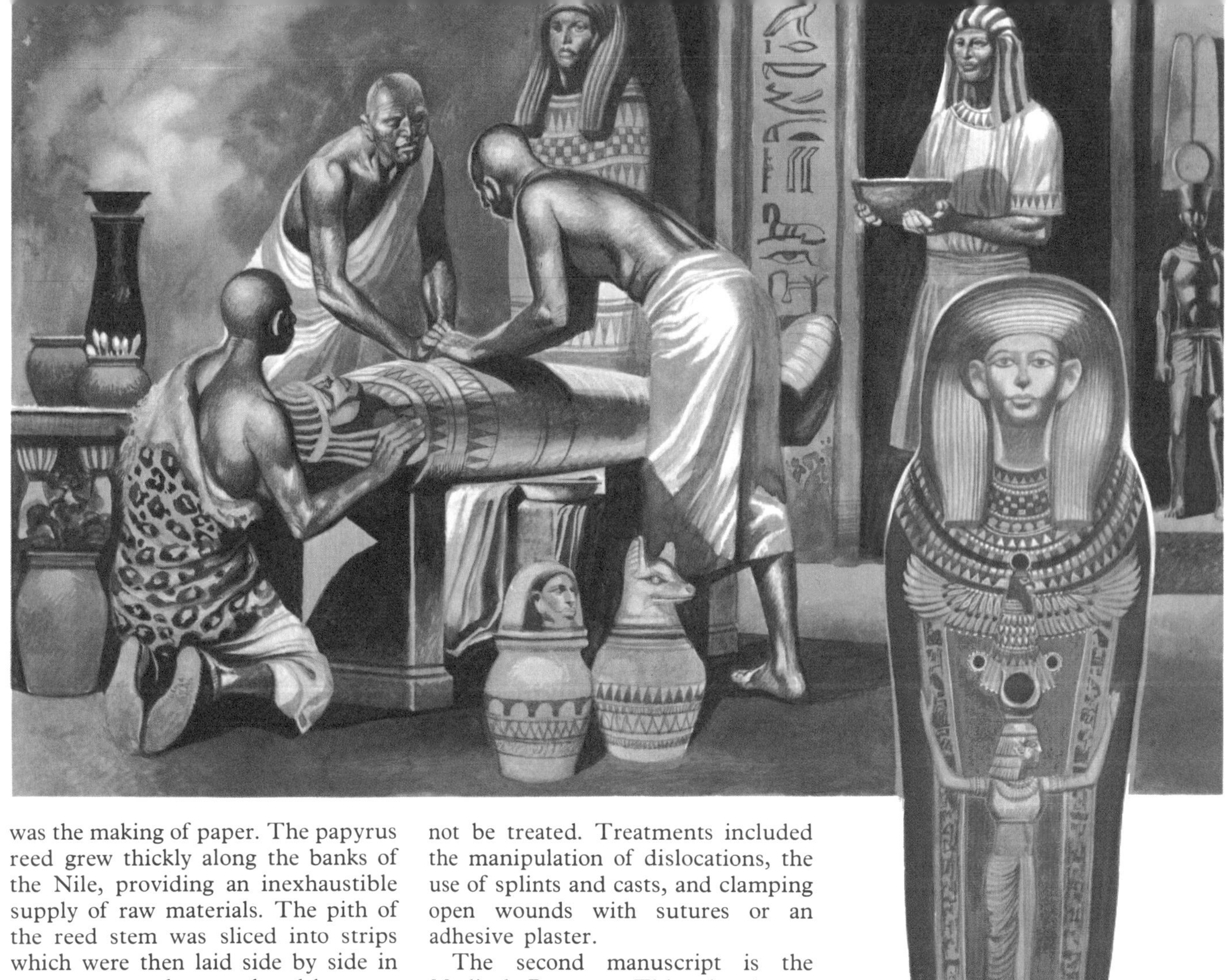

was the making of paper. The papyrus reed grew thickly along the banks of the Nile, providing an inexhaustible supply of raw materials. The pith of the reed stem was sliced into strips which were then laid side by side in two transverse layers, placed between cloth and hammered into a continuous sheet. The surface was then burnished with a polishing stone. Sheets were gummed together to form one long roll of paper. Before the introduction of book-binding, documents were always kept in a roll, often stored in a pottery jar. For a pen, the Egyptians used a reed cut like a quill, and ink was made with water and soot with a little gum added. This made Egyptian handwriting more flowing than the Sumerian cuneiform script incised in clay tablets, but they never improved on the Sumerian syllabic symbols. Despite the more flimsy materials of ink and paper, many Egyptian manuscripts have been preserved for us.

Medical Science

Apart from records and works of literature, preserved papyri include two famous medical manuscripts. The Surgical Papyrus deals with 48 cases of physical injury, beginning with ten cases of injury to the brain, four to the nose and so on continuing down the spinal column. Each injury is carefully described with the tests a doctor could use in diagnosis and the three possible conclusions he could arrive at: that the condition could be treated, that treatment was uncertain of success, or that the ailment could not be treated. Treatments included the manipulation of dislocations, the use of splints and casts, and clamping open wounds with sutures or an adhesive plaster.

The second manuscript is the Medical Papyrus. This also has a surgical section. There is another section dealing with the heart, and a third on the use of medicines. One of the remedies listed is the use of castor oil as a laxative. These two manuscripts indicate that Egypt was the first place in the world where medical practice first emerged from the incantations and ceremonies of the witch-doctor, though these too were practised in ancient Egypt. Certainly Egyptian doctors were famous far beyond the confines of their own country. Clay tablets have been found that indicate the despatch of Egyptian physicians to the courts of Assyria, Syria and Persia, and the use of their herbal remedies spread throughout the Mediterranean peoples.

Preserving the Dead

An interest in chemistry was stimulated by the Egyptian custom of preserving the bodies of the dead. No account of the mummification process has come down to us, but a little is known about it from the examination of mummies. Surgery was employed to remove the viscera and brains which were pickled and sealed in jars. The body was stuffed with fine linen and treated either with a brine of salt or natron (an impure form of soda) in solution. Spices and resins were also used.

Once the mummy of a pharaoh was embalmed it was placed inside a wood or stone coffin such as the richly decorated example shown.

Salt also continued to be used in the cooking and preservation of meat. Fermentation was always understood by the Egyptians, to whom vinegar was the strongest known acid. They used it with dung to generate the heat that turns lead into its basic carbonate known as white lead for the manufacture of paints.

Like Sumer, Egypt suffered an invasion by a Semitic people, the Hyksos, who ruled for about 200 years and introduced the horse-drawn chariot. But the national pride of the Egyptians enabled them to rally and expel their various conquerors until Alexander the Great bequeathed the country to his general Ptolemy. By that time, the old civilisation had gone into a decline, and Egypt came under Greek influence from which its reputation as a centre for learning took on a new stimulus.

The Indus Valley

When the lands of Sumer and Egypt were already well established on their road to technological and scientific progress, there were two other civilisations in the world based on metal-working, about which there is still some mystery. The first of these is known principally from two ancient cities discovered in the valley of the river Indus in India at Mohenjo-daro and Harappa. The people who built these two cities were already sufficiently civilised to be the first town planners. Yet nothing is known of their origin.

It seems probable that when the early farmers left the high Iranian plateau to farm the rich valleys of the Tigris and Euphrates in the west, some of their race at least went east to the valley of the Indus. What happened then, how their civilisation developed or even what they called themselves is unknown. All that has been found are the twin cities, perhaps the northern and southern capitals of two kingdoms. Both the cities were obviously laid out in the way these mysterious people thought a city of the times should be, rather as town planners today lay out a new satellite town. The streets ran north and south or east and west, forming blocks of houses that were built in line and not allowed to encroach on the street. The siting of the streets was probably dictated by the prevailing northerly winds which would ventilate them. At street intersections, the buildings were curved so that beasts of burden or carts would not run up against sharp corners. There were no windows, only narrow doorways and flat roofs, probably the best design for such a hot climate.

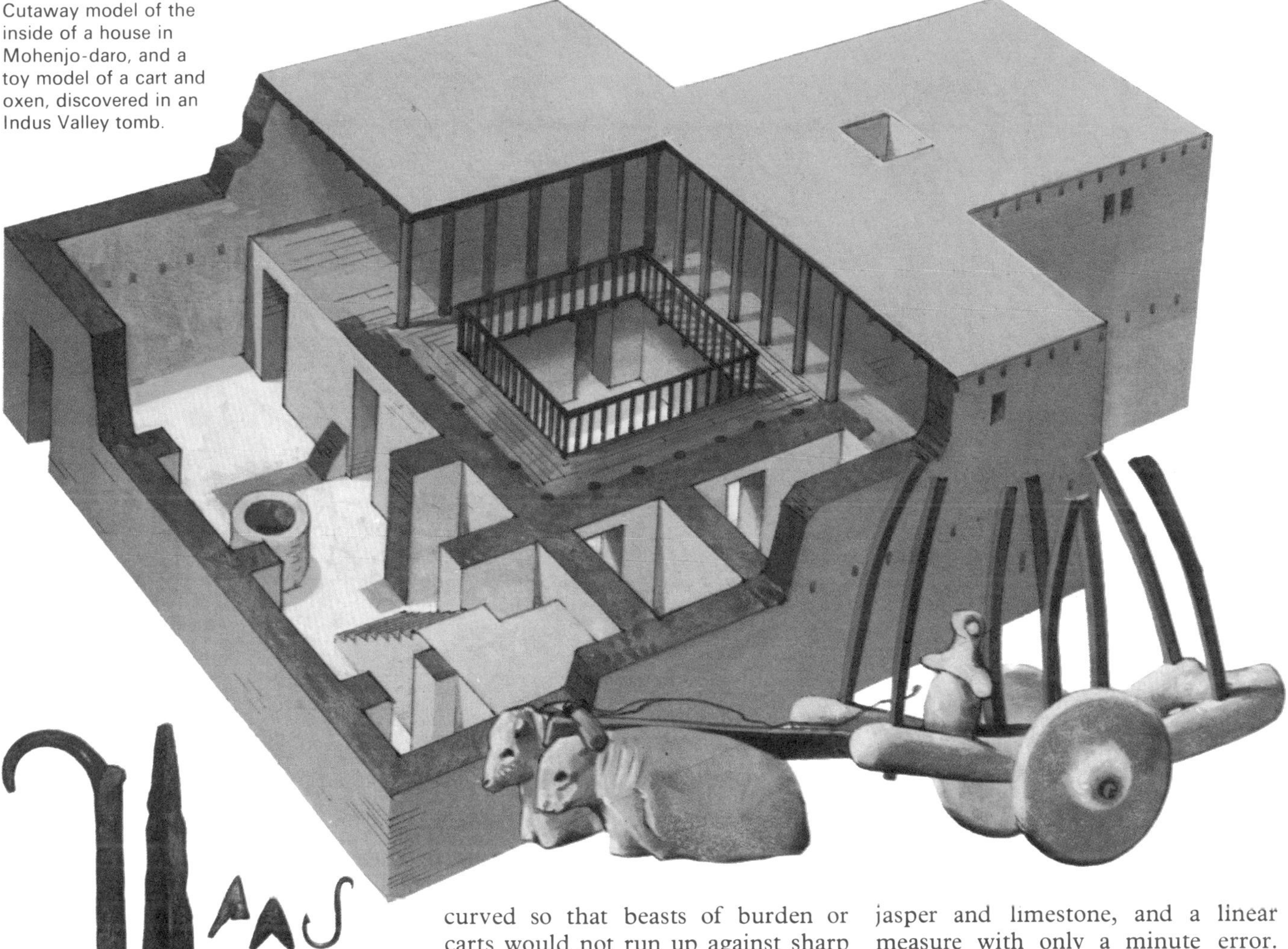

Cutaway model of the inside of a house in Mohenjo-daro, and a toy model of a cart and oxen, discovered in an Indus Valley tomb.

Implements recovered from the Indus Valley, where the civilisations of Mohenjo-daro and Harappa were based on metal-working.

Mohenjo-daro boasts a great bath-house which included arrangements for providing hot air, steam and water, a swimming pool and changing rooms, small bathrooms with running water and cold showers. Even the houses in both cities had baths, lavatories, main drainage and freshwater tanks. There was a huge granary at Mohenjo-daro with grain bins constructed to provide constant air ventilation to prevent dampness.

Jewellery and Metals

These people of the Indus valley made silver, copper and bronze vessels, jewellery of gold and silver, of electrum—an alloy of those two metals—and of copper and bronze, and also many semi-precious stones. They made bronze mirrors with wooden handles, used cosmetics and razors, and even invented the earliest known metal saw with serrated teeth. They had balances and weights made very accurately from alabaster, quartz, jasper and limestone, and a linear measure with only a minute error. They could spin and weave cotton, which they must have grown instead of the flax used in the Middle East.

The people of the Indus valley flourished from about 1700 B.C. until they were conquered by Aryans from the north in about 1500 B.C. There is considerable archaeological discovery to be made yet before we know how they came to plan their cities so ingeniously.

Warriors and chariot from ancient China, as suggested by excavations.

Ancient China

From the ape-like, cave-dwelling Peking Man of 350,000 years ago to the first Bronze Age civilisation of the Shang Dynasty founded about 1750 B.C., the progress of people in China is also shrouded in mystery. A village of four or five thousand years ago has been discovered at Yang Shao where the people had some kind of spinning wheel and cultivated fibrous plants, and where earthenware objects bear the imprint of woven cloth. They had bone and horn tools, fine-eyed needles, pots with slender necks and handles, and large urns decorated with pictures of dogs and horses and abstract designs.

The abacus was invented by the ancient Chinese as an aid to arithmetic. It was used widely throughout the world before the adoption of written symbols. It is still in use in China today.

Shang Dynasty

At Anyang in Honan Province north of the Yellow River, a city of the Shang Dynasty has been unearthed. Finds there show that the people used lines, rods and nets and used bait. They used arrows and spears, and horses to pull their carts. They grew millet and rice and cultivated mulberry trees. They cultivated the silkworm and wove fine silk fabrics. They knew how to smelt copper, tin, silver and lead.

How this civilisation came about, whether it learned its skills from the west or invented them for itself is not known. Certainly, everything it produced in fine pottery and metal castings has its own distinctive beauty and craftsmanship. The Chinese also devised their own system of writing, at first carved on bone but later painted with a brush on silk.

In one thing, however, the Chinese metalworkers were far in advance of the west. Early writings suggest that the smelting of iron first became known in China about the 7th or 6th century B.C., whereas it began in Asia Minor much earlier, about 1200 B.C. But a manuscript called the Tso Chuan talked about the casting of iron cauldrons in the year 512 B.C. Iron in the west could only be wrought at that time. The technique of casting was not known until the 14th century A.D. in Europe. Archaeological evidence of iron casting in China goes back at least as far as 400 B.C. In fact, iron moulds were cast for use in the casting of other metal objects such as bronze axes. Iron moulds for the casting of spades, chisels and chariot parts were found at Hsing Lung in Jehol Province in a foundry dating back to the 4th century B.C.

The crossbow, the last important advance in armament before firearms were produced, was probably invented in China about 200 B.C. at the same time as the building of the old part of the Great Wall was finally completed. Certainly, the Chinese crossbow, with its intricately fashioned bronze lock and its greater accuracy and range, was used from the wall, to devastating effect, against the Mongol attackers.

As time goes on, more evidence is being collected of what happened in early Chinese history and the nature of the contacts maintained with the west. The problems revolving around where the first advances were made in each technology will one day, no doubt, be resolved.

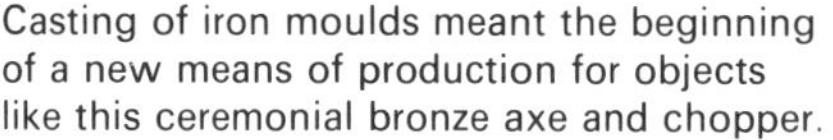

Casting of iron moulds meant the beginning of a new means of production for objects like this ceremonial bronze axe and chopper.

Minoan Crete

While the civilisations of Sumer and Egypt were flourishing, the people of western Europe lived in primitive huts and were barely beginning to learn farming. The spread of civilisation across Europe was a slow process over several thousand years. The first European civilisation blossomed on the island of Crete.

The first people to colonise Crete came from Asia Minor about 5000 B.C. They must have been daring sailors to trust themselves to the boats of the time in the open sea. It is not surprising, therefore, that they eventually became a powerful maritime nation. The cities they built between 2500 and 1400 B.C. were not fortified since they relied on their ships to protect them from invasion. It was their ships that provided them with the wealth on which their civilisation was based.

World Traders

For the first time, a civilisation was not based on a river valley and did not have an irrigation system. In fact, not enough food could be grown on the island to feed the increasing population. The answer the Cretans found to their problem was to develop the world's first sea-going trade. For a thousand years or more, they were masters of the Mediterranean Sea, their high-prowed ships holding a monopoly of trade between Egypt, Syria, Cyprus and the Aegean islands, Greece, Italy and Sicily. In some of these places, they established the first coastal trading posts.

Apart from the profits to be made from the transporting of cargoes by sea, the Cretan craftsmen made many things for export. The island was suitable for sheep farming, and fine woollen cloth was exported. Objects in ivory, gold, silver and bronze were manufactured. But their most famous product was their pottery, everything from the most delicately thin cups—comparable to modern china—to huge storage jars as big as a man. They created a luxury trade that brought them great wealth and a high standard of living.

They developed their own script which was used chiefly for the keeping of accounts, and they adopted a decimal system of counting in tens. For the figures 1 to 9, they used vertical strokes of the appropriate number. The figure 10 was one horizontal stroke, 20 was two horizontal strokes, and so on. They never devised a symbol for zero.

The cities they built were supplied with running water, baths and drainage. Their shops included smithies, potteries, carpenters' and shoemakers' workshops. They had oil refineries and textile factories. They had folding doors between rooms, and oil lamps ingeniously fed with a continuous supply of fuel. They loved to deck their womenfolk with jewellery, elaborate hair styles and flounced dresses. They can be credited with the invention of both the corset and the crinoline.

The Fall of Crete

About 1400 B.C., a mysterious disaster overtook Minoan Crete. Their cities were destroyed by fire. They may have been attacked by the Achaean Greeks, an Indo-European people who had flooded into mainland Greece and who perhaps resented the luxury and power of the Minoans. Whatever happened, they never recovered and remained under the dominance of the spreading Greek Empire.

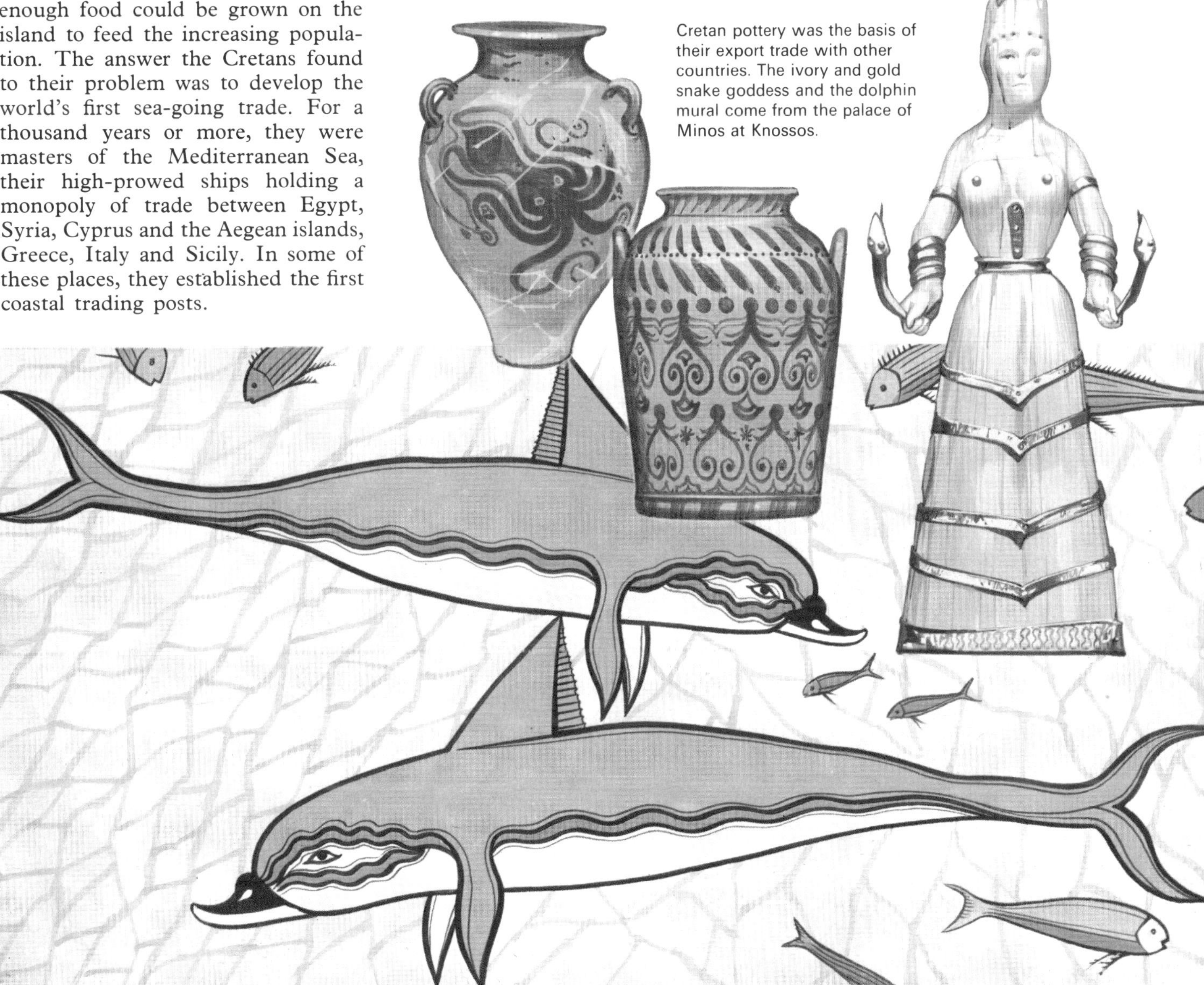

Cretan pottery was the basis of their export trade with other countries. The ivory and gold snake goddess and the dolphin mural come from the palace of Minos at Knossos.

The Hittites made great use of metal. These gold, bronze and silver objects were found at Alaca Hüyük in Asia Minor.

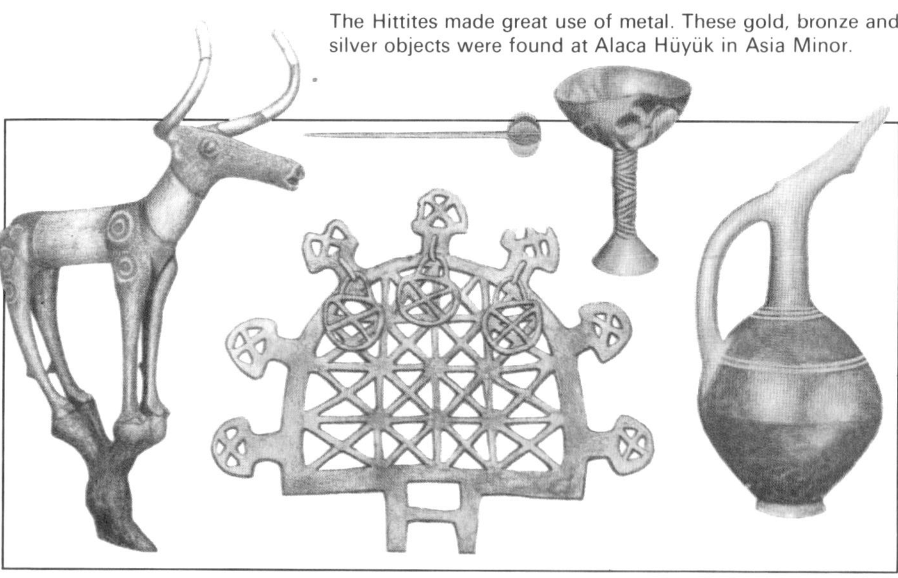

The Lion Gate at the Achaean city of Mycenae (above). Mycenaean building methods were similar to those used in constructing Stonehenge in England. Also shown are the head of a Mycenaean warrior and a gold cup from Vaphio.

The Invaders

The settled life of the first agricultural civilisations developed within each of them the seeds of their downfall. Good living made the people soft and easy-going. Greed and jealousy erupted into warfare among neighbours. The 'haves' of the world became ripe for conquest by the 'have-nots'. Barbarians or outsiders, living a tough nomadic life beyond the frontiers of civilisation, saw wealth and ease theirs for the taking.

From the north came the Indo-Europeans. The Achaeans swept into Greece, the Hittites into Asia Minor and the Aryans into India. From the south came the Semites: the Akkadians into Sumer and the Hyksos into Egypt. Invasion and conquest continued for a thousand years between 2400 and 1400 B.C.

From about 1200 B.C. the second wave began. First the Assyrians and then the Chaldeans came to rule Mesopotamia. They were overcome in their turn by the Medes and Persians. On the Mediterranean coast, the Phoenicians established their maritime empire. In the north, Teutons, Celts, Latins and Dorians spread into southern Europe.

Each conquest gave new life to the territory it plundered. For, in time, the conqueror always settled down to enjoy the way of life of the conquered. The pictures on these pages show some of the changes they brought with them.

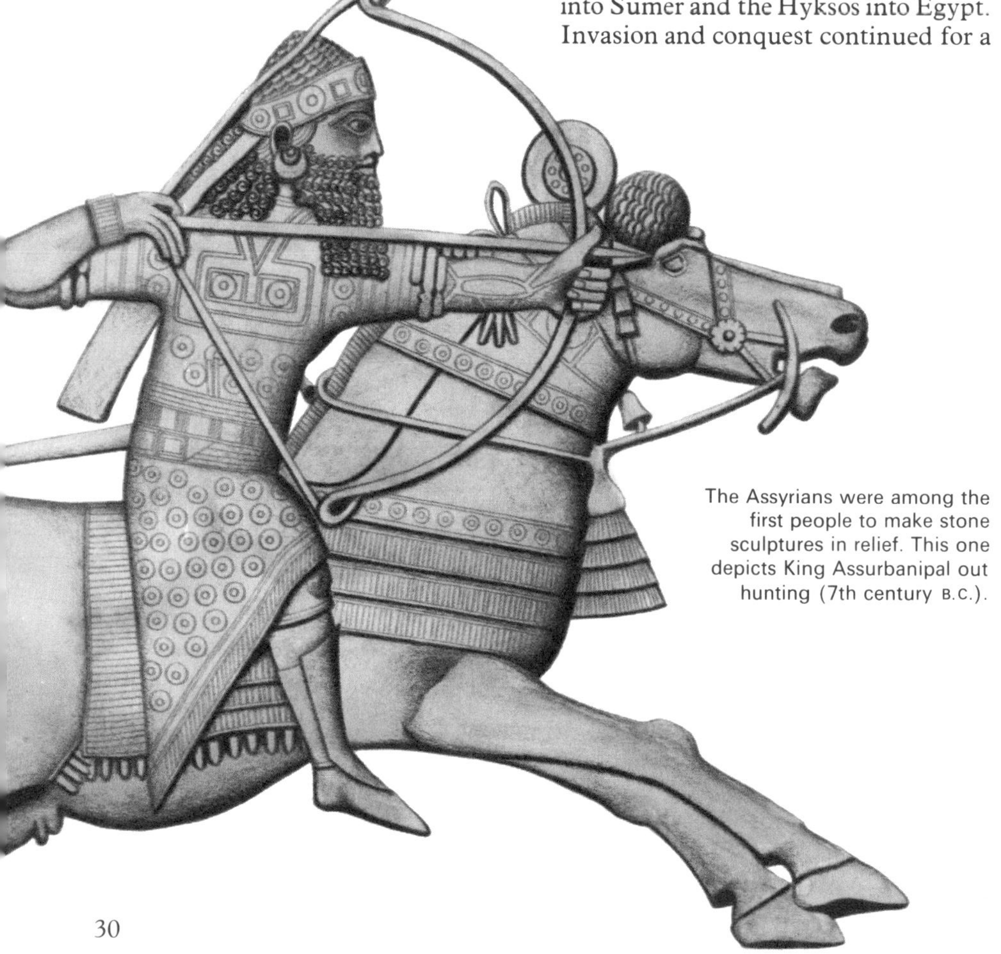

The Assyrians were among the first people to make stone sculptures in relief. This one depicts King Assurbanipal out hunting (7th century B.C.).

Forced to take to the sea in their struggle for existence, the Phoenicians covered the entire Mediterranean in their trading ships.

Gold coins first began to be used sometime about 700 B.C. Illustrated below is a Persian gold daric of the time of Darius the Great (522–485 B.C.) who amassed great wealth.

Bronze head of Sargon of Akkad, who founded the Akkadian dynasty about 2400 B.C., the first great empire of the ancient world.

The people of northern Europe developed the art of ornamental horse trappings. These examples of Celtic enamelled bronzes are thought to be bridle and harness decorations.

The chariot was introduced into Egypt from Asia by a race of invaders called the Hyksos, who dominated Egypt between the 12th and 18th dynasties. Realising its versatility as a war machine, the Egyptians later adopted the vehicle. The type seen here is of Egyptian design and construction.

The Greek Thinkers

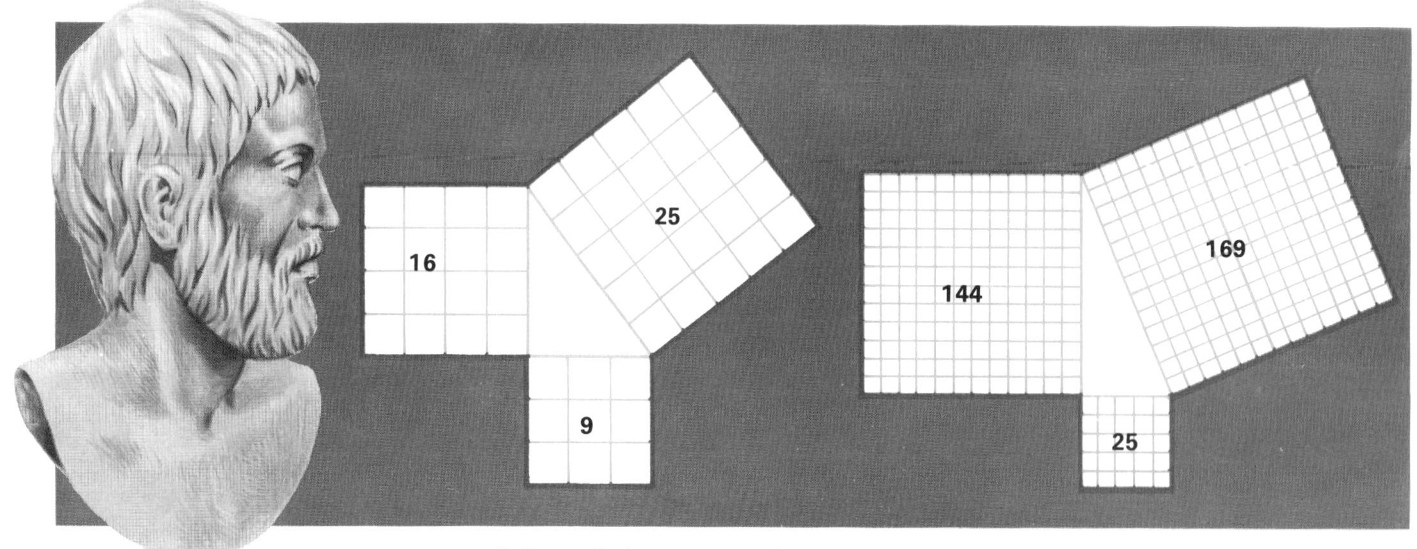

Pythagoras's theorem concerning the squares of the sides of a right-angled triangle still holds true.

Stone Age Man had invented the village and the farm. The Sumerians had invented the city with its individual god and priest administrators. Egypt had invented the nation with its ruler god called pharaoh. Sargon of Akkad and his Babylonian successors had invented the empire with its rigid code of law and military governors. The next people to exert a dominant influence over the eastern Mediterranean were the ancient Greeks who invented the city-state called the polis. The polis included the city itself and a large area of countryside around it, including a number of villages. Each polis was independant. To begin with, they had kings to rule them. The kings were later overthrown by the nobles, and the city-states were ruled by a few rich and powerful men, a system called an oligarchy. Gradually, other citizens began to demand the right to some say in their own government. Important decisions began to be put to the vote of the assembled citizens and the majority opinion acted upon. Thus democracy was born.

This was not the democracy we know today. Not every adult living in the city-state could vote at the public assemblies. The Greeks had at first been invaders of the territories where they set up their city-states. The natives of the conquered territories were taken into slavery, as also were prisoners of later wars. The slaves did all the manual work on the farms and in the craft industries. The citizens with the right to vote were the slave-owners: merchants, legislators and landowners. Yet democracy did emphasise the importance of the individual, at least among the free citizens.

This attitude to the individual created a new kind of scientist. No longer were people ruled by the fear of gods or a military dictatorship. There arose great orators, skilled in the art of swaying the citizens' votes towards their own opinions. People listened more to those with a reputation for great learning. Thinkers began to question the fundamentals of existence, the nature of the universe and the things in it, living or inanimate. The philosopher had arrived.

Greek Philosophers

The word philosophy comes from the Greek and means a love of learning. The Greeks were not great inventors of practical things. They had slaves to do the hard work, and a slave was usually cheaper than a labour-saving machine. What technological progress was made during this period came probably from inventions of the slaves themselves. The Greek philosopher was a man of standing in the community, often with legislative problems, but always with a love of learning and discovery for their own sake. Nor was he in awe of the gods.

Among the first of the Greek philosophers were two friends from Miletus, a city of Ionia on the coast of Asia Minor. Their names were Thales (636–546 B.C.) and Anaximander (610–546 B.C.). Thales was a local statesman and legislator, and has been credited with such public works as the building of bridges, the diverting of rivers and the compiling of almanacs. He is supposed to have predicted, from existing Babylonian observations, the eclipse of the sun in 585 B.C. The two friends can be said to have invented geometry. They found a way of estimating the height of a pyramid from the length of its shadow. The length of a shadow cast by a stick was first measured, then the distance from the centre of the pyramid to the end of its shadow. The proportion between the first and second measurements was therefore the same as the proportion between the length of the stick and the height of the pyramid. In other words, if the shadow cast by the stick was one-twentieth of the pyramid's shadow,

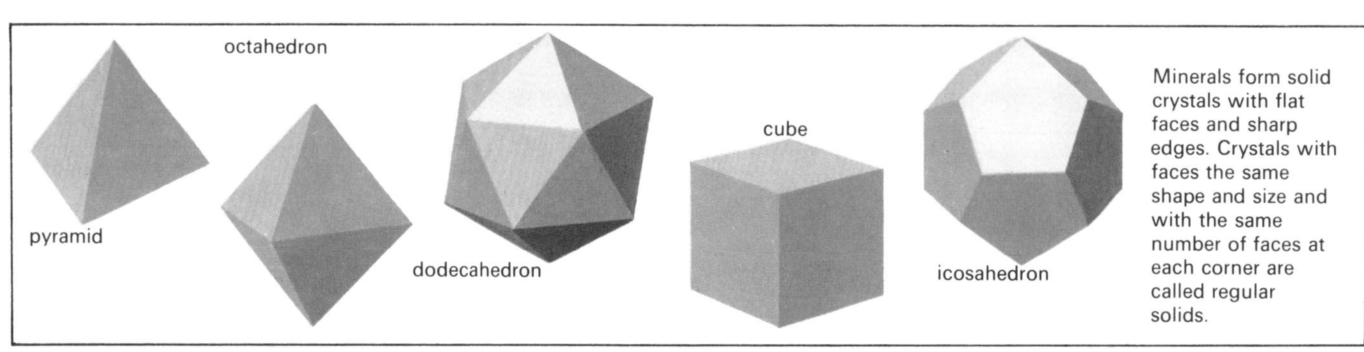

Minerals form solid crystals with flat faces and sharp edges. Crystals with faces the same shape and size and with the same number of faces at each corner are called regular solids.

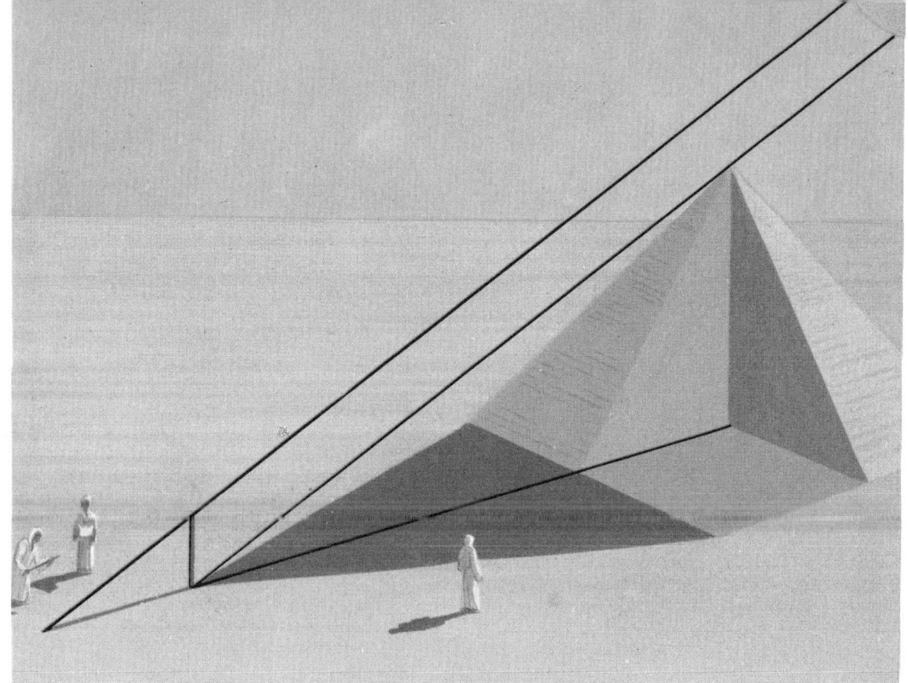

Thales and Anaximander discovered how to measure the height of a pyramid from its shadow.

The Greeks 'invented' democracy. In this sculpture symbolic figures represent Democracy crowning the people of Athens.

then the pyramid was twenty times the height of the stick. Similarly, they showed that the distance of a ship from the shore could be calculated by taking two sightings a known distance apart and making a scale drawing to find the point of intersection of the two lines of sight.

Earth, Air, Fire and Water

Thales thought of the universe as being composed of a region of air above the earth with a region of fire above that and, beyond that, the vault of heaven. He called celestial phenomena *meteora* meaning 'above the air' or in the upper atmosphere of fire from which lightning, for instance, came. He thought of the earth as a disc floating on water, though he never explained what supported the water. All things, he considered, were derived from water which deposited them as it dried out. All things contained gods with certain powers or properties. This idea came to him from studying the properties of a magnet and the behaviour of static electricity formed on a rubbed rod of amber.

Anaximander also believed that the land was once covered in water, and gave as his evidence for this the discovery of fossil shells on dry land. Creatures arose, he thought, as the land dried up from evaporation caused by the heat of the sun. These first creatures had a sort of protective bark to prevent their own evaporation. Man, he supposed, must have been at one time a fish-like creature, perhaps suckled by some kind of sea mammal. He took Thales's view of the universe much farther, describing our universe as an eddy in a vast flood, shoreless and endless, with our eddy just one of many. The eddy itself is the god and creator of all physical things, and derives its power from the great infinite flow which he called the Unbounded.

An analogy he might have made was that of the winnower's sieve. When it is rotated, the heavy grain gravitates to the centre, while the chaff is thrown out towards the rim. In the same way, the eddy causes contrary things to separate out, the earth going to the centre and fire to the outside, with air and water in between. The fire on the outside causes the water to boil, and the steam created pushes back the fire. Here and there, the fire shows through, which explains our view of the sun and the moon. Anaximander used his primitive geometry to estimate the belt of fire containing the sun to have a diameter 27 times that of the earth, while the diameter of the cooler belt containing the moon was eighteen times greater.

The Harmony of Nature

Pythagoras (582–507 B.C.) was the founder of Greek mathematics. He was born on the island of Samos, and later founded a colony of his disciples in Italy. He searched for a unifying element in nature, and thought he had found it in numbers. He came to this belief when he discovered that harmonious sounds are produced when a vibrated string is divided along its length into exact divisions of whole numbers. If a string is vibrated, a note is produced. If the string is held firm at the exact centre, it is in fact divided by two, the two halves produce vibrations with a note harmonious to the first note. Vibrating a portion of the string which is a division by three or four produced two more notes in harmony with the first two. Any division of the string which is not by a whole number produces a discordant note.

Therefore simple numbers must express harmonies, and the harmony of nature is a matter of numbers. So thought Pythagoras. His famous theorem derives from the attempt to express the relationships in space in terms of numbers. It had long been known that certain lengths of the sides of a triangle produce a right angle, which is the relationship between the horizon and the vertical fall of an object through space. Such a relationship was important to ancient builders who needed to achieve a right angle in their buildings. Masons' set squares were constructed on the dimensions that had been found to give them a right angle, but the exact

The great orator Demosthenes suffered from a weak voice. He is said to have trained himself by declaiming loudly in the open air with his mouth full of pebbles.

relationship between these dimensions was not known. Four right angles were known to complete the circle. Pythagoras showed that four masons' set squares could be arranged to form either a hypotenuse, or an L-shaped figure made up of two squares, each with sides of the length of one or other of the remaining sides of the triangles. The well-known right angle triangle with sides of 3, 4 or 5 units can be shown to prove this by numbers:

$$5 \times 5 = 25$$
$$3 \times 3 + 4 \times 4 = 25$$

In such ways, Pythagoras sought to express through numbers the natural harmonies of space and the relationship of forms moved through space. It is the language of modern mathematics.

Physics and Medicine

Anaxagoras (500–428 B.C.) was born at Clazomenae in Ionia. About 463 B.C., he went to Athens where he taught for about 30 years. He developed a theory of physics that assumed an original 'mixture' containing the 'seeds' of all natural substances. From this mixture, identifiable substances were separated out by the action of *nous* which was the name he gave to the matter composing the living mind. He described the sun as being a mass of hot iron bigger than the whole of the known world, and he is said to have originated the idea that light from the moon is a reflection of the sun's rays.

Democritus, whose atomic theory of the universe was revived by modern scientists.

Hippocrates (460–375 B.C.), a native of the island of Cos who travelled widely throughout Greece and died at Larissa in Thessaly, has been described as the father of modern medicine. *Pharmakos*, the Greek word from which we get pharmacy, was the scapegoat magically laden with all the sins of the city in times of trouble and driven out of the gates. Physicians of Hippocrates's time thought of the body containing four 'humours': phlegm representing coldness; blood representing heat; black bile representing moisture; and yellow bile representing dryness. Any imbalance in the proportions of these resulted in illness, and treatments were devised accordingly. Yet Hippocrates was a careful and observant doctor. He was not a scientist in the modern sense, but built up his art of healing from experience. He believed that a doctor's role was mainly to co-operate with the natural healing force of the body. He thought a patient should be told the course his sickness would take in order to boost his morale to face it. He was the author of the Hippocratic Oath, the first compilation of an ethical code for a doctor to obey.

Atomic Theory

Democritus (460–360 B.C.) came from Abdera in Thrace, a breakaway colony from the Ionian city of Teos. He travelled widely and lived to be over a hundred. His was altogether a remarkable mind, ranging over mathematics, biological and social evolution, geography, astronomy, meteorology and economics. He devised the first atomic theory. He thought of matter consisting of atoms of different sizes, shapes, positions and velocities moving through a void. Among his sayings are: 'Nothing comes about by chance, but all through reason and by necessity. Nothing can be created out of nothing, nor can it be destroyed and returned to nothing. There is no end to the universe, since it was not created by an outside power. There is nothing but atoms and the void between them.'

Eudoxus (390–337 B.C.) is credited with being the first scientist to estimate the length of a year as $365\frac{1}{4}$ days and the inventor of the sundial. He saw the universe as a series of concentric

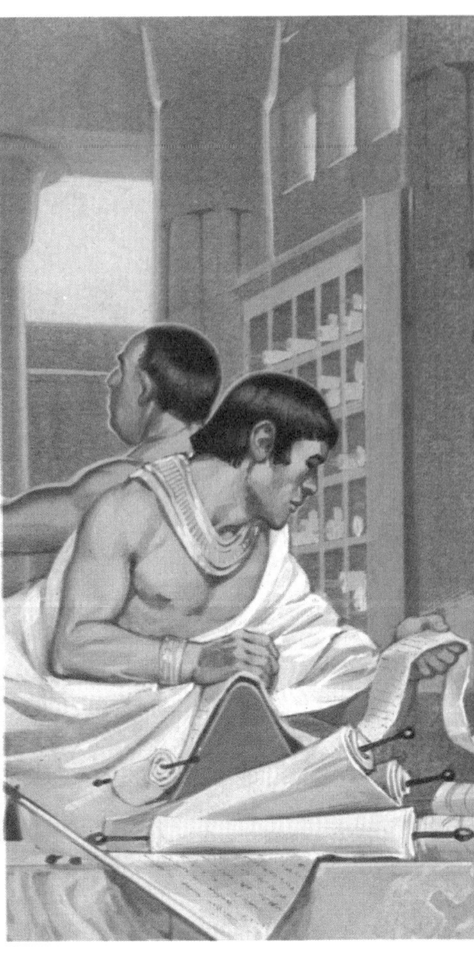

spheres of some glass-like substance with the earth at the centre. He designed and built an armillary sphere which is a model of the universe showing how the planets revolve in relation to the earth. Since the ancients thought of the circle as the perfect shape, they assumed a circular orbit for the planets. They could never satisfactorily reconcile this idea to the fact that the planets in their courses change speed. They wasted a great deal of time trying to find circular orbits that would explain the observed phenomenon.

The First Professor

Aristotle (384–322 B.C.) became the most influential of the Greek philosophers. He attempted to gather together all the learning of his time and to use the language of logic to form it into a coherent whole. He was the great organiser of knowledge, and his work formed the foundation of all education for the next two thousand years. He can be called the first professor. Yet most of his learning did not survive the 17th century. His value in terms of modern science is as a biologist, and as that he was greatly underrated. He was born at Stagira in Thrace. At seventeen, he went to Athens and

The library at Alexandria, founded by Ptolemy I, one of Alexander's generals.

Asclepius, god of healing, is seen tending a boy in this sculpture (4th century B.C.).

joined Plato's famous Academy. In 347 B.C. he opened his own school at Assos in the Troad. At about 344 B.C., he moved to Mitylene on the island of Lesbos where he devoted two years to the study of natural history, particularly marine biology. He brought to this study a new scientific system of meticulous observation. For instance, in the fourth book of his *History of Animals,* he describes minutely the day-to-day development of the chicken embryo inside a hen's egg. He taught that we must not recoil from the more unpleasant aspects of animal behaviour, but must fit every part into the pattern of the whole grand design. In 342 B.C., he was invited to the court of Philip of Macedon in northern Greece as tutor to Philip's son, who was to become Alexander the Great. In 336 B.C., when Alexander succeeded his father, Aristotle returned to Athens where he opened a school in the Lyceum.

The young Alexander of Macedon listens to his tutor, the great philosopher Aristotle.

Greek Learning

In 334 B.C., Alexander crossed the Hellespont from Europe into Asia and began the series of conquests which was to bring into his empire the whole of the civilised world as far as the Indus and beyond. Aristotle had taught the young Alexander that only the Greeks possessed the true humanity, that all other people were barbarous, fit only to be slaves and the living tools of the Greeks. But Alexander was to learn that there were base Greeks who let him down and men of other races who deserved his respect. He began to dream of one world, undivided by race or creed, a united federation of city-states each on the model of the Greek polis. The concept has been called 'cosmopolis'. Alexander and his successors, who divided his empire between them on his early death, did indeed set up city-states that were more populous and cosmopolitan than any that had gone before. All of them came under the influence of Greek learning and the teaching methods of Aristotle.

Alexander himself founded the city of Alexandria, which contained the Royal Museum, a name originally meaning not just a collection of things from the past but a place dedicated to the muses of all the arts and sciences. The museum at Alexandria contained exhibition rooms, lecture halls, laboratories, dissecting rooms, an observatory and a library which is estimated to have had, by ancient Roman times, a collection of 700,000 rolls. More importantly, it was a centre for some of the leading scholars of the day. The schools at Athens continued to flourish, but the principle rival to

Alexandria became Pergamum in Asia Minor. So great was the rivalry between the two centres of learning that Alexandria refused to supply Pergamum with papyrus. Pergamum devised a substitute from sheepskin and called it *pergamene* after the city. The word has since been corrupted to parchment. This new material had the advantage that both sides could be written on, so a way of fastening the sheets together was invented and led to our modern form of bound book.

Archimedes, lost in thought, ignored a Roman soldier's command and was killed.

Euclid's *Elements*

The spread of Greek learning in the post-Alexander period brought a new attitude to science. Aristotle had given it method and coherence.. Later scholars began to set it out in terms that everyone could understand and to apply it to the practical problems of the times. Euclid (330–275 B.C.) was born in Alexandria. In his treatise called *Elements,* he produced a textbook of mathematics which remained in use until recent times. It included books on plane and solid geometry, on proportion and on the properties of numbers. It was not all his own work, but a compilation including the work of his predecessors.

Aristarchus of Samos (310–230 B.C.) was less fortunate. His work was derided in his own times and had to wait for the support of Copernicus in the 16th century. He had the ingenious idea of measuring the angle of the sun in relation to the moon when the latter was half illuminated. At such times, the angle formed by the earth, moon and sun is a right angle. From this triangle, Aristarchus showed that the sun must be at least eighteen times farther away from the earth than the moon and must be at least 300 times larger than the earth. Such a huge body, he reasoned, must be at the centre of our universe and not orbiting the earth. It was an insight that was not to be accepted for many centuries, and even then was to lead, in 1634, to the trial of Galileo for heresy.

Mathematical Physics

Archimedes (287–212 B.C.) was born at Syracuse in Sicily. He was the founder of mathematical physics as we understand it today. Not until his books were translated and published in the 16th century did the study begin again. He established the principles of the lever and of the equilibrium between a floating body and the hydrostatic pressure of the liquid in which it floats. His famous law states that the apparent loss of weight of an object immersed in water is equal to the weight of water displaced. He turned his genius to the design of marvellous engines of war which were said to have held the Romans at bay when they laid siege to Syracuse. When the city was eventually starved into submission, Archimedes was put to death by the victors.

Eratosthenes (276–194 B.C.) was born at Cyrene and studied at Alexandria and Athens. About 235 B.C., he returned to Alexandria where he became chief librarian. He was both poet and writer on scientific subjects. His greatest achievement was his measurement of the earth's circumference. It was known that on a midsummer's day at noon the sun shone vertically down a well at Aswan. The distance between Alexandria and Aswan was about 5,000 stadia, and the two places were thought to be on the same meridian of longitude. By measuring the angle of a cast shadow with the vertical at Alexandria at midsummer's noon, he calculated that the distance between the two places was one-fiftieth of the total circumference of the earth which therefore must be 50 times 5,000 or 250,000 stadia, about 48,250 kilometres

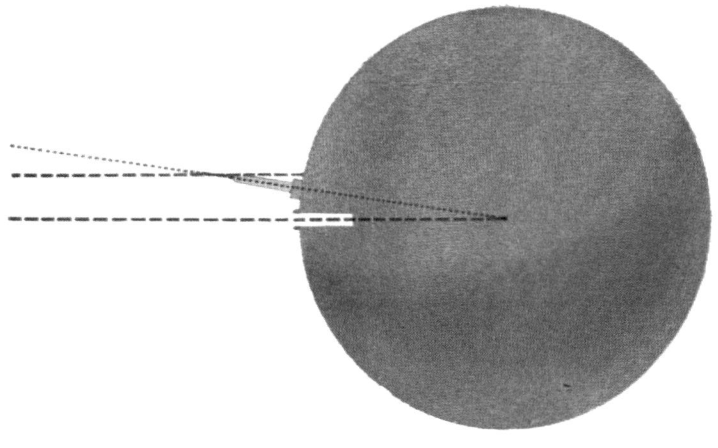

Eratosthenes measured the circumference of the earth from calculations based on the position of the sun and the angle of a shadow. His conclusions were almost accurate.

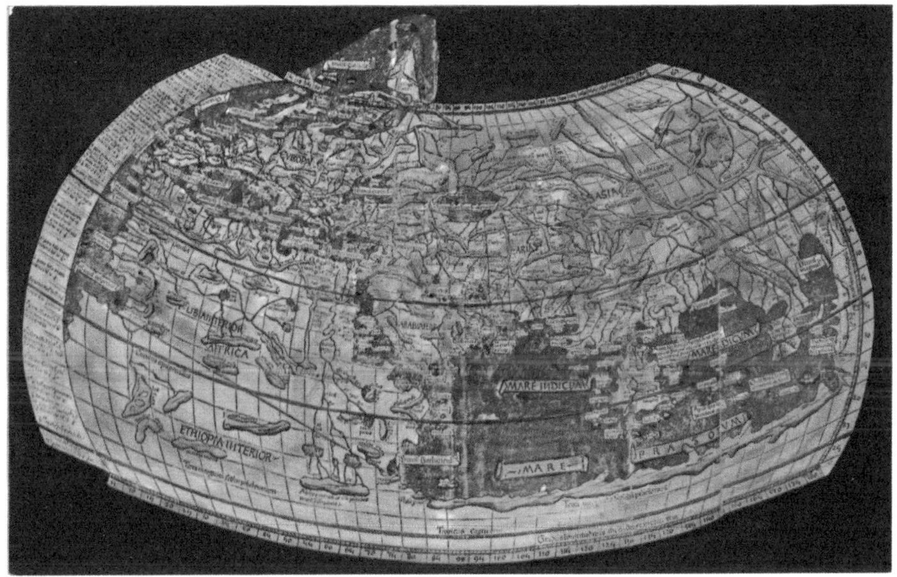

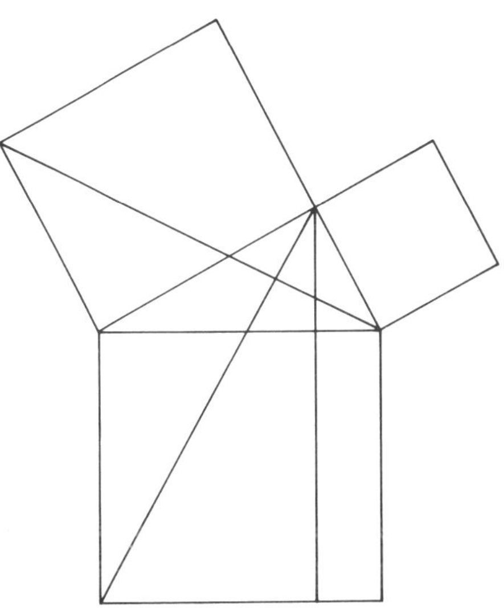

(Left) Map of the world by the Egyptian astronomer and geographer Ptolemy. One of the most famous proofs of Pythagoras's theorem was provided in the formal geometry of the Greek mathematician Euclid (above).

(30,000 miles). His calculations would give a polar diameter of about 12,600 kilometres (7,850 miles), which is only 80 kilometres (50 miles) less than the true polar diameter. This close result was achieved by two miscalculations which cancelled each other out. The two places were actually more than 5,000 stadia apart, but were not quite on the same meridian. Nevertheless, his method was valid and the achievement remarkable.

School of Engineering

Hero of Alexandria founded the first school of engineering in the first century A.D. He invented the first steam turbine engine in which a small boiler turned with the squirting of steam and water from two angled outlets. It was never put to practical use and was just a gadget like most of Hero's inventions. He wrote a vast technical encyclopedia, full of mathematical short cuts, some accurate, some approximations. His work gave us most of what we know about ancient technology until the discovery of the corroded fragments of a mechanism found in a sunken Greek ship near the island of Antikythera. These were shown, in 1959, to date back to 82 B.C. and belong to an astronomical computer of very advanced design.

Galen (A.D. 130–201) was a Greek physician born at Pergamum. He studied medicine there, and at Corinth and Alexandria. He went to Rome where he became physician to the emperor Marcus Aurelius. He wrote over 100 books of which more than 80 survive. They were considered authoritative for fifteen centuries. Next to Hippocrates, he can be considered the greatest physician of all time. Since human dissection was not permitted either in ancient Roman times or the Middle Ages, his anatomy was based on animal studies and was not superseded until the work of Vesalius in the 16th century.

Claudius Ptolemy was an astronomer and geographer who lived in Alexandria in the first half of the 2nd century A.D. Under the Arabic title of *Almagest*, his astronomical writings remained the authoritative textbook on the subject until the time of Copernicus. They represent the sum of knowledge of all his predecessors. Ptolemy still clung to the idea of the earth at the centre of things and the circular orbits of the planets about it. But, in order to find an explanation of the apparent variations in speed of the planets as viewed from earth, he introduced two new ideas, epicycles and eccentrics. An epicycle is where the planet has a separate circular orbit of its own along which it travels while at the same time that orbit is orbiting the earth, like a small cogwheel turning on its own axis and travelling round a larger wheel at the same time. An eccentric is where the centre of the planet's orbit is set at some distance from the earth, and this centre orbits the earth.

Plans exist of Hero's hot air engine for opening temple doors, although it is unlikely it was ever put into practice.

Alexander, whose head is seen on this silver coin (c. 290 B.C.) brought Greek learning and invention to all the countries he conquered.

Greek Invention

In practical terms, the ancient Greek civilisation gave us the invention of money in the form of coins, the first modern type of lathe adapted from the potter's wheel, and lighthouses such as the pharos at Alexandria which became one of the wonders of the world. The light from its wood fire, magnified by mirrors, was visible for 30 miles, and sirens operated by steam gave warning in bad weather. The ancient Greek philosophers gave us the first studies of pure science for its own sake. Rediscovery of these studies in the period we call the Renaissance led the new scientists to question once again the nature of existence and the physical universe, and to lead western European civilisation out of the Dark Ages.

The Roman Engineers

Unlike the Greeks, the Romans were not greatly curious about the nature of the universe. They were essentially practical men. Their empire was founded on military genius. Once established, it depended on good communications, just administration and strong military force to police its territories. Wherever the Roman legions settled, they dug themselves in. As well as his weapons every soldier carried tools to throw up earthworks and, later, to raise more permanent fortifications. It is not surprising, therefore, that the Romans became the greatest engineers of the ancient world.

Vitruvius, who lived in the 1st century B.C., began his career as a military engineer for Julius Caesar and went on to be an architect. Towards the end of his life, he wrote a celebrated work on architecture, building construction and mechanics from which we have gained much of our knowledge of Roman methods and the Greek buildings that have disappeared since his day. In his own life, Vitruvius represents well the practical skill of the Roman engineer.

Roads and Buildings

Under the emperors, beginning with Julius Caesar's nephew, Octavian, who in 27 B.C. assumed the title of Augustus Caesar, the empire was divided into provinces, each with its provincial governor. Each province had its centres of local government where cities on the pattern of Rome were built. The whole system was linked by a network of roads. The Roman roads were a fine engineering achievement. Trenches were dug and filled with coarse rubble to provide adequate drainage. A finer gravel was spread on top as a bed for the paving stones or cobbles. Lastly, the road surface was bound together by kerbstones. In the provinces more distant from Rome, the roads were often banked up to some height above the surrounding countryside. This gave a marching column a good view from which to avoid ambush. Building the roads straight, with only the gentlest curve to change direction, had the same advantage.

According to the availability of local materials, the Romans built their cities in stone or brick. Clay bricks were fired in kilns and the brick industry became a state monopoly. Stone was usually cut with copper saws, and the cut fed with abrasive sand or emery. Saws driven by water power appeared towards the end of the ancient Roman era. Shaping of the stones was often done by pounding with stone balls. The Romans developed cranes operated by human treadmills for raising the huge stone blocks used in their buildings.

Wherever the Romans went, they engaged in mining for the available ores of metals. For the drainage of mine shafts, they introduced the Archimedean screw. This was either a cylinder containing a rotating spiral up which the water was 'screwed', or a spiral tube working on the same principle. They also used scoop-wheels powered by treadmills.

In particular, lead became very cheap and was used extensively for plumbing and roofing. The Romans discovered a method of extracting gold by the use of mercury. The rock containing the gold ore was first crushed and then treated with mercury in which the gold became dissolved in an amalgam. The gold could then be separated out by distillation, and the distillation of mercury used again. Tin was alloyed with 30% lead to make pewter, a popular material for vessels used in Roman households. But most of the tin mined was made with copper into bronze. Roman copper and bronze ware, produced on a factory scale, found its way far beyond the confines of the empire. The centre for iron smelting was in Spain where the Catalan iron furnace was invented. This had two pairs of bellows to maintain a constant blast and directly produced a malleable iron. The best steel used by the Romans had to be imported from southern India by way of Abyssinia. This was called Seric iron and was a high-carbon crucible steel made into small round cakes. It remained scarce and expensive and was used only in the finest tools and weapons.

Concrete Walls

The city of Rome itself was built mostly of concrete. The Romans discovered that a volcanic earth called pozzolana, found extensively in Italy,

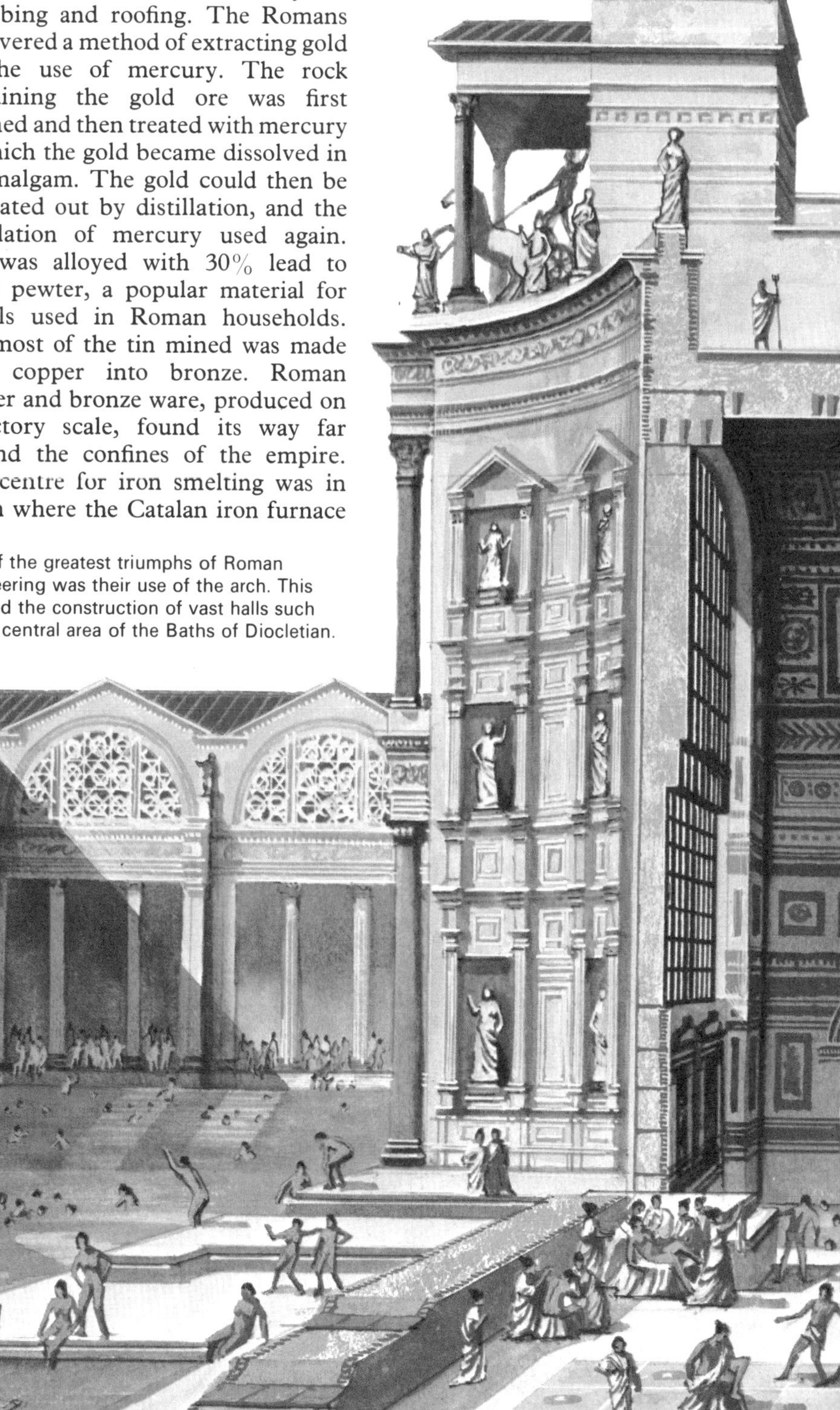

One of the greatest triumphs of Roman engineering was their use of the arch. This enabled the construction of vast halls such as the central area of the Baths of Diocletian.

when mixed with lime made a cement resistant to fire and water. Mixed with brick or stone rubble, it made a concrete as hard as stone itself. Walls were built by pouring this concrete between wooden shuttering. When the concrete set, the shuttering was removed and the concrete walls faced with brick or tiles, or for the grander buildings with marble. An even greater advantage of concrete was its lightness for the construction of vaults and domes.

The Romans took the arch from the Etruscans, their neighbours in Italy whom they conquered at the very beginning of their expansion. The Etruscans built small bridges with arches of wedge-shaped stones joined without mortar. The principle of the arch seems to have originated in the Middle East, yet it was never exploited by the Greeks. Their only method of constructing doorways or roofs was with the lintel and the beam. That is why Greek architecture is composed of so many closely set pillars and why the roofs of the larger remains have collapsed with the passage of time. Wood rots, and the length of a stone beam is limited by its own weight. The weight of a stone beam compresses the upper surface towards the centre and produces tension or a stretching force on the underside.

A semicircular arch, on the other hand, distributes the weight more evenly, much of it pressing directly down on the supporting columns. By constructing the arch of wedge-shaped stones or bricks, the weight is used to bind the separate parts more firmly together. Two arches joined by a curved roof form a vault. By the use of concrete in the roof, the Romans

Roman lettering engraved on a bronze table and (below) a marble relief of the Roman seaport at Ostia.

QVIDEMSTATIM·AB·ORIGINE·VRBIS·NOSTRAE·IN·QVOT·F
STATVSQVE·RES·P·NOSTRA·DIDVCTA·SIT

were able to construct long vaults which were light enough to require little support and, consequently, gave greater free areas of floor space beneath them. This made for lighter and airier buildings.

The dome, which can be thought of as a sort of three-dimensional arch, can also be constructed of concrete. The domed roof of the Pantheon at Rome is 42 metres (140 feet) across and has survived for 1,800 years. The use of the arch, the vault and the dome enabled the Romans to build on a huge scale, with a lightness and grace that was quite new. Their roads could bridge the widest rivers. Their aquaducts could carry water across broad valleys at a height to provide sufficient pressure for its distribution throughout a large city.

(Right) Diagram of a Roman hypocaust, a method of underfloor heating by the circulation of warm air from a fire.

Water Transport

Despite the elaborate road system, long journeys and transportation of heavy loads were still more convenient by water. In the time of the emperor Diocletian, the carriage of a load of hay by road for 50 kilometres (31 miles) could double the price, whereas a shipload of wheat could be carried from one end of the Mediterranean to the other and add only a quarter to the price. The Romans built harbours such as the one at Leptis, east of Tripoli, where the Saharan caravan routes ended. The stone quays were backed by colonnaded warehouses, and a great mole was built out to sea to protect the moored vessels. Rivers continued to be used as highways, and the Romans dug canals, such as the one between the rivers Rhine and Meuse.

In farming, the Romans appear to have developed the harrow, which began as a simple frame of thorn branches dragged across the ground to break up the soil. They also invented single-handed sheep shears. They developed rotary hand-mills and donkey-mills for grinding corn and oil seed. From the Celts, they borrowed the idea of hooped, wooden casks which were an improvement on pottery amphorae for the storage of wine. From the east, they introduced the water-mill which at first had a vertical shaft with horizontal paddles. It is Vitruvius who is credited with inventing the vertical paddle-wheel which we know today. From the East, too, came the padded horse-saddle which replaced the horse-blanket in the 4th century A.D.

The art of glass-blowing was introduced by the Romans from Syria. At first, it probably consisted of the blowing of vessels inside moulds. But as the glass-makers' skills improved, they dispensed with the mould. Glass was produced as a bubble on the end of the blowpipe and shaped with pliers. While still molten, the shaped glass was transferred on to another rod called the pontil which was thrust into, but not through, the glass. The blowpipe was then detached, leaving a mouth to be trimmed by shears. Flat dishes up to two feet in diameter could be blown, or even one small jug enclosed in a larger one.

Lastly, the Romans have given us the design which we still use today for our capital letters. Roman lettering was designed to be engraved on monuments and triumphal arches, and to be easily read from a distance. The same design, or variations of it, is still used for the same purpose nowadays.

The Eastern Empire

When the northern barbarians swarmed into the western half of the Roman Empire in the 5th century A.D., not all was lost. The eastern half continued for many hundreds of years to flourish from its capital city of Constantinople. In the south, the rise and spread of Islam preserved much of the learning of the Greek thinkers and the technological skill of the Roman engineers and builders. Only in western Europe did the abandoned cities crumble into ruin, and even there what was useful to the new agricultural communities was retained and developed.

Workmen carrying out repairs on a Roman road.

The Middle Ages

The upheavals that took place with the collapse of the Roman Empire gradually became subject to the unifying forces of the great religions. Christianity was split into two territorial halves. The Orthodox Church was centred on the Byzantine Empire with its capital city of Constantinople.

In western Europe, the Church of Rome slowly converted the invading Germanic tribes to Christianity. The various orders of monks took upon themselves the burden of education, and their Latin became the universal language of learning. Again, scientific enquiry gave way to theology. To begin with, the life of both monks and lay people was rural and agricultural. The Roman two-field system with half the land remaining fallow in alternate years gave way to the three-field rotation of crops which made a more intensive use of the land. Forest clearance took on a new urgency with the rise in population.

New Technology

In technology, most innovations came from the more prosperous East. For a time in the West, even the potter's wheel disappeared in some areas. It was reintroduced from the Rhineland, and the kick-wheel became characteristic of the Middle Ages. This was worked by the foot, leaving both the potter's hands free. Tubular spouts, formed by wrapping the clay round a stick or the finger, were introduced. The only independent development in the West was the stoneware which was made from a very fine clay fired at the unusually high temperature of 1,250°C. This causes partial vitrification of the clay, producing non-porous pots without glazing. Improvement in the design of kilns made these high temperatures possible.

In the 14th century, it was discovered that throwing salt over the pots at a late stage in the firing produced a hard salt-glaze. The finest white porcelain was brought by the Moslem caravan trains from China. A tin glaze, made from salt, powdered potash-glass and oxides of lead and tin, was invented in the Middle East to make a reasonable copy of the Chinese ceramics. Fired pottery was dipped in this tin glaze and fired again.

The great glory of western technology was the invention of the tall, pointed, Gothic arch. As well as giving greater height to vaulting and window openings, it carried the stresses of large buildings to the exterior framework where a further

The 12th century saw the beginning of a new era in architecture with the building of vast cathedrals in western Europe. The most notable features of these structures were the pointed arch, the rib-vault and the flying buttress. All of these allowed architects to achieve greater lightness and strength, and an upward movement in the planning of religious buildings which echoed the religious beliefs of the Middle Ages.

invention, the half-arch or flying buttress, was built to withstand them. The medieval masons did not know how to calculate these stresses. Intoxicated with their newly-discovered power, they went on building bigger and bigger structures, until the 45-metre (150-foot) vault of Beauvais cathedral collapsed in 1284, some years after it was built. Nothing as large was attempted again, although the 38-metre (125-foot) vault of Rheims cathedral, built in the 13th century, still stands. Egyptian and Greek buildings survive to this day by virtue of their mass and weight. But the Gothic cathedral had a new tension transmitted through a skeleton rather like the bones of an animal or the fibres of a tree. Its mechanics were not improved upon until the steel-reinforced concrete structures of our own time. The skeleton structure gave the medieval cathedral great spaces that could be filled with that other glory of the Middle Ages, stained glass.

Glass-blowing in the Middle Ages, with an example of enamelled glass from Syria (mid-13th century).

Stained Glass

Glass for the windows of houses was produced by spinning a hollow globe of blown glass until centrifugal force made it open out flat. The panes, left with the central crown where the glass had been fixed to the pontil (an iron rod which held the glass during the process of making), produced the well-known 'bottle-glass' windows. Glass for churches and cathedrals was produced by the more costly process of blowing a glass cylinder which was then opened out flat in the furnace. Clear glass was obtained by getting rid of the green or brown tinge from the iron content with the addition of manganese dioxide, the so-called glass-maker's soap. Greens and reds were produced with the use of copper though the best reds came from gold chloride. Adding iron produced browns and yellows, (adding metallic silver gave the best yellow). Blue was obtained from zaffre, an Arabic word for a mixture containing cobalt. The art of the stained glass window went on improving until about 1550. Then it was lost and never fully regained.

Another craft of the medieval glass-maker was the grinding of spectacle lenses for the correction of faulty vision, an invention dating back to about 1286. The first lenses were all convex and could assist only long-sighted people. Concave lenses for the short-sighted came about two centuries later.

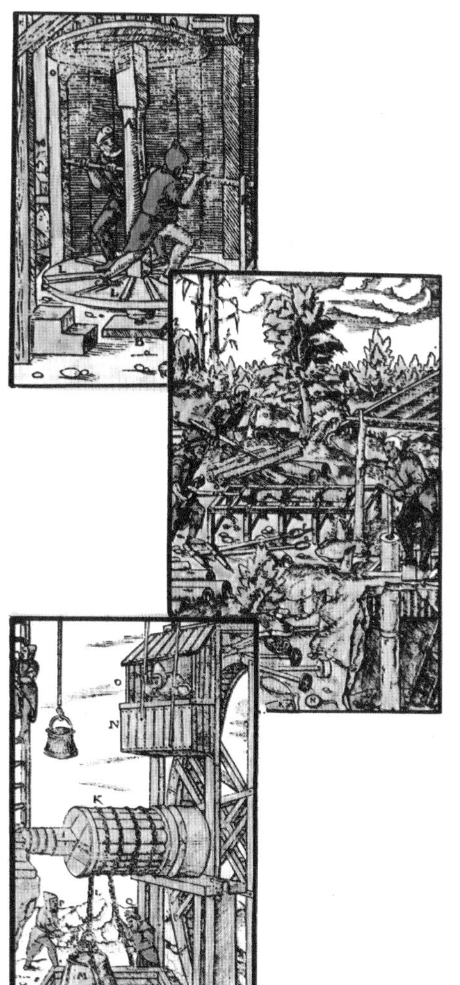

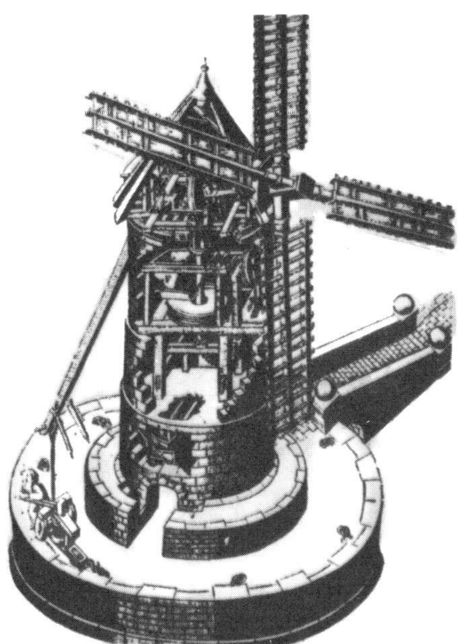

Three illustrations portraying mining techniques from Agricola's book *De re metallica*. These detailed drawings reveal much about medieval mining methods. On the right is a 16th-century windmill.

Mining Techniques

In 1556, twelve books under the title *De re metallica* were published. They were written by Georg Bauer who was a Saxon doctor practising in the Bohemian mining district of Joachimsthal and is better known under the Latin name of Agricola. He tells us a good deal about the development of mining techniques in medieval Christendom. For the transport of ores, trucks were used with wheels designed to run in grooves cut into wooden railways. Windlasses were used for drawing the loads up the shaft, with gear wheels harnessed to horse or water power. Ventilation was supplied by revolving fans and bellows. Rag-and-chain pumps were used to lift water. Stuffed balls were fixed at intervals to a chain. As each entered the barrel of the pump in turn, it acted as a one-way piston driving the water before it. Agricola mentions one mine with a series of three such pumps worked by 96 horses and raising water from a depth of 200 metres (660 feet).

Land transport had from Greek and Roman times relied heavily on the horse. In the Middle Ages, the breast-band was replaced by the stiff, padded horse collar. This took the pressure off the horse's windpipe. Together with the development of shafts and traces, which had been occasionally used in Roman times, the horse collar allowed for the harnessing of horses in file, one behind the other. Altogether, the load which horses could haul with the new harness was multiplied as much as five times.

Water-wheels

The water-wheel became the means of powering many new machines, including sawmills, ore-crushing plants, trip-hammers for metal-working, bellows for furnaces and the new fulling mills. Fulling is a way of thickening material by matting the fibres. The fulling mill caused hammers to fall on the cloth while it soaked in a bath of water containing fuller's earth and other alkaline materials. The windmill seems to have been a Persian invention of the 7th century A.D., but it may also have developed independently in the West. Windmills were common on the north European plain by the end of the 13th century. The early type was the post-mill in which the whole superstructure with sails and machinery was carried on a vertical post and could be turned to present the sails to the wind. Tower-mills were in use by the late 14th century. With these, only the top carrying the sails turned, reducing the effort required. Windmills were at first employed only for grinding corn. From the 15th century, their most important use was in pumping water, notably for the land reclamation schemes in Holland. Large cranes continued to use the manpower of the treadmill. All these machines greatly stimulated the development of cog-wheels as a means of gaining mechanical advantage. Some attempts were made to transmit their power over quite long distances, but the losses due to friction must have been considerable.

Moslem Science

In the southern Mediterranean, from about the 7th century A.D., the great unifying force was the religion of Islam whose militancy established the Moslem Empire. In the hundred years following the prophet Mohammed's capture of Mecca in 630, Islam spread to Spain and southern France in the west, and to the borders of India and China in the east.

Moslems gathered and preserved scientific ideas from all the conquered territories. Yet they never produced more than one really original scientific mind. This belonged to Ibn al-Hathem, more familiarly known to us as Alhazen, who lived in the 10th century. He understood the properties of lenses, of plane, spherical and curved mirrors. The Greeks had thought that light travelled from the eyes to the object observed. Alhazen was the first to recognise that light is reflected from an object, and that rays of light travel from every part of it to the eye. As the object moves closer to the eye, the angle at the apex of the cone of rays where they enter the eye widens, as does the base of the cone. This is why the object appears larger the closer it is to the eye. It is the foundation of perspective, which was to revolutionise both art and mathematics in the Renaissance of Europe, 500 years after Alhazen.

The alchemist, often thought of as a magician for his strange experiments, was chiefly concerned with the working of metals.

The horse collar and harness not only enabled horses to be harnessed in file, but made the farmer's ploughing more efficient.

From the East, the Muslim scholars brought another invention—the writing of numbers. Roman numerals simply added the digits together, so that MDCXVI means 1,000+500+100+10+5+1 which equals 1,616. This was cumbersome enough for simple addition. For division and

Fortification was essential during the wars of the Middle Ages, a fact illustrated by this detail from a 15th-century manuscript. Typical of the castles all over Europe are those at Apulia (top) and Harlech (below).

multiplication, it was a very unsatisfactory system. The new notation, which appears to have originated in India, gave the value of each digit according to its position, so that the first digit in 1,616, being four digits along, indicated a thousand. The first 6 represents hundreds, the second 1 represents tens and the last figure stands for units. Such a system requires a symbol to indicate there is no value in one of the columns, so a zero had to be invented.

The Moslems improved on the Greek invention of the astrolabe. This is an instrument for measuring the elevation of the sun or a star. With the use of star maps, the one observation can establish latitude, sunrise and sunset, the time for prayer and the direction of Mecca, towards which the prayers of a Moslem are directed. For many centuries the astrolabe was the only pocket-watch and portable calculator.

Tartars and Mongols

During the Middle Ages, India and China also had their upheavals. By the 10th century, the Moslem invasion of India had begun. Chinese expansion westward was stemmed by the Turks, and she was harassed in the north by the Tartars and the Mongols. The 13th century saw what were virtually the last great bandit raids of nomadic hordes into the more civilised territories. Genghis Khan had forged an irresistible force from his Mongol cavalry. They swept into China and India, and ravaged as far west as present-day Poland. Their nomadic, warlike way of life failed in the end because there was nothing for them to do but adopt the civilised ways of the people they conquered, to become Moslems or Buddhists or even Christians themselves. Settled peoples, enjoying the prosperity of civilisation, cannot indulge in the banditry of nomads. They must defend what they have. Military technology becomes an important branch of engineering.

The medieval metalsmiths became above all armourers. Chain mail had been introduced from the East. Rings of iron wire were riveted or welded together and shaped to cover the whole body, feet, arms and most of the head. By the 12th century, the head was completely encased in a helm of steel with holes for the eyes and nose. Plate armour began to reinforce chain mail until, by the 14th century, knights were completely encased in plate, often beautifully engraved and with the joints and hinges skilfully contrived to give the maximum protection. Mounted knights became the mobile tank divisions of medieval warfare.

Armoured knights took little part in siege warfare. Here, the engineers came into their own. Fortifications were devised to give maximum field of fire to archers, crossbowmen and the artillerymen of the time. Their catapults and huge siege crossbows were capable of hurling heavy arrows with iron heads and stone missiles, or

14th-century brass showing armour worn at the time of Edward III. A late 13th-century bascinet (helmet), two 15th-century swords, and an early 16th-century halberd.

inflammable material like the so-called Greek fire. Siege machinery was developed, such as mobile towers with drawbridges that could be lowered on to enemy walls, and massive mobile battering rams. Despite all this armament, sieges usually resolved themselves into a stalemate with the besiegers waiting for the besieged to be starved into submission or relieved from elsewhere.

Gunpowder

And then came gunpowder. From 500 B.C. in Europe, and from at least as early as the 10th century A.D. in China, inflammable mixtures were commonly used in warfare. From the 7th century A.D., the Byzantine Empire owed its successful defence from repeated attack largely to the use of Greek fire, the secret ingredient of which was probably highly inflammable naphtha. By the 11th century, the Chinese discovered the value of adding nitre (potassium nitrate) which gives off oxygen when heated. By 1300, mixtures of nitre, sulphur and charcoal were being used in artillery and later in small arms as the explosive charge.

Examples of jointed plate armour. 15th-century Maximilian suit from Germany (top), 16th-century suit, with mail skirt, from Milan, and a 16th-century German helmet.

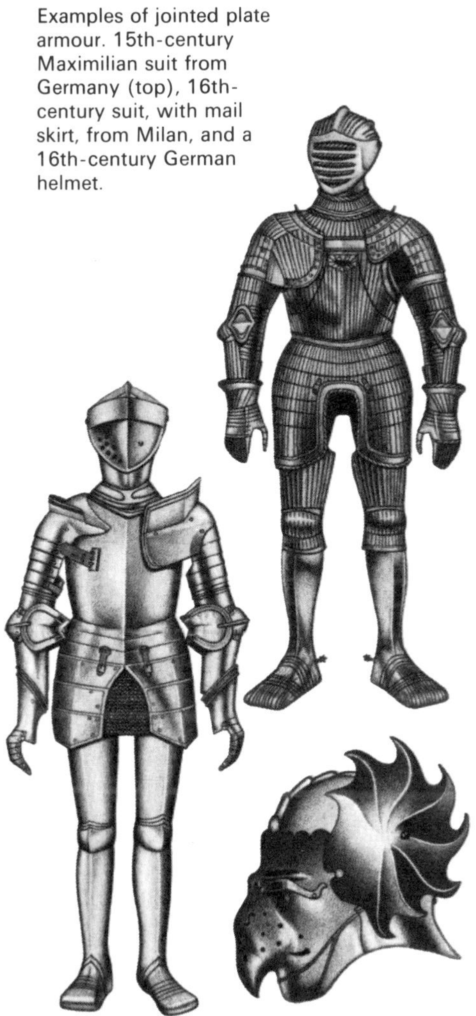

The ballista, used widely in eastern Europe for hurling stone missiles at the enemy's fortification (A.D. 1000–1200).

Siege cannon began to replace slings and catapults during the 14th century. The type shown here is from the 15th century.

The bombard, a stone-throwing machine used in sieges in Europe in the 15th century.

Charcoal had long been used as a fuel. Sulphur occurs naturally in a fairly pure form and, if further purification was needed, this could be achieved by distillation. Nitre was obtained from the earth of stables and pigsties, where it resulted from bacterial action on manure. Boiling in water, sometimes with the addition of potash or lime, separated out the impurities. As the solution cooled, crystals of fairly pure nitre would be formed.

Metal Casting

The bell-maker became the caster of bronze, and later iron, cannon. Improvements in the blast furnace allowed large iron castings to be made. Clay moulds were first shaped, reinforced with iron bars, baked and lowered into pits. Molten metal was poured in and allowed to cool. The mould then had to be broken to remove the casting, and the barrel bored for more precise alignment. Boring bits were usually turned by water-power. As they could be supported at one end only, their accuracy left a lot to be desired. Small arms were very inaccurate, designed only for short-range against close formations of the enemy. Sporting guns were more finely engineered, but too expensive to be used by armies. Words like matchlock and flintlock indicate that the locksmith added his skill to that of the gunsmith to provide trigger mechanisms. The cutting of a spiral groove (or rifling) of the inside of the barrel to spin the missile and make it fly with more accuracy had begun by the end of the 15th century.

Rises in Population

The waves of invasion, tending usually from east to west, resulted in sudden rises in population, particularly in western Europe. Improved methods of farming and vast forest clearance did not always provide sufficient food. In some places, land reclamation seemed to be the answer. Dykes were built, at first of boulder clay faced with seaweed, straw or reeds, later with wooden palisades, the spaces between them stuffed with bundles of faggots. The water inside the dyke was drained, often with scoop-wheels driven by windmills, into the ditch outside the dyke from where it was carried away into rivers or canals. In Holland, sluices were developed in the drainage canals. At certain times, when the pressure of tidal water on one side balanced the pressure of canal water, the sluices could be raised to allow boats to go through. By 1373 there was at least one pair of sluices forming a basin between them, the first example of the lock, which was to become an important feature of transport at the beginning of the Industrial Revolution.

Throughout the Middle Ages, the Mediterranean had provided the principal trade routes by sea, building the prosperity of Constantinople and such city-states as Genoa and Venice. The caravan routes had maintained the Moslem monopoly of trade with the East, particularly in spices. The end of the Middle Ages is marked by the change created by the development of ships and navigational instruments. The great navigators found ways to circumvent both the Mediterranean and the caravan routes. The world was about to be discovered.

Discovery of the World

The Portuguese caravel was broad-bowed, with a narrow, high-built stern and carried deck-mounted cannon. The ships of the great 15th-century explorers who opened up new sea routes were caravels and carracks.

Chinese terrestrial globe

The compass is believed to have been first used in China in the 11th century.

Viking warships were fitted with a steering oar, forerunner of the fixed rudder. Some Arabic ships were rigged with lateen (triangular) sails.

An astrolabe, used in Europe until superseded by the sextant in the 18th century.

Man's curiosity impels him to be forever pushing at the boundaries of his knowledge. New technology must be tested to its limits. So it was in the great age of discovery between A.D. 1450 and 1600.

Astronomers were already beginning to argue again the possibility of a global earth. If there was truth in their claim that the sun travels round the earth, then a sailing ship could do the same and reach the Spice Islands of the East by a westerly route. Was there not some half-forgotten tale of a landfall made in the far west by Norsemen of long ago?

Little by little, as ships and navigational instruments improved, so did the confidence of seafaring men. At last, on 8th September 1522, 31 seamen aboard the *Victoria,* all that was left of Magellan's fleet, arrived home in Seville having journeyed 40,000 miles in three years and circumnavigated the globe.

So the world *was* round. Its many strange lands were open to discovery and exploration. Thereafter ships poured out from European ports with adventurers and settlers bound for the virgin lands.

15th-century quadrant board, used for fixing the position of a vessel at sea by taking angles. Like the astrolabe it later gave way to the sextant.

The seal of Elbing in Germany (13th-century) bears the earliest known pictorial record of a ship's rudder.

The *Henry Grâce à Dieu*, or Great Harry, was flagship of Henry VIII's fleet, weighed 1,000 tons and carried 184 guns. She was one of the first ships to carry cannon which fired through portholes between decks.

Stern view of a Dutch galleon, highlighting the tall, castle-like deck structure. These 17th-century decorated ships sometimes had four decks.

The tainui, a double canoe with steering oars, was used by the Maoris when they migrated to New Zealand around 1350.

The Scientific Revolution

Aristotle's idea of the universe was as a series of revolving spheres with the earth at the centre.

The Old Science

The Scientific Revolution which exploded upon the intellectual world in the 17th century was touched off by a handful of geniuses working in western Europe, men like Copernicus, Vesalius, Galileo, Kepler, Harvey and Newton. The lives of these six span the two and a half centuries between 1473 and 1727 and carry us into the modern world. Yet to trace the origins of their thinking, to discover the stage of learning from which they began, we must go back to the 12th century. Before that, the Moslems had by far the most advanced civilisation the world had yet known. Then, with the aid of more efficient farming methods, western Europe began to emerge from the Dark Ages and enjoy a standard of living as high as any in the ancient world. Intellectuals began to examine and dispute fundamental problems of philosophy and relate them to Christian belief. These scholars grouped themselves into universities, such as those at Paris and Bologna, founded in 1160, Oxford in 1167, Cambridge in 1209, and Padua in 1222.

Moslem Scholarship

It is not known how much Moslem scholarship added to the scientific ideas of the ancient Greeks, since much of our knowledge of the latter comes from works in Arabic. Contact between Islam and Christianity was made principally in Spain and, to a lesser extent, in Sicily. The commentaries on Aristotle by the Islamic scholar Averroes (1125–98) were translated into Latin and eagerly studied by Christian intellectuals. St Thomas Aquinas (1226–74) attempted to reconcile both Aristotelian and Christian thought. Up to the 16th century, most men's ideas of the universe were based on those of Aristotle and the Alexandrian astronomer Ptolemy whose *Almagest* (from the Arabic word for 'greatest' to distinguish it from other, lesser works) was also translated into Latin.

Aristotle had placed the earth at the centre of the universe and surrounded it by eight crystalline spheres, to which later astronomers had added two more. The earth remained motionless while these spheres revolved around it. The first sphere contained the moon, the next Mercury, then successively Venus, the sun, Mars, Jupiter, Saturn and the eighth, the fixed stars. The ninth and tenth spheres carried no heavenly bodies, their movements being used to account for certain changes taking place over the centuries in the positions of the fixed stars as seen from the earth. Each sphere had just sufficient thickness for the heavenly bodies to move from the outermost surface when farthest from the earth to the innermost surface when nearest, thus accommodating the epicycles and eccentrics assumed by Ptolemy (previously described). The spheres were kept in motion by the angels and beyond them was heaven, the home of the elect, with the throne of God.

The armillary sphere is a 'skeleton' globe made up of metal hoops which represent the motions of the heavenly bodies.

According to Aristotle, all the heavenly bodies were composed of perfect and incorruptible matter consisting of the 'quintessence' or fifth essence. Their circular movements were the most perfect motion. Matter in the earth and its atmosphere, on the other hand, consisted of the four elements of fire, air, earth and water. These elements, unlike the unchanging material of the heavens, were subject to change, and their natural motion was vertical, upwards for fire and air, downwards for earth and water. Natural motion did not always take place, as for instance when the elements were mixed together or when they were subject to outside forces such as man's interference.

The Bodily Humours

The attitude to man himself was based on the works of the second century physician Galen, who believed in the four bodily humours already described. Following the vertical motion of the four elements, Galen thought of the blood flowing upwards and downwards in the body. There were two kinds of blood, the bright red kind which governs muscular activity and ebbed and flowed through the arteries, and the dark red blood which controlled the digestive processes and was contained in the veins. A circulating system through the heart was not considered because that would imply circular motion not possible on the imperfect earth.

Basic assumptions about the nature or 'essence' of things were made by the ancient Greek scientists. Such were the assumptions of circular motion of the heavenly bodies and vertical motion of those on earth. From these, logical deductions were made. In the 13th century, scholars began to question these assumptions and to present problems in a different way. The first to outline the new method clearly were the Oxford scholar Robert Grosseteste and his follower Roger Bacon. They suggested that observed phenomena should first be collected, and a theory then be devised to explain them. Once formed, the theory should then be either verified or disproved by appropriate experimentation. This new scientific method of enquiry spread throughout Europe and became an essential ingredient in the Scientific Revolution.

Law of Acceleration

In the 14th century, Nicole Oresme, a French scholar who became Bishop of Lisieux, questioned the assumption of a fixed earth around which the heavenly bodies revolved. He showed that the daily rotation of the earth could not be disproved either by argument or observation. A group of scholars at Merton College, Oxford, began to consider the problems of free-falling bodies, of acceleration and of the motion of projectiles. One of them, William Heytesbury, in about 1335 made the first correct law of acceleration. In effect, he said that, for example, a falling body accelerating from rest at a uniform rate would cover three times the distance in the second half of the time of travel than during the first half of that time. Time was the important factor in the equation. Nicole Oresme used graphs to prove this fact, and it has been claimed that his system of graphs to some extent anticipated mathematical calculus by three centuries.

One of the scenes of contemporary English life from the 14th-century Luttrell Psalter. The introduction of a spinning wheel revolutionised textile production.

In the 15th century, the work on optics of the 10th-century Moslem philosopher Alhazen reached the Renaissance artists of Italy. From it, by 1425, Brunelleschi had worked out a system of perspective as a means of depicting the three-dimensional world on a two-dimensional surface. In 1435, Alberti published a book on the system and said that no painter can paint well without a thorough knowledge of geometry. Thereafter, so much did artists practise mathematics that they were called upon to become architects, engineers, and even ballistic experts. The greatest of these artist-scientists was Leonardo da Vinci (1452–1519) who dissected bodies and made anatomical drawings from them; analysed the flight of birds and invented a model flying machine; worked as a civil and military engineer and studied fossils while constructing canals; and made drawings of quick-firing and breech-loading guns. Mathematics as a means of explaining the universe became the new enthusiasm from which the Scientific Revolution was about to spring.

Leonardo da Vinci was a man of colossal genius. He excelled as a mathematician, painter, sculptor, architect and engineer. He constructed models from some of his plans of various machines, but probably none of these was ever built to full scale.

The New Instruments

What speeded up the spread of scientific enquiry and lit the fuse that turned it into a revolution was the development of what was probably a previous invention. This was in the German city of Mainz in about 1450 when Johaan Gutenberg began printing with movable type. Until then, books had to be laboriously copied out by hand. Printing meant that scientific books could be quickly made available throughout Europe. By 1500, printing presses were at work in every European country except Russia. There were by that date over 1,700 presses in about 300 towns, and an estimated nine million printed books were already in circulation.

Paper had been made in China from such materials as linen, cotton, straw and wood since A.D. 105. In the middle of the eighth century, some Chinese papermakers were taken prisoner by Moslems, and Arab manuscripts written on paper survive from the ninth century. In the 12th century, a paper industry was established by the Moors in Spain from where it spread into Christian Europe. The raw materials were beaten to a pulp and mixed with water in a stamp-mill which used tappets to raise and drop pestles into mortars. Spikes were later added to tear the pieces of rag which were among the raw materials. A frame with 28 or more tightly stretched wires to the inch was dipped into a vat of the pulp and, as the water drained away, the fibres felted together to form a sheet of paper. Laid with others between layers of cloth, the sheet was squeezed in a press and hung up to dry. A suitable printing ink was made from linseed oil and lampblack or powdered charcoal.

Wood-block Printing

Printing from wood blocks goes back to ancient Roman times. Metal engravings were used as early as 1346. These processes were for the printing of pictures, playing cards and the like. What the Gutenberg invention did was to perfect a process for producing letters of the alphabet that could be assembled to form words and sentences, and the same letter used over and over again. Steel punches, familiar from their use for coining, began the process. The punch bearing the letter was struck with a hammer into a softer metal such as lead, which was then inserted into a type mould. Molten metal, probably a tin alloy such as that used for 15th century pewter, was poured into the mould,

By the 16th century, printing houses were established in many European cities.

Illustration from the world's oldest known book, the Diamond Sutra (A.D. 868), from China.

The Chinese have been skilled in paper-making for nearly 2,000 years.

and the foot of the cast type, the end farthest away from the letter, built up to an exact height. Including capitals, joined letters and abbreviations, more than 150 characters had to be cast for each size of type.

The cast type was picked up letter by letter in tweezers and set in line along a composing stick. The lines were made up into pages and clamped into chases. Setting up a single page might take as long as a day. From two to sixteen pages, according to size, were printed on one sheet of paper. A tympan, a parchment-covered frame to which the paper was attached, was hinged down in such a way that the paper came squarely into contact with the inked type. Pressure was then applied with a screw-press. Many copies could, of course, be taken from the same set of type pages by simply re-inking. The type itself could be re-sorted and used again and again until it wore out. Further type could then be cast, using the original punches or moulds. The original 'Gothic' type based on the German handwriting of the day was gradually superseded by the clearer 'Roman' type which is universally used nowadays, as in this book.

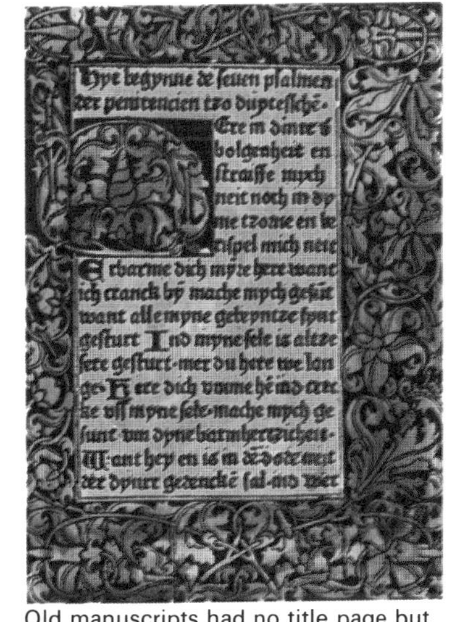

Hye begynne de seuen psalmen
der penitencien tzo duytesche.
Here in dinre v
bolgenheit en
straiffe mych
neit noch in dy
me tzorne en be
rispel mich neit
Erbarme dich myn here want
ich cranck byn mache mych gesunt
want alle myne gebeyntze synt
gesturt Ind myne sele is altze
sere gesturt. mer du here we lan
ge. Here dich vmme hē ind erre
ke vß myne sele. mache mych ge
sunt vm dyne barmhertzicheit.
Want hey en is in dē dode neit
der dyner gedencke sal. ind wer

Old manuscripts had no title page but the first page opened 'Here beginneth'. This one was printed in Cologne in 1485.

Science of Navigation

Among the readers of the new books were the literate sea captains anxious to learn about any new development in the science of navigation. The voyages of discovery in the 15th and 16th centuries were to become a great stimulus to both astronomers and cartographers. The seaman of the time was poorly equipped with navigational aids. By the 13th century, he had a pivoted compass needle to give him direction, though until the 16th century no means of distinguishing magnetic from true north. The astrolabe was used on land to measure the elevation of the sun or a star, but was difficult to use at sea. The 15th-century navigator had the sea-quadrant which measured the angle of elevation of the pole star seen through pin-holes with a plumb-line passing over a graduated scale. The time correction could be made by reference to the changing position of the Guards, two stars in the Lesser Bear. These were also used with an early 16th-century invention called the nocturnal which could be set to indicate the number of hours before or after midnight from their position. Another instrument for measuring elevation, the cross-staff, was improved upon in 1595 by John Davis's invention of the back-staff which had the advantage of allowing the user to turn his back when sighting the sun and so avoid the dazzle.

Reliable Timekeepers

These instruments gave the navigator his latitude, the distance north or south of the equator. His position relative to east and west, his longitude, could not be accurately measured until the production of a reliable timekeeper whereby noon at his port of embarkation could be compared with the number of hours ahead or behind that time when the noon of his present position occurred. Such a timepiece was not produced until the 18th century. Before that, the navigator had to plot his longitudinal position from the number of miles he had sailed east or west. This estimate was made from the logging of his speed. A piece of wood was thrown overboard attached to a rope with knots tied at intervals. The number of knots that passed over the side in a given time indicated his speed, hence the term knots still used for a ship's speed.

Maps of the known world and seamen's charts were at first drawn assuming the earth to be a flat plane. The voyages of discovery had proved the earth to be a sphere. If a navigator was to plot his course accurately in straight lines on a chart and position his landfalls for those who came after him, a map was necessary that allowed for the world's curvature. Mercator's world map, published in 1569, met the requirements. It was produced by projecting from the centre of the globe through each point on its surface and beyond on to, as it were, a cylinder of paper touching the globe only at the equator. Distances were thus accurately to scale when measured from east to west, but became progressively exaggerated the farther north or south the map continued. However, a curved line across the surface of the globe became a straight line on the map. With some modification, Mercator's projection is used to this day.

A 16th-century map (above) showing part of Europe, Asia and Africa.

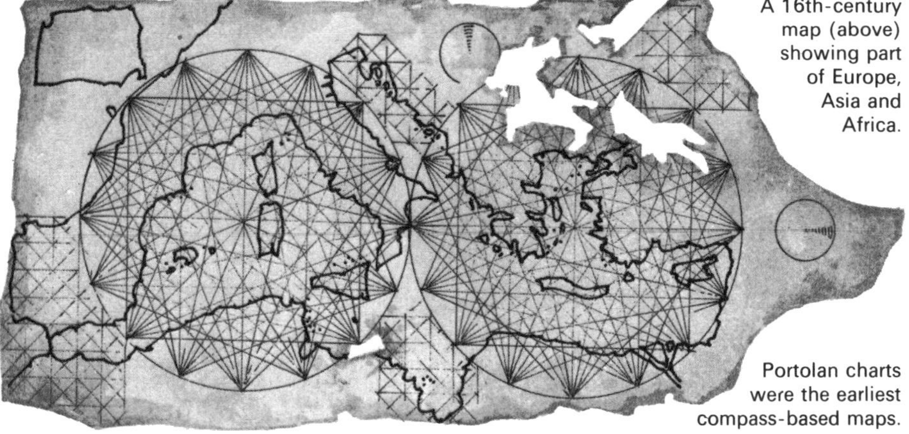

Portolan charts were the earliest compass-based maps.

Advances in Mathematics

There were great advances in mathematics during the 16th and 17th centuries. Most of the symbols used today as essential to the writing of mathematical problems were invented or came into general use during these two centuries: signs that we take for granted nowadays, such as those for addition (+), subtraction (−), multiplication (×), division (÷), equal to (=), greater than (>) and less than (<). The enclosing of figures or letters in brackets, to indicate that these should be dealt with first, began in the 17th century. So did the use of a decimal point to divide the units from the tenths of a number.

François Viète, known as Vieta, who died in 1603, developed the Moslem use of algebra by rationalising the symbols used and reducing them in number. He raised mathematics from the specialised uses it had had before to a much greater level of generalisation, enabling it to cope with more abstract ideas. John Napier (1550–1617) invented logarithms. This involved a tabular system of numbers which replaced the ordinary processes of multiplication by those of addition and subtraction. Napier's friend, Henry Briggs (1561–1631) published the first table of 1,000 logarithms in 1617. In 1624, he published his *Arithmetica Logarithmica* containing the logarithms of 30,000 numbers worked out to fourteen places of decimals. Logarithms represent one of the greatest steps forward in practical mathematics. The French astronomer Pierre de Laplace (1749–1827) said that the invention, by shortening their labours, doubled the life of the astronomers.

René Descartes (1596–1650) was another mathematician who forged a new tool, this time in the service of dynamics. He combined together algebra and geometry, showing that many geometrical problems could be put into algebraic form and solved by the use of the standard rules of algebra and arithmetic. His technique was very useful with such calculations as those associated with ballistics, where accurate measures of the range of guns were required. It helped to solve many of the problems in the science of mechanics.

The Calculus

An even more useful mathematical tool was the calculus which was worked out independently by two men, Isaac Newton (1642–1727) and Gottfried Leibniz (1646–1716). The calculus made possible calculations involving continuous change. In mechanics and astronomy, for instance, where the changing movement of bodies is involved, the calculus is essential. Newton had to invent it to prove mathematically his theories of such things as the moon's orbit round the earth. He worked it out in the 1660s but did not publish his system, which he called fluxions, until 1704. Leibniz invented his form in the 1670s and published it in 1696. It is his superior notation which is used today. Leibniz also invented a calculating machine that could add, subtract, multiply, divide and work out the roots of numbers.

Blaise Pascal

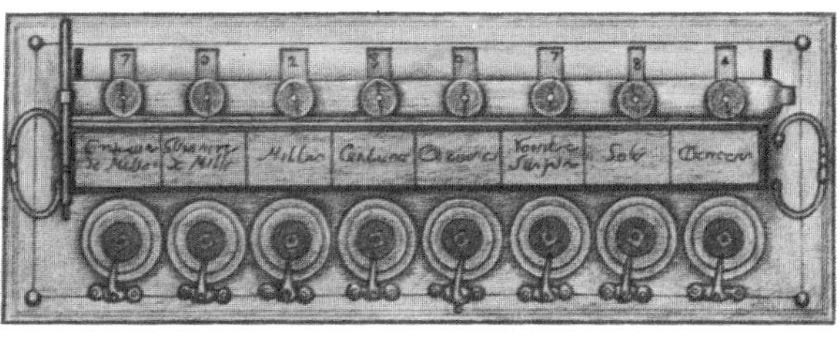

Adding machines constructed by the French scientist Pascal (1623–62) were the first to use counter gears. Seen below is a map of the world on Mercator's projection.

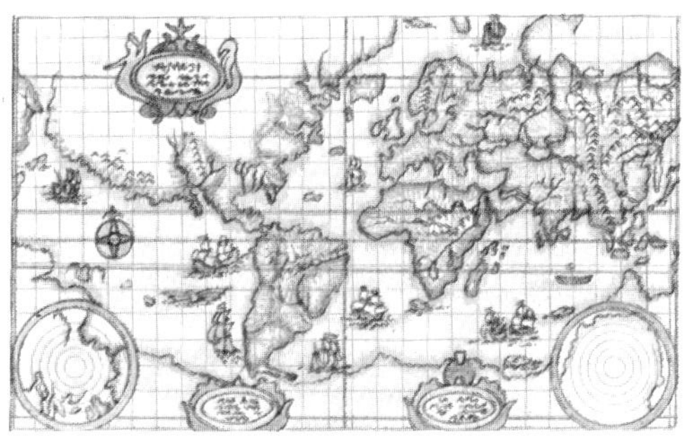

Gerhardus Mercator

Bacon and Descartes

The work of two men is important in the development of modern scientific method. The first of these was Francis Bacon (1561–1626). He made no scientific discoveries himself, but his books caught the imagination of other scientific thinkers and were widely read. He recommended the collection of masses of facts by observation and experiment, and the formation of general theories from them. He warned that the generalisation on a fact based solely on numbers was not good enough. For instance, all the swans ever observed by people living in Europe were white, but that did not mean that all swans are therefore white—a generalisation disproved when the black swan was discovered in Australia. He believed that the progress of mankind could only be achieved by the amassing of records of fact and experiment in every field of science from all over the world, and using this accumulation to advance into further experiment. Scientific progress on these lines would bring with it material prosperity.

The other writer on scientific method was René Descartes, the inventor of analytical geometry. He saw the mechanical universe as being subject to mathematical laws. Nothing was to be taken on trust except the primary self-evident fact: 'I think, therefore I exist'. From this beginning, he thought everything else could be proved by mathematical deduction.

Observation, experiment, precise mathematical calculation and deduction, these were the combined approaches of Bacon and Descartes. To them must be added the ability to form general imaginative concepts which such methods can prove. All these came together in the person of Galileo who could be described as the first truly modern scientist. Men like Galileo had to be more than scientists. Often, they had to invent and construct their own apparatus. Invention sometimes made the new science possible, and the new science stimulated invention. A typical example of this cross-fertilisation is the enquiry into air pressure.

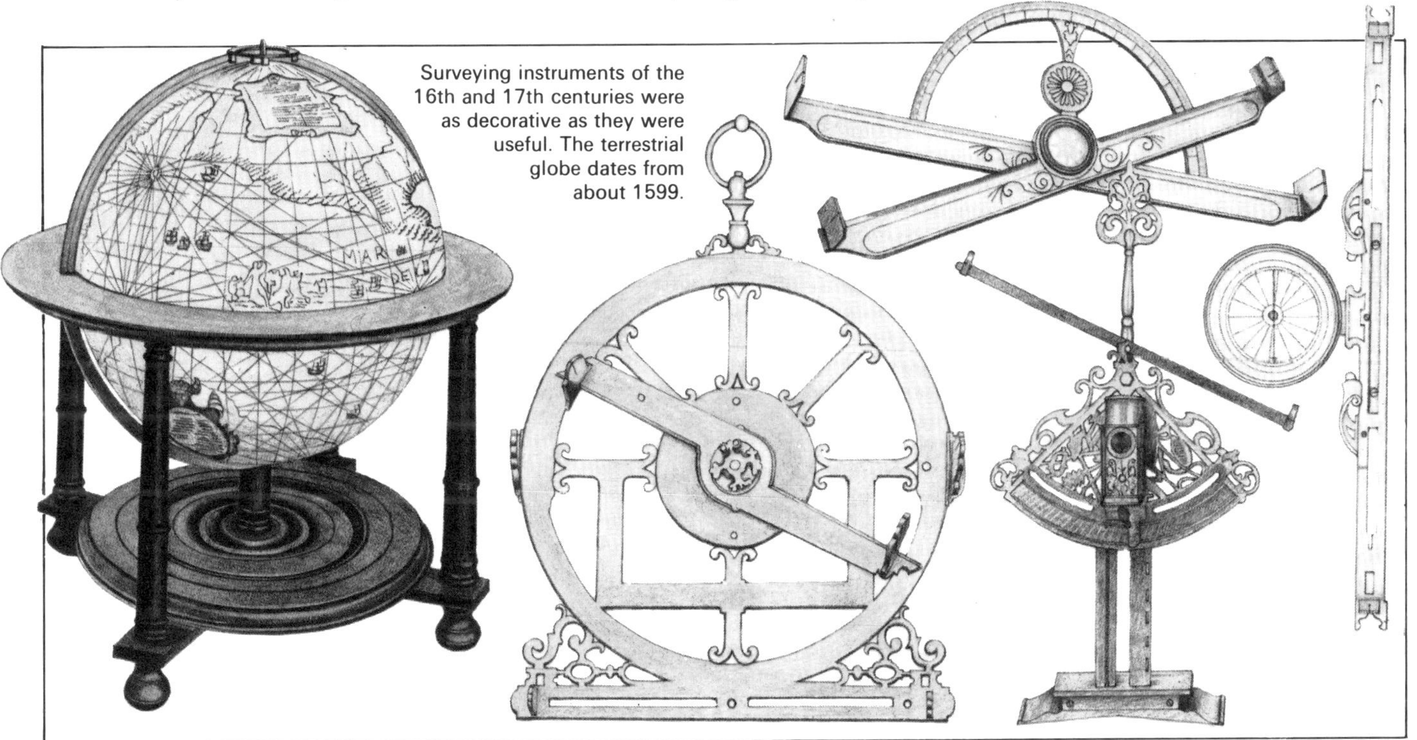

Surveying instruments of the 16th and 17th centuries were as decorative as they were useful. The terrestrial globe dates from about 1599.

One of von Guericke's experiments to show that two hemispheres placed together to form a sphere, with the air between them extracted, could not be pulled apart by heavy weights.

Galileo was asked why the ordinary lift-pumps of the day used in mines could raise water only 10·4 metres (34 feet). Experiments with columns of water 10·4 metres (34 feet) high present difficulties. Galileo's pupil, Evangelista Torricelli (1608–47), had the idea of experimenting with mercury instead, since it is about fourteen times heavier than water. He sealed one end of a glass tube about a yard long and filled it with mercury. He covered the open end with his finger, turned the tube over and immersed it in a bowl containing mercury. When he removed his finger, the mercury in the tube sank to a height of about 76 centimetres (30 inches), leaving a space above it which Torricelli believed, correctly, to be a vacuum. This could disprove Aristotle's theory that a vacuum cannot exist in nature. Torricelli believed that what held up the mercury to a particular height was the weight of air on the mercury in the bowl, there being no air pressing down on the column in the tube. He noticed that the height of the mercury in the tube varied slightly from day to day, and ascribed this to changes in atmospheric pressure. He had invented the barometer.

Pascal's Experiments

News of Torricelli's discovery reached Blaise Pascal (1623–62) who lived in Rouen, France. Pascal designed special apparatus and had it made at the Rouen glassworks. A glass tube over 12 metres (40 feet) long with one end sealed was lashed to a ship's mast. The glass tube was filled with water, and the open end stoppered. The mast was then lowered into a tub of water, stoppered end downwards, and the stopper removed underwater. A column of water 10·4 metres (34 feet) high remained in the tube. Pascal calculated from the different specific gravities of mercury and water that the equivalent heights to which columns of the two liquids ought to be held by the same outside pressures should indeed be 76 centimetres (30 inches) and 10·4 metres (34 feet) respectively. Then he attached a bag filled with mercury to a glass tube and immersed it in water. The mercury rose farther up the tube the deeper the bag was plunged, indicating a greater pressure at a greater depth. From this, Pascal reasoned that air pressure must be greater at a lower altitude since, like the deeper water, a greater weight of air is pressing down on the air at a low altitude than at a high altitude. He arranged for his brother-in-law to carry a Torricelli barometer to the top of the Puy de Dome, a mountain in Auvergne, to test if the column of mercury fell at the higher altitude. It did, by 7·6 centimetres (3 inches). There was even a small, measurable difference when the mercury tube was taken to the top of the highest tower in the church of Notre Dame de Clermont.

Producing a Vacuum

Quite independently, at Magdeburg in Germany, Otto von Guericke (1602–86) was trying experiments to produce a vacuum. He began with a water pump attached to a sealed cask full of water. Two strong men were set to pump out the water, von Guericke reasoning that a vacuum would thus be left inside the cask. The cask collapsed under the pressure of the air outside. He tried again with a stronger cask which made a sizzling noise as the air forced its way in. Finally, he used a copper globe and at last produced a vacuum. Then he invented and constructed an air-pump. With this, he drew out the air from two bronze hemispheres placed together. At a famous experiment in 1651, before the emperor Ferdinand III, he showed that two teams of eight horses each could not pull the hemispheres apart once the air inside them had been removed, proving the force of the air pressure on the outside. Von Guericke weighed a sphere with and without air to determine the density of air. He built a water barometer up the side of his house with a little manikin floating on top. From his observations of this, he forecast a severe storm in 1660. He also showed that light could pass through a vacuum but sound could not; also that a vacuum extinguishes a candle flame and kills small animals.

In Britain, Robert Boyle (1627–91), a rich aristocrat with a private laboratory of his own, heard about von Guericke's air-pump. Boyle's assistant Robert Hooke (1635–1703) made one of his own design. With this, they conducted many experiments, and Boyle formulated his famous law that the volume of a given mass of gas, at constant temperature, is inversely proportional to its pressure.

Measuring Time

It became important to the experimenters of the 16th and 17th centuries to be able to measure time accurately. From about 1500 B.C., the shadow-clock with a number of scales to be used at different times of the year; the water-clock or clepsydra which measured the flow of water from a small orifice into a large container; and the sand-glass, using sand on the same principle, were for thousands of years virtually the only time-keepers. Mechanical clocks first appeared in the 13th century A.D., driven by falling weights. Spring-driven clockwork, making watches possible, did not appear until the 15th century.

The force exerted by a falling weight is the same at the end of its fall as at the beginning. But a spring diminishes in force as it uncoils. To compensate for this, a fusee was used. This was a conical drum with a spiral groove so arranged that, as the spring uncoiled, a connecting cord exerted a greater moment of force on the shaft carrying the fusee. The timekeeping or escapement mechanism of early clocks was the verge, in which a pair of tongues on an oscillating arm engaged alternately with the cogs of a wheel geared to the falling weights. The verge was subject to a good deal of friction and did not keep time very accurately.

In 1582, Galileo discovered the principle of the pendulum, that the time taken by a suspended weight to swing to and fro is virtually independent of the extent of its swing. In 1641, he invented a pin-wheel escapement to go with the pendulum and

Torricelli believed that man lived 'submerged at the bottom of an ocean of air'. He sought to prove this by his invention of a simple apparatus which was the forerunner of the barometer.

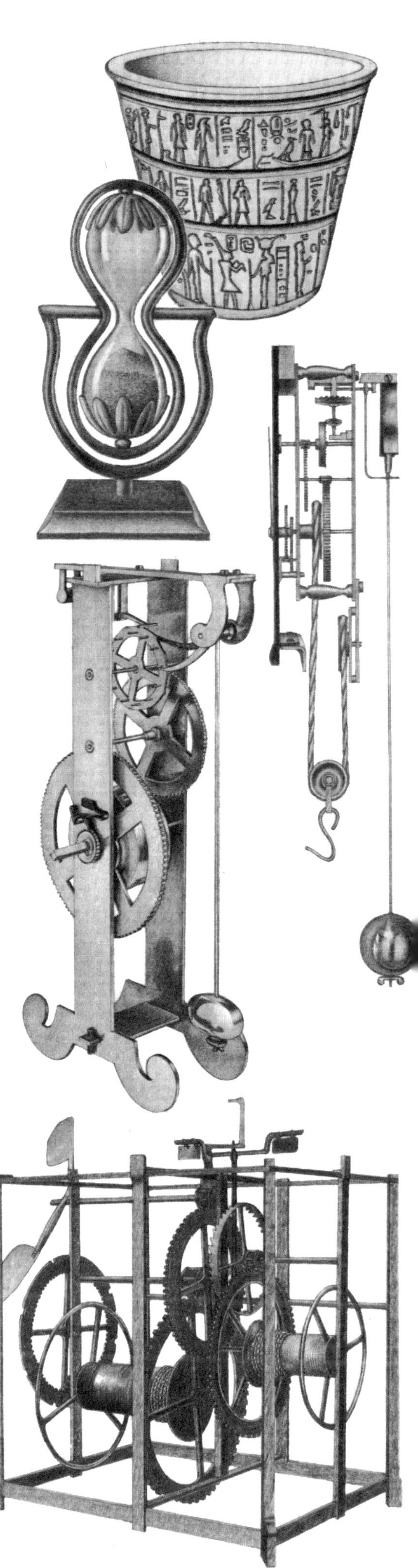

Since his earliest time on earth man has probably devised ways of marking the passage of time. At first his life was regulated by natural events; such things as sunrise and sunset. The earliest methods used to mark the passing of time included candles or pieces of cord marked off in sections so that when they were lit their rate of burning could be recorded. Other devices included water clocks, hour-glasses and shadow clocks which recorded the passage of the sun. Mechanical clocks began possibly as long ago as the 7th century A.D. Examples shown are (top to bottom) Egyptian water clock, an hour-glass, a pendulum mechanism, 17th-century pendulum clock by Huygens and the clock from Salisbury Cathedral in England.

The crest of the Royal Society, founded in 1662.

left behind him after his death detailed drawings for a clock mechanism prepared by his son. The principle of the pendulum was first developed in clock mechanisms by Christiaan Huygens (1629–95), a Dutch mathematician, astronomer and physicist. Huygens's clockmaker in the Hague, Salomon da Costa, made many of his clocks for sale, but all of them incorporated the old verge escapement. Better escapements, such as the anchor or recoil used by the London clockmaker William Clement from about 1671, interfered less with the swing of the pendulum. It also required less arc of swing, so the pendulum could be included with the driving weights in the long case of the so-called grandfather clock.

The Microscope

Another useful instrument that the 17th-century scientists had to make, or at least design, for themselves was the microscope. The use of lenses has a long history going back to the ancient Greeks. The invention of the compound microscope, using two or more lenses, did not occur until the end of the 16th century, probably in Holland. The ingenious Robert Hooke was one of the first microscopists. His microscope consisted of a tube about 16 centimetres (6 or 7 inches) long inside which another tube could slide, with an objective lens at the lower end and an eye lens at the top. A third lens could be introduced between these two to give a wider view. The object was fixed on a pin on the base, and the microscope could be focused with a screw thread at the lower end. Hooke found that a good deal of light was needed to make the enlarged image clear. By day, he used the sunlight from a window. At night or in dull weather, he used a small lamp, the rays of which were focused on the object through a glass sphere filled with brine. Hooke published his *Micrographica* in 1665 with his own beautiful drawings of a large variety of objects as seen through his microscope.

Another great English microscopist was Nehemiah Grew (1641–1712) who used the instrument to study plants. He discovered that the stamens of a flower are the male organs and the pistils female. Two Dutchmen were among the early microscopists. The first, Jan Swammerdam (1637–80) was an amazingly skilful dissector of insects. His scalpels, knives, lancets and scissors were so fine he had to sharpen them under a microscope. The second Dutchman, Anton van Leeuwenhoek, made most of his observations with a single lens giving 300 times magnification. He taught himself micro-dissection and could remove the brain from the head of a gnat. His most remarkable discovery was what he called his 'little animal-cules' which he saw swimming about in fresh water taken from a lake near his home at Delft. He described them as above a thousand times smaller than cheese-mites. He was, in fact, observing for the first time ever single-cell protozoa, the simplest form of animal life.

Galileo's Telescopes

Galileo may or may not have invented the thermometer which was developed in the 17th century, but he certainly had a great deal to do with the improvement of the telescope. He heard of such an instrument made by a spectacle-maker in Middleburg, Holland, called Hans Lippershey. At once, Galileo set himself the problem of constructing a telescope of his own, and solved it in a single night. The first instrument he constructed in his own workshop had a magnification of about three, no better than a superior opera-glass. Soon, however, he had improved this to a magnification of

When the French Academy of Sciences began their meetings in the Royal Library in 1666, the members were given pensions by Louis XIV, who also set up a fund for the purchase of instruments.

eight or ten, which is a real telescope. All Galileo's telescopes worked on the refraction of the image, bending it through a lens. In 1668, Isaac Newton made a telescope which reflected the image from a mirror. Newton's reflecting telescope was the prototype of all the largest ones used today.

Thus, the new scientists of the 16th and 17th centuries had the means of communication through the printed book, both by translations from the past and new works they contributed themselves. They had the stimulation of world discovery and the knowledge it brought. They had a growing appreciation of a new scientific method involving exact observation and carefully measured experimentation. Where suitably accurate instruments were not available to them, they had the skill to construct their own. Finally, they had the encouragement provided by the learned societies that began to spring up to back research and spread the knowledge of their discoveries.

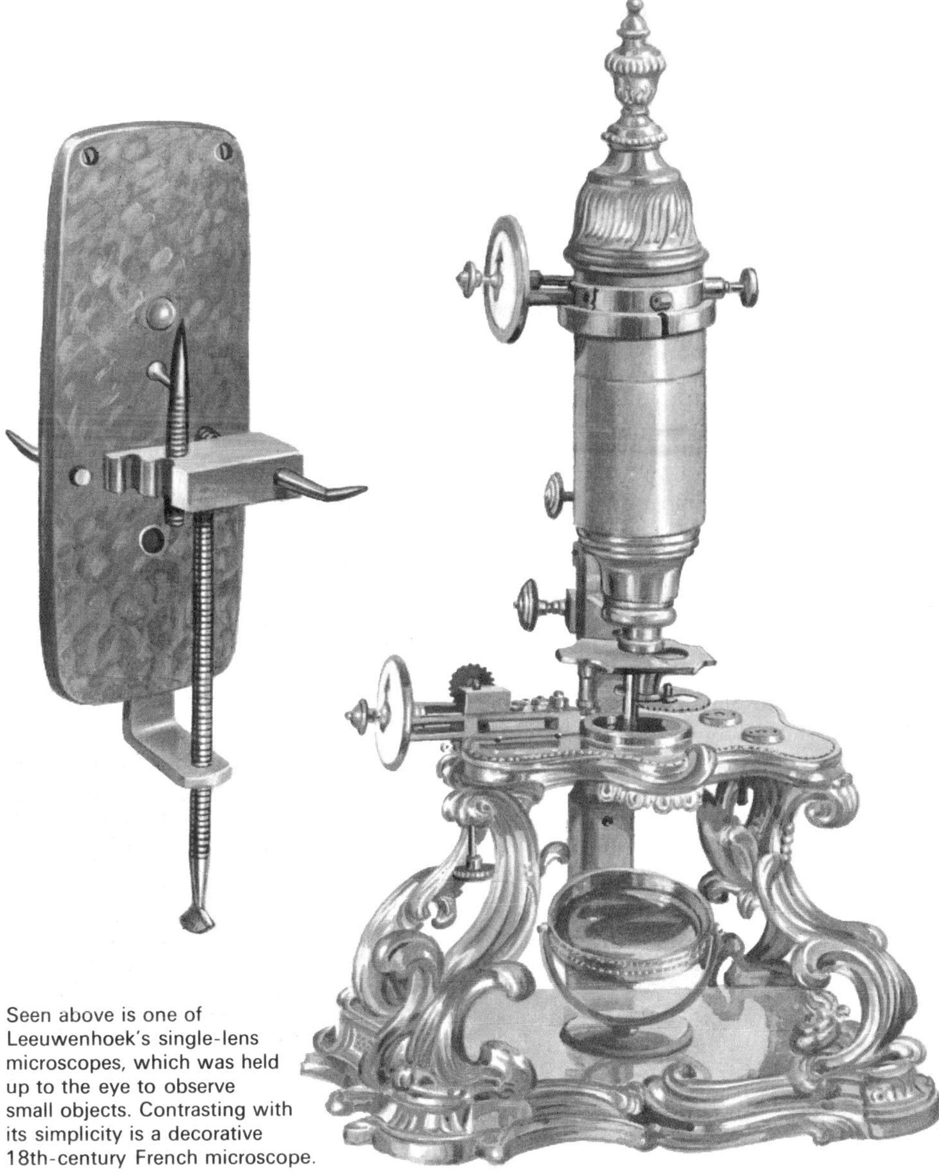

Seen above is one of Leeuwenhoek's single-lens microscopes, which was held up to the eye to observe small objects. Contrasting with its simplicity is a decorative 18th-century French microscope.

Scientific Societies

One of the earliest of these societies met in Rome between 1601 and 1630. It was called the Academy of the Lynx-eyed. Galileo was the sixth member and greatly valued the contacts he made there. Between 1657 and 1667, the Academy of Experiment flourished in Florence under the patronage of the Medici family. It published a book which became a laboratory manual.

In Britain, the Royal Society was founded by Charles II in 1662. It grew from a club formed in London in 1645 by men influenced by Francis Bacon's 'new philosophy'. Merchants played a considerable role. Committees were set up to study the history and technological requirements of such trades as shipping, mining, brewing and woollen manufactures. Most eminent men of the age were members. At the beginning, Bacon was the leading spirit. From his appointment as President in 1703, Isaac Newton dominated the Society.

In France, a small group centred around Father Mersenne who kept in communication with men like Galileo and Descartes. In 1666, the Paris Academy of Sciences was founded by the king's chief minister, Colbert, with twenty members, each of whom was paid a pension. In 1699, it was reorganised by Louis XIV to include most of the famous people interested in science, who met in the Louvre.

Perhaps the most valuable functions of the scientific societies were the publication of papers by the members and the contact maintained internationally between men of science. Oldenburg, secretary of the Royal Society, was forced to use the pseudonym Grubendol because his correspondence abroad aroused suspicion. Despite such precautions, during 1667 he spent two months imprisoned in the Tower of London.

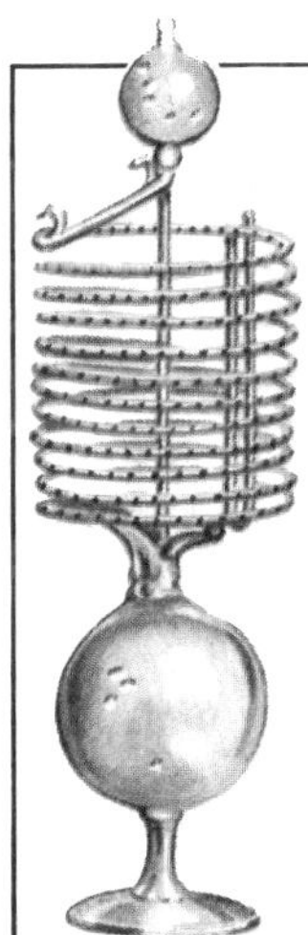

Galileo's thermoscope, an invention of 1593, was the beginning of the modern thermometer. His original instrument does not exist but there is a model in the Museum of Sciences in Florence. The spiral thermometer (left) was made in Florence in 1657. Such devices consisted of glass tubes twisted and turned into a variety of attractive shapes. Liquid rose or fell inside the tube as temperature altered.

The New Scientists

Throughout history, astronomy features prominently in the story of early science. It was so at Sumer. The Greek philosophers were absorbed by the subject. Even the Mayans who created the most advanced civilisation in the New World were concerned with it. It began the Scientific Revolution in western Europe. There were practical reasons, of course. Farmers needed to know when the appropriate seasons were due for preparing the ground and planting the seed. Attempts to produce an accurate calendar led to a system of mathematics to measure the movements of the heavenly bodies. A traveller seeking direction across the trackless land masses had to depend on the position of the sun and the stars. Sailors ventured out of sight of land with only sun and stars to guide them. Groups of stars were given personalities as an aid to memory, and a whole mythology was created around them. From the study of astronomy came the sciences of arithmetic, geometry, mechanics and physics.

The orrery (seen above) was a device which demonstrated the movements of the heavenly bodies and their relative positions. The model planets were rotated mechanically when the handle was turned. The instrument was named by its inventor George Graham in honour of the 4th Earl of Orrery.

The heavens have been studied in the East for many centuries, particularly in India. Observatories such as that at Jaipur (top of page) date from the 18th century. The stone stairways provided fixed angles to calculate the position of the stars.

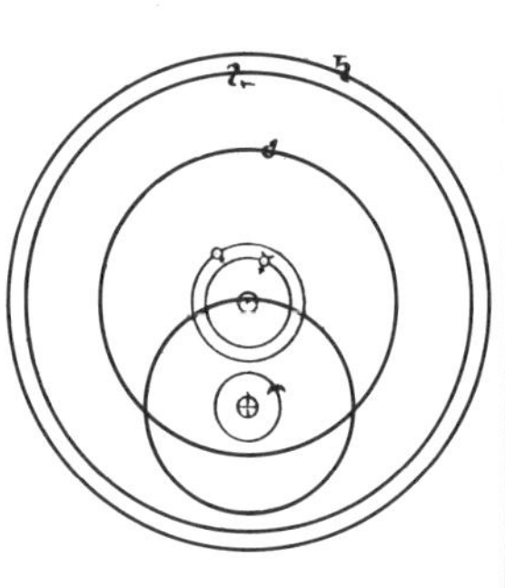

The Danish astronomer Tycho Brahe built an observatory at Uraniborg in 1576 (above left) where he worked for 21 years. The old print (left) shows Brahe inside the observatory. Far left is Brahe's idea of the solar system.

It was astronomy that gave the world navigators the confidence to embark on their voyages of discovery. Why was it the people of the Old World who set sail to discover the New? Why not the other way round? There were certainly great voyages made in the south Pacific, when primitive men discovered the Polynesian islands, for instance, or when the Maoris reached New Zealand. Such voyages were almost certainly accidental, the coastal vessels being carried off by strong currents or prevailing winds. The southern hemisphere has no pole star to guide a sailor home. When he made his chance landfall, he was stuck there.

The north American Indian was

trapped in his great continent by the retreat of the ice cap which created the Bering Strait. It is possible that he did not create a communication network on land because he never developed the great dynamic of the Old World, the wheel. Though he valued the power of the sun, his religion was directed towards Mother Earth, the giver of life and the place to which the dead returned. In the Old World, the wheel was symbolic of the revolving planets, with the earth at the hub. In its three-dimensional concentric form, as in the armillary sphere, it established the pattern of the universe.

Calculating Longitude

The 15th-century voyages of discovery gave a new impetus to astronomy. The calculation of a ship's longitude, the distance east or west of a fixed meridian, depended upon time. A difference in time of one hour measured one twenty-fourth of the circumference of the earth at the equator, or 15° of longitude. A great deal of observation of the moon's passage among the stars was recorded in the hope that the moon might be used as a clock. Calendar reform was needed in the 15th century, too. The Julian calendar introduced in 46 B.C. assumed a year of 365¼ days, whereas the year is shorter than this by 11 minutes and 14 seconds. By the 16th century, the discrepancy had accumulated to more than a week. The pope requested assistance in reform of the calendar from a Polish churchman and intellectual, Nicolas Copernicus (1473–1543).

Renaissance Man

Men of the Renaissance prided themselves on being interested in all the intellectual pursuits. Copernicus was a true Renaissance Man. He was born at the port of Torun in Poland and went to the university of Cracow where there was a flourishing school of astronomy. After five years, he went to Bologna in Italy to study law, mathematics and astronomy, and to learn Greek. Later, he studied medicine at Padua. The last 30 years of his life, he spent as canon of Frauenburg cathedral. Near the cathedral, on a slight hill overlooking the Baltic, was the tower where Copernicus made his astronomical observations. He must have come to many of the conclusions contained in his book, *The Revolution of the Heavenly Orbs,* many years before it was published. It seems he was afraid of the controversy it would arouse. At last, it was published in 1543, and it is said that Copernicus saw only one copy, given to him on his death-bed.

The title of the book was prophetic. In fact, it gave a new meaning to the word revolution that Copernicus had not intended. Against all the theories of Aristotle and Ptolemy, which were the official teaching of the Church, Copernicus put the sun at the centre of the universe, with the planets, including earth, revolving around it at different speeds. Such an arrangement would explain why Mars, for instance, sometimes appears to be moving backwards and sometimes forwards. If the earth, in a smaller orbit round the sun, were moving faster than Mars in its larger orbit, then sometimes the earth would be moving away from Mars and sometimes towards it. This would also account for the variation in the brightness of Mars which Copernicus had observed. The closer the earth's orbit carried it towards Mars, the brighter Mars would appear. The great argument against a universe with the sun rather than the earth at its centre was that the stars towards which the earth was moving would appear to move farther apart, and those from which it was retreating would appear to move closer together. Copernicus answered this by supposing that the stars were so far away from the earth that the difference in their relative positions would be too small to notice. The navigators discovered a far larger earth than they had imagined. Copernicus was suggesting a far larger universe than his predecessors had ever visualised.

Astronomical instruments at the 17th-century Jesuit observatory in Peking, China.

Copernicus in his celebrated book *The Revolution of the Heavenly Orbs* clearly demonstrated his belief that the sun was the true centre of the solar system around which all the planets including the earth revolved. Below is seen a room at Greenwich Observatory near London in the 18th century.

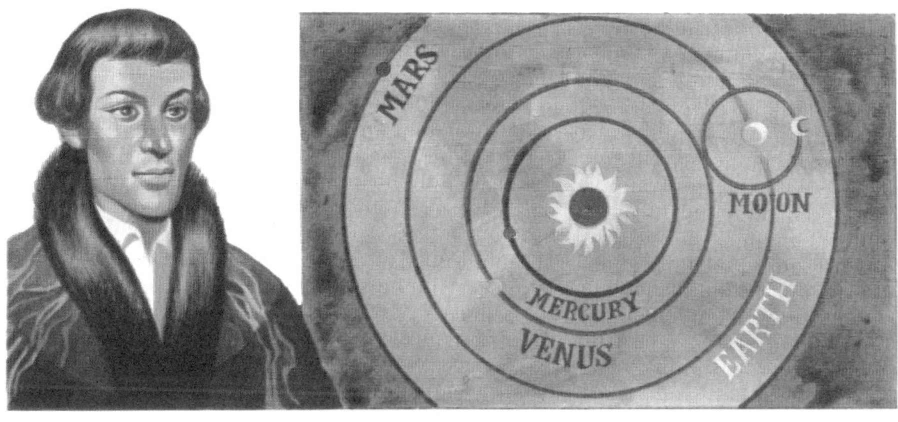

Brahe's New Stars

Yet Copernicus still clung to the circular orbits of the ancients, and his new system was complicated by the inaccurate data it was based upon. In November 1572, a new star made its appearance, an event Aristotle would have claimed to be impossible in the unchanging perfection of the heavens. The new star was noticed by a remarkable man, Tycho Brahe (1546–1601), a Danish nobleman who wrote about it in the following year. He claimed that he had known every star in the heavens since boyhood, and that there had never before been a star in the place where the new one had appeared. What he had seen was a very distant exploding star, but his account of it created a sensation at the time.

In 1576, Frederick II of Denmark offered him rent-free the island of Hveen between Copenhagen and Elsinore. There Tycho Brahe built an observatory complete with library, printing press, chemical laboratory and a workshop where most of his instruments were made. Then he set about making accurate records of the night-by-night position of all the planets. This regime he followed for twenty years. He had no telescope, of course, the positions of the planets were plotted with a quadrant, the moving arm of which could be sighted on the planet and the elevation read off on a graduated scale.

Tycho had lost the bridge of his nose in a student duel. He replaced it with a plate of gold and silver alloy. He had an egg-shaped head and a large handlebar moustache. He matched this piratical appearance with his arrogant manner. He quarrelled with King Frederick's successor, Christian IV, and was forced

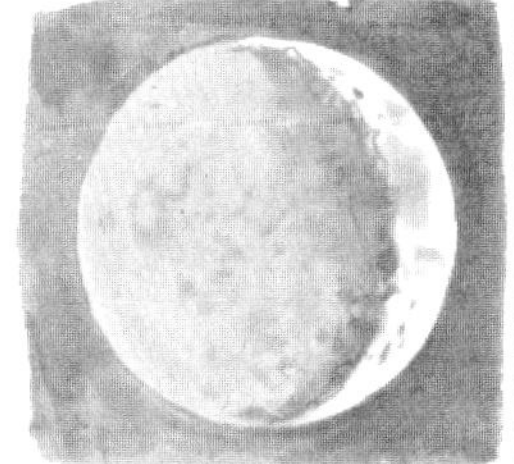

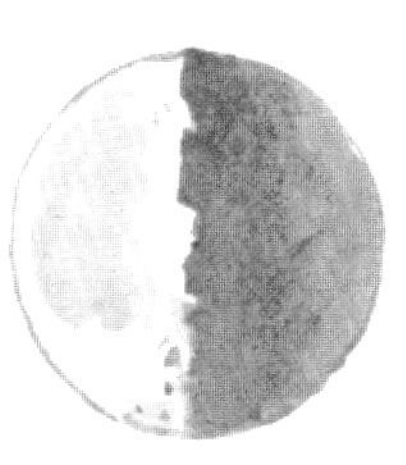
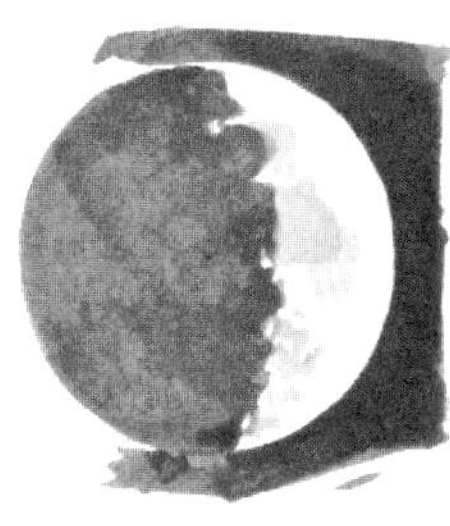

Galileo devised an idea for adapting a pendulum to control clockwork, although it is not known for certain whether he ever made such an instrument. The mechanism seen in this drawing is based on a 19th-century model made from original drawings. Below are reproductions of Galileo's drawings of the moon as he saw it through his telescopes.

to leave his island observatory in 1597. He wandered about Europe for a couple of years until the Emperor of Bohemia gave him a castle near Prague. It was there he met Johann Kepler (1571–1630), who was to inherit the records of Brahe's observations on his death eighteen months later.

Planetary Motion

Tycho Brahe did not believe that the earth moves. He thought the planets revolved around the earth-and-moon system. Though his observations of a comet in 1577 dealt a further blow to the Aristotelian theory of crystalline spheres which could never be penetrated by a moving body, his importance stems from the hitherto unsurpassed accuracy of his observations. With these, Kepler was able to formulate his laws of planetary motion.

Kepler was born at Weil in south-west Germany and was intended by his parents for the Lutheran ministry. His interest in astronomy and aptitude for mathematics decided him to abandon divinity before taking his final examinations. He took a job as teacher of astronomy and mathematics at Graz. His duties were light enough for him to write a book on his idea that the universe was built on geometrical lines around such figures as the pyramid and cube. He sent a copy to Tycho Brahe who invited him to join his work. Kepler accepted and came into possession of Tycho's papers.

The best observations were those of Mars. From these, Kepler tried to plot a circular orbit for Mars with its epicycles on the basis of Copernicus's system and found it would not work. At last, he decided to abandon the circle and try an ellipse. He had little hope of success since he thought that an elliptical orbit would already have been discovered centuries ago if it existed. The ellipse fitted the observed facts, not only of the motion of Mars but all the known planets as well (Uranus, Neptune and Pluto had not been discovered in Kepler's day). At last, all the complex of circles, epicycles and eccentrics was swept away. The answer had a beautiful simplicity. Each planet had a single elliptical orbit around the sun.

Elliptical Orbits

Thus Kepler established the fundamental law that the planets move round the sun in ellipses. He also discovered that each planet increases or decreases its speed along its elliptical orbit in such a way that it is

The German astronomer Johann Kepler and an illustration from his book on the laws of planetary motion.

moving at its greatest speed when it is closest to the sun, and at its slowest speed farthest from the sun. Finally, he devised a formula from which can be calculated the distance of planets from the sun and the periods of their orbits. For instance, Saturn's average distance from the sun is shown to be nearly 9·7 times that of the earth's, and the time taken by its complete orbit is about 30 times the earth's orbit or 30 years. The complicated calculations required to arrive at these conclusions involved immense labour. Like Pythagoras, Kepler believed in the mystical quality of numbers and wrote much nonsense about them. Yet for the first time, he had separated our solar system from the rest of the heavenly bodies and discerned the relationship of the planetary motions within it.

Experiments in Mechanics

Galileo Galilei (1564–1642) was born at Pisa and attended the university there, where he was appointed professor of mathematics at the age of 25. Three years later, he moved to a professorship at Padua, one of the most famous universities in Europe. Padua was in the republic of Venice, and Venice was the hub of the Mediterranean world. There, ambitious men were free to work without restraint. Galileo was able to pursue his experiments in mechanics. He took the 14th-century work of William Heytesbury on acceleration and the motion of projectiles to the point of mathematical formulae, and proved these equations experimentally.

The distance covered by a falling body is proportional to the square of the time taken. That is the mathematical theory. Galileo put it to experimental test. He 'slowed down' gravity by using an inclined plane instead of dropping the body vertically when, with the devices available to him, the time would have been difficult to measure accurately. He rolled a bronze ball down a sloping board with a groove cut in it. The ball was highly polished and perfectly spherical. The groove was lined with polished parchment. Everything was done to reduce friction to a minimum. To measure the time taken by the ball, a large vessel was filled with water and fitted with a pipe of small diameter. The water which flowed from the pipe during the ball's descent was weighed on an accurate balance. It was found that the ball rolling down a quarter of the length of the groove took half the time it did rolling down the whole length. Various lengths of the groove

Galileo's first thoughts on the pendulum were inspired by his observations of a swinging lamp in the cathedral at Pisa.

were tried, and these lengths were always in the same proportion to each other as the squares of the times taken for the ball to roll down.

A similar experiment was to roll a ball down one inclined plane and allow it to roll up another set at a less steep angle. Galileo found that whatever angle he set the rising plane, the ball always rolled up it to the same vertical height from which it had started on its downward path, allowing for a slight discrepancy due to friction. If the rising plane was at a very low angle, the ball would roll a considerable distance along it to achieve the height from which it had started. Galileo wondered what would happen if the second plane was horizontal and concluded that without friction or other causes to slow the ball down or stop it, it would continue to roll. This he ascribed to its inertia.

Inertia and Motion

The idea of inertia is that uniform motion is just as 'natural' as a state of rest, that the movement of a body will continue until other forces are applied to it to slow it down or accelerate it, change its direction or stop it. Observing what happened when a ball was rolled across a table and fell over the edge, Galileo realised that the horizontal and vertical motions were independent of each other. Disregarding air resistance, the horizontal motion would continue while the vertical force of gravity was acting to change the ball's direction. From this he showed that the path of the ball beyond the table's edge was a half parabola. He deduced, therefore, that the path of a projectile, again disregarding air resistance, is a full parabola. He still mistakenly believed that inertial movement, at least on a large scale, was circular like the movement of planets. But he had made a fundamental change in scientific attitudes. Before, scientists had sought to explain motion itself. Now, if it was natural for motion, once begun, to continue, then it was *changes* of motion that should concern the scientist.

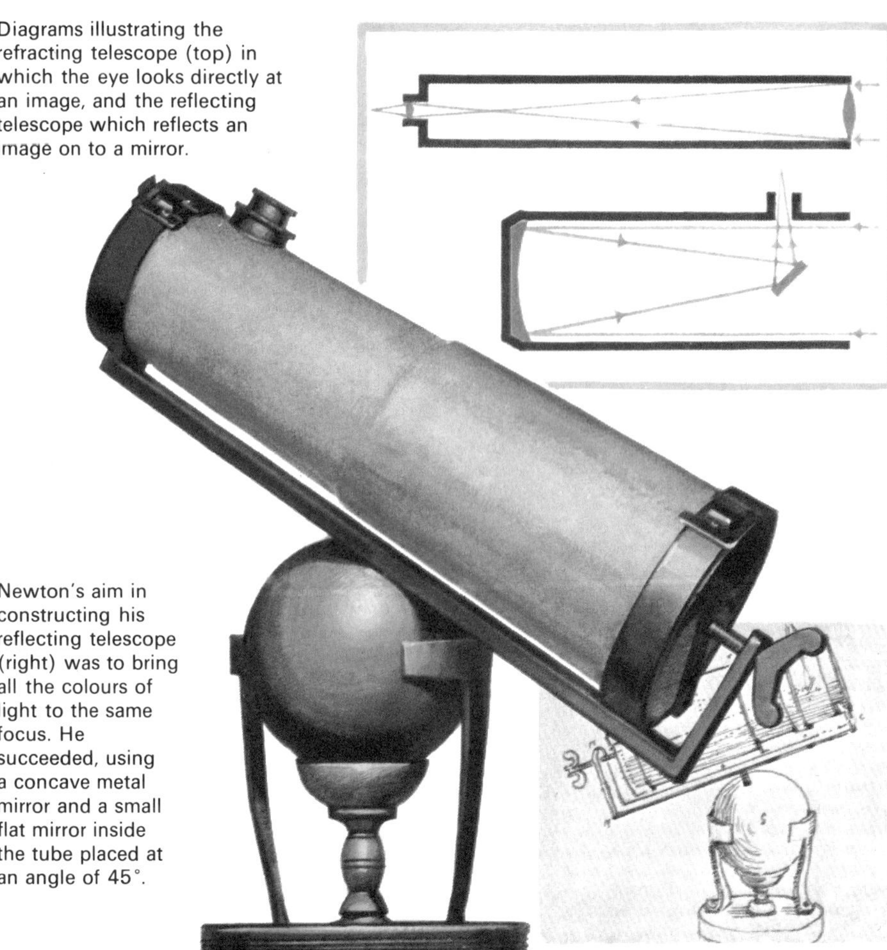

Diagrams illustrating the refracting telescope (top) in which the eye looks directly at an image, and the reflecting telescope which reflects an image on to a mirror.

Newton's aim in constructing his reflecting telescope (right) was to bring all the colours of light to the same focus. He succeeded, using a concave metal mirror and a small flat mirror inside the tube placed at an angle of 45°.

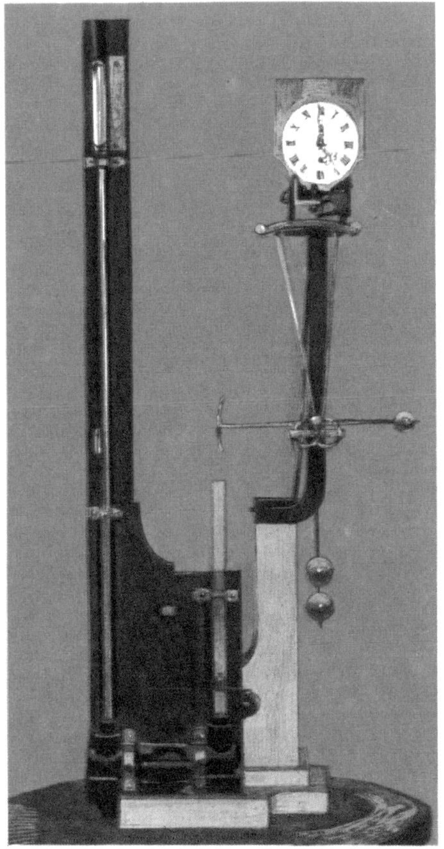

The invention of the barometer made possible the modern science of weather forecasting. This recording barometer, made in Florence, followed Torricelli's early experiments. In 1644 Torricelli first described his barometer, or 'torricellian tube'.

Sun-centred Universe

At the age of 45, Galileo began to make his telescopes. What he saw through them startled him. He looked at the moon and saw that it was not the perfect orb with smooth, polished surface made of the perfect material, the quintessence, of Aristotelian theory. He saw that it was much like the earth, with mountain ranges and valleys, craters and protuberances. He looked at the stars and saw what had not been visible to the naked eye, 'a host of other stars . . . so numerous as to be almost beyond belief'. Around the three stars of Orion's 'belt' and the six of his 'sword', he counted 80 other stars. Near the constellation of the Pleiades, made up of seven closely grouped stars visible to the naked eye, he counted 40 others, none more than half a degree away from any of the seven. He found the four largest satellites orbiting Jupiter, a Copernican system in miniature.

Galileo had long accepted Copernicus's idea of a sun-centred universe. With his work on the laws of motion and his astronomical observations, he thought he had found the proof. The Establishment of the day began to fear that science was undermining their authority with discoveries presented as new truth. Galileo was forbidden to hold or teach opinions that did not put the earth at the immovable centre of Creation. He wrote a book in which he presented both sides of the controversy, but the Establishment opinion was put into the mouth of a character called Simplicio, who was not given the best of the argument. Galileo was arraigned before the Inquisition and forced to sign a recantation, and he was put under house arrest for the remainder of his life. This harsh treatment brought to an end the position of Italy as a centre of scientific progress. Henceforth, the Scientific Revolution moved to northern Europe. Galileo's last book on the new sciences had to be published in the Netherlands. The year he died, totally blind from too much looking at the sun through his telescopes, Newton was born.

Isaac Newton

Isaac Newton (1642–1727) was born on Christmas Day in the small village of Woolsthorpe in Lincolnshire. His father had already died a few months previously and his mother married again. Young Isaac was brought up largely by his grandmother. He was something of a weakling physically, and grew up to be solitary and suspicious of his fellow men. As a boy, he was fond of making mechanical models. He made a little wooden windmill with sails turned by a mouse on a treadmill. He made a water-clock and sundials. Nearly all the apparatus he used in later life he made himself, grinding and polishing his own mirrors, for instance. He was not well taught at school, and most of his mathematics he had to work out for himself.

After he had graduated from Cambridge, there was an outbreak of bubonic plague, and the university was closed down for eighteen months, between the autumn of 1665 and the spring of 1667. Newton returned to Woolsthorpe during this time. In a burst of extraordinary creativity, he invented the calculus, made important discoveries in the composition of light and worked out his first ideas of the law of gravity as it applied to the moon and earth. Yet it was twenty years before he published his great work, *Mathematical Principles of Natural Philosophy*.

The Laws of Motion

Newton's use of the word philosophy in this title has the same meaning as the word science. The book, which is in three parts, took eighteen months to write and marks the second great period of creativity in Newton's life. In it, he presents first his three laws of motion which are the basis for all future dynamics. The first law says that a body remains at rest or continues in uniform motion in a straight line until forces impressed upon it change its state. The second law, dealing with acceleration, says that any change of motion is proportional to the force acting upon it and takes place in the straight line along which that force acts. The third law says that to every action there is always an equal and opposite reaction. In the second part of the book Newton demonstrates that, for the purposes of calculation, the heavenly bodies can be treated as though their entire mass were concentrated at their centres. The third book explains his law of gravitation, which is that every body or particle in the universe is attracted to every other body or particle by a force that is proportional to the product of their masses and, inversely, to the square of the distance between them.

Newton's laws sweep aside the

Isaac Newton was a man with many interests. In these pictures he is seen working at his garden furnace (top) and, as Master of the Mint, seeking new methods of coin production and forming a secret service to fight counterfeiters.

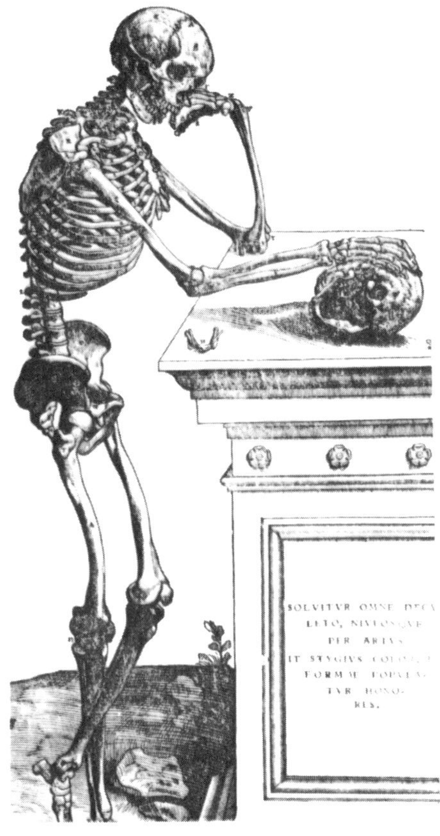

classical idea of natural motion being circular. Until and unless a force acts upon it, motion continues in a straight line. For instance, the path of the moon around the earth is compounded of two motions. The first is its 'natural' motion in a straight line, the second is its gravitational attraction to the earth. An apple falls to the ground from a position of rest in the tree, because the force of gravity acts upon it. The moon does not fall to the ground because it is already travelling at a certain speed in a direction away from the earth, this direction being in a straight line or a tangent to the curve of the earth's surface. It is as if the apple was hurled at such a speed that the arc of its fall towards the earth is never steeper than the curvature of the earth's surface. Since the earth is spherical, an apple travelling at such a speed would continue to travel round and round it. Newton worked out from the mass of the two bodies and the square of the distance between them how fast the moon would have to travel to remain in orbit. His first answer came to $27\frac{1}{4}$ days for a complete orbit by the moon, which is very close to the true figure.

One of the most famous books of the 18th century and one of the first comprehensive encyclopedias was the French *Encyclopedie* edited by Denis Diderot. Published between 1751 and 1780 it appeared in 35 volumes. Among its contributors were Voltaire, Rousseau and Buffon, whose work is illustrated on the opposite page. One of the drawings accompanying the article on anatomy in the *Encyclopedie* is shown (left above). Andreas Vesalius (left) caused a revolution in the history of anatomical study. Following the path set by Leonardo da Vinci who left some 1,500 anatomical sketches, Vesalius investigated the complete structure and architecture of the human body. With help from the painter Titian, Vesalius sketched his corpses as he dissected them. The result was the first really reliable book on anatomy published in 1543 at Padua. One of the anatomical drawings from the book is shown (below left).

The Grand Design

All the problems Newton set himself in the book on mathematical principles are solved like that by calculation. To work out all the mathematical proofs again, as he did in eighteen months, when writing the books, shows an astonishing mind capable of tremendous concentration. Small wonder that he suffered a nervous breakdown soon after publication. Yet Newton's view of the universe is a mechanical and geometrical one, rather like a huge clock with its wheels turning according to some Grand Design. It is based of necessity on the standpoint of an individual here on earth, which gives it an unreal simplicity. The information that is known to one small planet is based on messages received and these messages have each taken different periods of time to reach us. Messages from the heavens are sent by light waves. Unless we know how far away a star is, we cannot tell when the light we see tonight began its journey towards us. Nor do we know what is the speed and direction of our own movement relative to the speed and direction of the star. We cannot stop the universe long enough to plot a map of it. The scientists of continental Europe had such reservations about Newton's work, men like Leibniz who foreshadowed Einstein by saying that space is something purely relative like time.

In a darkened room Newton conducts his experiments with a prism to demonstrate the coloured components of white light. Only when all the colours are present does white light result.

Composition of Light

Newton was aware of the importance of an understanding of light and its composition. He invented the reflecting telescope because of the discolouration and distortion towards the edges of a lens in the older refracting telescope due to different angles of refraction. The edge of a lens, like the bevelled edge of a mirror, is a prism. Newton conducted experiments with prisms to show that the different components of white light were refracted at different angles, each component giving a light of a different colour. And these colours could not be changed by interposing materials of other colours along the beam. Obversely, he showed that only when all the coloured components came together was white light produced. He maintained that light was made up of particles from luminous bodies which gave rise to waves as they passed through space.

He published his *Opticks* in 1704. By that time, he was president of the Royal Society, a position to which he was elected annually until his death. In 1705, he was knighted by Queen Anne and became virtual dictator of the scientific establishment. Yet science was never the chief interest of this extraordinarily complex man. When he died, he bequeathed to his niece a collection of manuscripts amounting to over a million words, the result of vast researches into theology and alchemy. He was evidently searching for clues to the riddle of the universe from the Book of Revelation and the prophetic books of the Old Testament, from the measurements of Solomon's Temple and the alchemy of the ancients. His importance remains in his method of taking one phenomenon, such as motion, and applying to it concepts, such as mass and force, in terms of which the phenomenon of motion could be discussed. It was the method used by later scientists to formulate general laws for such phenomena as heat, light, magnetism and electricity.

Advances in Medicine

Alongside the advances in astronomy and mechanics was a parallel development in medicine. The first great challenge to the second-century anatomist and physician, Galen, came from a German Swiss named Theophrastus von Hohenheim (1493–1541). He was born near Zurich, the son of a doctor from whom he must have picked up an early knowledge of medicine. In his teens and early twenties, he travelled throughout Europe and the Middle East working as an army surgeon. He was a quarrelsome and conceited man, calling himself Paracelsus, meaning greater than Celsus, a famous Roman medical author of the 1st century A.D. In 1527, he was appointed physician and professor of medicine at Basle.

Paracelsus believed that the world was created by a chemical separation of Aristotle's four elements of air, fire,

The centre for botanical and zoological studies in France is the state-owned Jardin des Plantes in Paris founded in 1635.

The French naturalist Georges Buffon (top) produced his massive *Histoire Naturelle* between 1749/67. Its 36 volumes contained descriptions of every mammal and bird then known, illustrated with hand-coloured plates.

The medical amphitheatre at Padua university where Andreas Vesalius studied anatomy.

earth and water, to which he added three more—sulphur, mercury and salt. He also thought that the body repeated on a tiny scale the chemical reactions of the whole universe. He rejected Galen's idea that disease was caused by a disturbance of the four bodily humours. He taught that it had a local origin in one of the organs of the body. He was the first to claim that there are different diseases that can be classified. The chemical cause of disease, he thought, could be treated by chemicals. Though not the first to use chemical remedies, he placed such emphasis on their use instead of Galen's herbal medicines that he has been called the founder of medical chemistry. He stressed the use of exactly measured dosage and often used poisonous substances in small quantities. Though his ideas spread throughout Europe, they aroused considerable opposition. When he publicly burned the works of the medieval Moslem physician, Avicenna, there was such an outcry that he was driven out of Basle to wander for the rest of his life from town to town in Switzerland and Germany, quarrelling with the medical establishment to the end.

The Study of Anatomy

The importance of Paracelsus was in the diagnosis and treatment of disease. The man to make the breakthrough in the study of anatomy was Andreas Vesalius (1514–64), a Fleming who became professor of anatomy at Padua university at the age of 23. Galen had been forbidden by the opinions of his day to practise dissection on human beings. His anatomy was based therefore on that of animals. Vesalius discovered more than 200 anatomical errors in Galen's work and, in 1543, published his book *On the Fabric of the Human Body,* beautifully illustrated by one of Titian's pupils. Before Vesalius, professors of anatomy had not performed their own dissections, but left this to an assistant while they sat apart reading from the works of Galen. Vesalius performed his own dissections on human bodies during

William Harvey was physician to Charles I of England and here demonstrates his discoveries regarding the circulation of the blood to his royal master.

his lectures, and this practice was carried on by his successors at Padua, Fallopius and Fabricius. Vesalius himself gave up research when he left Italy in 1544 to become physician to the ailing emperor Charles V of Spain.

Circulation of the Blood

The university of Padua can be said to be the birthplace of the Scientific Revolution since Vesalius and Galileo were professors there, and among the students were Copernicus and William Harvey (1578–1657). The great step forward made by Harvey was his discovery of the circulation of the blood which he set out in his book, *An Anatomical Dissertation on the Movement of the Heart and Blood in Animals,* published in 1628. Before then, the movement of the blood was thought to be as described by Galen, with two separate systems, one ebbing and flowing in the veins, the other in the arteries. This was held to account for the different colours of venous blood and arterial blood. The heart was thought to act as a vat where a mixture of blood and vital spirits was brewed to give life and heat to the body.

Harvey proved that veins have valves which prevent the blood flowing backwards, and that the heart is a muscular pump keeping the system flowing. He did not discover the tiny capillaries, the only link between arteries and veins, but assumed that something like them must exist to complete the circuit. Four years after his death, capillaries were observed under a microscope by Marcello Malpighi (1628–94) in the lungs of a frog, water having been injected into the blood vessels to wash out the blood and make them more transparent. How venous blood was changed into arterial blood in the lungs was not fully explained until two more centuries had passed.

Chemical Experiments

One science that lagged behind the others during the Scientific Revolution was chemistry. In the 17th century, Robert Boyle did suggest that matter might be made up of simple forms or elements which combine to produce other substances, and he did a good deal of experiment on gases. It was realised that heat had a part to play in chemical reaction, and a curious theory was devised to explain combustion. It was first put forward by Johann Joachim Becher (1635–82) and developed by his follower Georg Ernst Stahl (1660–1734). They claimed that when a substance burned it gave off fire-stuff for which Stahl coined the word phlogiston from the Greek word phlox, a flame. A substance like charcoal that leaves very little ash behind was regarded as practically pure phlogiston. Some metals heated until they are molten leave a dross on the surface called the calyx. This was explained as some of the metal giving up its phlogiston to form the calyx. The calyx, however, is heavier than the metal from which it is formed. Therefore, phlogiston was considered to have levity or negative weight. Boyle established that air is essential to combustion and that, in a limited supply of air, a substance will burn only for a limited time. Thus it was assumed that the air absorbs phlogiston, but that the amount it can absorb is limited.

Prominent in chemistry and medicine in the 17th and 18th centuries were four scientists. Malpighi was a pioneer in microscopic studies of both animal and vegetable anatomy. He was chief physician to Pope Innocent XII. The Swedish astronomer Celsius constructed the centigrade thermometer in 1742. Descartes and Lavoisier were two of the greatest figures in scientific history. Descartes is perhaps best known as the father of modern philosophy, while Lavoisier has equal fame as the founder of modern chemistry.

New Substances

In 1756, Joseph Black discovered 'fixed air'. In 1766, Henry Cavendish published a scientific paper which described 'inflammable air'. In 1774, Joseph Priestley discovered 'dephlogisticated air'. It was left to the great French scientist Antoine Laurent Lavoisier (1743–94) to co-ordinate all this work in his *Elementary Treatise on Chemistry,* published in 1789. With the help of his colleagues, de Morveau, Berthollet and de Fourcroy, he gave the newly discovered substances their modern nomenclature. Fixed air became carbon dioxide, inflammable air became hydrogen, and dephlogisticated air became oxygen. The calyx of a metal became its oxide. The age of modern chemistry had dawned. But the full story of chemistry must take its place alongside that new burst of technological progress.

The Industrial Revolution

At the beginning of the 18th century, England must have seemed an unlikely place for a sudden burst of technological progress. Most of the population lived in rural communities, engaged in agriculture and cottage crafts. Technological know-how was largely imported from continental Europe. Mining engineers from Germany opened up the Cumberland copper mines. Canal builders from Holland drained the fenlands of East Anglia. French civil engineers advised on the establishment of the new turnpike roads. In the smelting of iron, England was behind even Russia. Sweden was then Europe's leading iron-maker both in quantity and quality. Yet what has been described as the most fundamental revolution in man's progress began in the north and midlands of England, in the lowlands of Scotland and in South Wales.

There were many reasons for this. England was a haven of religious freedom which attracted continental refugees, such as the Huguenots, who brought their technical skills with them. England had a population a third or even a quarter of France's, so there was a stimulus towards the invention of labour-saving devices. Particularly, this made farming in Britain highly efficient and released workers for the new industries. There was a much less rigid class system in Britain than elsewhere. Workers could advance by their own efforts to bring new vigour to a strong middle class. Landowners were ready to exploit their mineral resources and to invest in industry. Mill owners could buy country estates and were accepted into the highest society.

World Trade Centre

Geographically, Britain was well-placed to become a centre of world trade. Her long coastline provided ample ports, and navigable rivers were never far from the new factories. After 1745, new roads were constructed along which armies could be marched to deal with the aftermath of the Jacobite risings. Throughout the Industrial Revolution, Britain fought her wars abroad with professional soldiers. At home, industry was left at peace to get on with the job of creating wealth and to supply those armies and the navy for a programme of colonial expansion which itself created new markets for industrial products.

The English Revolution, as it has been called, began with improvements in agriculture and textile machinery. Dwindling supplies of home-grown timber stimulated coal-mining. Together with new puddling methods, the abundant deposits of coal and iron ore found close together created a rapid increase in the production of pig-iron. The power of wind, water and sheer muscle was slowly replaced by steam. New machinery that needed more power to operate it was assembled in factories. Instead of the work being distributed among the cottagers, workers were brought to the industrial centres where new towns mushroomed.

Continental Europe

All the new technology was available to the rest of Europe, but it was slow to take advantage of it. There was less mobility among the workers. There was serfdom in France until its own revolution of 1789, as well as in Germany, Austria and Russia well into the 19th century. Landowners were concerned only with agriculture, and a weak middle class was reluctant to invest in anything new. Despots like Frederick II of Prussia were obsessed with nationalised monopoly industries which have always stifled initiative. Powerful bureaucracies and trades guilds administered rules that restricted enterprise. National banks were conservative in their attitudes to new industry, whereas private banks in Britain had no difficulty in finding depositors and were eager for profitable investments. Wars that ravaged Europe upset trade and wasted both wealth and manpower.

It was inevitable that such rapid industrial expansion created new pressures. There were times of depression and unemployment. Workers were exploited by unscrupulous employers. Overcrowding undermined health. Factory chimneys polluted the atmosphere, and industrial waste destroyed the environment. Workers had to fight for their rights, for a fair share of the national cake, but at least there was a cake worth sharing.

From a basis of coal, iron and steam-power, the Industrial Revolution moved on to steel, electricity and the internal combustion engine. By that time, continental Europe and North America were catching up with Britain. Much of their early industrialisation had been started by British technicians and British-made machinery. Now others began to race ahead on their own initiative. As it had in Britain, a shortage of labour in America stimulated invention. Immigration from Europe, during the various periods of depression there, provided both a demand for consumer goods and a means of meeting it. In Europe, the spread of railways solved internal transport problems, and banking systems became more flexible. Innovations began to appear simultaneously in different countries. After 1850, it is often difficult to tell who invented what.

At the beginning of the Industrial Revolution, many of the inventors and innovators were artisans: spinners and weavers, blacksmiths and iron-mongers, millwrights and wheel-wrights. It was not long before the educated scientist became involved. For the first time, science and technology began to march hand in hand with the ambition to benefit the whole of society. This was to lead to the scientific research, backed by immense resources, that is such a feature of our own country.

For centuries coal mining in Britain was a small-scale industry, but increasing shortage of timber, which had provided charcoal for working iron, led in 1709 to the refinement by Abraham Darby of smelting pig iron with coke. From then coal mining was developed and Britain's supplies of both it and iron ore assured her lead in the Industrial Revolution.

Thomas Coke (1752–1842) improved crops and animal breeding methods on his estate.

Cottage and Country

An early 18th-century English village was an almost self-contained industrial complex. The corn-mill was its only custom-built structure to house large machinery, powered by wind or water. The blacksmith was the only engineer. The cottages were at the same time homes and mini-factories, where the spinning-wheel stood by the fireplace and the weaving-loom often took up more space than the family. Both machines had changed little since medieval times. In the early 16th century, a treadle had been added to the spinning-wheel to turn it with the foot by means of connecting rod and crank. This increased its output, but it still required between three and five spinners to supply one weaver.

In 1733, John Kay, a Lancashire weaver working in Colchester, patented his flying shuttle. It was rather like a toy boat on wheels that ran along a batten and carried the weft to and fro between the warp threads. It was operated by a cord attached to leather drivers running along metal rods. It enabled the weaver to drive the shuttle with one hand across a piece of cloth much wider than the span of his arms. One weaver could thus do the work of two, which intensified the search for a spinning machine to keep pace with him. The flying shuttle opened the way to a power-loom though it was entirely hand-operated at first. It also allowed the weaver to sit comfortably upright at his machine. Sadly Kay made little profit out of his invention which antagonised his fellow weavers and was pirated by unscrupulous employers.

Farming Methods

Meanwhile, improvements in farming methods were being pioneered by men like Jethro Tull, who, in 1701, invented a drill to plant seeds in rows. Horse-drawn and with a harrow attached behind, it covered the seeds it planted. Straight rows of growing corn made possible the use of a horse-drawn hoe which Tull introduced from France in 1714. He proved that continual tillage after sowing was particularly beneficial to root-crops, and he grew higher yields of wheat from less seed for thirteen successive years in unmanured fields.

The 18th century saw the end of the medieval three-field system which left a third of all agricultural land fallow each year. A new rotation of crops kept all the land under cultivation all the time. For this sort of intensive cultivation, landowners took to enclosing smaller fields with walls and hedges. There was a tendency to larger farms. Many smallholders and farmworkers were forced to leave the land altogether and seek employment in the growing towns. New crops were introduced to intersperse between grain crops. In England, these were particularly turnips, used as winter feed for animals, and clover, which fed the ground by fixing atmospheric nitrogen with the aid of bacteria in the roots, and also provided winter forage. The resulting increase in herds and flocks provided more manure for the further enrichment of the land. In 1747 a German chemist, A. S. Marggraf, discovered a beet with a rich sugar content. By 1840, there were 58 sugar-beet factories in France alone. They came much later to Britain who had ready access to the sugar-cane of the Caribbean.

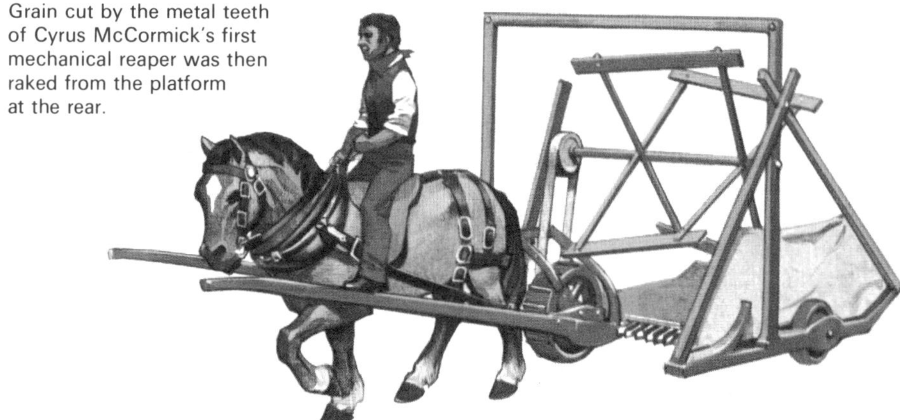

Grain cut by the metal teeth of Cyrus McCormick's first mechanical reaper was then raked from the platform at the rear.

The seed drill devised by Jethro Tull (1674–1741) was an efficient method of sowing and covering seeds in one operation.

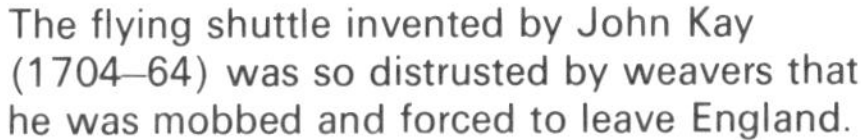

The flying shuttle invented by John Kay (1704–64) was so distrusted by weavers that he was mobbed and forced to leave England.

Animal Breeding

In most of this, Holland and Flanders, forced by lack of space to introduce mixed farming in compact areas, provided the pioneers. Once the enclosure of fields had made it possible, however, British farmers began to lead the way in animal breeding. Robert Bakewell of Dishley created his Leicester sheep by selecting a stock to develop the most desirable points. They were small animals, but provided the maximum weight of the most valuable joints. In Spain, the merino sheep was developed for its wool and its secret jealously guarded. Nevertheless, it spread into Western Europe. George III of Britain had his own flock, though the efforts of most British breeders were directed towards meat production.

Bakewell also bred the Midland black horse, very powerful in relation to its size. It became a popular coach and dray horse. He was less successful with cattle than Charles Colling of Ketton in Yorkshire who developed the Durham shorthorn. Ayrshire cattle in Scotland were also improved through importations from Holland. So much did beef and mutton become part of the regular diet of the British and Dutch that they were regarded as gluttons by other Europeans. In England, improvements were publicised and spread by men like Thomas Coke of Holkham in Norfolk, local member of Parliament for 55 years and first Earl of Leicester. Coke and men like the Duke of Bedford and Lavoisier in France created model farms to conduct their experiments. The ancient practice of covering a light soil with clay containing limestone, called marling, was revived. From Holland came the use of organic waste from industry: from soap-boiling and tailoring; even scraps of horn from the handle-makers in the cutlery trade were used as fertiliser.

There was a whole series of inventions to aid the farmer. The small Dutch plough with its curved mouldboard partly covered in iron plate was improved in Britain by Robert Ransome of Ipswich who designed the all-iron plough. In 1789, he produced a cast-iron share in which the under surface was cooled more quickly than the upper so that, as the two surfaces wore unevenly, the plough sharpened itself. A few years later, his iron plough was designed with easily replaced, standard parts. The flail was still the universal instrument for separating grain from husks and straw until Andrew Meikle, a Scots millwright, produced in 1784 the first machine. It consisted of a drum rotating close to a curved shield so that the corn fed between the two had its husks rubbed off. At first it was powered by horses. In 1842, the steam-driven threshing machine appeared. By then, a winnowing machine to separate grain and chaff had been invented. A handle rotated a fan and agitated sieves in a box through which the grain passed. With a steam locomotive to drag thresher and winnower combined through the countryside and to operate them under contract with the farmers, this bit of farming automation became a common sight at harvest time.

19th-century steam-powered ploughing: a cable running between two tractors pulled a double-ended plough from side to side of a field.

Reaping Machines

Cutting corn was the job which employed most labour on an arable farm. Yet the designs for reaping machines which began to appear in Britain and America from 1780 onwards came to nothing until the American Cyrus McCormick patented his famous invention in 1834. A few years later, Americans were mowing their hay with a machine which had a flexible cutter to compensate for uneven ground. Except for the thresher, most new machines were horse-operated. Attempts were made to introduce steam-ploughing whereby a stationary engine hauled the plough on the end of a cable. It was limited to suitable terrain and its high capital cost to the small farmer made it little more than a curiosity.

Advancements in farming technology and the manufacture of machinery for export kept Britain in the lead until the American Civil War began the rapid industrialisation of the United States. The war stimulated an increase in land use. Three successive years of bad harvests made Britain dependent on American imports. The New World rapidly overtook Europe in grain and meat production, and in the development of new machinery such as the first combine harvester, which cut and processed into sacks of grain twelve hectares (30 acres) of a standard crop in a single day. Between 1860 and 1900, over 160 million hectares (400 million acres) of land in the United States alone were newly brought under cultivation. This is an area ten times the total land mass of England and Wales. North America had become the granary of the world.

James Brindley (1716–72), a poorly educated millwright who became a brilliant engineer.

Canal-building

While the enclosure of fields and the new farming methods in 18th-century Britain were changing the face of her countryside, so were the civil engineers who set out to solve her transport problems. Among the first of these was James Brindley who began his career in 1733 at the age of seventeen as a repairer of millwheels. He worked out methods to improve the grinding of flints for the growing pottery industry. Travelling about in the course of his work, he began to survey England's waterways. The Duke of Bridgewater asked him to build a canal from the coal-mines on the duke's estate at Worsley in Lancashire to the growing town of Manchester 9·6 kilometres (6 miles) away. The finished canal was a remarkable engineering achievement including the first canal aqueduct to carry it at treetop height across the River Irwell.

Brindley went on to connect Manchester and Liverpool by water, and altogether laid out 640 kilometres (400 miles) of canal in different parts of the country. He was in many ways typical of the new generation of practical men who did so much to give Britain its industrial lead. He had very little conventional schooling. The men who dug canals were called navigators. It was because Brindley could not spell the word that the English for a labourer became navvy. Yet this untutored man worked out his own method of kneading clay to provide a waterproof bed for canal aqueducts. In 1805, the largest canal aqueduct ever built had an iron trough carrying the Ellesmere canal for a distance of 304 metres (1,000 feet) at a height of over 30 metres (100 feet) above the river Dee. It was engineered by Thomas Telford, another of the great Scottish canal-builders. By then, he had begun work on the Caledonian Canal in Scotland, the last major work before the railways began to take over.

Road-building

In road-building, the European leaders were the French, who had been the greatest canal-builders of the previous

Coping with the difficulties of canal building accelerated the development of civil engineering. The finance needed was raised by selling shares in specially created companies for every canal system, each with its seal.

To propel barges under bridges with no towpath they were 'legged' by two men who pushed against the walls on either side.

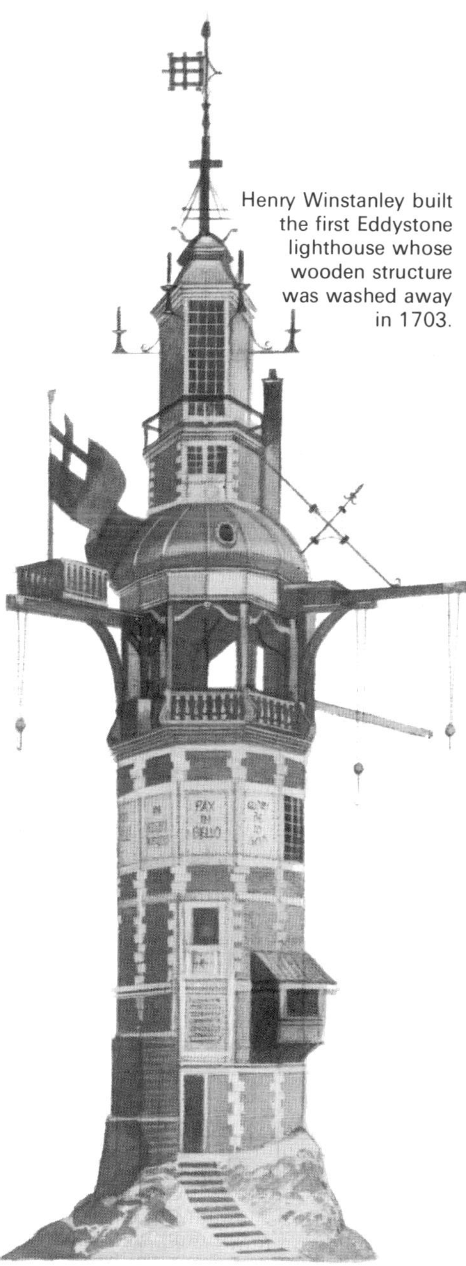

Henry Winstanley built the first Eddystone lighthouse whose wooden structure was washed away in 1703.

century. In a country controlled by all-powerful rulers, a national network of state-controlled highways was comparatively easy to establish. In 1720, a civil service was set up to look after roads and bridges. By the middle of the century, there was a training school for engineers in Paris. In 1776, France had built 40,000 kilometres (25,000) miles of state highways using the notorious *corvée* system of unpaid forced labour.

P. M. J. Trésaguet was the great 18th-century French road engineer. He invented a three-layer system in which a trench was dug and stones laid in the bottom on edge, hammered to form the contour of the final cambered surface. Two layers of smaller stones were then spread on top, the last of these, 7·5 cm. (3 inches) thick, composed of stones no bigger than a walnut. In Britain Thomas Telford, originally a stonemason, broadly followed Trésaguet's system, except that he started with a masonry pavement of large stones set on their broadest edge and the protruberances knocked off and used to fill intervening spaces. The two top layers of smaller stones were added in stages so that normal traffic could be used to impact the first layer before the second was added.

Bridges

France also had the first great bridge-builder, J. R. Perronet. He taught his engineers to flatten their arches to provide a gentle gradient for wheeled vehicles and to reduce the thickness of the piers. The temporary wooden centres used to support the arches as they were built were made of bolted pieces. When the bolts were removed, the whole temporary structure could be made to collapse into the river by pulling on ropes.

England had the first cast-iron bridge, built in 1779 across the river Severn by Abraham Darby of Coalbrookdale, third-generation owner of the famous ironworks there. Its main ribs were cast in sand-moulds with molten iron straight from the furnace. The bridge's parts were hoisted into position and held together by wedges without a single bolt or rivet. Though the masonry approaches have been repaired many times, the iron structure has stood the test of time and is still used by pedestrians today. America saw the first suspension bridge, built in 1800 in Pennsylvania by James Finley. It consisted of a deck hung on vertical rods from iron chains.

Harbours and Lighthouses

Men like Telford, laying new routes to speed the transportation of consumer goods, were not only road and bridge engineers, but also became involved in the improvement of harbours to which, on an island like Britain, the roads inevitably led. The Dutch, as might be expected, were the pioneers in the design of dredging equipment. About 1750, they invented the chain dredger which brought up the waste in buckets. With the later addition of steam-power, this became the system still essentially in use today.

In England, John Smeaton pioneered the technique of letting water do the work. In 1774, he began work on the entirely artificial harbour at Ramsgate in Kent. He enclosed an inner basin with six sluices from which water could be released at low tide. By sinking a barge in its path, the rushing water was made to gouge a way through the sand and deposit large quantities well beyond the harbour entrance. It was Smeaton who also designed the first of the great masonry lighthouse towers which are a feature of European coasts even today. Smeaton's new design was for the Eddystone rock which had had two previous lighthouses, mainly wooden structures.

By controlling the flow of water, sluice gates raised or lowered vessels to the next stretch of canal.

Factory and Town

The textile industry is the one usually chosen to illustrate the technological developments that gave rise to the Industrial Revolution. At first, the new technology was confined almost entirely to Britain. The appearance of the large textile factory was the first visible sign of it. A maritime nation, Britain's towns and cities were all on the coast or a river estuary. These were the centres of commerce, both for coastal shipping and international trade. It was not in such places that the factories first appeared. They were built in the villages where the textile crafts were practised. Here, labour (robbed since the enclosures of a livelihood from the land) was available, as was water-power from the rivers and streams. In time, these factory villages developed into the inland towns and cities of today.

Where the cottage industry had traditionally processed wool and linen-flax, the new material was cotton, imported in its raw state from the West Indies and the Middle East. It was this cheap raw material, available in large quantities, that stimulated the sudden spate of inventions. Cotton fibre had an elasticity that makes it easier than other fibres to spin by mechanical means. The old spinning-wheel was the bottleneck to any increase of output by the weaver. It was therefore the invention of spinning machines, particularly for cotton thread, that began the factory system.

Richard Arkwright was knighted in 1786.

Spinning Machines

The famous name in cotton-spinning is that of Lancashire-born Richard Arkwright (1732–92), who began his working life as a barber. His spinning machine may not have been his own invention. His patent rights in it were later taken from him in a court action. At the top it had four wooden bobbins set horizontally on which the raw cotton, cleaned and carded (i.e. combed out) was twisted. From these, a thread was drawn through two pairs of rollers, the second turning faster than the first so that the cotton was drawn out into a longer and finer thread to be wound on to lower bobbins. About the same time, in the 1760s, a carpenter and weaver called James Hargreaves invented his spinning-jenny. With this, the raw cotton was placed on bobbins at the bottom of the frame and drawn out by a bar that moved to and fro across the top. The spun cotton was taken up on spindles at the opposite end. About 1779, Samuel Crompton, a farmer who devoted more time to textiles than he did to his own land, invented the spinning-mule, a combination of the other two machines, incorporating both rollers and a moving bar.

At first, these machines were designed to be operated by hand, by water-power or by horses. In 1785, a steam engine was built to supply

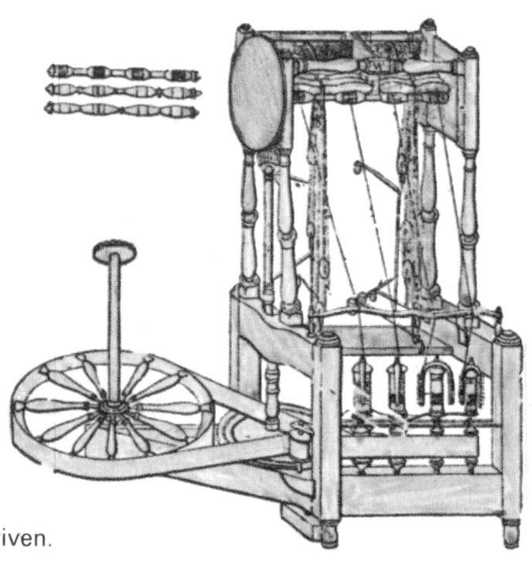

Arkwright's spinning frame was water-driven.

he interior of a 19th-century textile factory.

power to a spinning factory at Papplewick in Nottinghamshire. Its success led to a slow but continuous growth of steam-power for all the operations in textile production. Most of this development led to more and more factories being built. But steam-power came even to the cottage industry, as at Coventry where rows of silk-weavers' cottages each had their steam engines built behind them. This is not to say that hand-looms did not continue far into the 19th century. But the new pattern of life for most workers was fixed. Small factory towns began to mushroom wherever there was coal or water-power readily available.

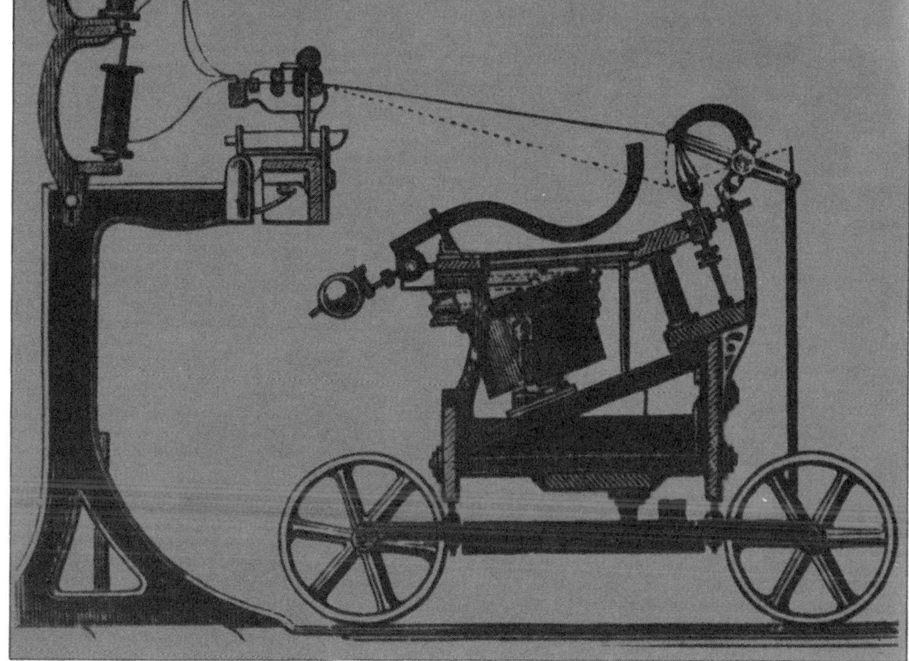

Samuel Crompton's spinning-mule was the first to produce a fine thread.

Power Looms

Speeding up spinning reversed the old bottleneck situation. Now weavers could no longer keep pace with the supply of thread or the demand for cheap cotton fabrics. A Leicestershire parson, Edmund Cartwright, became aware of the problem on a visit to the cotton-spinning valley of the Derwent in Derbyshire during the summer of 1784. He met some men from Manchester who were discussing the likely spread of spinning-mills when Arkwright's patents ran out. Cartwright had the sort of mind that delights in problems. He was used to doctoring his parishioners as well as preaching to them. Within three years, he had invented a power-loom and set up a factory of his own in Doncaster.

It would be nice to say that he prospered from his ingenuity. His machine had drawbacks, however, and his factory was forced to close within half a dozen years. A Manchester firm who took up the idea had their factory burned down by irate weavers afraid for their livelihood. Cartwright had shown the way though, and other inventors solved the problems of his machine. By 1809, there were more than 2,000 power-looms in Britain and Cartwright was awarded £10,000 by a grateful government. The march of progress could not be stayed.

In the years that followed, machines powered by water or steam were created for every operation in the textile industry. Men like Richard Roberts set up in business as machine-makers. Roberts spent £12,000 perfecting a fully self-acting spinning machine. It was Roberts who built the standard power-loom of his day, based on a system invented by William Horrocks of Stockport. A method was devised whereby cam-wheels operated levers to raise different sets of warp

Edmund Cartwright (1743–1823)

The loom invented by Jacquard (1752–1834) was the first machine to weave in patterns.

threads for weaving fancy fabrics. Soon, however, a French silk-weaving loom developed in 1801 by J. M. Jacquard at the command of Napoleon was adapted to the weaving of fancy worsteds. It had a punched-card system for lifting needles which controlled the threads to be raised. It was essentially the system still used today. Europe had followed Britain's lead in textiles, but was now beginning to make its own way.

Continental Pottery

In pottery, continental Europe was already ahead of Britain at the beginning of the Industrial Revolution. England's contribution from the beginning of the 18th century was the development of cheap, factory-produced soft-paste porcelain, particularly in the area of Staffordshire known ever since as the Potteries. China began to replace the use of vessels made from wood, leather and metals such as pewter. It was easier to clean and similar to cotton in improving the nation's health and opening up a vast new market among ordinary people. Continental pottery was much more of a luxury trade, centred on the production of finely-decorated, hard-paste porcelain in imitation of the high quality importations from China.

In 1710, J. F. Böttger, chemist to Augustus the Strong of Saxony, first found a process to rival the Chinese, whose secrets had been carefully kept since ancient times. He used powdered alabaster and marble with a particularly white china clay, using a new type of kiln giving temperatures as high as 1,400°C. Before, only soft-paste delftware had come anywhere near to the appearance of Chinese pottery, often directly copying its decoration. Böttger's discovery established the famous Dresden pottery at Meissen. His process was also kept secret until, in 1768, P. J. Macquer, chief chemist at the state-owned pottery of Sèvres in France, produced a hard-paste to rival Meissen. In the same year, a British chemist, William Cookworthy, made the same discovery. Two years later, he began manufacturing in Bristol from where his process spread to Hanley in the Potteries.

English Bone China

As well as at Delft, soft-paste porcelain was produced at Sèvres until the pottery there found out how to make the more highly prized hard-paste. England's contribution was in new ingredients such as soapstone (hydrated magnesium silicate) used in Worcester after 1752. In London, the pottery factories at Bow and Chelsea began using bone-ash as an ingredient. The idea came from Germany, but English bone-china quickly became famous throughout Europe. What first made the fortunes of the Potteries, however, was a development made by John Astbury about 1720. This involved mixing a white-burning clay with finely-powdered flint, the final product being known as stoneware. Canal-builder Brindley was involved in devising effective flint-mills. About 1750, double-firing was introduced, first at the so-called biscuit stage and then after dipping in a liquid glaze containing lead oxide. The flint lightened the colour of the final product and increased its hardness. Mills for grinding the flint were one of the earliest users of steam-power.

Staffordshire pottery was typical of many English innovations which together make up the beginnings of the Industrial Revolution. Cheap products in vast quantity were aimed at international mass markets. The leading name in this growing industry was Josiah Wedgwood, a potter's son who was himself throwing pots at the age of nine. Wedgwood improved the local cream stoneware, using no coloured decoration but adopting classical designs to shape his products. In 1762, Queen Charlotte accepted a set and this style of pottery became known as Queen's ware. Wedgwood was appointed royal potter. He employed John Flaxman to design white relief ornamentation on coloured backgrounds and revived the ancient use of moulds to speed production. With the invention of transfer printing of coloured patterns, the way was open to mass production with division of labour along a production line. The final improvement to bone-china came when the Spode family added felspar to the mixture at their factory in Stoke-on-Trent, creating the easily worked porcelain material still used today. An increasingly scientific approach developed with precise analysis of the raw materials, exact kiln temperatures and careful factory procedures.

18th-century porcelain. Top: a Wedgwood vase of 1786; a Sèvres plate of 1772. Centre: 'The Young Suppliant', a figure from the French pottery at Vincennes, 1752. Bottom: a tea-pot from St Petersburg; a Meissen piece 'The Allegro' dating from about 1740.

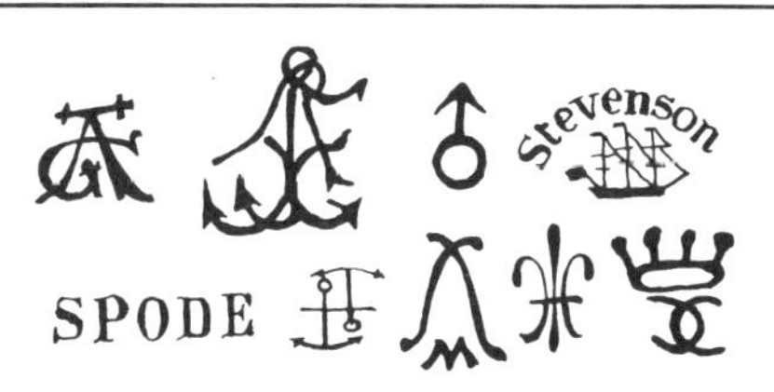

European 18th-century pottery marks.

Glass-making

In glass manufacture, an important scientific advance was made when John Dolland invented a lens which eliminated the rainbow effect of light refraction. He cemented a convex lens of crown glass to a concave lens of flint glass to produce achromatic lenses, patenting the process in 1758. This led to the large reflecting telescopes such as the twelve-metre (40-

foot) example built by William Herschel in 1789. The year before, P. L. Guinand of Switzerland had discovered that stirring molten flint glass with a fireclay stirrer distributed its heavy lead oxide content more evenly and produced a better optical glass. It also dispersed air bubbles in the mixture, improving light transmission. The secret of this process, developed in Munich in association with Joseph von Fraunhofer, was kept until both men died. Then it was purchased by the French glass-maker, Georges Bontemps, who brought it to England during the revolution of 1848 and formed a partnership with the firm of Chance Brothers.

It was in Germany and France that a new method of making sheet glass was first practised. A ball of glass, as much as eighteen kilograms (40 pounds) in weight, was blown into a globe and then rolled in a trench to give it a cylindrical shape. The two ends were cut off and the cylinder slit lengthways with a diamond-tipped tool. Reheated to soften it, the cylinder was then unrolled into a flat sheet. For better quality glass, the cylinder was opened out on a glass-covered stone, smoothed with a block of wood and hardened in a special kiln. The process was not introduced into Britain until 1832. Meanwhile, a plate-glass factory established in 1776 at Ravenhead near St Helens in Lancashire boasted a casting-hall with a floor area 118 by 45 metres (130 by 50 yards), one of the largest factory buildings of its time. As early as 1789, the new steam engines were used to power the grinding and polishing processes.

Industrial Glass

In these early years, Britain established a reputation for cutting and engraving the finest crystal glass and made several advances in colouring processes. These were confined to the luxury trade. The full industrialisation of glassware had to wait until 1887 when the first commercially-successful bottle-making machine came into use at Castleford in Yorkshire, to be improved in 1898 by M. J. Owens in America. Chance Brothers developed a semi-automatic process of producing plate-glass by pouring the molten material on to an inclined plate, passing it between rollers and then on to grinders and polishers. This depended for its mechanisation on the improved gas-fired furnaces recently developed by the German firm of Siemens. These eventually provided a continuous flow of molten glass. By then, as in the pottery industry, the chemical combination of the materials had been scientifically defined. Ernest Abbé, Otto Schott and Karl Zeiss joined forces in 1886 at the famous Jena glassworks in Germany to improve optical glass. By the end of the century, the company was producing about 80 different kinds of glass and had introduced 28 new elements into its composition.

The factory system did not just take the production of consumer goods away from the individual craftsman. To succeed, it had to make goods cheaper by producing them in greater quantity. The new work-force assembled in the factories was not made up entirely of skilled craftsmen. There were never enough of these available. As time went on, the speed of production required a precision of which even skilled hands were not always capable. New machines had not only to be invented, they had to be manufactured in sufficient numbers to meet the demand for them. It is not surprising, therefore, that this period

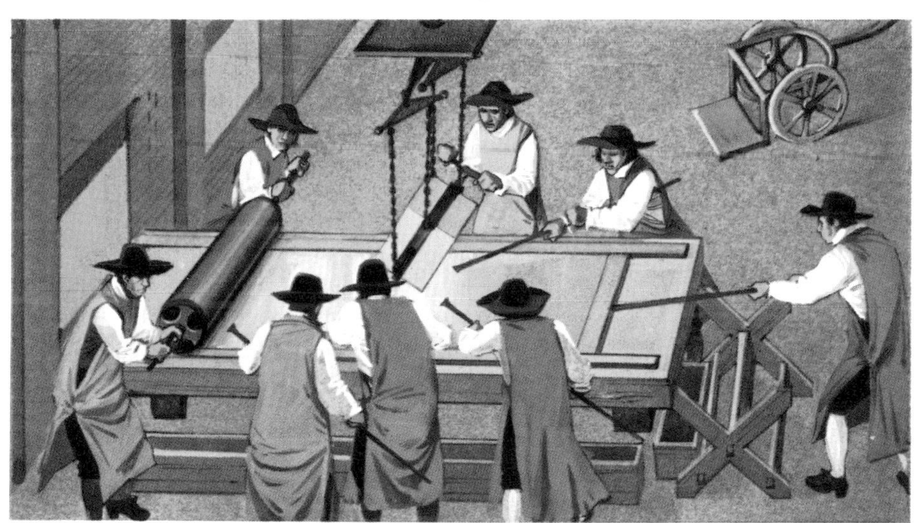

The 18th-century method of casting sheets of plate glass.

England's skill in engraving glass was developed in the late 17th century when a flint glass containing lead oxide was made. This was both brilliant and soft enough for cutting.

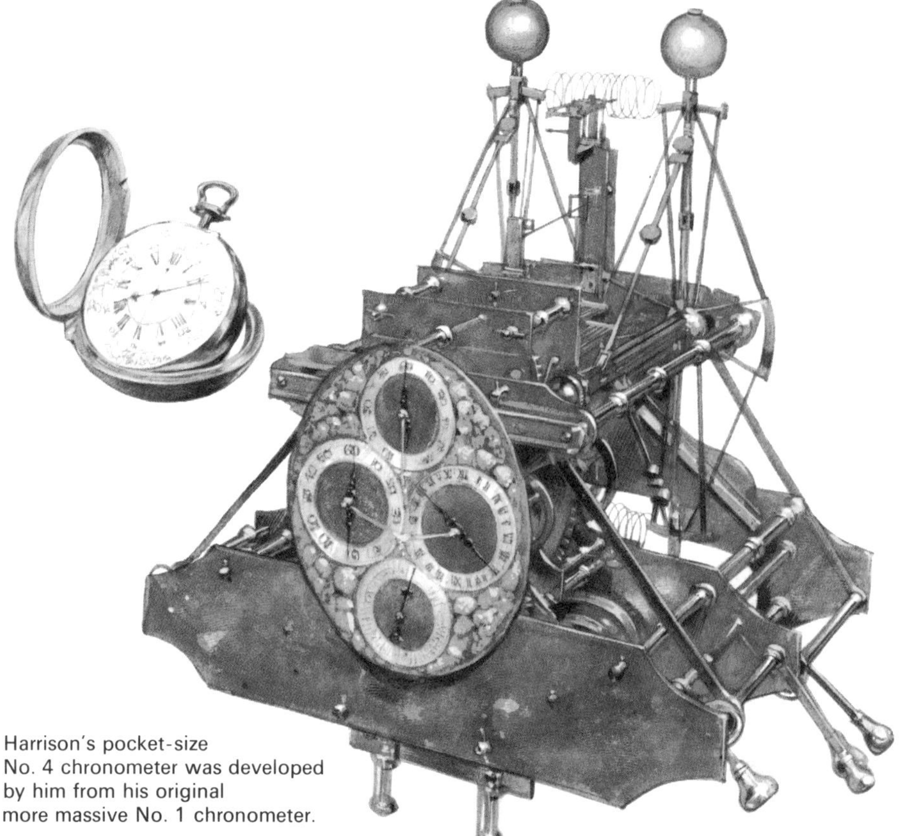

Harrison's pocket-size No. 4 chronometer was developed by him from his original more massive No. 1 chronometer.

saw the development of an entirely new machine-tool industry. The craftsman had often made his own tools. The factory worker was the operator of machine-tools that were themselves made in factories.

Precision Tools

It was the makers of clocks and scientific instruments who first found the need for precision tools. The French were the masters at producing automata, clockwork playthings that went through a sequence of beautifully flowing movements. They represent the beginning of modern automation. The British had a more practical turn of mind. In the early decades of the 18th century, clock-making progressed from a craft in the hands of a few skilled makers to a national industry that captured the European market. In 1759, John Harrison completed his famous chronometer No. 4. It won the £20,000 prize which had been offered by the Board of Longitude from as far back as 1714. This chronometer enabled seamen to estimate their longitude within an accuracy of half a degree.

Clock-making required accurate lathes that began to appear from 1700 onwards. In 1750, the Frenchman Antoine Thiout introduced a tool-holding carriage which moved the cutter across the workpiece. Jacques de Vaucanson invented an improved lathe and a drill working on the same principle. In 1770, an English instrument maker, Jesse Ramsden, devised the first satisfactory screw-cutting lathe with an accuracy sufficient for the screws used in measuring instruments like the micrometer. It was Ramsden, too, who produced the first dividing-engine for use on an industrial scale. In 1757, the sextant had come into use as an aid to navigation. Its graduated scale had to be marked off very accurately. Dividing-engines like Ramsden's speeded up the job. In France in the early part of the 19th century Henri Gambey was producing even more accurate instruments. His dividing-engine graduated a 2-metre circle at the Paris Observatory in 1840 which remained in use for 80 years. He even introduced remote control so that metal expansion from the body heat of the operator was avoided.

Machine Tools

The desire for accuracy was reflected in larger industrial machine-tools. In their manufacture a number of English engineers were the pioneers. In 1775, John Wilkinson set up his famous boring-mill in his father's ironworks in Denbighshire. A hollow boring-bar was supported in a bearing at one end and driven from a large wheel at the other. The cutter rotated with the bar and was moved along it by a rod within the bar. Originally designed for boring cannon, it was easily adapted to the production of accurate cylinders for steam engines, for which it had a monopoly for twenty years. Without it, the steam engine itself could never have reached an early state of efficiency, and its design remained much the same into the middle of the next century.

Another famous name in the machine-tool industry is that of Joseph Bramah, son of a Yorkshire farmer. Among other things, he invented a hydraulic press, a wood-planing machine, a machine for printing serial numbers on banknotes and a patent lock that remained unpicked for 67 years despite the standing offer of a 200-guinea prize. The American visitor who finally picked Bramah's lock took 51 hours spread over sixteen days. Bramah also built a spring-winding machine with a geared leading-screw which could be set to wind springs of predetermined pitch. From this, Bramah's foreman, Henry Maudslay, devised a screw-cutting machine. Finding that his ingenuity did nothing to raise his 30-shillings-a-week wage, Maudslay set up his own firm in 1797.

His first major order was for machine-tools for Portsmouth naval dockyard. Marc Brunel, a royalist refugee from the French navy, had designed machinery for manufacturing pulley-blocks. In 5½ years from 1802, Maudslay built 43 machines for sawing, boring, mortising and scoring three sizes of pulley-blocks. Driven by a 30 hp steam engine, these machines produced 130,000 blocks a year with ten unskilled men in place of the 110 skilled men employed before. It was another portent of the labour versus machinery controversy that has beset industry in the western world ever since.

Standards of Accuracy

Maudslay set a new standard of accuracy for all machine-tools, partly with his insistence on all-metal construction. He also trained the next generation of great machine-tool engineers, among them Richard Roberts who made the first metal-planing machine in 1817. A larger version was produced a few years later by Joseph Clement, another of Maudslay's employees. It became the main source of Clement's income, earning him as much as £20 a day, and remained for ten years the only machine of its kind capable of handling a workpiece 1·8 metres (6 feet square).

James Nasmyth was Maudslay's personal assistant until the latter's death, when he set up his own workshop. He invented several machines, but is particularly famous for his steam-hammer. Designed in 1839, it consisted of a hammer-head connected to the piston of an overhead cylinder. Steam admitted beneath this piston raised the hammer for each

'Fritz', a 19th-century German steam hammer for working st

stroke. Later, steam was also forced in above the piston to increase the power of the downward stroke. With this machine, iron girders and plates of a size never known before could be forged. Yet the great hammer could be controlled to descend with a force just sufficient to crack an egg. A version of Nasmyth's steam-hammer drove the piles for Robert Stephenson's Newcastle bridge at the rate of one blow per second instead of one every few minutes by previous methods.

Last of the these early pioneers was Joseph Whitworth who also worked for Maudslay for a short time. In 1833, he set up business as a maker and seller of machine-tools. This was a new idea, since all the other machine-tool engineers mentioned had been involved in using the machines they produced. At the Great Exhibition of 1851 in London, he had 23 exhibits of which one was a planing-machine with reversible tool-holder so that cuts could be made in both directions. He produced a measuring-machine accurate to ·0000025 centimetres (one-millionth of an inch) and worked towards standardisation of screw-threads, so that screws might become generally interchangeable.

Mining and Metals

Sir Humphry Davy (1778–1829) devised his safety lamp to show the presence of fire-damp. Before then canaries, more quick than men to react to the gas, were used to detect it.

Right: a Davy safety lamp. Centre: token money, like the coins minted by the ironmaster John Wilkinson of Bradley, was used to pay wages in the chronic absence of state coin. Bottom: the method of removing fire-damp, replaced by the Davy lamp.

In early 18th-century Britain, there was what could be described as a coal rush. Many landowners were involved. If coal was found even beneath the sweeping lawns and flower beds of a gentleman's estate, he had no compunction in ripping it all up to get at the black gold. When surface workings were exhausted, mines were sunk ever deeper.

The most common method of extraction in a deep mine was known as bord-and-pillar. Bords (an obsolete spelling of board) were the first excavations made at right angles to the seam, dividing the rest of the coal into pillars anything from 20 to 55 metres (22 to 60 yards) square. Slices about 5·5 metres (six yards) wide were cut from these. The roof was supported by timbers during the cutting and then allowed to collapse. In very deep mines, where the pressure was too great for the roof to be supported by timber, coal was removed in one go by the system known as longwall working. A wall of coal about 90 metres (100 yards) long was taken out and the roof above supported by stone piles as the cutting advanced.

Coal Hauling

Coal was hauled away from the face in wicker baskets loaded on to sledges. The baskets were then carried up the shaft by a series of ladders and landing stages, sometimes to a height of more than 30 metres (100 feet). While the men did the actual coal-cutting, their wives and children hauled away the coal. As distances became greater, pit ponies were introduced from about 1763. Towards the end of the century, trucks running on light rails were used, though more often than not women and children still did the hauling. Some galleries could be tunnelled with an upward slope so that loaded trucks could run to the shaft down an incline. Others had dips which increased the haulage difficulties, or were too low for a pony to stand upright. Steam-haulage was gradually introduced, even in level galleries, and power winding gear was used to raise coal and miners up the shaft.

Flooding and ventilation were ever-present problems. Again, steam-power was eventually used for pumping out water. Black-damp, air deficient in oxygen, was the main problem in shallow mines, but could be noticed quickly by the miner when his lamp

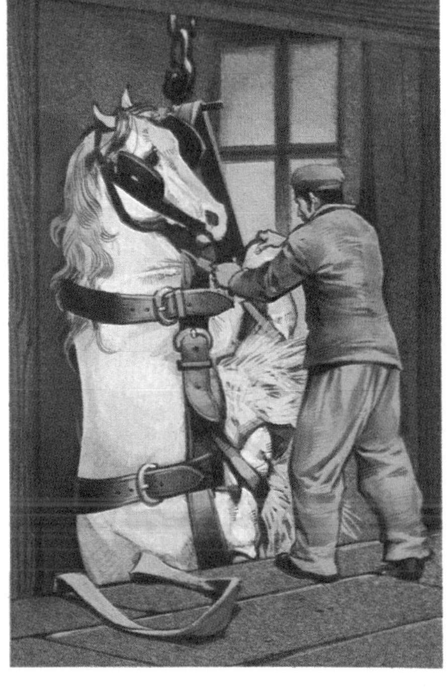

A French pit pony being lowered to its work in the mine.

dimmed. The use of explosives to get at and move the coal often caused after-damp, the product of incomplete combustion after an explosion. Fire-damp, a mixture of air and methane gas released from the cut coal, was a third hazard. A fireman was employed to go ahead of his companions, wrapped in wet sacks and holding a naked flame on the end of a long pole to burn away the gas. A flint-and-steel mill, which emitted a stream of sparks bright enough to work by, gave warning of explosive gas when the sparks grew bigger and brighter. A number of safety lamps were devised, the most famous of which was designed by the scientist Sir Humphry Davy. The flame was contained within a metal gauze cylinder which carried away the heat before it could ignite any gas. A second gauze was later added to avoid the danger when the first gauze became red-hot, as it could in a strong draught. Davy's experiments in this field illustrate how, for the first time, pure science was beginning to be applied to the solution of practical problems.

Mining Safety

Every improvement in mining safety and technique was slow in coming. By 1900, twelve-year-old boys still went underground. Disastrous explosions continued to be a frequent occurrence. No satisfactory coal-conveyor was introduced until 1902. The early mechanical cutters, like circular saws, were driven by compressed air. Electric coal-cutters were a later innovation. Well into our own century, the coal-face worker had to lie or crouch in wet or unbearably hot conditions, hacking a deep groove close to floor level, then pull down the coal mass with pick, crowbar or hammered wedge. For some, human muscle was still the prime force.

A growing shortage of timber in Britain had stimulated the coal rush. The use of coal for the smelting of iron-ore was to bring together the two great raw materials of the Industrial Revolution. When brewers tried to dry their malt by coal fires, the taste of the beer was ruined. We know now that this was because of the presence of sulphur. In the 17th century, some Derbyshire brewers had the idea of charring the coal to make coke, which has most of its sulphur removed, just as wood is charred to make charcoal. The result was a famous beer. Similarly, smelting iron-ore with coal introduced impurities into the metal, making it brittle and difficult to work. In 1709, Abraham Darby, who had served his apprenticeship to a malt-mill manufacturer, experimented with coke-smelting of iron. He achieved a reasonable success with the production of pig iron, but did not advertise his process. In 1748, his son of the same name, by careful selection of ores with low phosphorus content, managed to produce coke-smelted cast iron. Later, the quality of the iron was improved by remelting in foundry furnaces where the iron was not in contact with the coal burnt in them.

Coke in a blast furnace burned less easily than charcoal. John Smeaton partly overcame this by introducing blowing cylinders powered by water to provide more air for complete combustion. John Wilkinson in 1776 started the use of a steam engine to provide the air blast. In 1784, Henry Cort established the puddling process which essentially involves the raking, separating, stirring and spreading of the melted ore within the furnace to give the air complete and rapid access to it. The Clyde Ironworks in Glasgow introduced, in 1829, the hot blast which produced three times as much iron with the same amount of fuel. The principal metal for the new industries was becoming cheap and plentiful.

Progress in the production of other metals was somewhat slower. Benjamin Huntsman of Doncaster, a clock and instrument maker, produced an improved steel. He heated bar iron and charcoal in special heat-resisting clay crucibles for five hours at a very high temperature. This crucible steel gradually became adopted by the cutlers of Sheffield where Huntsman moved to exploit his invention. But steel remained a costly, small-scale process.

One notable new use of metal was the invention in 1742 by Thomas Bolsover of Sheffield plate, at first for making buttons. Thin sheets of silver were soldered or fused on to either side of a thick sheet of copper. This sandwich was then rolled into a thin sheet. Cheaper than pure silver, its use spread for such articles as tea and coffee services and candlesticks, especially after a technique was introduced for soldering a silver wire to cover the edges where the copper was exposed.

Sheffield plate was a popular substitute for solid silver and after 1784 had its own hallmark. Left: Until about 1900, children were used to drag coal from the face.

Modern Chemistry

By co-ordinating and extending the work of others, Lavoisier founded modern chemistry.

The study of chemistry could not advance until the processes of combustion and chemical combination were understood. This understanding was the great scientific breakthrough of the 18th century. We owe it to the work of one of France's most eminent scientists, Antoine Laurent Lavoisier (1743–94). Yet his years of experiment discovered no new chemical substance and established few new chemical facts. What he did was to interpret the discoveries of others, to formulate a new theory of combustion, to explain the basic simplicity of chemical combination and to give a start to the modern naming of such combinations and the elements comprising them. It was the foundation on which the modern study of chemistry was to be built.

When Lavoisier was beginning his chemical experiments, scientists still believed in the phlogiston theory put forward in the previous century by Johann Joachim Becher and developed by his disciple Georg Ernst Stahl. The theory stated that when a substance burns it gives off fire stuff or phlogiston. Something like charcoal which leaves very little ash behind was considered to be almost pure phlogiston. Lavoisier burned phosphorus in a bottle to the neck of which was attached a bladder of air and showed that a sizeable proportion of the air was absorbed by the burning phosphorus. He did the same experiment with sulphur with similar results. This seemed to contradict the phlogiston theory which claimed that when phosphorus and sulphur burn, rather than absorbing anything, they emit phlogiston.

When metals like lead and tin are melted, they leave a dross on the surface called a calyx, the process called calcination. It was known that this calyx was heavier than the metal from which it was formed. Adherents of the phlogiston theory explained this by saying that phlogiston has levity rather than gravity, or that it possessed negative weight. Lavoisier, believing that the increase in weight came from the absorption of air, heated some lead in a sealed vessel until there was no further calcination. Weighing the vessel before and after this process, he found no change in the weight. When he unsealed the vessel, he heard an inrush of air. The weight of the vessel and its contents had then increased by an amount equal to the increase in the weight of the calyx. These experiments showed that the amount of air available is the critical factor in the extent to which calcination takes place. Only a part of the air, about a fifth, is absorbed. What was the peculiar nature of this one-fifth of the air?

The answer came from the experiments of an English Unitarian minister called Joseph Priestley (1732–1804), interested in the investigation of gases. Priestley devised an apparatus with a retort attached by a tube through a bath of mercury to a gas-collecting vessel. With the aid of a powerful burning-glass, he heated some red calyx of mercury (mercuric oxide, HgO). He found that the calyx changed into mercury and that a gas was given off. This new gas caused a candle flame to burn with astonishing vigour. He put a mouse in a quantity of the gas. In the same amount of air, the mouse would be expected to live about fifteen minutes. It lived for half an hour. Taken out, apparently dead, it revived in front of the fire. Priestley called his new gas dephlogisticated air because, as a supporter of combustion it must readily absorb phlogiston. We, of course, call it oxygen.

Experiments with Air

Lavoisier repeated Priestley's experiments. He heated mercury calyx with charcoal and collected the gas that was emitted. This gas extinguished a candle flame and killed animals placed in it in a few seconds. It was obviously the gas discovered in 1756 by the Scottish chemist, Joseph Black, and called fixed air (carbon dioxide, CO_2). Lavoisier next heated mercury calyx by itself. This time, the gas given off made a candle flame flare up brilliantly and supported the breathing of animals. It seemed to be particularly pure air. Lavoisier concluded that what combines with a substance when it is burned or calcinated is this pure air. Eventually, he showed that ordinary air consists of two gases, one that supports combustion and respiration (oxygen) and another that does neither (nitrogen).

He heated mercury in a vessel connected to the air in a bell jar standing in a bath of mercury. The heating continued until no more red calyx of mercury appeared. Then by heating the mercury calyx and the air in a number of ways, Lavoisier disproved the phlogiston theory. This stated that heating mercury in oxygen made it release its phlogiston into the oxygen. Lavoisier demonstrated that, on the contrary, all the oxygen present was absorbed to create the mercury calyx.

Another great British experimenter, the eccentric millionaire Henry Cavendish (1731–1810) had discovered another gas obtained from the action of acids on metals. It was highly inflammable, and he called it inflammable air which we now know as hydrogen. In 1781, Priestley ignited a mixture of inflammable air and about a fifth of the ordinary air was changed into a liquid. The liquid had no taste or smell and left no deposit when evaporated. It seemed to be, and indeed was, pure water. Lavoisier repeated these experiments and laid claim to the discovery. He had not, of course, discovered the composition of water. But he did realise, as Cavendish did not, that water could no longer be regarded as an element as it had been from ancient times. He had the genius to perceive that inflammable air and dephlogisticated air are the true elements, and that their chemical combination produces water. It was this momentous explanation that eventually led chemists to look for the elements combined in all substances that were not themselves elements. Modern chemistry was born.

Lavoisier's Experiments

Lavoisier went on to name the substances that had been discovered. Dephlogisticated air became oxygen and the calyx of a metal its oxide. Inflammable air became hydrogen. Pure charcoal was called carbon and its salts carbonates. The combination of sulphur and oxygen became sulphuric acid and its salts sulphates, and so on. Lavoisier, as a rich man, fell foul of the revolutionary leaders in his country and was brought to trial. In his defence it was claimed that, as a scientist, he had brought honour to France. The President of the court replied: 'The Republic has no need of men of science', and Lavoisier went to the guillotine.

Henry Cavendish reconstructed the Torsion Balance experiment to determine the earth's specific gravity. He measured the torsion, or twisting, caused to a thread suspending two small spheres attracted by two large spheres.

Priestley's sympathy for the French Revolution led in 1791 to the wrecking of his house by a mob. In 1794 he emigrated to the United States.

The First Balloonists

Francesco de Lana's 1670 design for an aerial ship. Most early designs for flying machines were based on the use of birdlike wings, and it was not until the possibilities of lighter-than-air gases were realised that practical designs were produced. The first successful balloon used heated air to provide lift.

It was the 18th-century interest in gases and the discoveries resulting from them that began the new and often dangerous pastime of ballooning. The balloonists themselves approached their problems in a spirit of scientific enquiry, prepared to risk their lives in practical experiment. The Montgolfier brothers, Joseph and Etienne, French papermakers, began it all.

Oxygen and Hydrogen

Their first hot-air balloon was not designed to carry passengers, though big enough to do so. Their aerostatic machine, as they called it, was made of cloth lined with paper. It was spherical with a circumference of 34 metres (110 feet). A wooden frame 4·6 metres (16 feet) square held it fixed at the bottom. Its capacity was about 625 cubic metres (22,000 cubic feet), so it displaced a volume of air weighing 898 kilograms (1,980 pounds). The weight of the hot air that filled it they estimated at 450 kilograms (990 pounds) and the weight of the fabric of the machine at 227 kilograms (500 pounds). It was the 221 kilograms (490 pounds) difference between the balloon's total weight and the weight of air it displaced which caused it to rise. Two men could lift the structure to fill it with hot air from a fire on the ground. But once filled, it took eight men to hold it down. It remained ten minutes in the air. The hot air soon escaped through the buttonholes of the buttons that held it together, was replaced by cold and heavier air, and it floated gently down. At last, on 5th June 1783, aeronautics became a practical possibility. In September, 1783, the brothers' fourth experiment included the first living passengers, a sheep and some pigeons carried in a basket suspended beneath the balloon.

First Manned Ascent

The following month, the first manned ascent was undertaken by the Marquis d'Arlandes and Pilâtre de Rozier. This time, the fire that provided the hot air was slung under the balloon itself and a supply of straw for fuel was carried with the two passengers. The 25 minute flight carried them nearly 9 kilometres (5½ miles) across Paris. They landed safely, though de Rozier had to crawl out from under the enveloping folds of the collapsed balloon.

Almost as soon as the hot-air balloon had achieved its first success, the hydrogen balloon appeared. This was the invention of the French scientist Professor Jacques Charles. His first experiment was launched on 27th August 1783 without passengers. His balloon landed in the village of Gonesse, where the local people were so terrified by its sudden appearance that they hacked it to pieces with their scythes and forks. Professor Charles was the real creator of the balloonists' art. He invented the valve to control the gas content, the car to carry passengers, the sand for ballast, the coating of caoutchouc (india-rubber) to make the balloon airtight and the practice of carrying a barometer to measure altitude. Nevertheless, he only ever made one trip in a balloon, during which his companion left him at the first landing, while the professor flew on alone, the first solo aviator in the world.

It was a Frenchman, too, who made the first parachute descent from a balloon, on 22nd October 1797. His name was André Garnerin. His parachute was attached to the small basket in which he stood, and all this was suspended beneath the balloon. At 610 metres (2,000 feet), he cut the cord which connected the parachute to the balloon. At first he fell swiftly, but then the air caught in the parachute, opened it out and brought him gently to earth. Garnerin was eventually killed experimenting with a parachute, but his pioneer efforts and considerable courage certainly helped to save many lives in later years.

Ballooning Craze

The craze for ballooning spread throughout Europe and to America. In 1785, Blanchard and Jefferies made the first crossing of the English Channel. Soon the military authorities were beginning to take an interest. A balloon was first used for military reconnaissance at the battle of Maubeuge on 2nd June 1794. The French sent up the craft *Entreprenant* with two occupants to send down reports of the enemy's movements. The captain in charge was Jean Marie-Joseph Coutelle, appointed by Napoleon to form a balloon company, the first air corps in history. The first bombing raid was in 1849 when the Austrians sent a fleet of pilotless balloons to drop incendiary bombs on the beleagured city of Venice. The bombs had time-fuses and did considerable damage. Balloons were used for military observation in the American Civil War, the Boer War and the First World War.

Attempts were made to propel balloons and to direct their flight. The envelope was elongated into a torpedo shape. In 1852, the French engineer Henri Giffard experimented with a small steam engine driving a propellor. There was not enough power to give more than some aid to steering. In 1884, a balloon was fitted with an electric motor and specially designed lightweight batteries. It reached a top speed of 22·5 kph (14 mph) on a round trip of five miles.

A great measure of control was achieved when the rigid airship was developed. In this, a streamlined hull contained a number of gas-bags, and nacelles to carry passengers and crew were slung underneath. Count von Zeppelin gave his name to a whole series of such aircraft. They were used in bombing raids in the First World War, but were too vulnerable to the swift fighter planes that had already been developed by then. Their use continued after the war, but the difficulty remained of providing sufficient lift. Hydrogen is the lightest gas, but it is highly inflammable and, mixed with air, explosive. This was the cause of a number of disasters. Helium, the inert gas discovered in 1895, was available only in small quantities and had but a quarter of the lifting power of hydrogen.

Ballooning, particularly the inexpensive hot-air variety, continues to be a popular sport today. Balloons, because of their silent movement, have been used to study the migrations of wild animals and for filming them from particular points of vantage. Sporting events are filmed from the air and small airships are being developed to carry awkward loads to sites that might otherwise be difficult to reach. We have not yet seen the end of the aerostatic machine, in which the balloonists of the 18th century were the first to travel.

October 1783—de Rozier and d'Arlandes take off in a Montgolfier hot-air balloon to become the first men to fly.

The Charles brothers in their hydrogen-filled balloon, 1783. Hydrogen-filled balloons have the advantage of being able to remain aloft almost indefinitely.

Garnerin makes the first parachute descent in 1797. The principle of the parachute was set down by Leonardo da Vinci, but it was not until the development of the aeroplane as a weapon that its use became widespread. In modern jet aircraft the pilot is ejected still in his seat, and his parachute opens automatically.

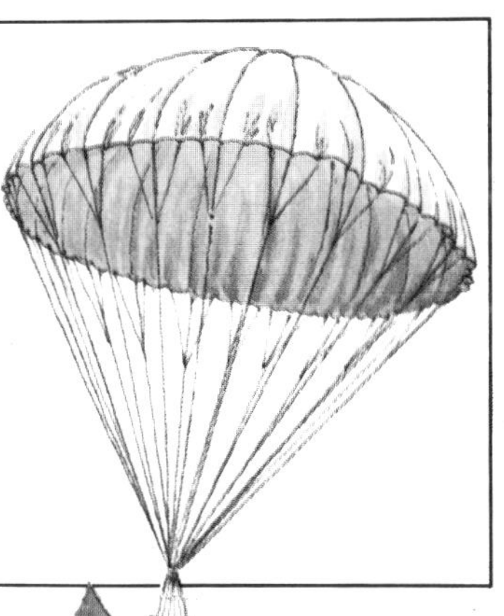

The Steam Engine

The idea of steam pressure as a motive force goes back to ancient times. Its practical realisation, however, came rather late in the progress of the Industrial Revolution. It had been known for some time that when heat converts water into steam its volume is expanded about 1,300 times. Thus, if steam is condensed back into water in a closed chamber, the result is a partial vacuum. Von Guericke demonstrated the force of atmospheric pressure on a vacuum. He produced a vacuum in a cylinder, one end of which was closed by a sliding piston. The strength of 50 men was unable to prevent the piston moving along the cylinder under the force of the atmospheric pressure outside it.

In France, in 1690, Denis Papin brought two principles together in a famous experiment. He put a little water in a cylinder with a moving piston. When the cylinder was heated to boil the water, steam pressure forced the piston to the top of the cylinder where a catch prevented it from being blown out. Jamming the piston in this position, Papin allowed the cylinder to cool. The steam condensed back into water, leaving a partial vacuum. When the piston was released, atmospheric pressure forced it rapidly down into the cylinder. Papin had created what should properly be called an atmospheric engine, since atmospheric pressure was the motive force.

The Miner's Friend

In 1698, the Englishman Thomas Savery patented an atmospheric engine which he described in a pamphlet entitled *The Miner's Friend*, since the engine's purpose was to pump water out of flooded mines. The essential part of Savery's engine was an oval-shaped vessel, at first filled with water. Steam entering this vessel forced out the water through an outlet valve which was closed as soon as the vessel was full of steam. Water from a tap was then poured over the vessel to condense the steam inside and produce a partial vacuum. A valve at the bottom was opened, and water from the flooded mine was forced in by the outside atmospheric pressure. The whole cycle then began again. There were two of these steam-condensing vessels working alternately. The operator, manually opening and shutting the valves at appropriate intervals, could work the engine at the rate of five cycles per minute.

Normal atmospheric pressure can raise a column of water only nine metres (30 feet) or so. Savery's engine had therefore to be built on a platform in the mineshaft about this distance above the flood water. To raise the water further, Savery used high-pressure steam. Water normally boils at about 100°C, the temperature at which the vapour pressure equals atmospheric pressure. In a closed vessel, the pressure above the water can be increased so that boiling takes place at a higher temperature. This is the principle of the pressure cooker, also invented by Denis Papin. Superheated water can generate very high pressures, for instance at 200°C steam pressure is fifteen times that of steam at 100°C. It would thus lift a column of water fifteen times higher than normal, about 135 metres (450 feet). Savery tried to use steam at eight to ten times atmospheric pressure, giving a potential lift of 90 metres (300 feet) or so. Unfortunately, construction problems associated with such high pressures could not, at that time, be overcome.

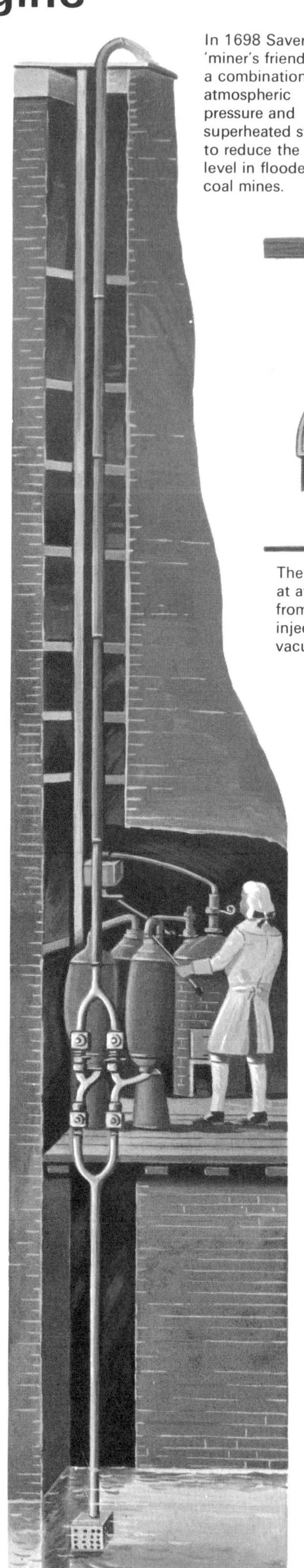

In 1698 Savery's 'miner's friend' used a combination of atmospheric pressure and superheated steam to reduce the water level in flooded coal mines.

James Watt at work in his Glasgow laboratory

The principle of the Newcomen engine. Steam at atmospheric pressure enters the cylinder from the bottom and is condensed by an injection of cold water. This creates a partial vacuum which draws the piston down.

Newcomen's Engines

Meanwhile, Thomas Newcomen, a Devon man like Savery but working in Dartford, Kent, as a blacksmith and ironmonger, was independently developing his own invention. His engine used the cylinder and piston method suggested by Papin. The piston rod was attached to one end of a large beam pivoted in the middle like a pair of scales. The other end of the pump-rod brought the piston to the top of the cylinder. Steam at atmospheric pressure was introduced from the bottom of the cylinder until it was full. Then an injection-valve admitted a jet of cold water to condense the steam. Atmospheric pressure forced the piston down into the cylinder, now a partial vacuum, completing the cycle. Opening and shutting of steamcock and injection-valve were automatically controlled by movement of the injection-pump rod which was itself connected to the oscillating beam.

Newcomen's first operating engine was installed in the colliery at Dudley Castle in Worcestershire in 1712. The beam rocked twelve times a minute, lifting with every stroke 45 litres (ten gallons) of water 47 metres (153 feet) through a series of pumps. This invention spread rapidly through Britain, and by the time of the inventor's death in 1729 had reached many countries in Europe. Its drawback was the difficulty at the time of boring accurate cylinders. Newcomen tried to overcome this by sealing the top of the piston with a leather disc covered with a layer of water.

James Watt

James Watt was working as a maker of mathematical instruments at Glasgow University in Scotland when he was given a model of a Newcomen engine to repair. He saw that its efficiency was limited by the necessity of cooling the cylinder to condense the steam between strokes. He hit upon the idea of a separate condenser into which the steam could be drawn by means of an air-pump. In the engine he finally developed, the cylinder was kept hot by means of a steam-jacket. As the piston reached the top of its stroke, the exhaust valve at the bottom of the cylinder opened and, at the same time, steam was admitted to the space above the piston by an inlet valve. A combination of steam pressure and atmospheric pressure drove the piston down. At the bottom of its stroke, the exhaust and inlet valves were closed. A special valve opened to equalise the pressure on both sides of the piston which was drawn up again by the weight of the pump-rod. Watt went on to make his engines double-acting by admitting steam alternately on either side of the piston. He also cut off the supply of steam early in the stroke so that its expansion did the rest of the work. Watt can thus be credited with the invention of the steam engine as

The first locomotive to run on a track was built in 1804 by Richard Trevithick at Penydarran Ironworks in Wales. Trevithick was one of the first to use high-pressure steam.

George Stephenson (1781–1848) is regarded as the foremost engineer of the railway era.

Top to bottom: the *Rocket*, George Stephenson's greatest engineering masterpiece, built in 1829; the *Best Friend of Charleston*, with a tender for carrying extra coal; and the *Novelty*, built by the Swede John Ericsson, with carriages.

Nicolas Cugnot in his 1769 steam tractor, which he drove round Paris until he hit a wall.

opposed to the atmospheric engines of his predecessors.

It was May 1765 when Watt thought of the idea of a separate condenser, but 1776 before his first two engines began work. One of these was built to supply air to the blast furnaces of John Wilkinson's ironworks at Denbighshire in Wales. In return, Wilkinson bored cylinders for Watt's engines on his recently invented boring-mill. Without the precision of Wilkinson's cylinders, Watt's engines could never have succeeded so dramatically, requiring as they did airtight operation at high working temperatures. From the to and fro action of the engines used to power pumps, Watt naturally moved on to using rotary motion to power other machinery.

High-pressure Steam

Watt had always considered the use of high-pressure steam to be too dangerous. Almost at once, high-pressure steam engines were developed simultaneously in the United States and Britain. By 1804 in Philadelphia, Oliver Evans was using a small engine with a steam pressure of 50 pounds per square inch. Two years earlier, Richard Trevithick, a Cornish mine engineer, had built a pumping engine with a steam pressure of 145 pounds or ten times the normal pressure of the atmosphere. It was Trevithick who first produced a steam locomotive to run on a railway. In Wales in 1804, his locomotive pulled five trucks loaded with 70 men and ten tons of freight the sixteen kilometres (ten miles) or so between Penydarran ironworks and the Glamorganshire canal at a speed of eight kph (five mph). In 1808, he was charging the public five shillings a trip on a circular track near Euston Square in London.

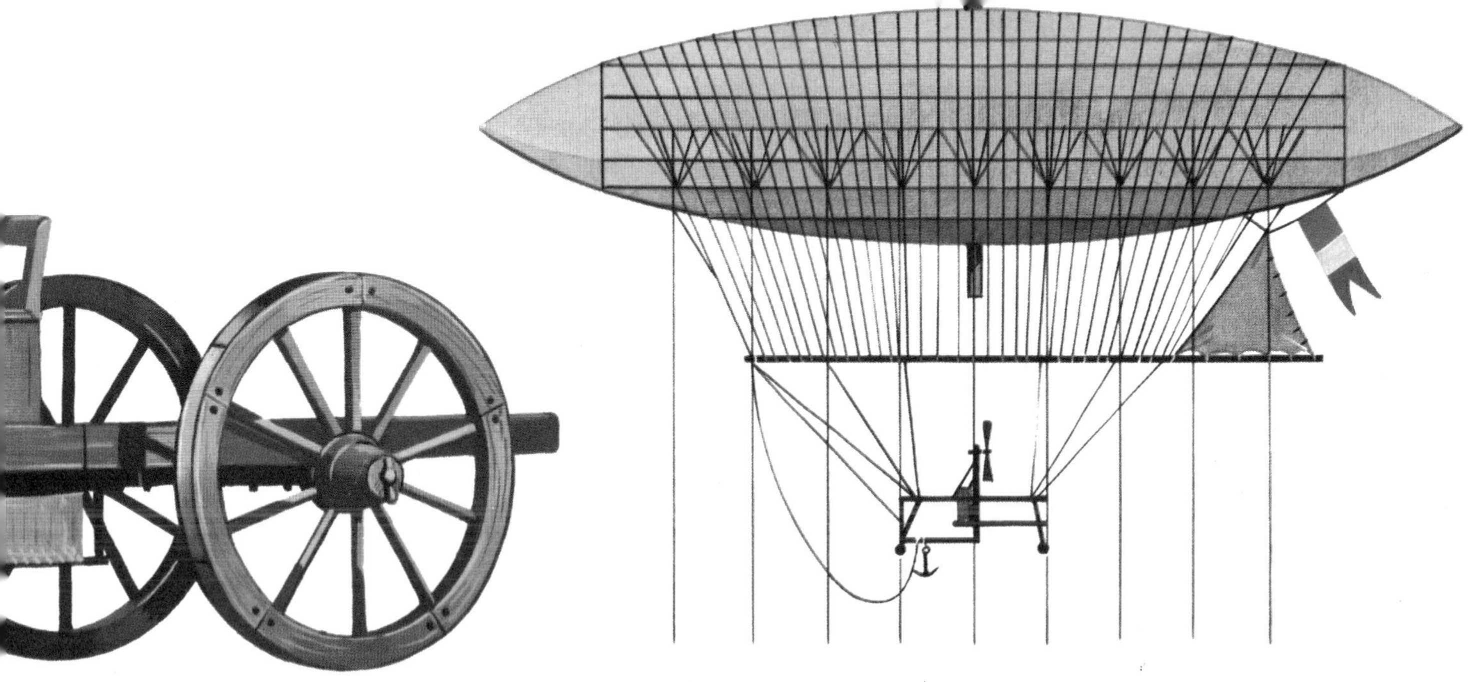

Giffard's airship, with a small steam engine driving a propeller, was too slow to steer.

The first powered vessel—the tug *Charlotte Dundas*, a paddle steamer built in Scotland in 1801–02.

The *Savannah*—first steamer across the Atlantic (1819). In fact she was a sailing ship with an auxiliary engine.

Above: the earliest Atlantic crossing under continuous steam power was by the packet-ship *Sirius*. It took 18½ days in 1838. Right: Robert Fulton's *Clermont* provided the first regular steamship service, on the River Hudson in 1807.

The development of the propeller was one of the most important advances in the history of the ship. Virtually all of the first steamships were powered by paddles arranged round wheels set either at the stern or on either side of the ship. At any given moment most of these paddlewheels is out of the water, and therefore doing no useful work. A propeller, on the other hand, is always totally immersed, so that almost all of the power fed into it through the driveshaft is used to push the ship forward. The picture shows the propeller of the *Great Britain*, one of Brunel's most famous designs, which is now being completely restored.

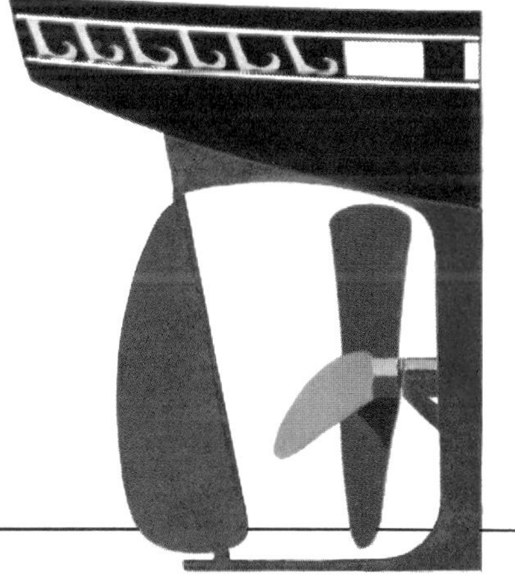

The joining of the Union Pacific and Central Pacific Railroads in 1869 gave the United States its first transcontinental rail link.

Transport

The railway was a very much earlier development than the steam locomotive. It was particularly used to ease the passage of coal trucks from pithead to canal. The motive power was either men or horses. The earliest rails were made of timber, which was first replaced by iron at Whitehaven in 1738. By 1767, cast-iron rails were being produced at Coalbrookdale, again in Britain, and their use began to spread. Both flanged rails for holding ordinary wheels on the track and flanged wheels on flat rails were early developments. Cast-iron is a rather brittle material, but from 1820 a method was devised for rolling wrought-iron rails which became the standard practice. In Britain, double-headed rails were keyed into special chairs fastened to the transverse wooden sleepers. In America, an inverted T-shape section was spiked directly into the sleepers.

The first public railway was a track for horse-drawn traffic which, by 1805, ran between Croydon and Wandsworth near London and was called the Surrey Iron Railway. In 1825, the opening of the Stockton to Darlington railway with steam locomotion began the world's modern railway system. By the 1840s in Britain, railway building had become a national mania. Steam engines improved in power and speed so rapidly that in 1849 there were five locomotives achieving average speeds of 80 kph (50 mph) between London and Bristol. Already, locomotives were happily coping with gradients of one in 38.

Signalling Systems

The increase in the railway network and the traffic that flowed along it required an elaborate signalling system. The French invention of the semaphore was adapted for the railways and used in conjunction with signal boxes placed at strategic intervals along the line. The first electric telegraph was installed between Paddington and West Drayton stations in 1839. Integrating the signal mechanism with that of the points first came into operation on the Hampstead Junction railway in 1859. Track was improved from 1862 when the first trials were made of steel rails at Crewe. All these developments took place in Britain but, by 1867, steel rails were being made in Pennsylvania for the rapidly expanding American network.

Early passenger coaches had four wheels or sometimes six. The bogie truck had been patented by an Englishman, William Chapman, in 1812. But the regular use of bogies at either end of a long passenger coach was an American invention. It made the coach able to take curves smoothly and avoided derailments on poorly aligned track. The Americans also led the way in passenger comfort with sleeping cars, dining cars and lavatory facilities.

The first American Pullman cars were imported into Britain in 1874, and one with electric lighting supplied by storage batteries was running between London and Brighton as early as 1881. Though Robert Stephenson invented a steam-brake in 1833, hand-brakes on tender or rear van were all that was deemed necessary for many years. During a test in 1875, the American Westinghouse compressed-air brake (first used in 1868) stopped a 200-ton train travelling at 80 kph (50 mph) in less than 300 metres (1,000 feet). Thereafter, the introduction of powered brakes not only avoided disasters but improved the timing of trains by making them pull up more quickly.

Roads and Waterways

The rapid expansion of the railway system in Britain replaced the horse-drawn coach-and-four sooner than in other countries. Yet road traffic increased in Britain as elsewhere, if only on short hauls from railway depots to town centres. The greatest world-wide influence on road-making was that of John Loudon McAdam (1756–1836), a Scot who had made his fortune in America and returned to his native Ayrshire. As Deputy Lieutenant of the county, he took an interest in the local roads. It was McAdam who established the principle that it was the native soil which bore the weight of traffic and, while it was kept dry, it would continue to bear the weight without sinking. He did away with the stone foundation, relying on the earth alone but making sure that there was good enough drainage to carry away any water or raising the road above water level. He also claimed that the thickness of the road was immaterial. What was needed was a waterproof and hard-wearing cover. He used small stones laid in three layers, each allowed to be compacted solidly by passing traffic. The macadamised surface spread throughout Europe and to America. Though nowadays his principles would be considered inadequate, his process was useful for repairing old surfaces.

In towns and cities, raised footpaths with stone kerbs began to appear in the second half of the 18th century. Roads carrying heavy traffic were covered with granite setts fitted together like masonry. Wood blocks were used in Russia at the beginning of the next century, and a creosoted type originated in America about 1867. Concrete road surfaces began in Austria in the 1850s and machinery for laying them was invented in Germany around 1879. The development of the asphalt road was carried on in France from 1832 with a mixture of powdered rock asphalt and bitumen from natural oil seepages. Sand-asphalt applied at temperatures between 150° and 200°C, and spread and rolled while still hot, provided a watertight surface. Tarmac, a mixture of coal-tar and small stones also laid hot and consolidated after cooling with a thin coat of sand, was first used in Britain in the 1830s. Such hot rolled surfaces became important, however, only when fast motor vehicles with rubber tyres began to break up macadamised surfaces.

Despite the growth of road and rail networks in the 19th century, canals and rivers did not lose their importance as means of transport. A great deal of work was done on European rivers bypassing rapids, deepening shallows and even straightening the watercourse. Some of this was laborious pick and shovel cutting and embanking. Sometimes a rough course was cut and the river turned into it to do the rest of the work, often with unintended results. Work on the great St Lawrence Seaway in Canada began in 1821 when the 13·5 metre (46-foot) Lachine falls were bypassed. The Welland canal was dug to bypass Niagara Falls and by 1847 the route from Montreal to Lake Ontario was completed. Between 1817 and 1824, the 585-kilometre (364-mile) Erie canal was built, linking New York with the Great Lakes. The 164-kilometre (102-mile) Morris canal in New York state had 23 inclined planes up which barges were hauled, mounted on a trolley which in its turn was pulled up rails by a cable-drum operated from a water wheel. For the digging of Ferdinand de Lesseps's Suez Canal, opened in 1869, a trough-dredger with long

Right: the badge of the North Eastern Railway Company. Below: a Crampton locomotive used on Belgian railways in 1846. The driver was still out in the cold.

A railway navvy, 'ready for anything'. Navvies often lived for years in camps which moved with the railhead all over the country.

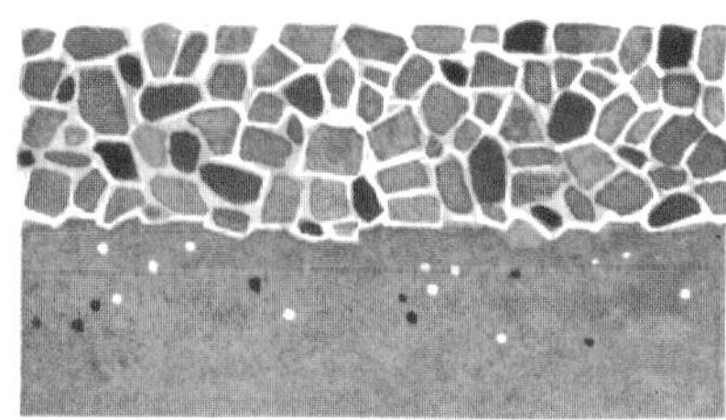

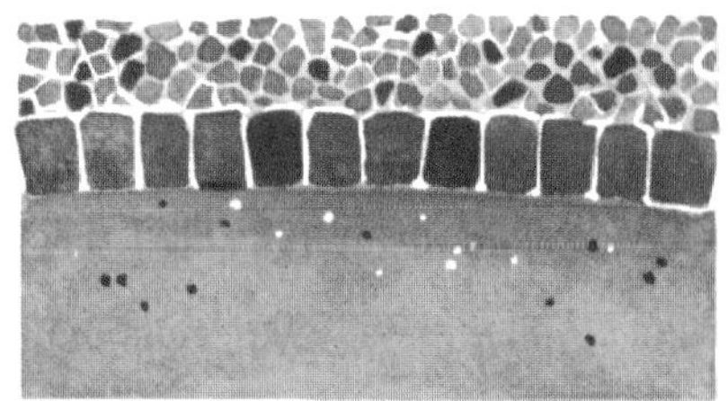

Techniques of road-building have kept pace with increasing numbers and weights of vehicles. Three early surfaces were (left to right) those of Telford, McAdam, Tresaguet.

Suspension bridges have to be specially reinforced to resist the pressure of side winds. The Brooklyn Bridge was one of the first to use the Roebling technique.

chutes for depositing silt was devised. A floating sand-pump was invented, and chisel-pointed rams broke up the rock. By 1867, 60 dredgers were moving 1·5 million cubic metres (56 million cubic feet) a month.

Bridge-building

In the techniques of bridge-building, there were a number of important improvements, stimulated by the growth of rail and road networks. In 1830, Sir Thomas Cochrane (later tenth Earl of Dundonald) introduced compressed-air caissons for the building of foundations on marshy ground. The principle was to lower a chamber on to the river bed and pump air into it to counter-balance the pressure of water outside. The men digging inside passed the waste up through an air-lock. As the caisson sank so it was built upwards to maintain a height always above water level.

Suspension bridges were built with longer and longer spans. There were many collapses until it was realised that the suspended deck needed reinforcement to avoid excessive movement in high winds. The most important advance was made by John Roebling, a German immigrant to America, with an arrangement of wire cable patented in 1841. Previous wire ropes were weakened by the twisting together of individual wires. Roebling proposed instead bundles of thick wires bound together after hanging. For the Brooklyn Bridge in New York, loops of galvanised steel wire were hauled across in both directions. Men on catwalks adjusted them for correct level and uniform sag. Then they were bunched into four main cables and bound together.

The cantilever system, in which the main structure is built outward from both sides and the intervening space linked by a girder span, was known in a crude form to the Chinese from ancient times. The system was fully employed in the Firth of Forth railway bridge in Scotland in which three main piers were established and each extended on either side simultaneously to preserve the balance. The 107-metre (350-foot) gaps between the cantilevered arms of the main piers were then built out to meet in the middle. When the ends came to be joined, such precision was achieved that improvised packing only was needed to expand the metal slightly to enable the final bolts to be inserted.

Tunnelling

An improved method of tunnelling through soft materials such as sand was introduced with Marc Brunel's shield used in the first tunnel constructed under the Thames in London and opened in 1843. It had two intermediate platforms enabling 36 men on three levels to attack the face simultaneously. It was moved forward a short distance at a time by jacks working against the completed masonry behind it. For the Mont Cenis tunnel through the Alps, a distance of twelve kilometres (eight miles) through solid rock, gunpowder was used for blasting and pneumatic drills were operated by water-powered compressors. The rate of advance, working from both ends, was 0·8 of a kilometre (half a mile) a year. The St Gothard tunnel, completed twelve years later in 1882, doubled this rate by using rock-drilling machinery from the start and the new dynamite for blasting.

Using a boring machine in the Mont Cenis tunnel, 1856–71.

Engineering

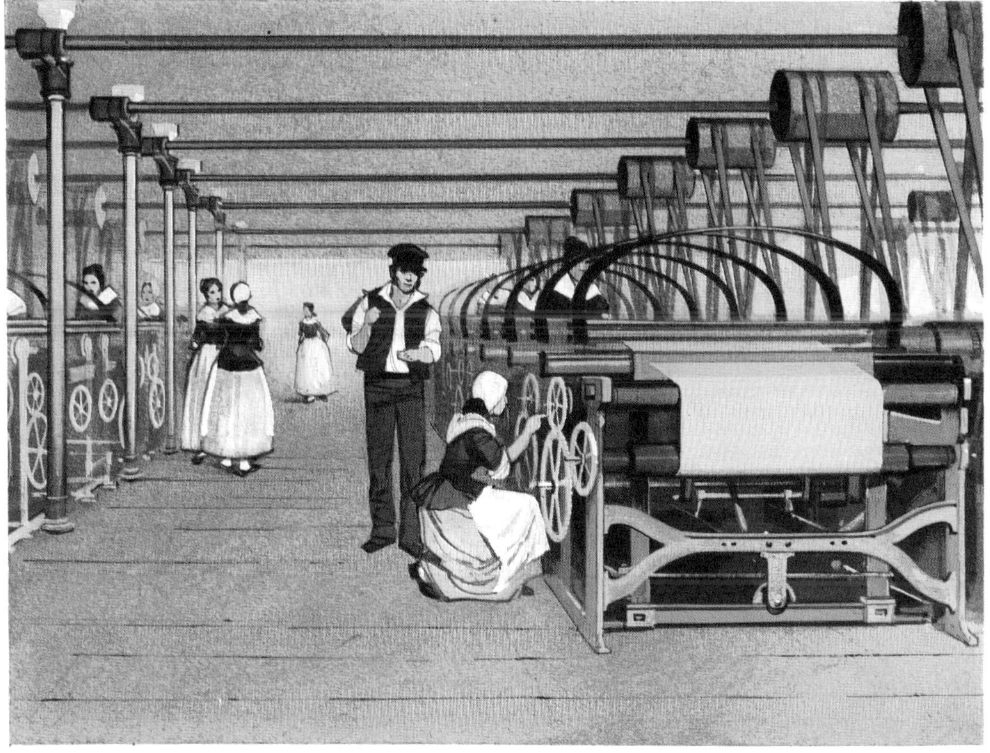

Power looms in a factory. The development of machinery to perform the repetitive tasks of weaving brought about enormous reductions in manufacturing costs.

Eli Whitney (1765–1825), American inventor of the cotton gin. He made very little money from his invention, and later manufactured the first muskets to have standardised interchangeable parts.

Perhaps the most important technological development in machine engineering in the 19th century was what has come to be known as the American system of interchangeable parts. It had begun, in fact, in Europe as a means of increasing production of muskets. The parts of the flintlock mechanism were designed for mass-production with sufficient precision to make assembly a comparatively unskilled job. In the United States, Eli Whitney, who had been unable to make sufficient profits from his cotton gin patented in 1794, turned to the production of muskets on the same principle. At a factory near New Haven in Connecticut, Whitney began making muskets using the new methods in 1798. Progress was slow at the beginning as machines had first to be invented and then built which would turn out uniform parts. When the government grew impatient, Whitney pointed out that once the machines were made and operating the assembly of the guns would be a simple and speedy matter. To prove his point he assembled a number of muskets before government representatives with parts chosen by them at random from piles of spares.

The idea of interchangeable parts spread to all small arms. Samuel Colt, inventor of the revolver, by 1853 had a factory using 1,400 machine-tools. As the century advanced, the system was used in all newly invented machines for which there was a mass demand. America, chronically short of skilled labour, continued to lead the way, pouring out cheaply manufactured machinery of increasing sophistication such as harvesters, sewing-machines and typewriters.

Textile Factories

In factories, mechanisation continued to develop, particularly in the textile industry where much of it had begun. Steam power was at first used to pump water for the operation of wheels which drove the actual machinery. In time, more and more steam engines were used to drive the machines directly. All the processes of preparation of raw materials, spinning, weaving and finishing off the cloth gradually surrendered to the mighty machine. Even the allied trades of hosiery, knitting and lacemaking began to be mechanised.

In Britain, John Heathcoat, a framesmith in the hosiery industry, invented the first satisfactory lace-making machine in 1809. John Leavers adapted the Heathcoat machine to make patterned lace in 1813. Finally, about 1840, Hooton Deverill in Nottingham made the first successful application of the Jacquard loom to lace-making. Net curtains appeared at every window and lace peeped from every petticoat.

Mechanisation of the knitting process for the making of stockings was longer delayed. In the 1840s Matthew Townsend of Leicester invented a circular rib-frame for making non-fashioned seamless hose. But it was William Cotton of Loughborough who produced a machine capable of making a dozen hose simultaneously and knitting fashioned garments of various kinds. At last, in 1887, inventors in America produced a power-driven sewing machine which could provide

When the manufacture of textiles ceased to be a craft industry and became a matter of tending machines, the employment of child labour became widespread. It was common for a child to work for twelve hours per day.

a seam for any knitted garment, working at 3,000 stitches a minute. Before this Elias Howe, a Massachusetts mechanic, had invented the lockstitch, the principle on which sewing machines were developed. His machine could sew only straight seams of limited length. In 1851, Isaac M. Singer of Boston produced the first practical domestic sewing machine using a straight needle and worked by a foot-treadle. The same year, the alternative chain-stitch was invented.

A draw-loom had been used in Kidderminster as early as 1735 for the weaving of carpet. Ninety years later, the Jacquard loom was adapted for the same purpose. The big breakthrough came when E. B. Bigelow of Massachusetts invented his Brussels power-loom. Strong wires with looped ends were automatically inserted and withdrawn to raise the looped pile, while thinner wires with a knife blade at the end raised and then cut the loops to produce the thick pile. The machine was improved in England to produce the famous Wilton carpet.

Machine-tool Industry

An important innovation in the machine-tool industry was the American invention of the turret lathe in the 1840s. A number of different tools could be locked into the octagonal turret which the operator could rotate to bring each tool in turn to bear upon the workpiece. Within twenty years, a mechanism was in use to rotate the turret automatically so that the lathe could go through a series of operations without further attention. At the same time, a means was devised of feeding in further metal bars to be worked without stopping the lathe. The way was open to a fully automatic lathe, machining a number of components simultaneously.

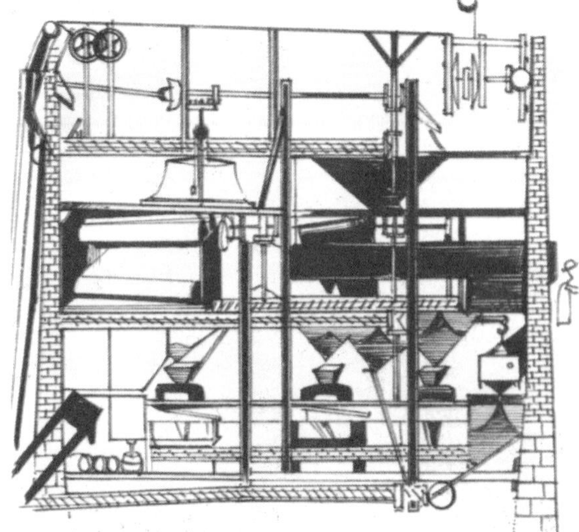

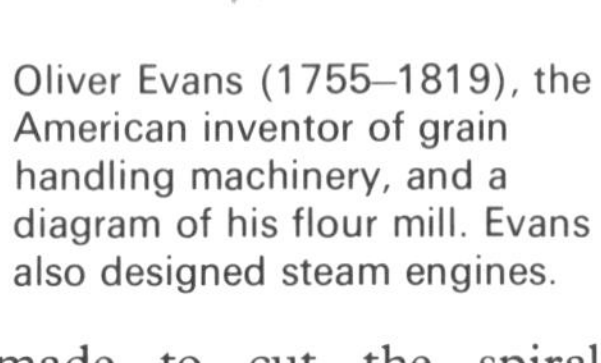

Oliver Evans (1755–1819), the American inventor of grain handling machinery, and a diagram of his flour mill. Evans also designed steam engines.

Precision Tools

These same principles were applied to drilling machinery. In 1862, Nasmyth produced a slot-drilling machine which was a valuable innovation. Previously, slots could be cut in metal only by boring two round holes and chipping away the metal in between. Further developments were in large vertical boring machines in which the part to be worked was clamped in a horizontal rotating table. About 1862, the first fully effective milling machine was designed in America by Joseph Brown. It was originally made to cut the spiral grooves in a twist-drill, but was quickly adapted to many other uses previously requiring hand-work. It eventually led, in the 1870s, to the automatic cutting of gearwheels which were beginning to play such an important part in the development of all machines, particularly as faster operation was the continual aim. Great advances in industrial development were made possible by the precision of the new machine tools. Watt's partner, Matthew Boulton, was so impressed with the accuracy of a cylinder bored by John Wilkinson in 1776 that he remarked it 'doth not err the thickness of an old shilling'. Yet Joseph Whitworth's machine, invented in 1856, was capable of measuring to one-millionth of an inch (·0000025 centimetres)—an extraordinary advance in precision.

Luddites, 1811. Fear that the new textile machinery was jeopardising jobs led to violent riots and the destruction of several mills. This riot is led by a man dressed as a woman.

The Chemical Industry

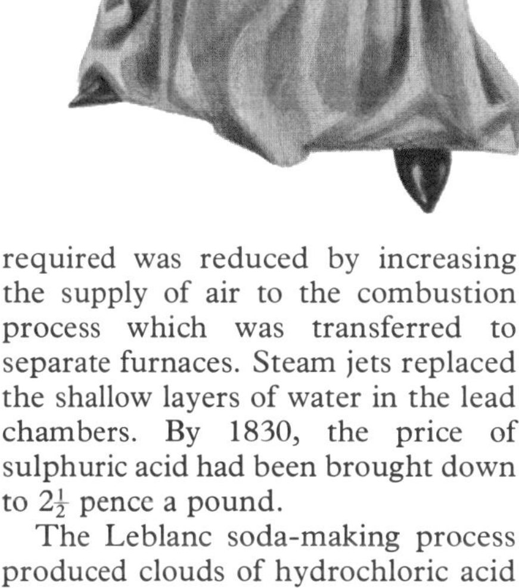

New dyes for new fashions. The 'mauve decade' of the 1890s.

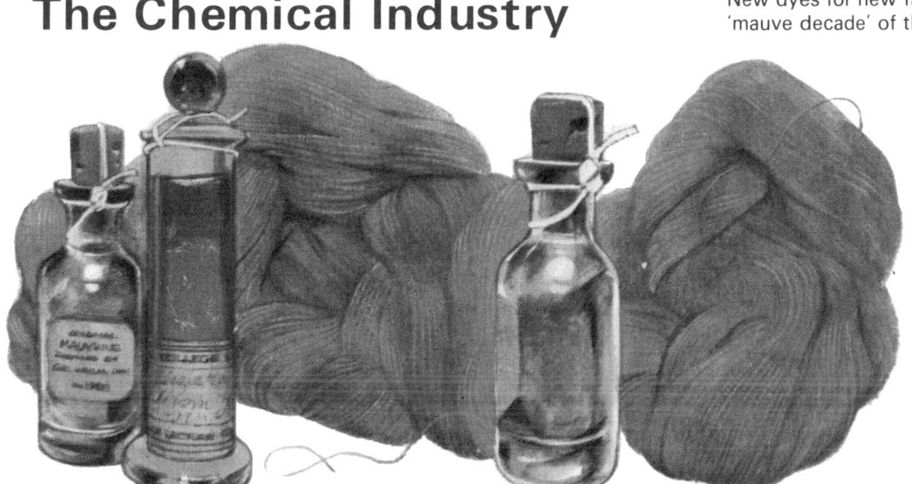

William Perkin's first synthetic dye.

The Industrial Revolution created a demand for large supplies of chemicals, particularly for the cleaning and bleaching of textiles, for glass-making and for soap-boiling. The demand was to create the modern chemical industry. One material in short supply, particularly in France, was soda. The French Academy offered a prize in 1775 for a method of making soda from salt. The problem was solved in 1787 by Nicolas Leblanc, physician to the Duke of Orleans. In his process, common salt was treated with sulphuric acid and the resulting sodium sulphate mixed with coal and limestone. The mixture was roasted and the soda extracted from the 'black ash' with water. The solution was evaporated in the atmosphere in open pans.

A purer product, for use in glass-making for instance, could be obtained by crystallisation.

Though he opened factories at St Denis, Rouen and Lille, Leblanc was dispossessed by the revolution and committed suicide in poverty in 1806. James Muspratt brought the process to Britain, though the soap-boilers who eventually became his best customers were suspicious of synthetic soda. Muspratt had to give it away at first and even supervise its use. In 1828, Muspratt formed a partnership with Josias Gamble and they set up a new works in St Helens, Lancashire, which has ever since been a centre of the British chemical industry. In 1825, Charles Tennant began manufacturing soda by the Leblanc method in Glasgow where his St Rollox works became the biggest chemical factory in Europe. By the 1830s it employed 1,000 workers, covered 40 hectares (100 acres) of land and had a chimney 139 metres (455 feet) high which was a famous local landmark.

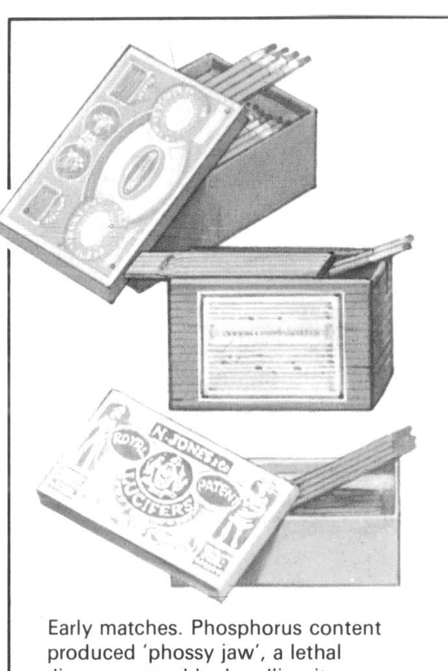

Early matches. Phosphorus content produced 'phossy jaw', a lethal disease caused by handling it.

Acid Production

Sulphuric acid played an important part in the production of synthetic soda. The centre for its manufacture has long been Nordhausen in Saxony where it was distilled from green vitriol (ferrous sulphate). But the process was expensive. In 1737, Joshua Ward began manufacture in Britain at Richmond by burning sulphur and saltpetre in the necks of glass vessels containing a little water. As the water became dilute sulphuric acid, it was concentrated by distillation. He reduced the price of the acid from £2 to two shillings a pound (0·4 kilogram). John Roebuck improved on the process by replacing the glass vessels with chambers made of lead, one of the few cheap metals resistant to sulphuric acid. Lead chamber factories were built in Rouen, France, in 1766 and in Philadelphia in the United States in 1793.

The original process was quickly improved. The quantity of saltpetre required was reduced by increasing the supply of air to the combustion process which was transferred to separate furnaces. Steam jets replaced the shallow layers of water in the lead chambers. By 1830, the price of sulphuric acid had been brought down to 2½ pence a pound.

The Leblanc soda-making process produced clouds of hydrochloric acid gas which is an unpleasant and destructive pollutant. In 1836, William Gossage, a Worcestershire chemical manufacturer, invented a tower in which the gas was absorbed in falling water. The resulting hydrochloric acid became a valuable by-product since its use had already been established in the manufacture of bleaching powder. The traditional way of bleaching textiles had been treatment with butter-milk and exposure to sunlight, a slow process taking months to complete. In

1785, the French chemist Berthollet showed that passing chlorine through potash made a solution with a strong bleaching action. In 1799, Tennant improved the process by passing chlorine over lime. The production of cheap bleaching powder gave a boost to the cotton industry without which it could not have expanded so rapidly.

Synthetic Dyes

A later, important development in the chemical and textile industries was the replacement of vegetable with synthetic dyes. This began when the German chemist August Wilhelm von Hofmann went to London in 1845 to be the first superintendent of the Royal College of Chemistry. Hofmann was interested in the chemical composition of coal-tar, a substance becoming cheaply available from the growing gas industry. He found a way of obtaining aniline cheaply from nitrobenzene, a coal-tar product, though he had no idea what could be made of it. A student of his, William Perkin, experimenting with aniline in the hope of producing quinine, found himself with some purple crystals which could be used to dye silk a brilliant mauve. By 1857, Perkin had his own works near Harrow to produce the first synthetic dyes.

Explosives

Alongside the dyestuffs industry, developments were taking place in explosives. Up to the middle of the 19th century the only important explosive for both military and civil engineering use was gunpowder. C. F. Schönbein discovered that cellulose treated with nitric acid produced an explosive material. It was called guncotton because cotton was the source of the cellulose. In 1846, it was manufactured in Britain by Schönbein in association with John Hall and Sons of Faversham but a disastrous explosion put an end to the enterprise. Nitroglycerine, discovered by the Italian chemist, A. Sobrero, was also a dangerous explosive to handle. It was Alfred Nobel who made it safe by absorbing it in a clay called Kieselguhr. His product became known as dynamite. Handled with reasonable care it is perfectly safe, but can be exploded by the use of a detonator such as fulminate of mercury.

Alfred Nobel (1833–96), famous both for the invention of dynamite and the prizes named after him. The Peace Prize medal is shown.

Another chemical industry was the manufacture of artificial fertiliser. Treating bones or mineral phosphate with sulphuric acid produces superphosphate, one of the most important agricultural fertilisers. It was manufactured by James Murray in Dublin from 1817. The large-scale industrial production of superphosphate was begun in 1834 by John Bennet Lawes in a factory at Deptford Creek near London. With J. H. Gilbert, he carried out extensive experiments on his agricultural estate at Rothamsted.

The chemical industry was also to bring important contributions to the field of medicine. Nitrous oxide, made by heating ammonium nitrate, was first used to alleviate pain in 1844 by a Connecticut dentist, Horace Wells. An American surgeon, C. W. Long, was the first to use ether in a minor operation. Its volatile nature, however, led Long to search for a substitute which resulted in the discovery of chloroform. In Britain, the pioneer work of Joseph Lister in the use as antiseptic of carbolic acid obtained from the distillation of coal-tar eventually led to the general use of iodine from 1878.

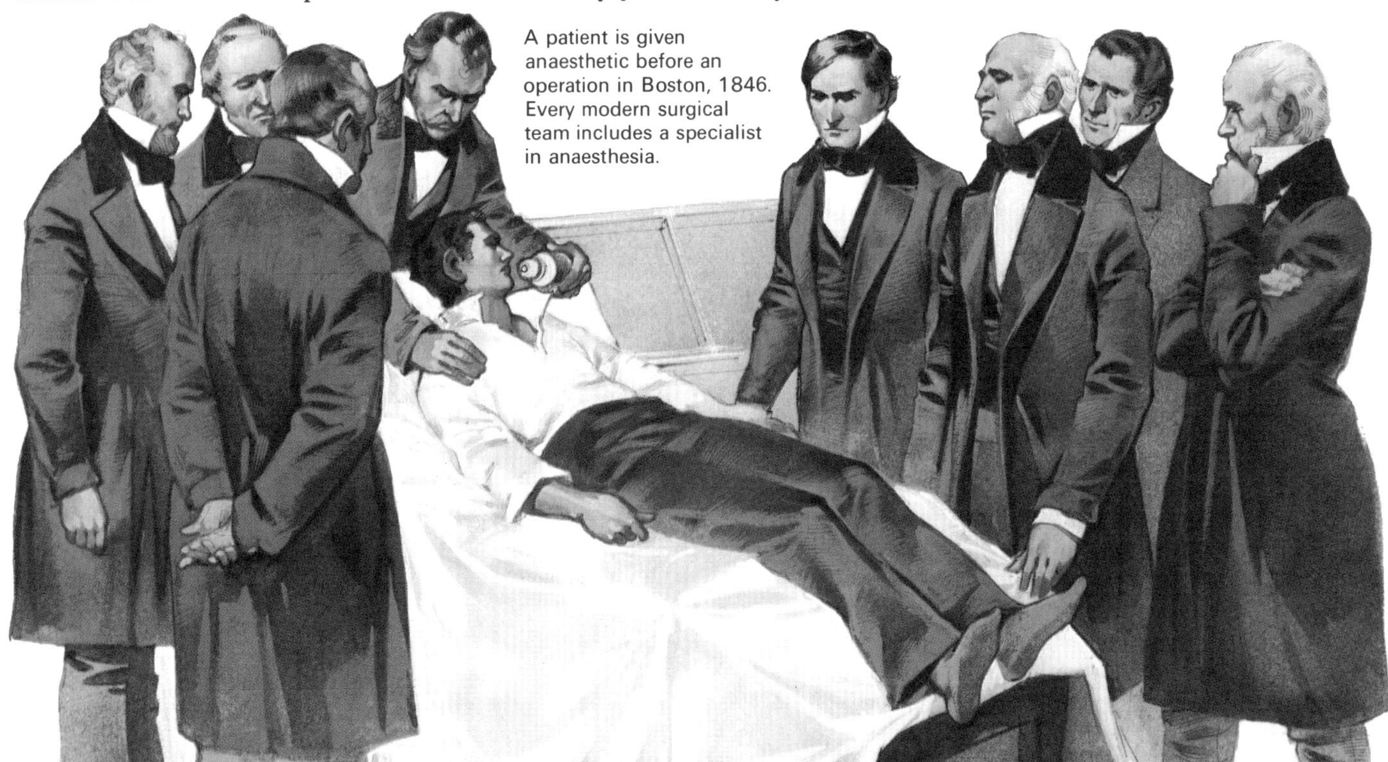

A patient is given anaesthetic before an operation in Boston, 1846. Every modern surgical team includes a specialist in anaesthesia.

Rubber

A material that was slow to be absorbed within the general progress of the Industrial Revolution was rubber. It had been known to Europeans since the discoverers of the New World had found natives cutting rubber tree bark and collecting the latex that oozed from the wound. The difficulty was doing anything with such an elastic material after it had coagulated and dried into a solid shape. Caoutchouc, as the substance was called, was brought back in the form of bottle-shapes or large balls, but could not easily be reformed into anything else. In 1770, Joseph Priestley found use for it in rubbing out pencil marks. In France, at the time of the revolution, it was softened with oil and wrapped round a bar to produce tubes useful to surgeons. In Britain, there was some experimentation in waterproof fabrics and air-beds. Rubberised fabric was used for a balloon in 1783.

J. B. Dunlop (1840–1921), who took out a patent for his pneumatic bicycle tyre in 1888. He made a fortune from the enormous popularity of cycling and, later, motoring.

Sheet Rubber

It was Thomas Hancock who first began to achieve some success with invention of his masticator in 1820. This consisted of a hollow cylinder with a solid roller inside which produced cylinders of rubber that could be pressed in iron moulds to any desired shape or size. Hancock began to make sheet rubber by shaving slices off a block. Slices could be joined by warming them and laying them edge to edge. Rubber thread was made by cutting rubber tubes spirally on a lathe. These could be used to make elastic webbing. Hancock also experimented with mixtures of rubber and tar which gave a cheaper product.

The Macintosh

Charles Macintosh, a Glasgow chemical manufacturer, first found a suitable solvent for rubber in coal-tar naphtha. Rubber dissolved in naphtha made a waterproof varnish that could be brushed on to cloth. By making a sandwich of two layers of cloth with the rubber coating between them, a tacky surface was avoided. Macintoshes were first produced in a Manchester factory opened in 1824. Hancock improved Macintosh's process by using masticated rubber. In partnership with Macintosh, he invented a machine for making rubberised fabrics.

Charles Goodyear, a Philadelphia hardware merchant, experimented with rubber and found that heating it with sulphur produced a substance no longer affected by heat or cold. The process was called vulcanisation. It allowed a lighter waterproof garment to be made. Vulcanised rubber was ideal for shoes, conveyor-belting and hoses. By the middle of the century, Hancock was manufacturing rubber tyres for road vehicles. These were solid and attached by metal hoops or stretched and held in position by a flange. A patent was taken out in the 1840s for pneumatic rubber tyres with an outer casing of leather. Known as aerial wheels, they were tested successfully in Hyde Park, London, and in New York. Yet the invention was completely forgotten until J. B. Dunlop's bicycle tyres of 1888. Michelin produced his first motor tyre in 1895 and Dunlop his in 1900. Fortunes were made in durable rubber compounds until synthetics replaced them.

Charles Macintosh (1766–1843), inventor of the rubberised waterproof cloth which still bears his name.

An 1895 Lutzmann with solid rubber tyres. The body is sprung independently of the chassis.

Coal-gas and Oil

Coal-gas, as fire-damp, had long been a hazard to miners. It was the year 1760 before an attempt was made to light a room with it in a house in Newcastle. The gas was produced in a kettle and passed along the stem of a clay tobacco pipe. It was ignited at holes made in the clay. A French engineer, Philippe Lebon, took out a patent in 1799 for lighting from the gas obtained by heating wood. James Watt's son, Gregory, went to Paris even though his country was at war with France, to investigate. Already in 1792 an engineer working for the firm Boulton and Watt, William Murdock, had used coal gas to light the rooms of a house in Redruth, Cornwall. Called back to the firm's Soho works in Birmingham, Murdock lit the main building there for several nights. By 1804, the firm was ready to look for customers for Murdock's process. In 1806–7, a large Salford cotton mill had 900 gas lights installed in the factory, along a stretch of private road and in a private house.

Large-scale Lighting

Having got into the business on the ground floor, so to speak, it is surprising that in 1814 Boulton and Watt decided to give up. From that year, Murdock is no longer associated with the story. Instead, it passes to Samuel Clegg who had been apprenticed to Boulton and Watt but had left the firm in 1805. It was Clegg who made the first important improvement by putting lime in the water through which the gas passed in the retort thus ridding it of its unpleasant smell. He was also installing gas lighting in factories. He fitted it in the premises of Rudolph Ackermann, the London art publisher, who had two cast-iron retorts with a capacity of a hundredweight of coal each, serving 80 burners for both lighting and heating.

A lecture on gas lighting in a London theatre, showing the retort used to provide gas for the burners. Although the first attempt to use gas for illumination was made in 1760, it was not until 1814 that the idea was pursued on a large scale.

In 1808 Pall Mall in London became the first street to be lit by gas.

The idea of a central generating station to distribute gas throughout a whole district was first devised in 1806 by a German immigrant to Britain, F. A. Winsor (formerly Winzer). In 1812 he was given a charter for his Gas Light and Coke Company and shortly afterwards secured the services of Samuel Clegg. On 1st April 1814, the parish of St Margaret's in Westminster was lit by gas. By the end of 1816, London had 42 kilometres (26 miles) of gas-mains. In the same year Baltimore began gas lighting in the streets and was followed by Boston and New York. Gas lighting began in Paris with the Palais Royal in 1819. A British company introduced it into Berlin in 1826, and by 1866 it had reached Moscow.

Heating and Cooking

As early as 1802, a Moravian, Z. A. Winzler, inspired by Lebon, was giving dinner parties with food cooked on a gas-stove in a dining room heated by gas. But gas cooking and the heating of water with geysers was a rarity until the 1870s. By then, the gas companies were approaching the time when there was serious competition from electricity. As an illuminant, coal-gas's smoky flame was saved from extinction by the incandescent gas-mantle invented in the 1880s by an Austrian, C. A. von Welsbach.

This was a gauze cap impregnated with thorium oxide and a little cerium oxide which gave a cleaner, brighter light. It carried gas lighting into the 20th century when the companies began to concentrate on selling their produce for heating and cooking, where it still functions efficiently.

Petroleum Products

Petroleum products from the earth's natural seepages have a very ancient history. Our concern here is with their application to the period of the Industrial Revolution. The demand was for improved lighting which had stimulated the gas industry. Oil lamps became more efficient after 1783 with the introduction of a flat-woven wick. Later there came the circular oil-burner with a cylindrical wick and glass chimney, named the Argand after its inventor. But the introduction of gas lighting served only to emphasise the poor quality of both the vegetable and animal oils available.

The first oil rig in Pennsylvania, 1859. Although previous rigs had frequently struck oil when drilling to find salt, it had never been extracted because at that time it had no commercial value.

Victorian improvements such as the cylindrical wick and the chimney greatly increased the efficiency of oil lamps.

In 1848, James Young began to develop a lubricant from a spring of crude oil that appeared for a short time in a Derbyshire coal mine. Later, he manufactured paraffin oil by dry distillation from a brown shale called torbanite, but again supplies of the raw material ran out. In the late 1850s, he was selling 'paraffin illuminating oil' made from coal tar naphtha, while American competitors were making so-called 'coal-oil' from an asphalt-like mineral found in New Brunswick, Canada.

Meanwhile, Abraham Gesner, a London doctor interested in geology, took out patents for a distillation of asphalt rock which produced a liquid that could be purified by treatment with sulphuric acid and lime and then redistilled. This new oil, called kerosene, sold well together with a new lamp with a flat wick and a chimney. Gesner hoped that it would completely replace whale-oil. The situation was entirely changed, however, in 1859 by the drilling of the first American oil well.

Oil Drilling

In the early part of the century, drilling had been undertaken in the search for salt or for water. In 1830, the introduction of the derrick made drilling easier and, by 1850, the steam engine was being used as a source of power. Between 1840 and 1860 in America, borings in search of salt had, on at least fifteen occasions, struck petroleum. The American industrialist, G. H. Bissell, began to consider the possibility of deliberately boring for oil. In 1854, he sent a sample of oil from a natural Pennsylvanian seepage to Benjamin Silliman Jr, professor of chemistry at Yale university. Silliman's report showed that by heating the crude oil in a still, several new products apart from illuminating gas, paraffin wax, lubricants and lamp-oil could be obtained. Bissell therefore ordered his contractor, Edwin L. Drake, to go ahead. After drilling through only 21 metres (69 feet) of bedrock, oil was struck on 27th August 1859 and the great Pennsylvania oil field had begun. Within fifteen years, annual output had reached ten million 163-kg (360-pound) barrels. In the years that followed, hollow drilling pipes could remove samples to reveal the structure of underground rock formations so that prospecting for oil became independent of chance oil seepages on the surface. Methods of refining to maintain the maximum yield of products from particular varieties of crude oil also advanced rapidly.

Steel

The discovery of another great raw material for industry was also made in America though its inventor gained nothing from it and is hardly remembered today. Iron had served its turn in the Industrial Revolution. The need now arose for a cheap steel of uniform quality for the new generation of precision machines and instruments. William Kelly was a manufacturer of sugar-kettles for farmers in Kentucky. His pig-iron was refined in a charcoal furnace, but the price of charcoal was rising even in timber-rich America. Kelly made the accidental discovery that a blast of air playing on molten pig-iron produced more heat when the iron was not covered with charcoal. The carbon in the pig-iron could therefore be blown out by air alone, the carbon already present acting as the fuel. By retaining more of the carbon than was needed for wrought iron, this air-boiling process could be used to make a steel.

The quantity of carbon retained in the iron is what gives steel its hardness. This had been realised by the Swedish metallurgist, T. O. Bergmann, as early as 1750. It is therefore surprising that Kelly's process had not been discovered before. But making steel from pig-iron without fuel seemed absurd to the ironmasters of the day. From 1851 onwards, Kelly built a series of converters and patented his invention in 1857. In the same year, he went bankrupt, and his patents fell into the hands of Henry Bessemer in Britain.

The Bessemer Process

Bessemer was a prolific inventor who had made a fortune from his patent of a process for making gold leaf cheaply. Another of his discoveries was a method of casting sheets of glass. The demand for new ways of casting cannon during the Crimean War (1854–6) had interested Bessemer in the subject of steel manufacture. Steel had been produced in small quantities for some time but the process made it very expensive.

Bessemer had been working on the same lines of 'boiling' the molten iron with a strong blast of air. In 1860, he invented his famous tilting converter. During the actual conversion of the molten iron into steel, the blast of air comes from the bottom and is forced right through the molten metal. When the metal is being run in or out of the converter, the 'wind box' is swung up to the top where it is out of action.

Open-hearth Furnaces

In 1861, Frederick Siemens invented a gas-producer which used low-grade coal to produce a gas that could be used as a fuel. His patent stated the possibility of using the invention to melt steel in an open-hearth furnace. It led to making steel from mixtures of cast iron and malleable iron called the Siemens-Martin process, and the decarburising of cast iron with iron ore to make steel which is called the Siemens process. These open-hearth systems had the advantage of attaining very high working temperatures. They were economic because scrap iron and cheap coal were used. They were comparatively slow processes so they were more easily and strictly controlled.

The majority of the iron in Britain is phosphoric, and non-phosphoric iron had to be imported from Scandinavia in order for the new process to work satisfactorily.

Both the Bessemer and the Siemens processes needed to use ores containing no phosphorous. Getting rid of phosphorous was a discovery made by S. G. Thomas and his cousin, Percy Gilchrist. They included limestone with the firebricks and this combined with the phosphorous to form a slag. The slag could be easily removed and, incidentally, could be pulverised to

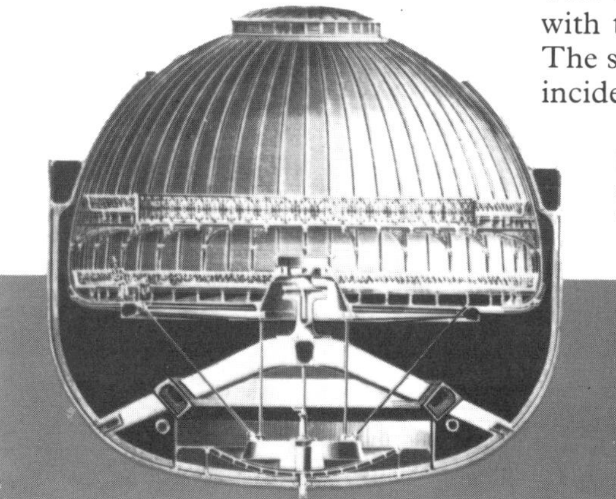

Bessemer's design for a hydraulically stabilised ship's saloon. The idea was never put to the test.

Henry Bessemer (1813–98), and a Bessemer converter in action.

The Bessemer conversion process. Molten pig iron is run into the converter, and air is blown through it. This oxidises the impurities in the iron, releasing heat which keeps the mass molten.

When conversion is complete, the converter is tilted and the molten steel pours out.

form the basis of a valuable agricultural fertiliser. The cousins' process virtually doubled the world's steel production.

Rolling Mills

With the increase in the supply of cheap steel, the development of rolling mills was not far behind. From these came the bars, sections and plates for the construction industry. The universal mill which began to appear from 1884 had enormous power. It could take an unhammered cast-steel ingot and convert it into a plate or a bar of any required width. Plates were produced for boilers and the new iron and steel ships, even heavy armour plate for the warship. By the turn of the century, the great Krupp's steelworks in Germany could take a thick steel ingot weighing more than 130 tonnes and roll it into a thinner plate measuring about three by thirteen metres (eleven by forty-three feet).

For a time, the South Wales and Monmouthshire steelworks had the virtual monopoly of the production of tinplate. For this, steel was rolled to a thickness of ·025 centimetres (one-hundredth of an inch). Hot rolled sheets were annealed, pickled and immersed in oil before dipping in the molten tin. They were then rolled again to regulate the thickness of the tin covering which even in best quality tinplate was less than ·0005 centimetres (one five-thousandth of an inch). As tinplate rusted quickly out of doors and was used mainly for food containers and the like, another sheet metal was developed. This was galvanised iron in which the sheet was dipped in molten zinc. Galvanised wire was used for fencing, often as barbed-wire.

Steel Alloys

Steels alloyed with other metals were at first produced accidentally by the smelting of mixed ores. Faraday made experimental samples of chromium and nickel steel as early as 1819. Tungsten steel was produced by the Austrian, F. Köller, in 1858. Ten years later R. F. Mushet, an ironmaster from the Forest of Dean, was manufacturing high-carbon tungsten-manganese steel which gave tools made from it five or six times the life of ordinary steel. Chromium steel for armour plate and shells was produced in France from 1877. Manganese steel, hardened from a temperature of 1000°C by quenching in water, was discovered by Robert Hadfield in Sheffield. Nickel steel was produced by the Le Creusot ironworks in France from 1888. F. W. Taylor of Philadelphia invented a high-speed steel that became harder the faster it cut.

Between 1870 and the end of the century, the world output of steel had grown from half a million to 28 million tons. Most of the growth was in America, where began the period producing a quarter of Britain's output and ended it producing double the British total. Together with the addition of electrical power to the earlier steam power, steel was the dynamic of the latter half of the Industrial Revolution, its various forms contained in all the busy tools and humming machines of the world's manufactories.

The Specialist Scientists

Dalton lecturing on his atomic theory.

The Structure of the Atom

While the engineers and inventors were busy advancing their various technologies, scientists were beginning to specialise in different aspects of the physical world. In the 16th century Vesalius had begun to list the elements of which all matter is composed. The next step was to discover the parts of an element and what made one element behave differently from another. The ancient Greeks had put forward the idea of atoms, tiny indestructible particles so small that in solids and liquids there seemed to be no space between them. Aristotle and Plato were against the idea. It fell into disrepute throughout the later years of antiquity and the Middle Ages. It was not revived again until the 17th century when men like Descartes and Newton began to explain phenomena in terms of the mutual interaction and movement of particles.

Dalton's Atomic Theory

The man who devised the primitive structure on which modern atomic theory rests was John Dalton (1766–1844). He was the largely self-educated son of a Cumberland hand-weaver and became a teacher of mathematics in the New College of Manchester. He was a member of the Literary and Philosophical Society of Manchester and later became its secretary and president. It was his ideas rather than his personality that brought him fame. As a lecturer he was not good at devising the kind of experimental demonstration which impressed the audiences of so many contemporary scientists. When he did include a demonstration, his experiments often went wrong.

In 1803, he began to apply his conception of atoms to chemical analysis. He decided that the difference between the atoms of different elements might be a difference of size and weight. He showed that eight parts by weight of oxygen combined with one part of hydrogen to form water. Assuming that a compound atom (now called a molecule) of water consisted of one atom of hydrogen and one of oxygen, it followed that the atomic weight of oxygen was eight times that of hydrogen. We now know that *two* atoms of hydrogen combine with one of oxygen to form water. Dalton's estimate of the atomic weight of oxygen was thus half the true value. Yet his theory led him to draw up the first table of atomic weights. He was correct in thinking that all atoms of the same element have the same weight, and that the compound atoms of any particular substance always contain the same number and kinds of atoms.

Chemical Symbols

Dalton's work inspired the great Swedish chemist Johan Berzelius who

Hydrogen	Strontium
Azote	Barytes
Carbon	Iron
Oxygen	Zinc
Phosphorus	Copper
Sulphur	Lead
Magnesia	Silver
Lime	Gold
Soda	Platina
Potash	Mercury

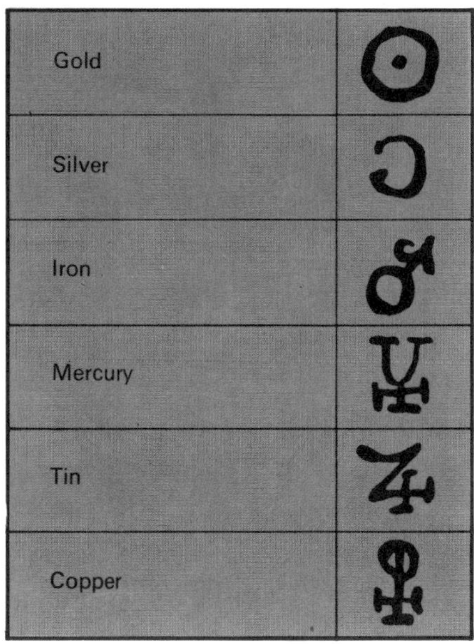

H	Hydrogen	Fe	Iron
C	Carbon	Zn	Zinc
O	Oxygen	Cu	Copper
P	Phosphorus	Pb	Lead
S	Sulphur	Ag	Silver
Mg	Magnesium	Au	Gold
Sr	Strontium	Hg	Mercury

Symbols for the elements used by (left) John Dalton, (centre) the early alchemists, and (right) Johan Berzelius. Modern scientists use Berzelius's system, which was adapted to show the exact composition of chemical compounds by the addition of numbers.

put the whole theory on a firm experimental basis. Between 1810 and 1820, he analysed over 2,000 inorganic compounds. He also gave us our modern chemical symbols, using the initial letter (or two letters where necessary) of each element's Latin name. In a compound, each symbol represented one atom and, where there was more than one, a figure was added. Thus H_2SO_4 tells us that sulphuric acid consists of two atoms of hydrogen, one of sulphur and four of oxygen. But Dalton's atomic theory gave no way of knowing how many atoms of each element occurred in the molecule of a compound. He himself gave the formula for water as HO instead of H_2O, and for ammonia as NH instead of NH_3. There was much confusion among chemists on this score for another 50 years.

Dalton was obsessed with the idea of the combination of different elements by *weight*. In 1808, the French chemist Joseph Gay-Lussac published the discovery that gases combine in simple proportions by *volume*. For example, two volumes of hydrogen and one volume of oxygen provide two volumes of steam. Three years later, the Italian Amedeo Avogadro adapted this law to the atomic theory by putting forward the hypothesis that equal volumes of all gases, at the same temperature and pressure, contain equal numbers of molecules. The word molecule is important here because his hypothesis distinguished between an atom and a molecule just as we do today. He suggested that oxygen and hydrogen, for instance, each consist of two atoms bound together, giving the molecules H_2 and O_2. Thus in the example of Gay-Lussac's law given above, $2H_2$ (2 volumes of hydrogen) $+0_2$ (1 volume of oxygen) $= 2H_2O$ (2 volumes of steam).

Avogadro's Law

It was not until 1860 that another Italian chemist, Sanislao Cannizzaro, published a pamphlet showing how Avogadro's hypothesis could be used to resolve the confusion about atomic weights and chemical formulae. All that was needed was to weigh all the compounds of an element that were gaseous and compare them with an equal volume of hydrogen. For instance, of three gaseous compounds of nitrogen, nitrous oxide is 44 times the weight of hydrogen, nitric oxide is 30 times, and ammonia seventeen times. By experimental analysis, the proportion by weight of nitrogen in each compound can be found. Nitrous oxide will be found to contain $\frac{28}{44}$ of nitrogen, nitric oxide $\frac{14}{30}$, and ammonia $\frac{14}{17}$. It can thus be assumed that the atomic weight of nitrogen is fourteen as compared with the unit weight of hydrogen and that nitrous oxide contains two atoms of nitrogen, giving the formula N_2O. Avogadro had died a year or two before his hypothesis was thus promoted into the important law that bears his name.

From the tabulation of the atoms of different elements in terms of their atomic weight and the analysis of compounds into their atomic formulae, the next step was the investigation of the atom itself. As early as the 1830s, the English chemist Michael Faraday had shown that compounds could be split by an electric current in the process known as electrolysis. Like a number of his contemporaries, he thought that electricity provided the force which combined elements into molecules. The discovery of the electrical forces within an atom was made through experiments in the conduction of electricity by low-pressure gases. In gases at ordinary atmospheric pressure, electricity can be conducted only in the form of a short spark. Conductivity over a distance, as in forked lightning, requires enormous voltages. If the pressure of the gas is reduced, say to a hundredth of atmospheric pressure, an electric current passing through gives off a luminous glow as in the discharge tubes used for modern lighting.

If the pressure is reduced to one hundred-thousandth of an atmosphere, the gas itself becomes dark and the glass of the tube gives off a faint green light. Anything placed in the tube will cast a shadow on the end farthest from the cathode, which is the metal electrode connected to the negative pole of the electrical supply. Invisible rays must be coming from the cathode. In 1876, the German physicist, Eugen Goldstein, gave them the name cathode rays.

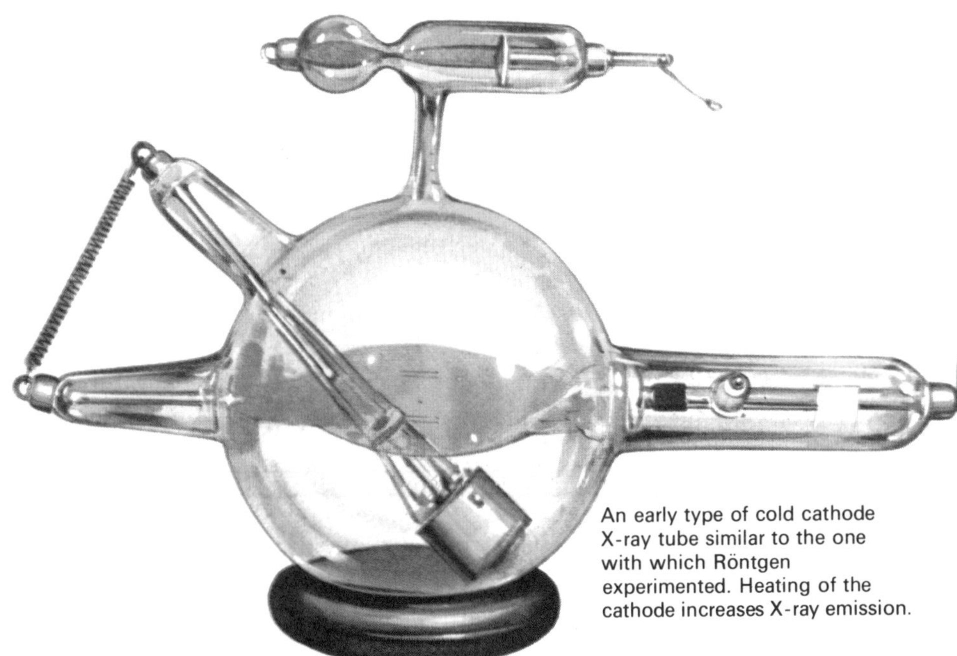

An early type of cold cathode X-ray tube similar to the one with which Röntgen experimented. Heating of the cathode increases X-ray emission.

X-Rays

In 1895, Wilhelm Konrad von Röntgen, professor of physics at Wurzburg in Germany, was experimenting with electrical discharges

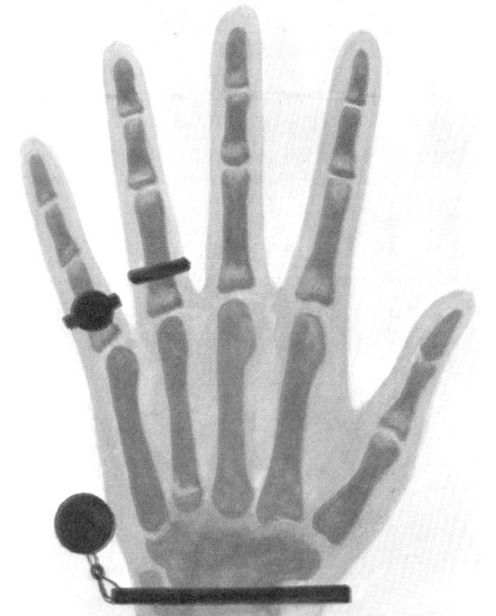

Röntgen (1843–1923), and an X-ray photograph of a hand showing rings and an identity disc.

Ernest Rutherford at work in the Cavendish laboratory, Cambridge, and a portrait of J. J. Thomson, who discovered the electron.

Apparatus used to break up nitrogen nuclei.

through low-pressure gases when he noticed a number of dramatic phenomena. A screen of barium platinocyanide fluoresced brightly when placed near the discharge tube. When he put his hand between the tube and the screen, a shadow of the bones of his hand appeared. Though wrapped in brown paper, photographic plates were fogged by the discharge. A key resting on a box of plates was reproduced when the plates were developed. Within a few weeks of the discovery, X-rays were being used in hospitals to examine broken bones and to trace objects swallowed by patients.

The nature of cathode rays and their importance in the discovery of atomic structure was explained mainly by the work of Joseph John Thomson (1856–1940) and his research team at the Cavendish laboratory in Cambridge. He discovered that X-rays caused a gas at ordinary atmospheric pressure to become a conductor of electricity. It was already known that positively and negatively charged particles, flowing in opposite directions, carry an electric current through a liquid. Such charged particles are called ions. It seemed that X-rays ionised the gas in a discharge tube. Thomson became convinced that cathode rays were streams of negatively-charged gaseous ions. When he measured their deflection in a magnetic field and saw the sharp outlines of the beam, he began to think that the particles were much lighter than atoms. Thomson performed a number of experiments to prove that the electrical charge on the individual particles of a cathode ray was equivalent to that of an ion in a liquid, but that the mass of the particle was very much less than that of a hydrogen atom.

A Model of the Atom

He had proved the existence of the electron. He showed that they could be produced not only in discharge tubes and by irradiating a gas with X-rays, but that they could be struck off a metal plate by ultra-violet radiation and were given off by incandescent metal filaments. They seemed to be part of all matter. Thomson put forward his model of the atom as a central positively-charged nucleus surrounded by rings or shells of electrons. He suggested that it was the outermost shell that gave an element its particular properties, irrespective of the total number of electrons it contained. Thus, elements with a complete outer shell were all chemically inert, those with one electron missing from the outer shell had similar chemical properties, as did those with two missing and so on.

Radium

In 1896, the French physicist Henry Bequerel decided to investigate whether all phosphorescent substances emit rays similar to X-rays. He discovered that salts of uranium affect a photographic plate. He put some uranium salt on an aluminium medallion on top of a photographic plate covered by an envelope and left them in a dark drawer for a number of days. When the plate was developed, there was an image of the medallion. The uranium obviously emitted a penetrating radiation. The phenomenon was to be named radioactivity by Marie Curie (1867–1934).

She was born in Warsaw and went to Paris to study science at the

Sorbonne. She met and married Pierre Curie, a teacher at the Paris school of Physics and Chemistry. She chose radioactivity as the subject for her doctoral thesis and went on to devote her life to it. She discovered that the ore of uranium, called pitchblende, is four times as radioactive as pure uranium. The ore must therefore contain some other unknown radioactive element. The Curies eventually analysed six tons of pitchblende from which they extracted only 0·1 of a gram of the new element which they called radium. They had provided the world with a treatment for cancer and, in 1902, were awarded the Nobel prize jointly with Becquerel.

Pierre and Marie Curie devoted their lives to the study of radioactivity.

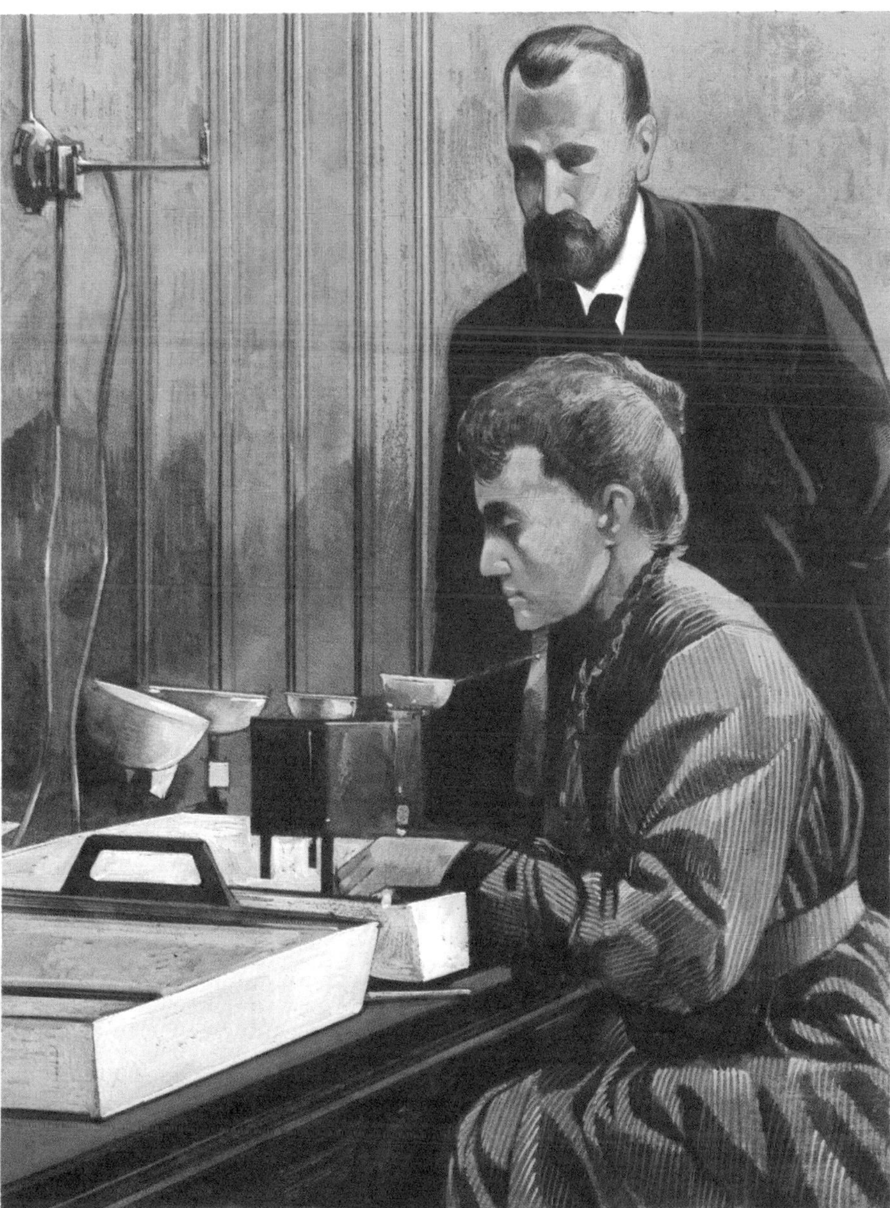

Radioactivity

In 1897, a young New Zealander, Ernest (later Lord) Rutherford (1871–1937) began work on radioactivity at the Cavendish laboratory. He discovered three different types of radiation from uranium salt. The least penetrating one he called alpha-radiation, a more penetrating one which consisted of electrons he called beta-radiation, and the third, similar to X-rays and emitted during certain radioactive changes, gamma-radiation. Rutherford discovered that when radioactive atoms emit alpha-particles, which are charged helium atoms, their atomic weight is reduced and they change into a new family of lighter elements with different chemical properties. His assistants, Geiger and Marsden, bombarded a sheet of gold foil with alpha-particles and discovered that about one in ten thousand actually bounced back. From this, Rutherford developed his picture of the atom as a miniature solar system with orbiting electrons and a positively-charged nucleus which repulsed those alpha-particles that penetrated close to it. The work of another of Rutherford's assistants at Manchester University, H. G. Moseley, showed that each element in an ascending scale has an extra positive charge in the nucleus of its atom balancing its extra orbiting electron. Thus the lightest atom, hydrogen, has a nuclear charge of +1 and one orbiting electron, helium has a nuclear charge of +2 and two orbiting electrons, and so on to uranium with +92. The number of the positive charge is now called the element's atomic number. Gaps in the table discovered by Moseley were later filled by the discovery of the new elements hafnium (atomic number 72) and rhenium (atomic number 75). The particles representing individual positive charges within the nucleus were called protons.

The English nuclear physicist Sir John Cockroft working in the Cavendish in 1932.

Now the discovery had been made that the nucleus of an atom was itself made up of particles, Rutherford began experiments to see if protons could be knocked out of the nucleus of one element to transform it into another. He bombarded nitrogen with alpha-particles and noticed particles leaving the nitrogen with a longer range than the original alpha-particles. Nitrogen atoms had been disintegrated and converted into oxygen.

The Rutherford model of an atom has been superseded by the more elaborate models of today's scientists. However inadequate his description of atoms may seem today, in its time it gave rise to the nuclear reactor and the atomic bomb.

Theories of Light

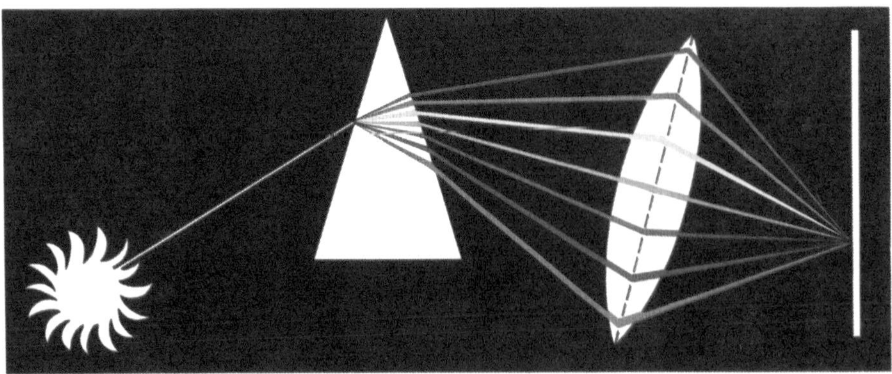

The composition of white light. The prism refracts the ray into a spectrum of different wavelengths, and the lens focuses them.

The problems of the transmission of light exercised some of the keenest analytical minds of the 18th and 19th centuries. The wave theory was perhaps founded by the Dutchman Christiaan Huygens (1629–95) who spent much of his life in Paris and had great success with his efforts to improve the telescope. He thought of light waves as the vibrations of the tiny spheres of matter comprising the 'aether', each vibrating sphere passing on the movement to its neighbour. He thought of such waves radiating from every point of a candle flame and crossing each other without interference. If light consisted of particles, he argued, they would be continually colliding with each other. Light to him was like sound waves. Sound cannot pass through a vacuum whereas light can.

Newton's Rings

In 1704, Isaac Newton published his *Opticks* which explained light as the movement of particles in straight lines. Reflection consisted of the bouncing of these particles from a surface. Refraction, or the bending of light, was due to their attraction towards the surface of a medium such as glass or water. If a lens is placed on a flat piece of glass, rainbow-coloured rings are seen round the point where lens and plate are in contact. Newton observed that rings of alternate blue and black were formed by blue light, alternate red and black by red light. The blue rings were about half the radii of the corresponding red rings. Newton supposed that the rings were due to the air between the two surfaces of glass being in some places prone to transmit light and other places to reflect it, and that this was caused by tremors or waves in the aether set up by the light particles striking it. In this case, Newton was suggesting a combination of particles and waves.

Thomas Young (1773–1829) examined Newton's idea that, if light consisted of waves, it would not travel in straight lines and sharp-edged shadows would be impossible. Young maintained that light wavelengths could be very short, that the spreading of light round corners would be very slight and therefore shadows would be sharp. He also introduced the theory of light interference which is the basis of modern wave theory. If two light waves are out of phase, that is if the crests of one wave-form coincide with the troughs of another, then they cancel each other out. This would account for the dark areas in Newton's rings.

Augustin Fresnel (1788–1827) in France showed that Newton's rings could be accounted for by the principle of interference. He further explained polarisation, which is the passing of a light through crystals in line with each other and the blocking of light when one crystal is opposed at right angles to the other. Fresnel suggested that light waves, rather than being to and fro pulsations in line with the direction of travel, were actually up and down vibrations at right angles to the direction of travel, like the waves in a length of rope that has one end moved steadily up and down. Such waves, operating in all directions, would be polarised into one direction as they passed through a crystal. Thus they would not pass through a second crystal set in opposition to that direction.

Huygens believed that light was a wave form emanating from every particle of matter. The theories of Planck and Broglie show that neither he nor Newton was completely right.

Modern light theory postulates waves similar to those of electromagnetic radiations and confined within the visible spectrum. But quantum theory also admits the possibility of particles found in the path of such a wave. The exact relationship between waves and particles is yet unknown.

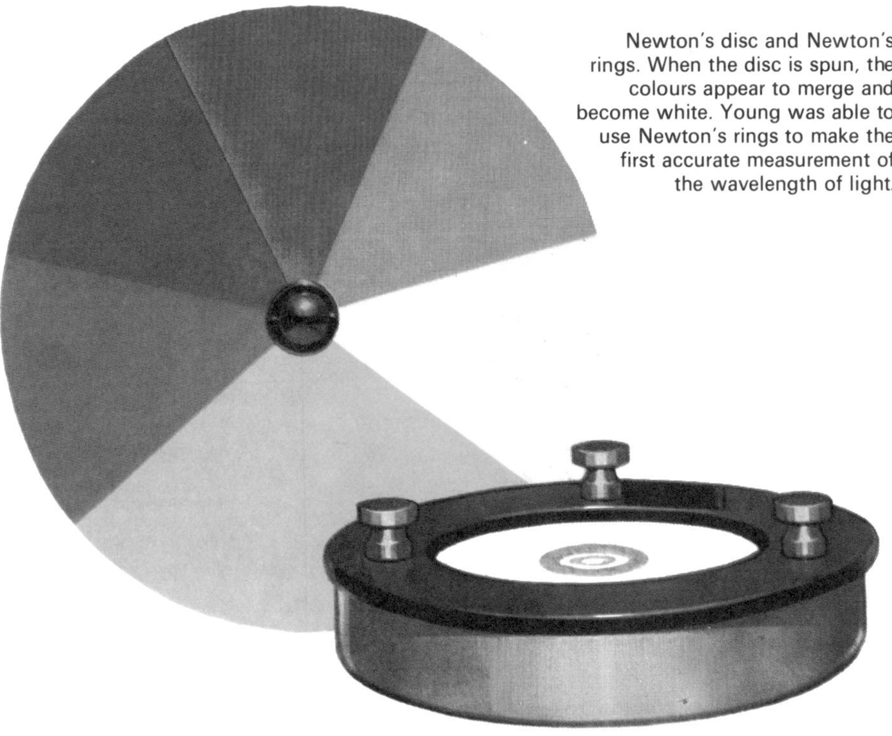

Newton's disc and Newton's rings. When the disc is spun, the colours appear to merge and become white. Young was able to use Newton's rings to make the first accurate measurement of the wavelength of light.

Energy

The two concepts of the conservation and dissipation of energy apply to all its forms, but they were perceived and formulated largely through a study of heat. In the 17th century, heat was correctly thought to be the energy of movement of the particles of which a substance is formed. In the following century, this theory fell out of favour. The great French scientist, Lavoisier, thought of heat as a virtually weightless and indestructible fluid that could flow from one substance to another. He called this fluid caloric. After his death, his widow married the man who was to show that caloric could not exist. His name was Benjamin Thompson, Count Rumford (1753–1814). In a colourful career, Rumford fought for the Americans in the War of Independence, founded the Royal Institution in London, became minister of war to the Elector of Bavaria and a count of the Holy Roman Empire.

Noting how much heat was produced by the boring of cannon at the Munich military arsenal, in 1798 he set up an experiment in which a blunt steel bit was used to bore a brass cannon in a bath of water. After two and a half hours, the water boiled. The supply of heat from the experiment seemed inexhaustible. Rumford wrote that if heat could be produced in this manner and without limitation, then it could not be a material substance. He believed that only motion could have created the heat, which had not previously been present in either the cannon or the water.

Top: Rumford proved that heat could not be a material substance; centre: Joule proved that energy is always conserved; bottom: Clausius formulated the first two thermodynamic laws.

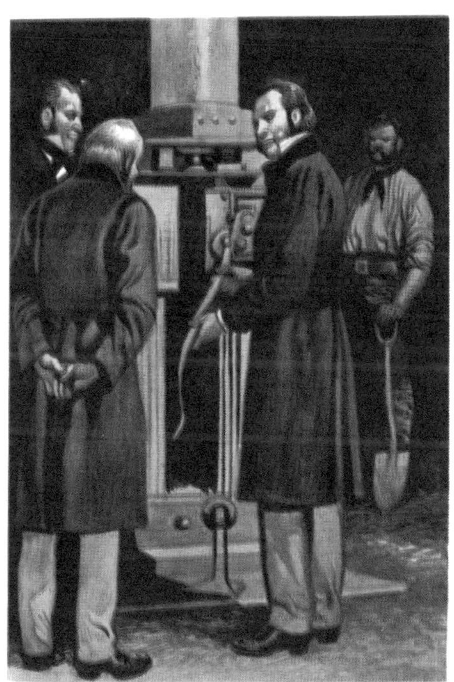

Lord Kelvin, as well as developing the science of thermodynamics, was a prolific inventor.

At the time, Rumford's findings made little impression on other scientists. About twenty years later, Nicolas Carnot (1796–1832), a French military engineer, began to study the steam engine with a view to improving its efficiency. He imagined an ideal engine working without friction and showed mathematically that the highest efficiency was obtained by the greatest drop of temperature between the hot, expanded gas and the cooled, condensed gas. He compared the fall from a high to a low temperature with the fall of water on a water-wheel from a high to a lower level.

Transformation of Energy

In England about 1837, James Prescott Joule (1818–89) began research to improve the recently invented electric motor. He realised that the source of electricity had to be cheap in relation to work done by the motor if it was to replace the steam engine. His experiments taught him that the loss of chemical energy from his batteries was equivalent to the heat generated in a circuit. He also noticed that when an electric motor was running it created a greater resistance to the flow of current than when it was at rest. The chemical energy from the battery required to overcome this increased resistance was equivalent to the mechanical work done by the motor. He was beginning to show the relationship between chemical energy, heat and mechanical energy. This led him to measure, with remarkable accuracy, the heat generated by mechanical work in such forms as the movement of pistons, the compression of air in a pump and the disturbance of water by paddle-wheels.

However, it was not Joule who first put forward the idea of the conservation of energy. This honour must be given to the German physicist Julius Robert Mayer (1814–78). On a journey to Java as ship's doctor between 1840 and 1841, he made the first draft of his paper on the subject. He received little attention, and others began to express similar ideas. For Mayer, proving that the original idea had been conceived by him became an obsession. He was confined to an asylum and put in a straitjacket.

In 1847, Joule gave a lecture at Manchester which was a landmark in scientific history. He expressed his ideas on the conservation of energy—that energy cannot be either created or destroyed. He showed how energy can be transformed from one kind into another, that mechanical energy, heat, electrical energy and chemical energy are all equivalent to each other. He established Mayer's idea by the careful experiment which Mayer's studies had lacked. Joule's work aroused the interest of William Thomson, later Lord Kelvin (1824–1907), who had worked in Paris and was familiar with Carnot's theories. Thomson was attempting to reconcile Carnot's work with Joule's when Rudolf Clausius (1822–88) announced to the Berlin Academy of Sciences his two laws of thermodynamics. Thomson went on to develop the new science of thermodynamics, which is the study of heat in relation to other forms of energy, and to state Clausius's laws in clearer terms.

Albert Einstein (1879–1955) was exiled in 1933 by the Nazis. The remarkable tower shown here was built for him by the pre-Nazi government.

Thermodynamics

The first law of thermodynamics is that energy cannot be either created or destroyed and is the principle of the conservation of energy. The second law of thermodynamics is that heat, of itself, cannot pass from a colder to a warmer body. This second law cannot be proved and is what is known as a statistical law. The temperature of a body is made up of the *average* velocity of the molecules contained in it. Some molecules will be travelling faster than this average speed and some more slowly. When a cold gas or liquid is brought into contact with a warmer one, *some* of the molecules in the cold substance will be moving fast enough to pass into the warmer substance, but the *average* speed will favour movement from warm to cold so that the temperatures are eventually equalised. In other words, it is the very large numbers of moving molecules which make the second law of thermodynamics true in practice. Thomson went on to show that only part of the heat of an engine is converted into useful work, and that the remainder is dissipated into the air. Though the lost heat has not been annihilated, it cannot be recovered. Since all heat tends to pass from a higher level to a lower one, all the world's energy is tending to fall towards a uniform level. When that happens and no more energy is available for work, the earth will have become uninhabitable. Thus, the second law of thermodynamics embodies the principle of the dissipation of energy.

$E = mc^2$

Scientists in the 19th century had, of course, no idea of the vast amounts of energy locked up in the smallest quantities of matter. It was Albert Einstein, in the early years of our own century, who expressed this by linking the principle of the conservation of energy with that of the conservation of mass. He did this in his famous formula: $E=mc^2$. This means that the energy in ergs (E) is equal to the product of the mass in grams (m) and the square of the speed of light in centimetres per second (c). For example, a gram of any substance, if entirely converted into energy, would yield about 25 million kilowatt-hours.

Today, we believe that the sun's energy comes from annihilation of mass and that it loses about four million tons every second. This loss occurs during the transmutation of hydrogen into other elements. It can be calculated that a transmutation of a tenth of the sun's mass will take another 10,000 million years.

James Dewar demonstrates the liquefaction of hydrogen. In the course of his work he invented the Thermos flask.

Magnetism and Electricity

The phenomenon of magnetism was almost certainly known to man in the early Iron Age. Lodestone, the ore of iron known as magnetite, was used by the ancients as a direction finder. The ancient Greeks knew something of static electricity, as for instance, when amber is rubbed vigorously, it attracts particles of dust. Our modern word electricity is derived from *elektron*, the Greek word for amber. Benjamin Franklin, the American statesman, knew that like charges of electricity repelled each other and unlike charges attracted. He gave the two kinds of static electricity the names positive and negative to distinguish them. In 1752, he proved that a stormcloud was charged with static electricity when a kite flown into it drew a spark from a key tied to the lower end of the string. With this experiment, he invented the lightning conductor and proved himself one of the most foolhardy experimenters who ever lived.

Above: Luigi Galvani, the anatomist who first showed the connection between electricity and muscle movement. Right: Benjamin Franklin flies a kite to prove that thunderclouds are electrically charged.

Galvani and Volta

Luigi Galvani (1737–98), anatomy professor at Bologna University in Italy, first recorded the effects of electrostatic induction in 1780. He was dissecting a frog with a steel scalpel when an assistant produced a spark with a static-electricity machine. A momentarily induced current flowed through the scalpel, making the frog's legs twitch. Galvani tied the legs of a frog to a brass hook and hung it on an iron fence during a thunderstorm. He intended to prove that lightning would make the frog's legs twitch but found they did so whenever they touched the iron fence, whether there was any lightning or not. Galvani thought that the frog's legs contained what he called animal electricity. It was Alessandro Volta (1745–1827), professor of physics at Pavia University, who showed in 1800 what had really happened.

The experiment which led Galvani to propose his theory of 'animal electricity'.

He demonstrated that the chemical action of moisture (contained in the frog's legs) and two dissimilar metals (like brass and iron) will generate an electric current. He went on to construct a pile of alternate silver and zinc discs separated by material soaked in salt solution, thus not only inventing the electric battery, but also producing the first man-made supply of electric current.

Still no connection had been made between magnetism and electricity. That was to be the great achievement of the 19th century, together with the means of transforming mechanical energy into electrical energy and vice versa. In 1807, the Danish scientist, Hans Christian Oersted (1777–1851), attempted to connect magnetism with electricity. He reasoned that the flow of an electric current through a wire should have a magnetic effect. To detect this, he placed a wire across and at right-angles to a compass needle, and then caused a current of electricity to flow through the wire. He expected the compass needle to line up with the wire, just as two bar magnets would tend to line up with opposite poles facing each other. Nothing happened. The compass needle did not move. It was not for another thirteen years that Oersted accidentally discovered that

Alessandro Volta demonstrates his 'voltaic pile' before Napoleon.

the compass needle had to be placed *in line* with the wire conductor to make it turn at *right angles* to it when a current flowed. At last, he had proved that an electric current did indeed set up a magnetic field, though not in the direction he had first supposed.

Magnetic Fields

A year later, the French physicist, André Marie Ampère (1755–1836), discovered that one electrical wire produced a magnetic effect in another electrical wire lying parallel to it. Two wires with currents flowing in the same direction attracted each other, while two wires with currents flowing in opposite directions repelled each other. Ampère had confirmed Oersted's finding that an electric current creates a magnetic field around itself. Could a magnetic field therefore create a flow of electricity? The discovery that it could was made in 1830 by Joseph Henry (1797–1878) in America, but at the time he did not publish it. The following year, the discovery was made again by somewhat different means and quite independently in London. The British scientist who did it and to whom can be credited the invention of the electric generator was Michael Faraday (1791–1867).

Faraday was the third child of a London blacksmith and received only the most basic education. He went to work as errand boy to a bookseller who later made him an apprentice bookbinder. He began to educate himself through his employer's wares. A customer at the shop took him to a lecture given by Sir Humphry Davy at the Royal Institution. Faraday wrote to Davy asking to join him in his research. It happened that a few days later Davy dismissed his laboratory assistant for misconduct. The job was offered to Faraday, who jumped at it. Within seven months, he was embarking on a journey through Western Europe as Davy's secretary and valet, during which he met most of the leading men of science. By 1821, Farday had made himself master of the study of electro-magnetism. In 1823, he was elected a Fellow of the Royal Society, and two years later replaced Davy as Director of the Royal Institution.

Michael Faraday at work in his laboratory. Faraday's discoveries explained the connection between magnetism and electricity and included the invention of the dynamo. They formed the basis for the modern electrical industry. He also formulated laws of electrolysis. Below: Faraday was a brilliant lecturer, and inaugurated the Christmas lectures for young people at the Royal Institution, of which he became director.

The First Generator

Three significant experiments of the many Faraday performed concern us here. On the 29th August 1831, he wound two coils of wire round opposite sides of an iron ring. One coil was connected to a loop of wire passing alongside a compass needle. The other coil was connected to a battery and switch. When the current was switched on in the one coil, it induced a current in the other coil which flowed only momentarily as shown by the deflection of the compass needle. When the current was switched off, again this induced current flowed momentarily. Faraday had discovered that induced currents were set up only by the *changes* of magnetism in the iron ring. On 17th October, he produced a current in a coil of wire by moving a bar magnet in and out of the coil. On 28th October, he rotated a copper disc between the poles of a large horseshoe magnet. By means of sliding copper contacts, one at the rim of the disc, the other at the axle, he drew off the induced current to be measured by a galvanometer. The flow of current was continuous. He had created the first generator of electrical energy from mechanical energy.

All his working life, Faraday believed in the physical existence of lines of force of magnetism and electricity operating within the aether. James Clerk Maxwell (1831–79), who converted Faraday's experiments into the precise mathematical formulae they had lacked, believed in a similar theory. It was left to Heinrich Hertz (1857–94), professor of physics at Karlsruhe Polytechnic in Germany, to show that electro-magnetic waves are the same as light waves. In 1880, he produced electro-magnetic radiation, opening the way to radio broadcasting.

Organic Chemistry

By the end of the 18th century, mainly through the work of the Swedish chemist, Johan Jakob Berzelius (1779–1848), scientists were beginning to distinguish between inorganic and organic matter. The first was concerned with mineral or non-living materials such as water, gases, metals, salts, certain acids and oxides. These are composed of small molecules which can be broken up into their elements, joined in new compounds and returned to their original forms. Organic matter, products of the animal and vegetable world such as wood, sugars, fats and oils, remained a mystery. They burned or charred easily and could apparently never be returned to their original forms. Lavoisier attempted to analyse them by burning them in known quantities of oxygen and measuring the carbon dioxide (CO_2), hydrogen, nitrogen and water (H_2O) produced. From this it became known that organic matter was composed mainly of carbon, hydrogen, nitrogen and oxygen. At first it was thought that some living force gave combinations of these elements their peculiar properties. It was further discovered that two or more substances with entirely different chemical properties could have an identical composition of elements. Berzelius gave these different compounds of the same atoms the name isomers from the Greek for 'equal parts'.

Organic Compounds

In 1828, one of his former pupils, Friedrich Wöhler (1800–82), heated silver cyanate with ammonium chloride in solution to produce ammonium cyanate. When this was evaporated, he was left with clear crystals of urea, one of the constituents of human and animal urine. It was the first time that an organic compound had been created from chemicals that had not been derived from living matter. From that moment, the idea that a living force made some compounds different from others began to decline. The French chemist, Marcellin Berthelot (1827–1907), took the matter even further when he treated a number of alcohols in the glycerol family with acetic acid, producing entirely new fats unknown in nature.

Another French chemist, Jean-Baptiste Dumas (1800–84), made the discovery that the atoms of hydrogen

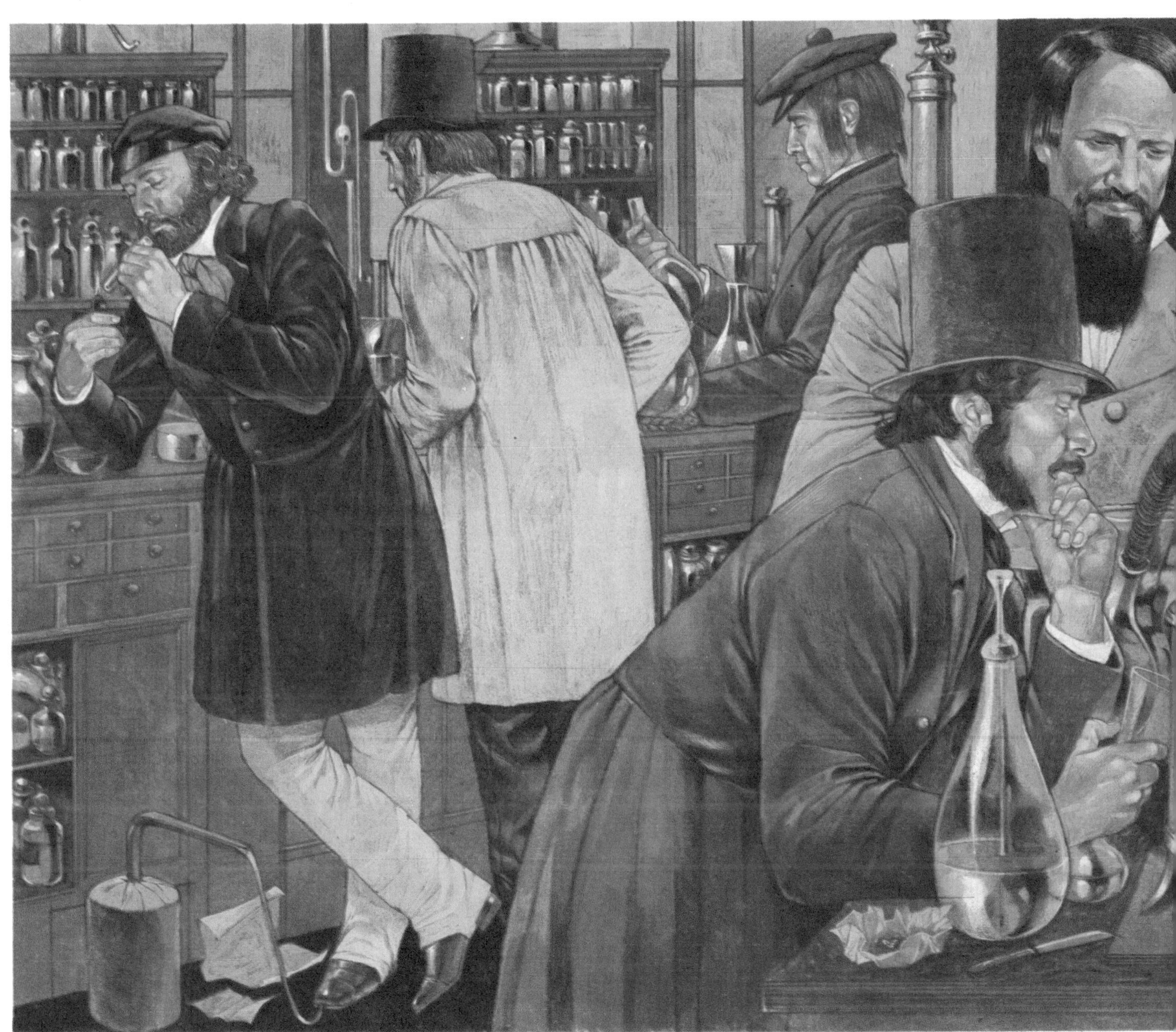

Liebig's laboratory at Giessen, where many of the groups of atoms known as 'radicals' in organic chemistry were first isolated.

in an organic compound could be replaced by chlorine, atom by atom, to produce a whole new series of compounds. For instance, the highly inflammable methane gas, CH_4, can have one atom of hydrogen replaced by chlorine to produce chloromethane, CH_3Cl, used as a refrigerant. The substitution of three chlorine atoms produces trichloromethane, $CHCl_3$, the anaesthetic chloroform; and the substitution of four chlorine atoms produces carbon tetrachloride, CCl_4, a chemical used in fire extinguishers. Dumas met so much hostility from his fellow scientists that he gave up chemistry in disgust and went into politics.

In Germany, Wöhler founded a school of chemistry at Göttingen University, while his lifelong friend, Justus von Liebig (1803–73), founded another at Giessen. They decided to conduct research together in an attempt to put some order into the vast number of organic compounds that existed in nature and could be created in the laboratory. Liebig had worked in the laboratory of Gay-Lussac in Paris. The latter had discovered that united carbon and nitrogen atoms could be transferred from compound to compound without themselves breaking apart. Liebig and Wöhler isolated many of the groups of atoms that behaved in this way, retaining their identity when combined with other atoms and acting like single atoms. These groups became known as radicals from the Latin for 'root', because from them more complicated molecules appeared to grow.

Combination of Atoms

An important step was taken in 1852 by one of Liebig's former pupils at Giessen, Edward Frankland (1825–99). He showed that atoms of certain

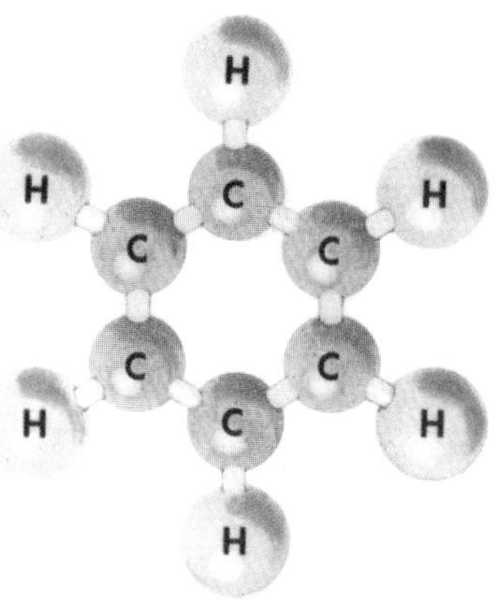

A benzene ring. Any or all of the hydrogens may be replaced by other radicals to form compounds including dyes and explosives.

An industrial chemical works in 1865. Less than a century later the chemical industry had become indispensable as a supplier of raw materials for countless essential commodities.

elements combine with a fixed number of atoms of other elements. The combining capacity of an element or radical is now called its valency. Atoms with a valency of one, such as hydrogen or chlorine, combine with one univalent atom as in hydrochloric acid, HC_1. An element with a valency of two, such as oxygen, combines with two univalent atoms as in water, H_2O. An element like phosphorous has two valencies, three and five, and can produce two different compounds.

The man who brought all this into the pattern of organic chemistry that we recognise today was August Kekulé (1829–96) who had also been one of Liebig's students. Kekulé recognised the importance of valency. He established that carbon has a valency of four and that carbon atoms can link with each other. This is why modern organic chemistry is concerned principally with the compounds of carbon, rather than merely with the molecules of living matter. In the 1850s, Kekulé was working as a laboratory assistant at St Bartholomew's Hospital in London. On the top of a bus between Islington and Clapham, he fell into a daydream in which atoms dancing before his eyes suddenly formed themselves into chains. He tested the idea and found it worked. It can be illustrated by the series of hydrocarbons that begins with methane, ethane and propane, in which each heavier molecule includes an addition to the chain.

The chain pattern worked for the aliphatic compounds, so-called from the Greek word for 'fat', but not for another group called, because of their characteristic odours, the aromatics. It was found that the simplest aromatic compound, benzene, had six carbon atoms. This did not suggest a chain structure. Again, Kekulé had a dream, this time sitting by his own fireside. Again, the atoms danced before his eyes, forming into chains and then serpents. Finally, one snake gripped its own tail to form a ring, and Kekulé knew he had the answer. Kekulé linked the atoms of benzene in a ring with alternate single and double bonds to account for the four bonds of each carbon atom.

Synthetic Materials

Modern chemists have modified Kekulé's chains and rings to take into account the three-dimensional reality of molecules which limits the number of possible isomers. Yet from his models all the new materials in common use today have been built up. Beginning in 1856 with the first synthetic dye, chemists have created synthetic drugs, fibres such as rayon and nylon, plastics like bakelite and perspex, synthetic rubber, insecticides and weed killers, detergents, explosives, lubricants and fuels. It would seem only a matter of time before the organic chemist synthesises the highly complex molecules of enzymes, hormones and genes to create in the laboratory even the living cell itself.

Germs and Disease

Left: Pasteur in his laboratory, where he exploded the myth of spontaneous generation of microbes. Right: Lister's carbolic acid spray.

Halfway through the 19th century, most of the medical profession thought that contagious diseases came from bad air, from a fatal miasma arising from decaying rubbish and the open sewers of cities. To combat epidemics of typhus, typhoid, dysentery and cholera, filth was cleared and laws passed to compel property-owners to provide proper drainage. To a certain extent it worked, since the places where microbes bred were cleaned up.

By the 1860s, it was becoming obvious that disease could be spread also by food and water, even from people's hands. A Hungarian doctor, Ignaz Semmelweis, had already reduced childbed fever in a Vienna maternity ward by insisting that attending physicians and midwives should wash their hands in chlorinated water. At the same time, the micro-organisms called bacteria were coming under the scrutiny of scientists such as Louis Pasteur (1822–95).

Louis Pasteur

A chemist with no medical training, Pasteur was asked to investigate the diseases that affect wines. His microscope showed him that, apart from the living yeasts that grow on the skins of grapes and cause healthy fermentation, there could be other micro-organisms. He became convinced that the latter were the reason for ill-flavoured wine. He tried antiseptics to destroy them, but found heat more effective, thus inventing the process later to be called pasteurisation. He also showed that micro-organisms were not spontaneously generated and indeed did not appear in truly sterile conditions. From this, he deduced that the diseases of both men and animals were spread by germs carried on dust particles in the air.

Vaccination against smallpox had been introduced into Europe by Edward Jenner (1749–1823). In 1796, he inoculated a small boy with matter from a cowpox sore on a milkmaid's hand. The boy contracted the relatively mild disease of cowpox. Inoculated with matter from a smallpox sufferer, he proved immune to the disease.

Pasteur tried the inoculation method as a preventive treatment against chicken cholera (no relation to human cholera). In broth, he made cultures of the microbes responsible and discovered that one such culture, several weeks old, gave chickens a mild form of the disease and thereafter immunity from fresh, more virulent cultures. Pasteur called his weakened culture a vaccine in honour of Jenner. In a similar treatment of anthrax, a deadly disease of sheep and cattle, he was forestalled by Robert Koch (1843–1910) who was to make Germany a world centre of medical science. It was Koch who, in 1882, isolated the tubercle bacillus, the first time a specific microbe was shown to produce a specific human disease.

Pasteur went on to cultivate the virus of rabies which he obtained in a weakened strain from the spinal cords of rabbits. He inoculated a nine-year-old boy, Joseph Meister, who had been bitten by a mad dog. Meister survived to become gatekeeper at the Pasteur Institute in Paris, founded to further the great man's work.

Antiseptics

Meanwhile in Britain, Joseph Lister (1827–1912) was applying Pasteur's principles to antiseptic surgery. By using a carbolic spray to kill germs in the air during an operation, Lister was able to use surgery in cases where the danger of blood poisoning, particularly hospital gangrene, had been previously too great. Nowadays, Lister's antiseptic methods of *destroying* germs have been replaced by aseptic surgery, the *exclusion* of germs from a sterilised operating theatre. Yet it was this great triumvirate of Pasteur, Koch and Lister who first put mankind on the winning side against disease by revealing the micro-organisms that are the true enemy.

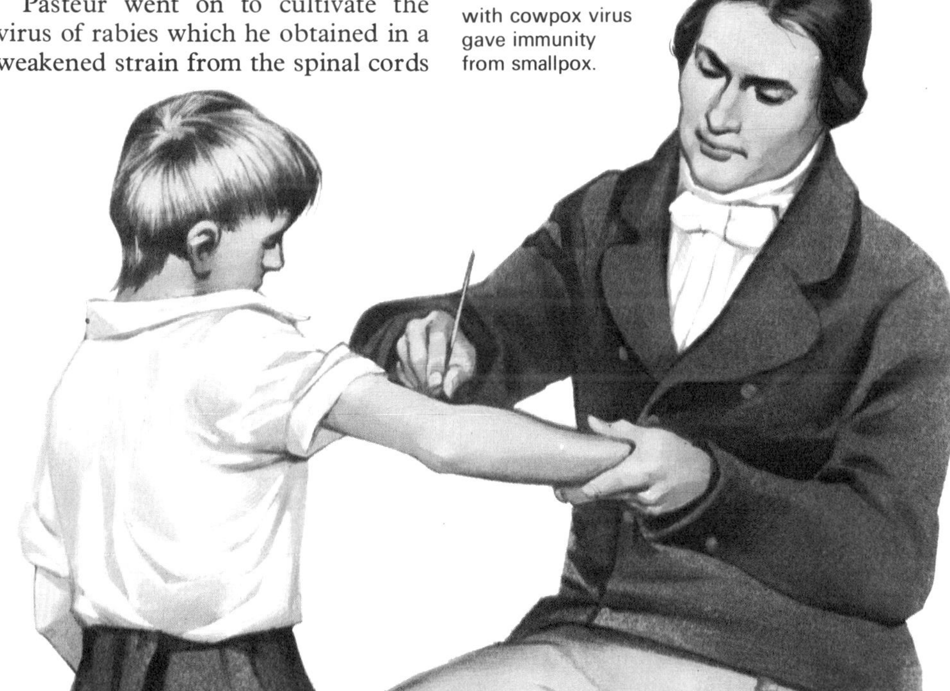

Jenner discovered that inoculation with cowpox virus gave immunity from smallpox.

The Great Exhibitions

As the Industrial Revolution progressed, nations began to display their new technologies in exhibitions designed partly in a spirit of self-congratulation and partly to attract export markets. The idea began in Paris where the first exhibition to claim any national importance was instigated by the Marquis d'Avèze in 1798. It presented the wares of all the art factories of France, particularly porcelain from Sèvres and the tapestries and carpets of the Gobelins. Exhibitions continued to be mounted in Paris at intervals throughout the following century.

The Great Exhibition of 1851, held in London, was a milestone of history for several reasons. It marked the peak of British technological achievement during the Industrial Revolution and the beginning of Britain's decline as the leading industrial nation. By then, thirteen European, thirteen American and seven other countries excluding British colonies were able to show their own innovations. Though the space allotted to the United States was not filled, the American system of interchangeable parts which heralded that country's future lead in mass-production and automated techniques was on show. So also were the American inventions of McCormick's labour-saving reaper, the sewing machine and the Colt revolver. Type for the catalogue was cast on the latest machinery from the United States. Hungary displayed the largest porcelain dish ever made. Krupp's of Germany showed a cast steel cannon and a 2,150-kilogram (4,740-pound) block of crucible cast steel, the biggest ever produced up to that time. Britain showed, among many other items, 23 of Whitworth's machine tools and the new amorphous phosphorus which was to become the material on the box for igniting safety matches.

The Crystal Palace

The main building, the Crystal Palace, was an entirely new construction of wrought-iron members prefabricated and erected at an unheard-of speed. It began a fashion for specially designed exhibition buildings that culminated in the Eiffel Tower in Paris built for the Universal Exhibition of 1889 and the Ceramic Palace in the same city in the following year where the interior was entirely constructed of Sèvres porcelain. The Crystal Palace itself was moved from the original site in Hyde Park to Sydenham in South London where it remained for many years as a somewhat melancholy reminder of a bygone pre-eminence.

An Otis elevator in the Eiffel Tower. Otis's invention of a safety brake made the building of skyscrapers feasible.

The Paris Exhibition of 1867 illustrated how far other countries had overtaken Britain in the industrial race. It was here that the great German electrical firm of Siemens showed their first large dynamo and Krupp's demonstrated their mastery of steel-casting with a 50-ton cannon. In Vienna in 1873, the first exhibition of the application of electricity to machine tools took place. In Berlin in 1879, the

When the Eiffel Tower was erected in 1889, it was condemned as ugly and unsafe. For 40 years it was the world's highest building.

Above: the Crystal Palace after its reconstruction at Sydenham in 1854. It was almost completely destroyed by fire in 1936. Centre: Prince Albert (left) whose initiative led to the 1851 Exhibition, and the Palace's designer, Sir Joseph Paxton. Bottom: erecting the great arch of the Crystal Palace at Hyde Park. The Palace was one of the first fully prefabricated buildings.

first example of electric traction was on display in Siemens's electric railway. In 1880, the first electric lift, another Siemens invention, was in use at the Mannheim industrial exhibition. At the Paris Electrical Exhibition of 1881, the same firm unveiled its electric tram, the first of its kind which ran commercially in Berlin in the same year. Thus had continental Europe ushered in the age of steel and electricity that was to replace iron and steam.

American Centennial Exhibition

Yet as late as 1876, at the American Centennial Exhibition held in Philadelphia, the American engineer Corliss was showing his steam-powered nine-metre (30-foot) flywheel, which drove machine tools. In 1878, there was yet another Paris exhibition where the new fuel, paraffin, was shown as a cooking agent in a modern stove that sold half a million in the following decade. America launched the first of a long series of world's fairs with the Chicago World Exhibition of 1893 which celebrated the 400th anniversary of the discovery of America. According to Thomas Edison, the most impressive exhibit on that occasion was a new machine for making seamless tubing from metal rods. The century was brought to a triumphant conclusion with the great Paris Exhibition of 1900. As well as the Ceramic Palace, there was a Palace of Electricity, and the exhibition attracted 39 million visitors.

With the growth of technology and the spread of world trade, the tradition of world's fairs has continued through the 20th century. The modern tendency, however, has been towards specialist exhibitions, often held annually and confined to particular aspects of the arts, sciences, industry and agriculture. In these, the new industrial giants, such as Japan and Russia, are beginning to take their place.

A New Age of Invention

From its pioneer days, the steam engine did not alter fundamentally, though it greatly improved in efficiency, particularly in the ratio of weight to power. From Britain, railways spread to all parts of the world, and the United States became a centre of locomotive manufacture. Some improvements came from continental Europe. For instance, Marc Seguin, the French pioneer railway engineer, invented the multitubular boiler in which steam was raised more quickly by passing water through a network of heated pipes. Another French engineer, Henri Giffard, designed the first injectors which provided a means of introducing water into the boilers and avoided much of the delay in getting up steam again after an engine had been stationary for some time.

Inventors turned their attention to steam-powered road vehicles. The first of their kind had been built in France by N. J. Cugnot in 1769. It moved at a mere walking pace. In 1800, Trevithick had run his first steam carriage, and three years later demonstrated one in the streets of London. But it was not until 1831 that Sir Goldsworthy Gurney perfected a steam carriage, providing a regular passenger service between Gloucester and Cheltenham. The 14·5-kilometre (nine-mile) journey was completed in 45 minutes. Within three years, the first London steam bus was covering a 12·8-kilometre (eight-mile) route in under an hour on one sack of coke. In 1858, Thomas Rickett invented his road steamer which seated three behind the tiller and had a stoker standing on a platform at the back.

Steam Carriages

In France, Léon Serpollet invented a steam-generator with water pumped through coils of nickel-steel tubing which were made red-hot. He adapted this to a four-cylinder engine for a steam carriage produced from 1894. It became a familiar sight in both France and Britain. Meanwhile, in America the Stanley brothers had designed a two-cylinder engine for a wooden two-seater vehicle. Stanley steamers became very popular until they were swept into obsolescence by the model T Ford. Serpollet had been

Three steam vehicles, top to bottom: Bordino's steam carriage, 1854; Stanley's Steam Car, 1899; Trevithick's carriage, 1802. Early steam carriages were slow to raise steam and were charged punitive rates on toll roads: but the steam engine may still eventually replace the petrol engine on the roads of the future.

a manufacturer of steam tricycles which also enjoyed some popularity in the last two decades of the century.

Powerful railway interests were anxious to keep mechanical transport off the roads. For instance, in Britain in 1865 and again in 1878, acts were passed limiting such road vehicles to a speed of 6·4 kph (four mph) and insisting on a crew of two with a third man walking ahead to warn of their approach. It was thus the steam-traction engine that achieved the longest life. It had begun with the steam plough, a stationary engine used to pull a plough on the end of a cable. It was soon realised that it was more convenient to use a locomotive. The power of heavy-duty traction engines was much greater than the early petrol lorries. As a means of driving fair-ground machinery and adapted as steam-rollers for road building and repair, they remained in use into our own times.

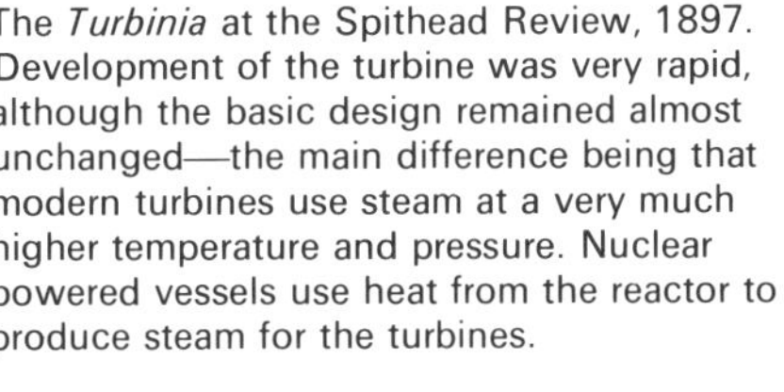

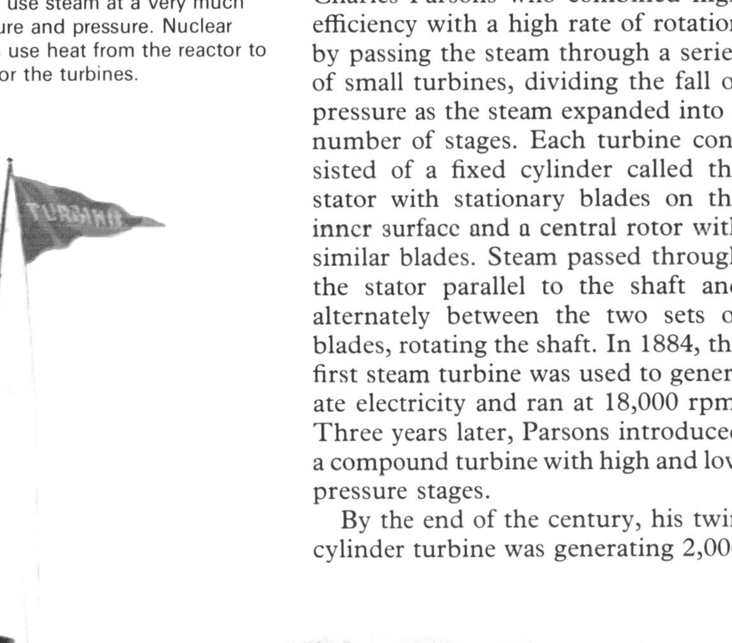

The *Turbinia* at the Spithead Review, 1897. Development of the turbine was very rapid, although the basic design remained almost unchanged—the main difference being that modern turbines use steam at a very much higher temperature and pressure. Nuclear powered vessels use heat from the reactor to produce steam for the turbines.

Steamships

A more steady and lasting progress was made in the development of steamships. At the beginning of the 19th century, iron was already replacing wood as the material for sailing ships. By the end of the century, the steel steamship was queen of the oceans. In 1858, the *Great Eastern*, designed by Isambard Kingdom Brunel and the largest ship of the century, was launched. It combined iron construction, steam power and both paddle and screw propulsion. It was not a success, requiring much higher coal consumption than had been anticipated. Among early steel ships were those built by the Confederates in the American Civil War as fast blockade-runners. The great Cunard liners of 1893, *Campania* and *Lucania* had steam engines developing 30,000 hp, four times that of the *Great Eastern*.

By then, an entirely new prime mover had appeared, the steam turbine. The idea of steam-jet propulsion had been suggested by the Greek mathematician Hero as long ago as the 1st century A.D. Trevithick had produced a 'whirling engine' in 1814 which consisted essentially of two hollow arms mounted on a shaft. Steam escaped at a tangent from small holes at the end of each arm, whirling them round. The maximum of 250 rpm, however, represented only about a fifth of the potential power of the steam used.

Steam Turbines

The modern steam turbine was developed by the British engineer Charles Parsons who combined high efficiency with a high rate of rotation by passing the steam through a series of small turbines, dividing the fall of pressure as the steam expanded into a number of stages. Each turbine consisted of a fixed cylinder called the stator with stationary blades on the inner surface and a central rotor with similar blades. Steam passed through the stator parallel to the shaft and alternately between the two sets of blades, rotating the shaft. In 1884, the first steam turbine was used to generate electricity and ran at 18,000 rpm. Three years later, Parsons introduced a compound turbine with high and low pressure stages.

By the end of the century, his twin cylinder turbine was generating 2,000 kw for the German town of Elberfeld.

Parson's first attempt in 1894 to develop a steam turbine marine engine failed because the high rate of rotation could not provide the screw propeller with the necessary thrust. In 1896, he tried a system with three shafts each carrying three screws driven by a connected series of turbines. There was also a separate turbine driving the central shaft for reversing. Altogether, the engines of his ship, the *Turbinia*, developed 2,000 hp, and when she first appeared at the Jubilee Navy Review in 1897, she reached the unheard-of speed of 34½ knots. Later systems included reduction gearing so that the engine could run at its most efficient and highest speed, while the screw propeller had reduced revolutions for maximum thrust.

Electricity

Early batteries suffered from a fall in voltage as the chemical products accumulated and the expensive copper plates were eroded. The first major improvement was the Leclanché cell of 1866, in which the electrodes were rods of carbon and zinc in a solution of ammonium chloride, materials used in the dry batteries that appeared towards the end of the century. The Daniell cell of 1836, in which electrodes were immersed in different electrolytes separated by a porous pot, was improved by J. C. Fuller in 1853. It gave a longer period of constant voltage and was used in the telegraph services into the 1870s. These were all primary cells with a limited life. In the 1860s, a Frenchman, R. D. G. Planté, developed a storage cell or accumulator based on electrodes in the form of large lead plates in sulphuric acid. It came into general use from 1880. During the charging period, lead peroxide formed on the plates. During discharge, the chemical reaction was reversed. A limitation to storage batteries was their weight, an accumulator for a simple lighting system often weighing as much as 113 kilograms (250 pounds).

Electric Generators

Immediately after Faraday had shown the way, mechanical generators of electricity began to appear, the first designed by Hippolyte Pixii and shown in Paris in 1832. It was turned by hand and had fixed coils with a rotating magnet. Rotating coils within a fixed magnet became general practice thereafter. These early generators provided alternating current, though a mechanical commutator to convert it into direct current was invented by Ampère and fitted to an early Pixii generator. Fluctuations of output voltage were evened out by the use of a combination of coils, called an armature, in which the maximum voltage was generated in each coil in turn. Electromagnets powered by battery had been known since 1825. Applied to generators, it was shown by C. F. Varley in 1866 that the electromagnet could be powered by diverting some of the generator's output and that sufficient residual magnetism was retained in the soft-iron core for the generator to be self-activating. In other words, a generator had only to be turned to produce continuous electricity.

When the steam engine was added to provide the motive power, the large-scale use of electricity was assured. In 1875, a generator was installed at the Gare du Nord in Paris to power

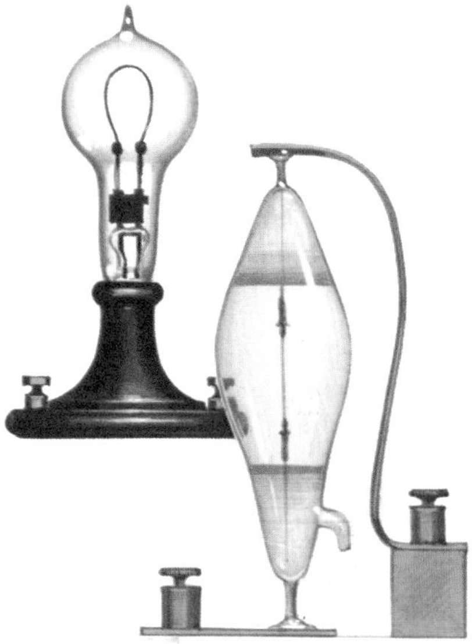

Thomas Edison with (left) an early carbon filament lamp and (right) Joseph Swan's lamp.

Electric street lighting in the City of London, 1881. The convenience and flexibility of electric lighting were quickly appreciated.

arc-lamps. In 1882, Edison's Pearl Street generating plant in New York was operating. In 1883, a small power station lit the Grosvenor Gallery in London and surplus electricity was sold to local customers. The power station designed by S. Z. Ferranti and built at Deptford in 1889 by the London Electricity Supply Corporation had four 10,000-hp steam engines driving 10,000-volt alternators and two 1,250-hp engines driving 5,000-volt alternators. It was the prototype of the modern power station. Ferranti invented a meter to measure customers' consumption. By 1886, work had been started on the first great hydroelectric installation at Niagara Falls using water turbines as the motive power.

Electric tramcars were a common sight in most large cities until they were made obsolete by the more manoeuvrable buses.

Electric locomotives made the building of underground railway systems possible.

Electric Railways

The principles of the electric generator and the electric motor are the same, the one working in reverse of the other. In 1873 in Vienna, Z. T. Gramme demonstrated two generators arranged so that either could be used to produce power to operate the other as a motor. These were direct current generators, and alternating current had become more common for large-scale generation. The first A.C. motor was invented in 1888 by Nikola Tesla and manufacture begun by Westinghouse of America. By the end of the century, machine-tool manufacturers were incorporating electric motors as an integral part of their machines, gradually doing away with the elaborate system of driving shafts, endless belts and pulleys that had been the factory's inheritance from water and steam power. In 1879, the first electric railway, 275 metres (300 yards) long and with current supplied to its three-hp engine by a central rail, was presented at an exhibition in Berlin. By 1884, Germany had the first electric trams with overhead power lines. In 1890, the first underground railway, the City and South London which passed under the River Thames, was operated by 150-hp electric locomotives.

Early electrical illumination was by arc lamp. As early as 1802, Humphry Davy had noted that a spark struck between two carbon electrodes gave a brilliant light. Yet it was not until 1857, when the steam-driven generator had appeared, that Frederick Holmes gave a demonstration of arc lighting suitable for lighthouses to the Brethren of Trinity House in London. Arc lamps were fitted into the South Foreland lighthouse in 1858 and four years later into Dungeness lighthouse.

Arc lamps lit by batteries had been originated in 1846 by W. E. Staite. One of his problems was that carbon electrodes burned away, increasing the gap between them and changing the intensity of the light. He overcame this with a mechanism driven by a falling weight which was controlled by the expansion of a copper rod as the heat from the arc increased with the length of the spark. In 1876, Paul Jablochkoff, a Russian engineer who had settled in Paris, devised a new arc lamp with the electrodes placed side by side vertically instead of end to end. The arc was struck across the tips which wore evenly as alternating current was supplied from a generator. A later improvement was to copper-plate the carbon electrodes.

Incandescent Lamps

The incandescent filament lamp was developed simultaneously by Thomas Edison in America and Joseph Swan in Britain. Swan's lamp used a filament of carbonised, mercerised cotton, while Edison used a sliver of carbonised bamboo. Such filaments had a long life only if heated in the absence of air, so evacuated glass containers were necessary. Platinum wire was used to lead the current to the filament because it was the only metal available with the same expansion when heated as the glass. If the two materials had expanded at a different rate, cracking of the glass would have been inevitable and the vacuum impaired. Swan overcame the blackening of the bulb by deposits of carbon by removing the last traces of air with a 'flashing' of the filament just before the bulb was finally sealed. Blocked by a rivalry of patents, the two inventors formed the Edison and Swan United Electric Light Company.

Carbon filament lamps quickly replaced arc lamps for general use. In 1898, von Welsbach, who had pioneered the incandescent gas mantle, developed a lamp with a filament of osmium which has a melting point of 2,700°C. By the end of the century, tantalum with a melting point of 2,996°C was in use. Tungsten (melting point 3,410°C) became the common metal for electric light filaments from 1911.

Guglielmo Marconi (1874–1937) received the Nobel Prize for Physics in 1909 for his work in advancing wireless telegraphy.

The Telegraph, Telephone and Radio

The first practical use to which electricity was put was the sending of messages by telegraph. Early ideas involved the use of an electrostatic machine to charge wires which then agitated a pith ball at the receiving end. As early as 1753, a system had been proposed using 26 wires, one for each letter of the alphabet. Later schemes reduced the wires to one and used a code. The invention of the electric cell attracted the German inventor S. T. von Soemmering to devise a telegraph. He demonstrated it to an attaché at the Russian Legation in Munich, Baron Schilling, who attempted to develop it. The establishment of a connection between magnetism and electricity suggested to Schilling an electromagnetic receiver based on the movement of a single needle allied to a code. One of his instruments was seen by William Cooke who, on his return to London, went into partnership with Charles Wheatstone, professor of natural philosophy at King's College.

Cooke and Wheatstone patented their first five-needle telegraph in 1837. The following year, they designed a two-needle version to connect West Drayton with Paddington station on the Great Western Railway. Four years later, the telegraph was extended as far as Slough. In 1845, it attracted enormous publicity when a suspected murderer was seen boarding a London train at Slough and the information was telegraphed to Paddington where the police arrested him. This type of telegraph required a code, and the one that was adopted eventually throughout the world was the invention of Samuel Morse. He had the good fortune to establish the first telegraphic link between Washington and Baltimore the day before the Democratic Convention met to choose its presidential candidate, and the election result was the first important news transmitted by it. From such dramatic beginnings, the telegraph spread rapidly. A submarine cable linked Britain with the Continent in 1851. After considerable difficulties, a transatlantic cable was operating by 1866. In 1872, when the mayors of London and Adelaide, Australia exchanged messages, cables linked many cities.

As early as 1845, a method of printing the message was devised. Wheatstone patented his printing telegraph in 1860. Meanwhile, the German physicist, Hermann Helmholtz, was researching into the reproduction of sound. Though an electric telephone was demonstrated in Germany in 1861, the first practical device was invented by Alexander Graham Bell and patented in 1876. In both microphone and receiver, Bell used electromagnets with pivoted armatures attached to metal diaphragms. Variations in strength of current varied the magnetic pull on the armature, setting up vibrations in the diaphragm of the receiver which transmitted the sound waves through the air. Conversely, sound waves impinging on the microphone diaphragm produced fluctuations of induced current in the electromagnet for transmission along the wire.

Samuel Morse (1791–1872), whose code of telegraphic signals is still widely used today, with (above) a Wheatstone perforator, which prints out telegraphic signals on a paper tape, and (below) a morse key.

The *Great Eastern*, for 30 years the world's largest liner, was used to lay a transatlantic cable.

The Phonograph

In 1859, Leon Scott demonstrated his 'phonautograph' to the Royal Association in London, proving that sound was a form of energy. The phonautograph consisted of a funnel with a diaphragm at the end attached to a stiff bristle which rested on a revolving cylinder coated with lamp-black. When the diaphragm was vibrated by sound entering the funnel, the bristle drew corresponding patterns on the cylinder. Scott's great discovery was that similar sounds made similar patterns, though he could see no practical application of the fact. It was Thomas Edison who, in 1877, saw the possibility that a permanent imprint of the patterns could be cut in a cylinder in such a way that the process could be reversed and the sound waves played back. Edison used a cylinder covered in tinfoil. The cuts in it were made vertically on a 'hill and dale' principle. Later, Tainter and Bell substituted a wax-covered cylinder.

The modern record player owes its origin to Emile Berliner, a German emigrant working in Washington. He replaced Edison's cylinder with a flat disc in which the cuts were made from side to side in a spiral groove, in contrast to the variations in depth of the cuts in Edison's early machines. Thus he combined Edison's idea of a permanent imprint with Scott's 'writing in sound'. Edison adapted his phonograph to incorporate the advantage of Berliner's method of cutting, but it was eventually the flat disc, with its technical superiority, that prevailed. Berliner began by etching the recording on glass, but soon changed to zinc. By 1888, he had found a way of making a master from which copies could be taken. Recordings were made mechanically, directly from the sound waves, for many years. Electrical recording was not invented until 1925.

Meanwhile, an even more revolutionary method of electrical communication was slowly emerging throughout the 19th century. Faraday's work on electromagnetism had propagated the idea of lines of force along which magnetism and electricity acted. James Clerk Maxwell, who translated much of Faraday's theory into mathematical terms, put forward the idea that electrical disturbances through space resemble the transmission of light. It was left to the German physicist, Heinrich Hertz, to produce in the laboratory the electromagnetic waves that Maxwell's theories postulated. He showed that a flow of current in one circuit could induce a similar flow in another circuit not directly connected but tuned to the first. Hertz proved that the difference between electromagnetic waves linking the two circuits and waves of light was merely one of wavelength.

Radio Signals

In 1895, Ernest Rutherford used electromagnetic waves to transmit messages over a distance of 1·2 kilometres (three-quarters of a mile) at Cambridge. Even then it was not considered possible to transmit radio waves over a great distance because of the curvature of the earth's surface. It was thought the waves would just fly off into space. Then, on 12th December 1901, Guglielmo Marconi, an Italian engineer largely ignorant of the physics involved, transmitted a radio signal across the Atlantic. Though Marconi did not know it, his success had been made possible by the ionosphere reflecting back his signals to earth. It was left to others to discover the existence of the so-called heaviside layer in the upper atmosphere. Marconi had used transmissions in the 300 to 3,000 metres waveband. It was not until much later that short waves, such as the 24 cms used by Hertz in his laboratory experiments, were found to be most suitable for long-distance communication.

Edison with an early phonograph. In 1877 he recorded himself reciting 'Mary had a little lamb'.

Photography and Printing

Above: 19th-century street photographer. Below: Louis Daguerre (1789–1851), the inventor of the first practical photographic process.

The world's first photograph was taken in 1826 by Joseph Niepce from his window at Chalon-sur-Sâone, France, with an eight-hour exposure. The light-sensitive material was a pewter plate coated with bitumen of Judea, a kind of asphalt. The picture was developed by using oil of lavender to dissolve away the bitumen where it had not been hardened by light during the exposure. Areas of undissolved bitumen provided the light areas of the picture and the underlying pewter the shadows. The process was improved by Niepce's partner, Louis Daguerre. The daguerreotype, as it was called, was taken on a silvered copper plate coated with silver iodide. Exposure in sunlight was not more than half an hour. Development then took place in a box containing vaporised mercury which clung to the areas affected by light. Excess silver iodide was washed off with sodium thiosulphate, known as hypo, leaving the silver underneath to form the shadows.

Calotype Process

Copies could not be made of daguerreotypes, but meanwhile in Britain, William Fox Talbot had produced his calotype process. This also used silver iodide, but on thin paper brushed with solutions of silver nitrate and potassium iodide and sometimes gallic acid. A negative image was formed after heating and fixed with hypo. Positive prints could then be made from this paper negative. In 1851, the wet collodion process, invented by the London sculptor F. S. Archer, was introduced. A glass plate coated with potassium iodide and collodion (nitrocellulose in ether) was dipped in a solution of silver nitrate just before the picture was to be taken and exposed while still wet. In 1878, a dry plate with an emulsion of gelatine containing nitric acid, cadmium bromide and silver nitrate was produced and sold in quantity. In 1889, the American George Eastman finally succeeded in producing the first celluloid roll film. Sold with his Kodak camera, one roll could take a hundred pictures which were developed and printed by Eastman's firm and the camera returned to its owner reloaded. Photography had become a universal leisure activity.

In France, Etienne Marey had begun in 1882 to take twelve exposures per second on a rotating glass plate, each exposure being 1/720th of a second. With the invention of paper film, he was able to build what was essentially the first ciné camera. It had a handle to turn the film from one spool to another, a shutter rotated between lens and film, and a brake mechanism to stop the film each time

Above: the first Kodak camera, which made photography available to the general public for the first time. Below: a daguerreotype camera, and (left) a daguerreotype being taken. The main disadvantage of the daguerreotype process was that no copies could be made.

Left: an early rotary printing press. Right: portrait of Aloys Senefelder, the inventor of lithography.

the shutter was opened. It took ten to twelve shots per second. Thomas Edison saw Marey's work in Paris in 1889, and two years later had patented his own camera. He opened his Kinetoscope Parlor on Broadway in New York in April 1894. It was a sort of peep-show where a single viewer looked through a hole at a film lit from behind and turned by an electric motor at a rate of 46 frames a second. Finally, the brothers Louis and Auguste Lumière invented a projector, working at sixteen frames a second, that began towards the end of 1895 to show moving pictures to audiences of 2,000 a night in the basement of a Paris cafe. From 1896, Georges Méliès, an expert conjuror, began making his fantasy films, and two years later a movie cameraman followed Kitchener's army to the Sudan.

Type Casting

In printing, the first machine for casting type appeared in America in 1838. It brought the moulds for each character up to a pot containing molten type-metal, opened the mould for the metal to flow in, closed it to shape the end and tilted out the finished character. Later rotary casters had 100 moulds and cast 60,000 characters in an hour. Type was no longer re-sorted after use, but thrown straight back into the melting pot. Typesetting machinery, using a keyboard to operate it, progressed slowly through the century towards the linotype machine, invented by Otto Mergenthaler, a German watchmaker who had emigrated to America. Single-letter matrices or moulds were brought together to form a line of type. Wedge-shaped spacers were knocked in to spread the line to the required standard width and the whole line cast in one slug of metal, hence the name 'line o' type'. A later refinement was the Monotype system with which the operator produced a roll of punched tape. This was fed into another machine which had a matrix-holder brought into position by the paper perforations and the molten type-metal forced into the mould by compressed air. With this method, each character was a separate piece of metal allowing single letters to be corrected individually.

A 'typographer' was invented in Detroit in 1829. Letters were mounted on a semicircular band of metal which moved to bring the required letter into position for printing. The first typewriter to have each letter mounted on a separate bar was invented in Marseilles in 1833. The American printer, C. S. Sholes, used the same principle with a horizontal platen and an inked ribbon. To avoid the clashing of type bars, he arranged the letters in such an order that those occurring frequently together were placed widely apart. His was substantially the keyboard used today.

The printing press itself became faster, bigger, more powerful and more automatic in all its operations from feeding in the paper to cutting and folding the finished product. The big breakthrough came with the development of the rotary press invented by Richard March Hoe, an American immigrant from Leicestershire. His prototype had one large cylinder to carry the type surrounded by four smaller cylinders to carry the paper to it. The type was fastened in cast-iron beds with wedge-shaped rules between the columns to prevent it flying off with the centrifugal force. The next big improvement was in stereotyping, with the original type used to make papier maché moulds from which solid plates could be cast. These plates were curved to fit the cylinder.

An eight-feeder rotary press. Modern presses are 'web-fed' straight from the paper roll.

Picture Reproduction

Finally, photography and printing were brought together for the reproduction of pictures. A negative made from an artist's line drawing was lit in contact with a sensitised zinc plate and then rolled with printer's ink in a dark-room. All the sensitive material could be washed off except where the lines of the drawing appeared. The plate was then etched with acid, leaving these lines in relief. Half-tone blocks could be made by introducing a screen of crosslines in front of the negative plate so that light passing through it made the heaviest dots in the darkest areas. This permitted reproduction in colour by use of three half-tone blocks for yellow, red and blue respectively, printed on top of each other. Photogravure, invented by Fox Talbot in 1852, was used for colour printing by the end of the century. A screen was printed on top of a positive image on a copper plate and the plate was etched to make tiny pits or cells which were deepest in the darkest areas. When the plate was inked and wiped, ink remained in the cells to be drawn out by paper pressed against it.

Internal Combustion

Like many early motor cars, this 1892 Peugeot owes much of its design to horse-drawn carriages. The driver sits in the back seat with passengers facing him.

Fuel for the early stationary internal combustion engines was usually coal-gas, mixed with air. The first fully successful gas engine was designed by Nicholas Otto in Germany in the 1870s. It worked on what became known as the Otto cycle and was adopted for almost all but the lowest powered internal combustion engines after 1890. It is based on a piston and cylinder with intake and exhaust valves and consists of four strokes: 1, explosive mixture drawn into the cylinder; 2, mixture compressed by piston and ignited; 3, explosion forces piston back; 4, returning piston drives out exhaust gases, and the whole cycle starts again.

Gottlieb Daimler (1834–1900) first put the Otto engine to use.

Karl Benz (1844–1929) is credited with building the first motor car.

Meanwhile, another fuel, at first used for lighting and heating, was able to compete in price with coal-gas. This was petroleum, which had the enormous advantage of being easy to transport. A fairly heavy kerosene oil was at first used for internal combustion. This had to be either vaporised by heating or atomised into a fine spray and mixed with air to form the explosive material. It could then be spontaneously ignited by extreme compression. The name chiefly associated with the oil engine is Rudolf Diesel, a German engineer who was nearly killed when his first engine exploded, and who finally disappeared mysteriously from the Harwich steam ferry on his way to London. In 1897, his engine managed to achieve the high compression ratio required, though diesel engines need to be of robust and heavy construction, making them most useful for heavy land transport, marine and large stationary engines.

Daimler and Benz

Two Germans can be said to have developed the petrol engine for use with the lighter, more volatile fuel-oil. One of these was Gottlieb Daimler whose single cylinder vertical engine worked on the Otto cycle with fuel ignited by a heated tube in the cylinder head. By 1886, it had been fitted to a bicycle and a carriage. The other engineer was Karl Benz who made engines specifically for motor cars. His engine was horizontal and had electrical ignition supplied by an induction coil from an accumulator. This was fitted with a rotary contact breaker driven from the engine to ensure accurate timing for the spark which was produced in a plug essentially the same as the one used today. After 1893, the modern float-feed carburettor, invented by Wilhelm Maybach, came into general use. The float worked a needle valve. Suction from the cylinder drew petrol through a fine nozzle into the air intake.

The first petrol-powered vehicle with an engine mounted on a handcart is credited to an Austrian inventor, Siegfried Markus, and given the date 1864. Nothing came of it, however, and Benz is usually considered the pioneer

An 1897 Daimler with the front engine, rear wheel drive layout which soon became standard.

The development of the bicycle. Top: the machine which started it all—an early 19th-century dandy-horse, which the rider pushed along with his feet on the ground. Centre is a tandem tricycle, with two sets of pedals but no brakes. The tricycle was very stable, especially in comparison with its contemporary the penny-farthing. Bottom is a modern bicycle with brakes, gears, mudguards and pneumatic tyres. The picture (left) shows a late 19th-century bicycle club outing. The introduction of the pneumatic tyre at the end of the century brought about a tremendous upsurge of interest in the bicycle as a cheap and convenient means of transport. Although the advent of the mass-produced motor car reduced the demand, there is renewed interest in the bicycle now as cities become more congested and the costs of motoring continue to soar.

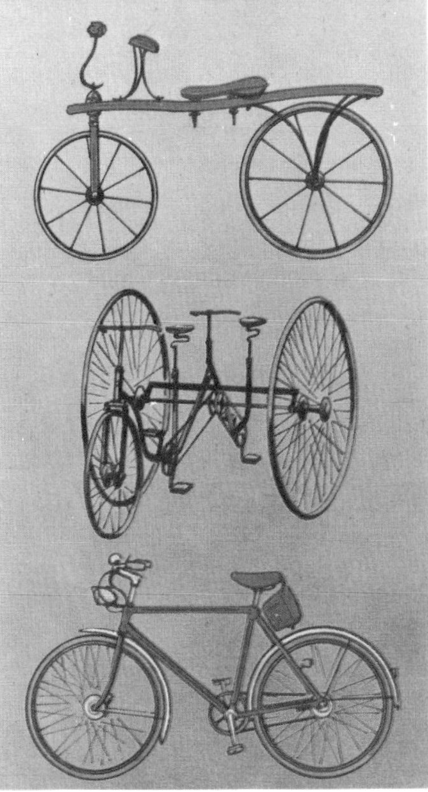

of the motor car. In 1885, he built a light vehicle with a single cylinder engine, a vertical crankshaft and a belt-drive which could be moved from a fixed to a loose pulley thus acting as a primitive kind of clutch so that the engine could idle in neutral. The vehicle had a single front wheel steered by a tiller. Within eight years, Benz had developed a four-wheeler with a horizontal crankshaft, a design which was being manufactured in hundreds by the end of the century.

Meanwhile, in 1886, Daimler was trying out his high-speed engine, the first of its kind, on a motorcycle. A year later, he fitted one to the rear end of an experimental carriage. His four-wheeled motor carriages, ancestors of the Mercédes cars, were produced at the famous Canstatt works near Stuttgart.

Early motor cars were made for the enthusiast and the well-to-do. In 1896, Henry Ford made his first car. In 1903, he founded the Ford Motor Company. By 1908, he had designed the Model T for mass production. In nineteen years without major design changes, it sold over fifteen million. The motoring age had dawned.

The Bicycle

Even after Ford and others had provided a cheap motor car, the bicycle remained a popular means of transport and, perhaps more particularly, an instrument of healthy exercise. Wheeled vehicles propelled by hand or foot go back to the 18th century. An early bicycle appeared in Paris about 1808 and an improved version of ten years later was designed by Baron von Drais at Mannheim in Germany. It was called the *draisin* or, more popularly, the dandy-horse. It consisted of two wheels running in the same track, joined by a wooden bar on which the saddle was mounted well forward. There was a rest for the forearms and a steering lever in front of that. The machine was propelled by the rider pushing each foot in turn against the ground. About 1840, cranks were fitted to the rear wheels with levers to operate them, by a Scottish blacksmith, Kirkpatrick Macmillan, who also thoughtfully added a brake.

A Frenchman, Pierre Michaux, first put cranks and pedals directly on the front wheel in the 1860s. He formed a company to manufacture his velocipedes. By the eighties there were more than 200 different kinds on the market, including tandems, bicycles with two parallel wheels, tricycles and even four-wheelers. The most common type was the penny-farthing on which the rider balanced rather dangerously above a front wheel that was made as large as possible so that the maximum distance would be travelled for each revolution of the pedals fixed directly to the wheel. The next step was the introduction in 1885 of a chain-drive geared to the rear wheel. This invention was known, understandably, as the safety bicycle and is credited to J. K. Starley of Coventry.

Early bicycles had steel tyres, from which some types were known popularly as boneshakers. The pneumatic tyre had been patented in 1845, but had to be reinvented by a Scottish veterinary surgeon, J. B. Dunlop, in 1886, to improve the comfort of his ten-year-old son's bicycle. There followed a boom in bicycle manufacture and many hastily formed companies going bankrupt. The bicycle had established itself as a firm favourite. It was the universal vehicle for the young, and initiated a vast array of touring clubs and sporting events.

Powered Flight

Lighter-than-air machines, such as balloons and airships, are dealt with elsewhere in this volume. Here, we are concerned with the heavier-than-air flying machines and the application of motive power to them. The ancient Chinese probably had kites big enough to carry a man, and they certainly had toy helicopters. Early ideas about human flight were based on the flight of birds and involved aircraft with flapping wings called ornithopters. Model ornithopters have actually flown, but none large enough to carry a human. Yet from the time around 1500 when Leonardo da Vinci began to take them seriously, much effort was expended on them.

The beginning of the modern aeroplane dates from the work of Sir George Cayley (1773–1857). He worked out the problems of aerodynamics and aerostatics and set about solving them by experiment. He kept records from which later inventors could follow his progress. He saw at once, unlike most of the other pioneers, that a fixed wing was essential. He made model gliders from 1804 and throughout the following 50 years, flying them from hilltops. He is believed to have been successful on two occasions in building and flying a glider over a short distance with a human pilot. His findings were published and encouraged others to attempt to solve the remaining problems of sustained and controlled flight.

Man-carrying Gliders

Success with man-carrying gliders was eventually achieved by the German, Otto Lilienthal, and his English follower, P. S. Pilcher. During the early 1890s, Lilienthal made more than a thousand flights in his so-called hanging glider. Pilcher also flew towed gliders. Both men were killed in gliding accidents, Lilienthal in 1896 and Pilcher in 1899.

Meanwhile, from 1827, attempts were made to produce a man-carrying monoplane kite. Success was not achieved until L. Hargrave in Australia produced in 1893 a box kite with two fixed lifting surfaces. This design was being studied by Pilcher at the time of his death. A French engineer, Octave Chanute, also experimented with both the box kite and gliders. He passed his design for a trussed biplane structure to the Wright brothers and gave them encouragement in other ways. In 1848, a lacemaker from Chard, John Stringfellow, managed to fly a model fixed-wing aeroplane on the end of a wire, though it is believed that his design was fundamentally unsound. Others produced powered models that took off from the ground and used many different power sources, including rubber bands, clockwork, steam and compressed air. By 1866 when the (now Royal) Aeronautical Society was founded in Britain, most of the vital theories of aerodynamics had been published. There was even a dart-shaped design which it was suggested could be powered by a steam jet, anticipating by nearly 100 years modern ideas of rocket propulsion. The model aeroplane enthusiasm culminated in a design by an American professor of astronomy, S. P. Langley, whose 4·8-metre (sixteen foot) wingspan, steam-powered monoplane flew for a distance of 1·2 kilometres (three-quarters of a mile).

Powered Flight

By that time, the development of the petrol engine was beginning to show promise as the final solution to the problem of powered flight. Two bicycle manufacturers, the brothers Orville and Wilbur Wright, had been experimenting with gliders. They built and flew three in 1900, 1901 and 1902 respectively. At last, in 1903, they fitted a twelve hp petrol engine to a tailless pusher biplane. On 17th December near Kitty Hawk in North Carolina, Orville took it with reasonable control of height, speed and direction through its first twelve-second flight, covering a distance of 36·5 metres (40 yards). Yet this historic event was virtually ignored by the American press. It was not until 1908 that an improved version of the Wright's biplane flew in Europe, and the western world began to take note of their achievement.

Before that, in 1906, the Brazilian

Above: Octave Chanute's box-kite glider, which shows the basic trussed biplane structure.

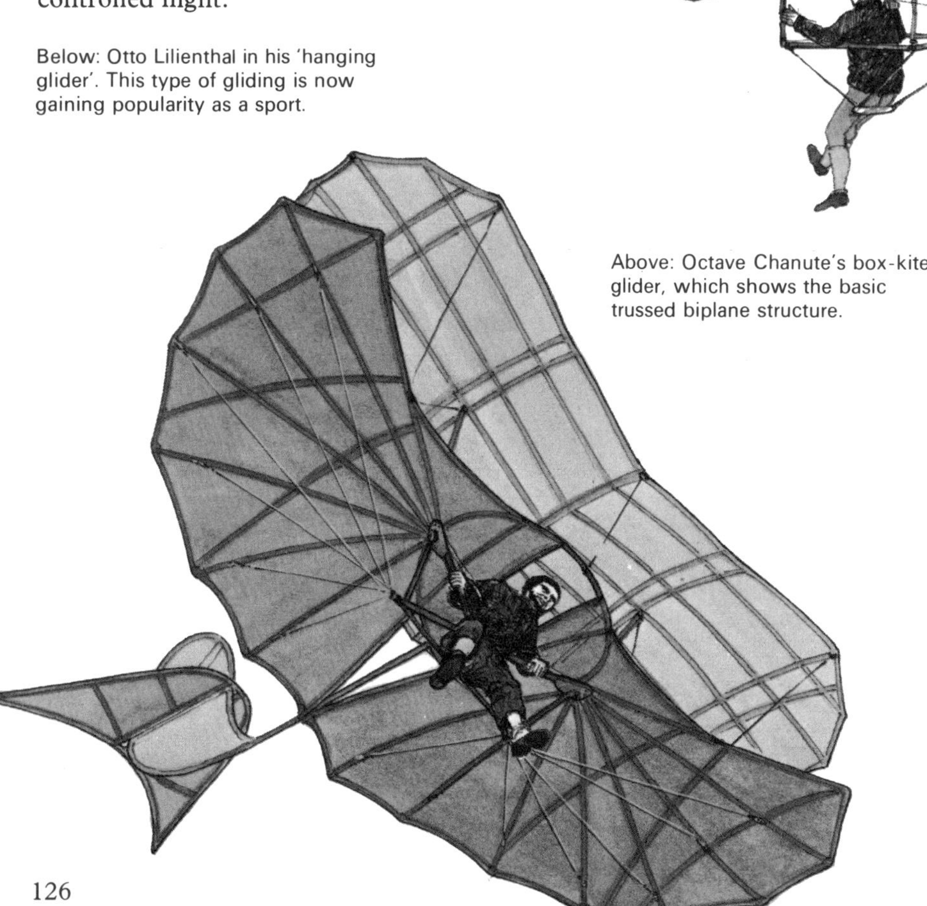

Below: Otto Lilienthal in his 'hanging glider'. This type of gliding is now gaining popularity as a sport.

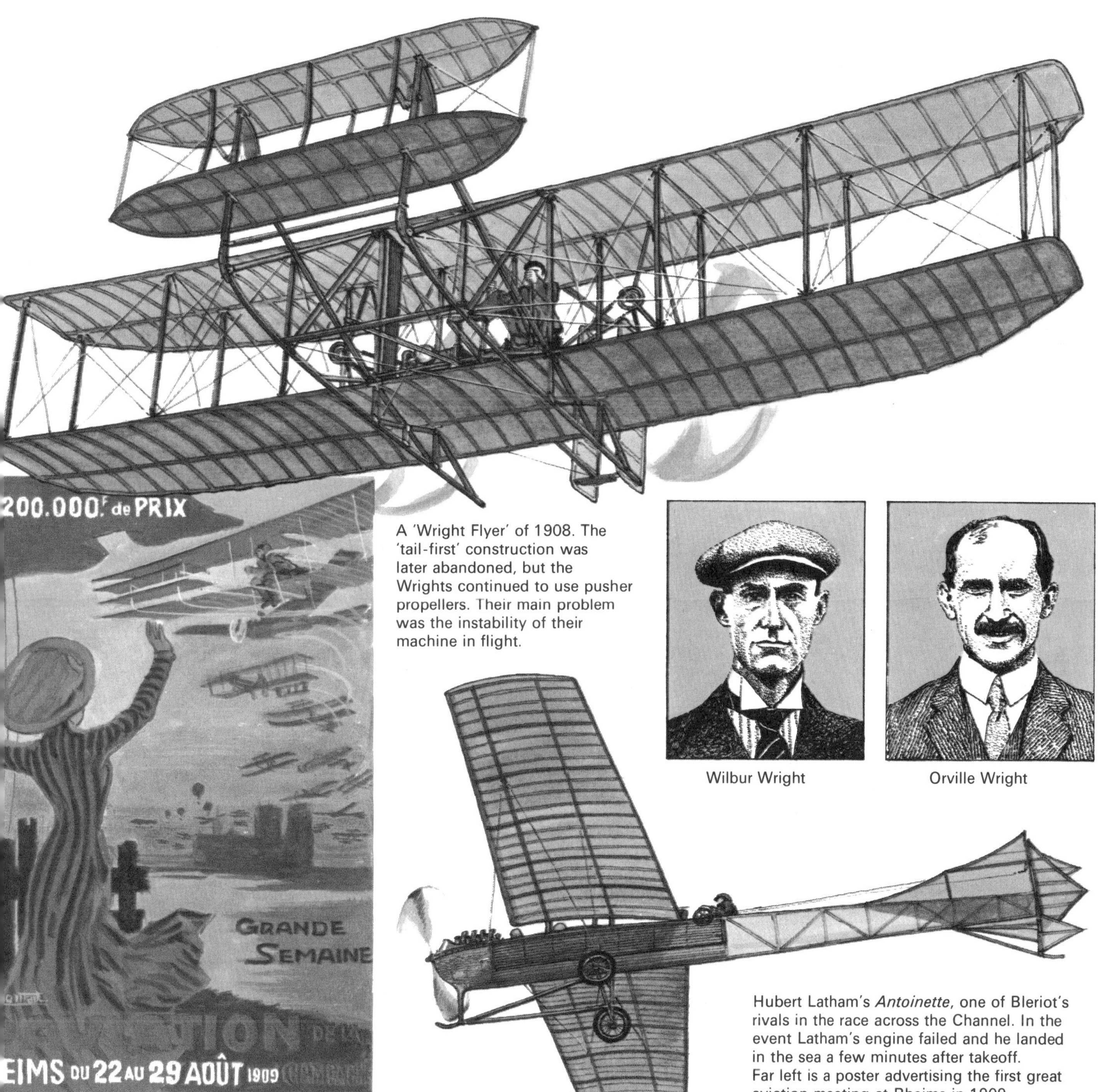

A 'Wright Flyer' of 1908. The 'tail-first' construction was later abandoned, but the Wrights continued to use pusher propellers. Their main problem was the instability of their machine in flight.

Wilbur Wright

Orville Wright

Hubert Latham's *Antoinette*, one of Bleriot's rivals in the race across the Channel. In the event Latham's engine failed and he landed in the sea a few minutes after takeoff.
Far left is a poster advertising the first great aviation meeting at Rheims in 1909.

Alberto Santos-Dumont had made the first powered flight in Europe in his independently designed biplane which was, however, much inferior to the Wrights'. The Voisin brothers, in their factory in France, were building their box-kite biplane which formed the basis for many later double-winged aircraft. Louis Blériot was also at work on his monoplane. In 1909, he flew it across the English Channel. The publicity attending this event not only focused attention on the aeroplane as a possible weapon of war, but also established the monoplane design which was eventually to gain the supremacy. The biplane continued for a number of years because its wings were easier to brace. For speed, thin wing sections were usually used, though the designer Anton Fokker showed that a thick wing section could be used for cantilevered wings braced internally.

Aeroplane Design

The First World War gave a tremendous impetus to aeroplane design. Though their aerodynamic design did not make much progress, the power of petrol engines specially constructed for aircraft increased considerably. Already floats had been fitted in place of wheels so that aeroplanes could take off from water. Machine guns synchronised to fire between the blades of the rotating propeller were devised, as also were bomb and torpedo release mechanisms. When the war was over, efforts switched largely to passenger-carrying aircraft, and regular scheduled routes were opened up around the world. By 1930, the largest airliners had four engines and could carry 30 passengers at cruising speeds of 193 kph (120 mph). The flying boat was developed with a watertight hull and a planing surface along the bottom.

In the 1930s, the biplane of largely wooden construction gradually disappeared. Aircraft were built with a skeleton of light alloys covered by a stressed skin. Such airliners as the American DC-3 introduced refinements like wingflaps to increase lift for take-off and drag for landing, variable-pitch propellers, retractable undercarriage to reduce drag in flight and supercharged engines to increase speed at high altitudes. Safety devices were also included, such as radio contact with ground control, the radio compass, radio beams as landing guides and heaters to combat icing. Flying was set to take over long distance travel from other transport.

Science Today

We are made aware of objects and events around us through our five senses, which react in different ways to matter or energy. For instance, we taste and smell through direct contact with matter placed in the mouth or inhaled through the nose. Our sense of touch also reacts to direct contact with matter. We feel its smoothness or roughness, its warmth or its coldness, its wetness or dryness. The sense of touch can react, without direct contact, to energy radiating from an object in the form of heat. In the case of light energy to which our eyes react, or sound energy to which our ears react, again there is no direct contact. The human brain is capable of analysing all these sensations and making deductions from them. From this process, a body of knowledge is built up which we call science.

A scientist makes a molecular model based on atomic structure.

This model of a nylon polymer, only part of which is seen here, contains about 1,700 atoms. The coloured shapes represent carbon (black), nitrogen (blue), hydrogen (white) and oxygen (red).

Scientific knowledge has never been absolute and probably never will be. We are limited first by the range of our own sensations, which are themselves the interactions of matter and energy. The instruments we invent to aid our senses have unavoidable limits built into them. There are limits both to the smallest detail and to the farthest object we can see, and to the speeds and changes of direction we can measure and record. As research continues, these limits are pushed further, but they remain as limits. This book can describe only some of the limits that scientific knowledge has reached at the present time, and even that description is limited by the language used to describe them. To explain how the intimate reactions between matter and energy take place, the scientist has to invent models. These models can only represent approximately what happens. As our knowledge advances, new models will be necessary to replace the old. Just as the schoolroom globe is a model of the earth we inhabit, so the diagrams given within this text are models representing our present state of knowledge.

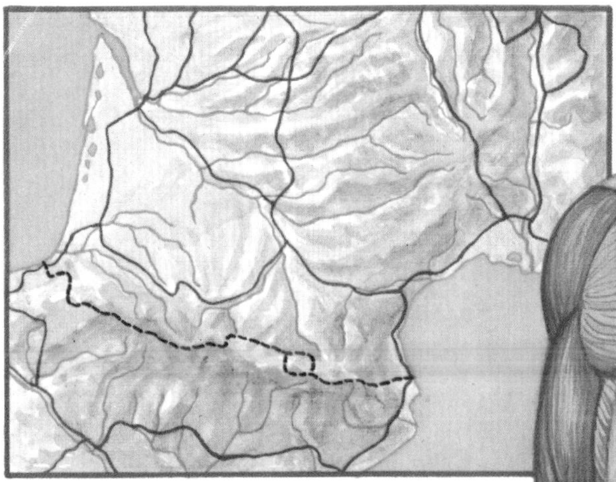

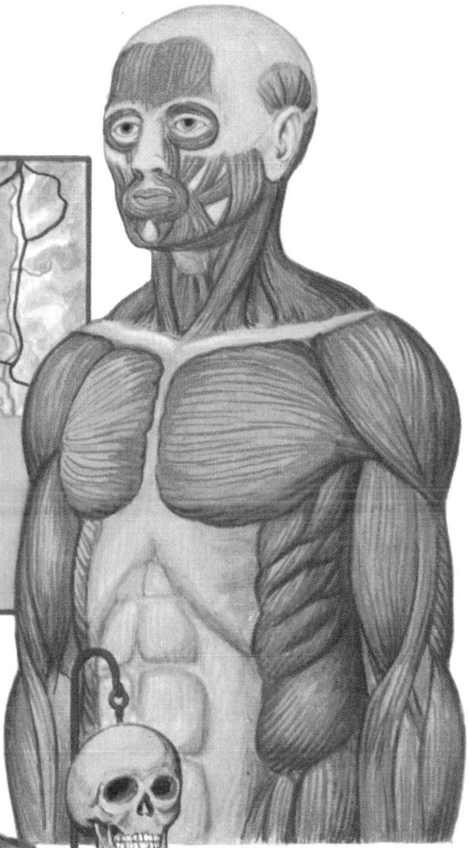

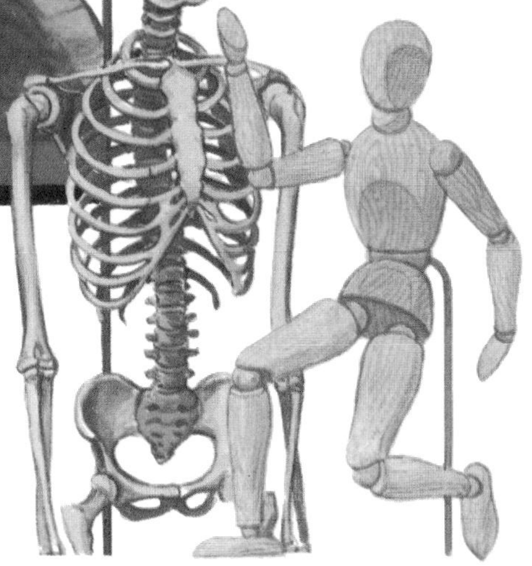

Right, examples of various models: a contour map, a three-dimensional image of the earth's surface, the human muscular structure, a skeleton, and an artist's lay figure.

Matter and Energy

The most fundamental advance in scientific knowledge in this century has been in the understanding of the relationship between matter and energy. The modern idea is that there is no absolute difference between them, that matter exists only when energy is present in certain forms. In an atomic explosion, matter reverts to energy. When the energy of a body increases, as for instance when its velocity is increased, its mass or the amount of matter it contains also increases. In other words, matter can become energy and energy can become matter. Nevertheless, it is more convenient to divide this study into two sections, the first dealing with matter or the science of chemistry, and the second dealing with energy or the science of physics. In these two sections key words and phrases which set out certain scientific facts are fully explained when they first appear in the narrative. For easy reference they are printed in bold type.

The final part of this volume gives a general description of how the new understanding of matter and energy has created the modern Technological Revolution. Exploitation of the forces that bind atoms and molecules together has produced new manufacturing materials. New forms of energy have been harnessed to bring about these reactions and to drive industrial machinery. The inventive mind of man has devised new methods of controlling and speeding up production so that every marvel is quickly and cheaply made available to us. Communications systems exist to link all humanity as members of the vast crew of Spaceship Earth. We must each of us understand something of the science that has created our age if we are to be responsible members of that crew.

Matter

Scientists arrange the 105 elements into a periodic table which groups them into related 'families' indicated by the different colours. Hydrogen, which has unique qualities, stands alone, the simplest and most common of all elements. The others are: 2 Helium, 3 Lithium, 4 Beryllium, 5 Boron, 6 Carbon, 7 Nitrogen, 8 Oxygen, 9 Fluorine, 10 Neon, 11 Sodium, 12 Magnesium, 13 Aluminium, 14 Silicon, 15 Phosphorus, 16 Sulphur, 17 Chlorine, 18 Argon, 19 Potassium, 20 Calcium, 21 Scandium, 22 Titanium, 23 Vanadium, 24 Chromium, 25 Manganese, 26 Iron, 27 Cobalt, 28 Nickel, 29 Copper, 30 Zinc, 31 Gallium, 32 Germanium, 33 Arsenic, 34 Selenium, 35 Bromine, 36 Krypton, 37 Rubidium, 38 Strontium, 39 Yttrium, 40 Zirconium, 41 Niobium, 42 Molybdenum, 43 Technetium, 44 Ruthenium, 45 Rhodium, 46 Palladium, 47 Silver, 48 Cadmium, 49 Indium, 50 Tin, 51 Antimony, 52 Tellurium, 53 Iodine, 54 Xenon, 55 Caesium, 56 Barium, 57 Lanthanum, 58 Cerium, 59 Praseodymium, 60 Neodymium, 61 Promethium, 62 Samarium, 63 Europium, 64 Gadolinium, 65 Terbium, 66 Dysprosium, 67 Holmium, 68 Erbium, 69 Thulium, 70 Ytterbium, 71 Lutetium, 72 Hafnium, 73 Tantalum, 74 Tungsten, 75 Rhenium, 76 Osmium,

1.0080 H 1								
6.939 Li 3	9.0122 Be 4							
22.990 Na 11	24.312 Mg 12							
39.102 K 19	40.08 Ca 20	44.956 Sc 21	47.90 Ti 22	50.942 V 23	51.996 Cr 24	54.938 Mn 25	55.847 Fe 26	58.93 Co 27
85.47 Rb 37	87.62 Sr 38	88.905 Y 39	91.22 Zr 40	92.906 Nb 41	95.94 Mo 42	(99) Tc 43	101.07 Ru 44	102.9 Rh 45
132.91 Cs 55	137.34 Ba 56	57-71 Rare Earth Metals	178.49 Hf 72	180.95 Ta 73	183.85 W 74	186.2 Re 75	190.2 Os 76	192.2 Ir 77
(223) Fr 87	(226) Ra 88	89-103 Actinide Metals						

138.91 La 57	140.12 Ce 58	140.91 Pr 59	144.24 Nd 60	(147) Pm 61	150.3 Sm 62
(227) Ac 89	232.04 Th 90	(231) Pa 91	238.03 U 92	(237) Np 93	(242 Pu 94

(223) — Atomic weight
Fr — Symbol
87 — Atomic number

The whole of the matter contained in the universe is made up from combinations of different kinds of **atoms** called the **elements**. At the time of writing, 105 elements are known and a list of these is given here, together with the internationally agreed abbreviations used to represent them. In the universe the simplest element, hydrogen, is the most common. On the surface of the earth, however, oxygen is the commonest element. Taking the earth's outer crust together with the seas and the atmosphere, approximately 98% is composed of only eight elements in the following proportions: oxygen 49%, silicon 26%, aluminium 8%, iron 5%, calcium 3%, sodium 3%, potassium 2%, magnesium 2%. All the remaining elements together make up only 2%. Even such an apparently common element as copper constitutes only 0·01% of the earth's surface.

Units of Matter

The atom is the smallest part of an element that can exist and still maintain the properties of the element, though as we shall see changes can take place in the structure of a particular atom, and the atoms of one element can be transmuted into atoms of another element. From the purely chemical point of view, however, atoms are the smallest units of matter.

Though there are only 105 elements, there are millions of individual chemical substances consisting of two or more elements which are called **compounds.** In a particular compound, the proportions of the different elements composing it are always the same. For instance, water is a compound made up from the elements hydrogen and oxygen. For every oxygen atom, there are two atoms of hydrogen. Using the abbreviations for these two elements given in the table, the chemical formula for water can therefore be written H_2O. This combination of two atoms of hydrogen with one atom of oxygen forms the smallest possible quantity of water, called its **molecule**. Thus, in the chemical sense, matter is composed of the atoms of elements or compounds of these atoms into molecules.

Some elements under normal conditions exist as gases. Such elements rarely appear in nature as single atoms, but combine like compounds into molecules. Hydrogen and oxygen, for instance, are gases at normal temperature and pressure. They exist as molecules, each composed of two atoms combined as in a compound, giving the formulae H_2 and O_2 respectively. These are called **diatomic molecules**.

Mixtures of Atoms

In nature, **mixtures** of atoms or molecules are common. Unlike a compound, a mixture can be separated into its different parts by purely physical means without any chemical changes to the molecules. For instance, a mixture of salt and pepper can be separated out by tipping it into water. The pepper will float on the surface, while the salt will sink to the bottom and begin to dissolve in the mixture. The air we breathe is a mixture of oxygen, nitrogen and the inert gases. The oxygen and nitrogen, mixed in the approximate proportions of 23% and 76% respectively, can be separated from the air by freezing, since each has a different freezing point. The proportions of the different parts of a mixture often give that mixture its particular properties.

77 Iridium, 78 Platinum, 79 Gold, 80 Mercury, 81 Thallium, 82 Lead, 83 Bismuth, 84 Polonium, 85 Astatine, 86 Radon, 87 Francium, 88 Radium, 89 Actinium, 90 Thorium, 91 Protactinium, 92 Uranium, 93 Neptunium, 94 Plutonium, 95 Americium, 96 Curium, 97 Berkelium, 98 Californium, 99 Einsteinium, 100 Fermium, 101 Mendelevium, 102 Nobelium, 103 Lawrencium, 104 Rutherfordium, 105 Hahnium. The last two elements, 104 and 105, have not yet been fully identified and are omitted from the periodic table.

								4.0026 **He** 2
			10.811 **B** 5	12.011 **C** 6	14.007 **N** 7	15.999 **O** 8	18.998 **F** 9	20.183 **Ne** 10
			26.982 **Al** 13	28.086 **Si** 14	30.974 **P** 15	32.064 **S** 16	35.453 **Cl** 17	39.948 **Ar** 18
58.71 **Ni** 28	63.54 **Cu** 29	65.37 **Zn** 30	69.72 **Ga** 31	72.59 **Ge** 32	74.922 **As** 33	78.96 **Se** 34	79.909 **Br** 35	83.80 **Kr** 36
106.4 **Pd** 46	107.87 **Ag** 47	112.40 **Cd** 48	114.82 **In** 49	118.69 **Sn** 50	121.75 **Sb** 51	127.60 **Te** 52	126.90 **I** 53	131.30 **Xe** 54
195.09 **Pt** 78	196.97 **Au** 79	200.59 **Hg** 80	204.37 **Tl** 81	207.19 **Pb** 82	208.98 **Bi** 83	(210) **Po** 84	(210) **At** 85	(222) **Rn** 86

151.96 **Eu** 63	157.25 **Gd** 64	158.92 **Tb** 65	162.50 **Dy** 66	164.93 **Ho** 67	167.26 **Er** 68	168.93 **Tm** 69	173.04 **Yb** 70	174.97 **Lu** 71
(243) **Am** 95	(247) **Cm** 96	(247) **Bk** 97	(249) **Cf** 98	(254) **Es** 99	(253) **Fm** 100	(256) **Md** 101	(254) **No** 102	(257) **Lw** 103

For a compound to be formed a **chemical reaction** must take place. Thereafter, the molecules of the compound cannot be altered unless another chemical reaction takes place with other atoms or molecules. It is a chemical reaction when hydrogen and oxygen form the compound water. Two diatomic molecules of hydrogen (H_2) react with one diatomic molecule of oxygen (O_2) to form two molecules of water (H_2O). The simple way to write the formula is: $2H_2+O_2 = 2H_2O$. This is called a **chemical equation**. Two molecules of hydrogen are necessary for every single molecule of oxygen because the molecule of water is composed of one oxygen atom combined with two hydrogen atoms. In a chemical reaction, though molecules change, atoms cannot disappear. The two sides of the chemical equation must contain the same total number of atoms, in this case four of hydrogen and two of oxygen.

Simple Models

Though the atom is the smallest particle of matter than can take part in a chemical reaction, it has in itself a particular structure. To understand atomic structure, it is necessary to invent a simple model and to begin with the simplest atom, that of hydrogen, thus:

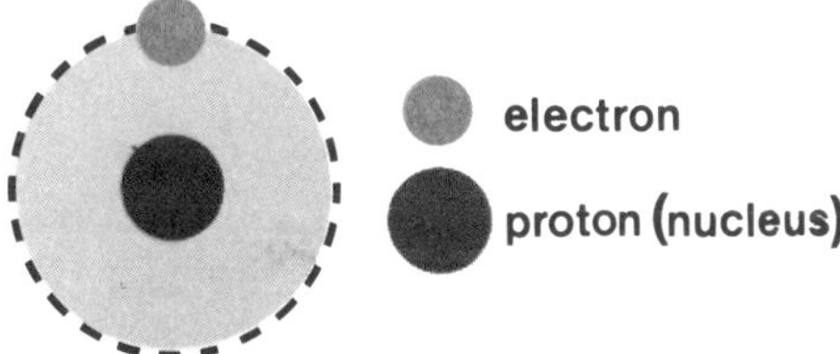

This must be regarded purely as a diagram, not drawn to scale. It represents a tiny planetary system with a central **nucleus** composed of one **proton** with one **electron** in orbit around it. If the nuclear proton were the size of a tennis ball, then the electron's orbit would be going on for 800 metres (half a mile) in diameter. In fact, an atom is only about one ten-millionth of a millimetre across, and its nucleus measures about one ten-thousandth of that. An atom is much too small to be seen by even the most powerful microscope. The particles of which it is composed are only a tiny proportion of it, the remainder consisting of empty space between them. We know that these particles exist only because of the way they behave. In attempting to describe them, we are pressing at the very limits of our present knowledge.

The electron is a tiny mass of concentrated energy. A thousand, million, million, million, million electrons are needed to make up a weight of one gram. An electron is charged with negative electricity. It is thought that the energy of this electric charge is what gives the electron its mass. But we cannot explain an electric charge, except in terms of its behaviour. We know, for instance, that one negatively-charged particle will repel another and attract a positively-charged particle. In some circumstances, an electron behaves like a particle of matter. It has weight, for instance.

Electrical Charge

The proton which forms the nucleus of the hydrogen atom is about 1,850 times heavier than an electron. It is charged with positive electricity. This positive charge is equal though opposite to the negative charge of the electron. The words negative and positive in this sense are used merely for convenience to express their opposite effects which, being equal, cancel each other out so that the atom as a whole has no electrical charge. All atoms are electrically neutral because they all contain equal numbers of protons and electrons. It is this number of protons contained in the nucleus that gives a particular element its chemical properties. It gives the element what is called its **atomic number** as shown in the table of elements. For instance, hydrogen has one proton and one associated electron, so its atomic number is one. The heaviest element that occurs in nature is uranium with 92 protons and 92 electrons. Its atomic number is therefore 92.

So far we have looked only at one form of hydrogen, the simplest, with its single proton and single orbiting electron. There is another, though far less common, form of hydrogen called deuterium or heavy hydrogen. On the same basis as our model of the lighter hydrogen atom, an atom of deuterium can be illustrated thus:

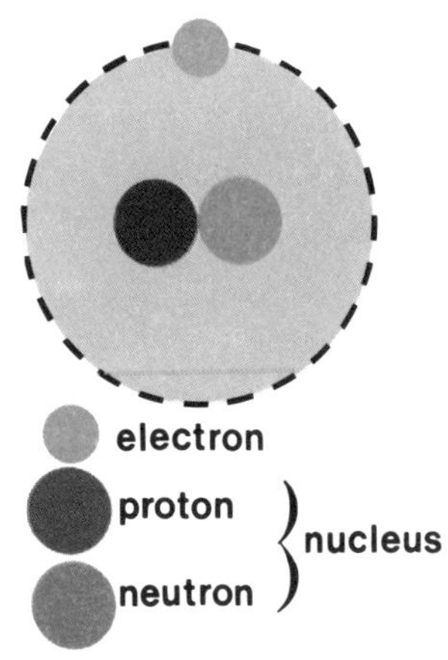

The **neutron** associated with the proton in the nucleus of a deuterium atom is a particle with a mass nearly as large as the proton but with no electrical charge. Because of this lack of electrical charge, the neutron does not alter the chemical properties of an element, but it does add to its mass and therefore its weight. Neutrons are present in at least one form of every one of the 105 elements. Elements are usually mixtures of these different forms of atoms, with or without neutrons. The different forms of an atom are called its **isotopes**.

In order to calculate **atomic weight**, an average of the weights of different isotopes must be taken, allowing for the proportions of each isotope normally contained in a quantity of the element. There is a complication in assessing atomic weight because the combination of neutrons and protons usually results in a loss of mass and the release of energy. It is this release of energy that provides the explosive power in a fusion or hydrogen bomb. In 1966, by international agreement, the carbon isotope which contains in its nucleus six protons and six neutrons, called carbon-12, was adopted as the standard and given an exact value of 12. All other weights, up and down the scale, are relative to the atomic weight of carbon-12, and these atomic weights are given in the table. To sum up the figures given in this table, the atomic numbers progress in whole numbers because each succeeding element contains one more proton than the previous element. The atomic weights, however, do not necessarily progress in this regular manner because some elements contain mixtures of isotopes which may have on average fewer neutrons than elements of a lower atomic number. For example, potassium (No. 19) has one more proton than argon (No. 18), but potassium contains more abundant isotopes with fewer neutrons, therefore its atomic weight is less than that of argon.

Electron Orbits

The electrons in an atom are not arranged haphazardly. They occupy specific orbits which are called **electron shells**. As successive atoms in the table of elements become heavier, extra electron shells are placed at successively greater distances from the nucleus. The first electron shell can hold no more than two electrons, but the second and third can hold up to eight electrons. An example of the structure of an element heavier than hydrogen is that of aluminium, which may be represented thus:

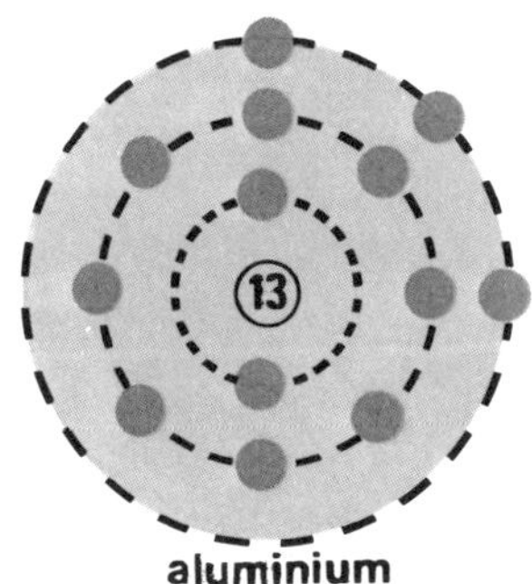

aluminium

The number written in the central nucleus in the diagram indicates the number of protons balancing the number of orbiting electrons and therefore the atomic number of the element. Other isotopes of each element will, of course, contain additional neutrons in the nucleus. The nucleus of a particular isotope is called its **nuclide**. Again, it must be emphasised that this diagram of an atom is not to scale and is a simplified model only. In elements with atomic numbers over twenty, the arrangement of electrons becomes more complicated. Third, fourth, fifth and sixth electron shells can contain more than eight electrons each, provided they are not the outermost shell. An example is uranium, the model of which looks like this:

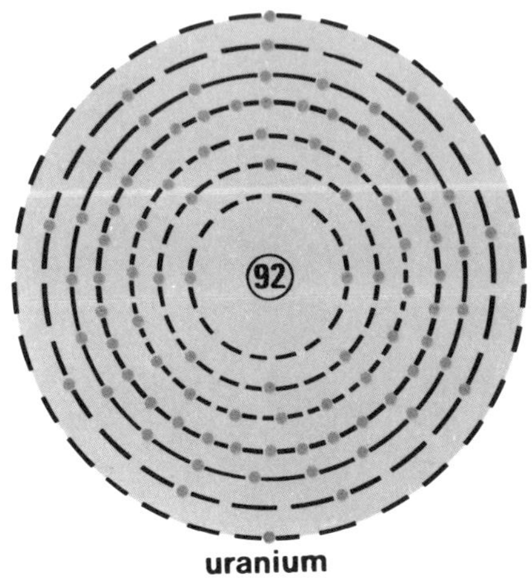

uranium

92 electrons in seven shells

92 protons as nucleus

The outer shells of these elements can accept more electrons before the inner shells are complete. In no case, however, can there be more than eight electrons in the outermost shell, and it is the number of electrons in this outer shell that gives the element its chemical properties.

All the elements are arranged by scientists into a **periodic table** of groups or families which share certain characteristics. All atoms with the same number of electrons in their outer shells exhibit similar chemical properties. The more complete the outer shell towards the full complement of eight electrons (as in neon and argon), or two in the case of helium, the more stable the atom. Thus helium, neon and argon, the so-called **inert gases**, are particularly stable, and only recently have compounds been produced which include them. Further on in the periodic table, the arrangement of groups is more complicated as atoms with incomplete inner shells introduce a number of sub-groups.

Atoms behave in such a way that they appear to be striving towards greater stability by adding electrons to the outer shell where the number falls short of eight. They try to find other atoms to give them or share with them enough electrons to complete their outer shell. Thus those with eight electrons already in their outer shells rarely combine, whereas those which have not form chemical compounds in two distinct ways.

The first is called the **electrovalent method of combination**. An example is the combination of the elements sodium and chlorine to produce the compound sodium chloride or common salt. The process can be illustrated like this:

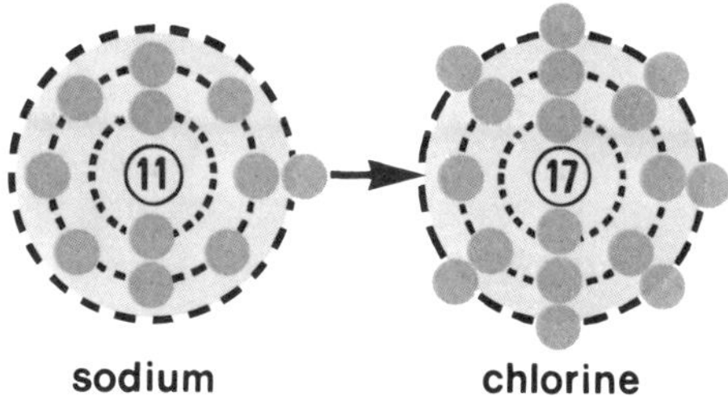

The single electron in the outer shell of the sodium atom moves across to complete the outer shell of the chlorine atom, increasing the number of atoms in its outer shell from seven to eight. But there is now one less negatively charged electron in the sodium atom to balance the eleven positively charged protons in its nucleus, so that the atom becomes charged with positive electricity. On the other hand, the chlorine atom has gained a negatively charged electron, thus making the atom as a whole electrically negative. These opposite charges attract each other, binding the atoms together so that they arrange themselves into the characteristic crystals of salt. Strictly speaking, they are no longer atoms and have become what are called **ions**. They break apart easily when dissolved in water and enable the solution to conduct electricity by the process known as **ionic conduction**. Thus water can become a good conductor of electricity by the addition of salt or by adding any other **electrovalent compound.**

Atomic Compounds

The second way in which atoms form compounds is called the **covalent method of combination**. In this case, electrons do not transfer from one atom to another, so there is no electric charge or ionisation produced. Electrons are simply shared between the two different atoms without leaving their original orbits. This can be illustrated by the combination of two atoms of hydrogen with one atom of oxygen to form the compound water. This combination can be illustrated like this:

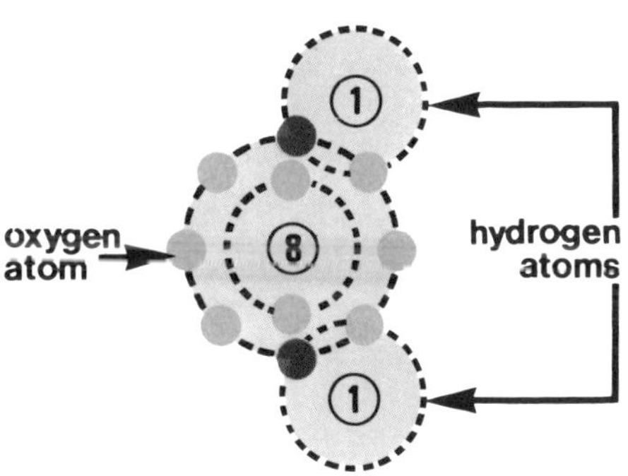

The hydrogen atoms have effectively completed their single shells with two electrons, while the oxygen atom has completed its outer shell with eight electrons. The result is a stable molecule of water. The diatomic molecules of hydrogen and oxygen are similarly formed by covalent combination, thus:

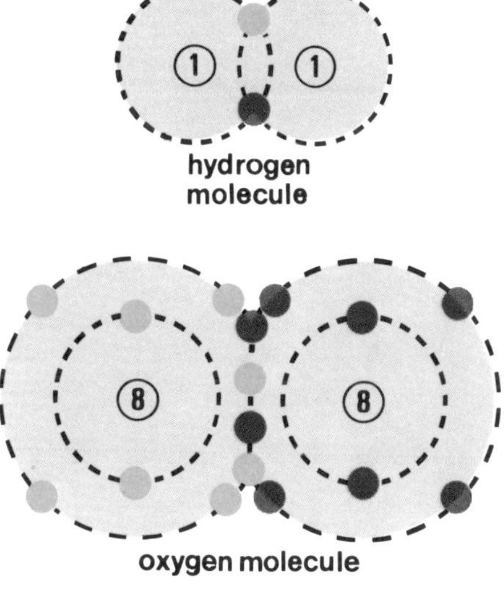

All the compounds found in the universe are formed by one or other of these two methods of combination or, in some cases, by both together. The number of atoms of a particular element that can combine with another atom is limited by the number of electrons in its outer shell. Hydrogen, with only one electron, can combine with only one other atom. Oxygen, with six electrons in the outer shell, can combine with two other atoms to complete the maximum of eight. The number of atoms of hydrogen with which a particular element can combine is called its **valency**. Since valency is dependent upon the number of electrons in the outer shell of an atom, it follows that all those elements with the same number of outer electrons have the same valency. There are, however, certain elements that can combine with others in more than one way, and these can have more than one valency.

Of the 105 elements listed in the table, those with atomic numbers from 93 upwards are produced only artificially in nuclear reactors or the laboratory. They are called **transuranic elements**. The heaviest naturally occurring elements are uranium, protactinium and thorium. Even in the natural state, these three have unstable nuclei. They are continually breaking down into other elements lower down in atomic number until they become the stable element lead (atomic number 82). This process of degeneration into lighter elements is due to the emission of radiant energy, and such elements are called radioactive. There are three distinct kinds of radiation called respectively **alpha**, **beta** and **gamma** from the first three letters of the Greek alphabet.

Radiation

Alpha radiation is caused by combinations of two protons and two electrons emitted from the radioactive nucleus in streams at high speeds. These combinations are called **alpha particles**. They slow down in the atmosphere after colliding with molecules in the air and collect orbital electrons as they do so, forming themselves into atoms of helium gas.

Beta radiation is caused by a process of transforming a neutron in the radioactive nucleus into a proton. This process is called **beta decay**, and the energy released is formed into an electron travelling at almost the speed of light.

Gamma radiation is caused by the disturbance of the radioactive nucleus as it emits alpha or beta particles. These gamma rays are very short wave X-rays and will be examined more fully in the section on radiant energy.

The radioactivity of the heaviest elements is not affected by temperature, pressure or chemical reaction and is a very slow and uncertain process. The time taken for half a given weight to be changed into a lighter element is called its **half-life**. In the case of uranium and thorium, the half-life is thousands of millions of years, which is why these elements still exist in nature. For the most common isotope of protactinium, the half-life is about 30,000 years, so this radioactive element is extremely rare.

The Three States of Matter

This chest of drawers is a solid object made up of atoms and molecules, the structure and temperature of which determine its solidity.

Matter also exists as a liquid when the molecular forces hold the particles loosely together so that they will fit themselves to the shape of a container, for example as water in a glass. Finally, matter may exist as a gas when it has 'boiled dry'.

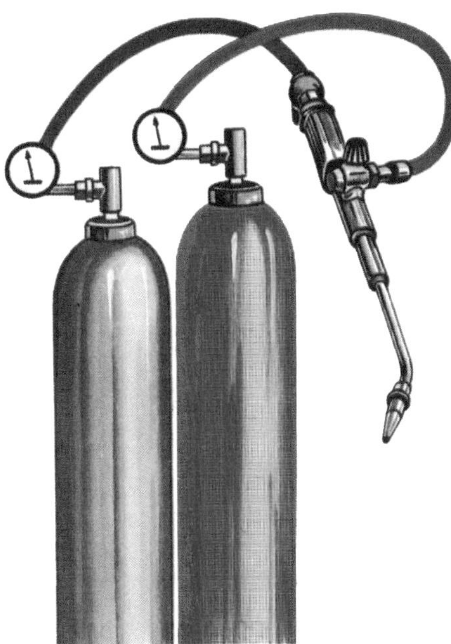

We have looked at the various particles which make up the structure of an atom and the methods of combination of atoms to form molecules. Now we must consider how atoms and molecules behave in association with each other. This brings us to the forms of matter we meet in our everyday lives. There are three physical states in which matter can exist: as solids, liquids or gases, and each state is dependent upon temperature.

A **solid** is a collection of atoms or molecules whose temperature has fallen below what is caled the **freezing-point** of that particular element or compound. In this state, the atoms or molecules have slowed down their movements relative to each other and become drawn so close together that elementary atoms or the atoms of which each molecule is composed arrange themselves into rigid patterns called **crystals**. In a crystal, each individual atom or molecule is still moving in relation to its neighbours, but it is vibrating about a fixed position. There is still considerable empty space between the atoms or molecules, but the limited movement permitted to them gives the crystal a framework called its **lattice**. Lattices can be based on squares, triangles, parallelograms, hexagons and other shapes which give each element or compound its internal structure. Solids usually break along the lines of their lattices. The forces that bind the components of a lattice give us three main types of crystals.

Electrovalent crystals do not really exist as atoms or molecules, but as ions held in a lattice structure by electrovalent forces. We have already seen how the electrovalent combination of sodium and chlorine produces negative and positive ions held together by the attraction of opposite electric charges. The structure of the crystal of salt (sodium chloride) thus formed can be illustrated like this:

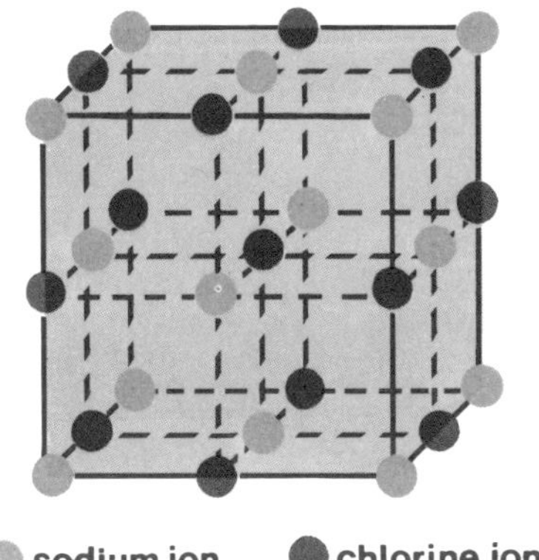

It must be remembered that the ions contained in this crystal are not stationary as shown, but vibrating about the positions they have been given. Apart from the simple cubic lattice of which salt is an example, there are two other cubic lattices, the **body-centred** with an additional ion at the centre of each cube, and the **face-centred** with an additional ion at the centre of each face of the cube. Altogether, there are fourteen different lattice systems occurring in nature.

Crystallisation

Electrovalent crystals can be much more complicated than the salt crystal. Copper sulphate ($CuSO_4$), for instance, contains one ion of copper and one of sulphur for every four of oxygen, together with five molecules of water, called the **water of crystallisation**. All crystals, however, have a repetitive lattice on a similar principle to the one shown. All electrovalent crystals dissolve in water, when the ions liberated from the lattice move freely about the solution and increase its conductivity of electricity.

Covalent crystals can be divided into two main types. The first has molecules as the basic units of its structure. The atoms are linked together into molecules by the covalent method of combination already explained. The molecules are brought together as the temperature falls, and their movements slow down. Between them are two electric forces, one attracting them together and operating over a limited distance, rather like the force of gravity, the other force which repels and operates within a much closer range. It is a kind of balance between these two forces which holds the molecules in their crystal lattice, though still vibrating about the positions they have taken up. Since these **molecular forces** are much weaker than electrovalent linkage of ions, covalent crystals of this type are softer and more easily fused. Most **organic compounds** form this kind of crystal.

Giant Molecules

The other kind of covalent crystal is that in which a giant molecule is itself the crystal. Since the atoms forming the giant molecule are linked by the strong covalent bond, such crystals are very hard and difficult to fuse. As an example, atoms of carbon can be bonded by covalent combination into a giant molecule that produces crystals called diamonds.

Snowflakes are formed by ice crystals and have six points.

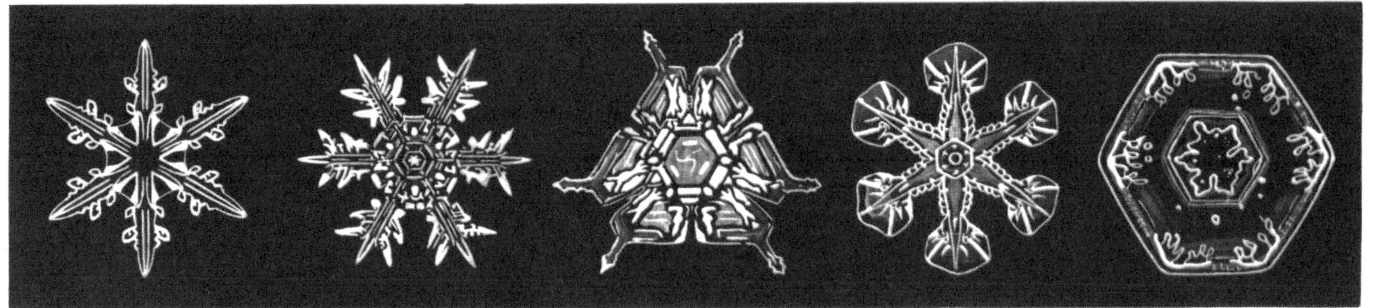

Metallic crystals are formed by the ionisation of elementary atoms which are then held together by forces similar to those between the molecules of a covalent crystal. Since all the ions in a metallic crystal carry a positive charge, they cannot be held together by either electrovalent or covalent combination. The electrons which have escaped from the outer shells of the elementary atoms can move about freely within the lattice, so the ions can be thought of as being suspended in a cloud of electrons. It is these free electrons which make metals good conductors of electricity. According to the strength of the bond between neighbouring ions, the metal is either soft or hard.

There are some substances, like glass and certain resins, that do not form crystals. They have no definite freezing-point, but become gradually more pliable when heated until they eventually assume all the properties of a liquid. Such substances are called **amorphous** and, in the solid state, are best described as **super-cooled liquids.**

Melting and Freezing

As heat is applied to a crystal, the ions or molecules within the lattice begin to vibrate with greater speed and through a greater distance. This increases the average distance between them, which accounts for the characteristic expansion of solids when heated. As the heat is increased, ions or molecules begin to move together out of position, sliding over each other. The substance is then said to have reached its **melting-point** (0°C in the case of ice changing to water). From the point of view of temperature, this is the same as the freezing-point. In the first instance, heat is increasing to raise the temperature and melt the substance. In the second, heat is diminishing to lower the temperature and freeze the substance. When the entire lattice has broken down with the application of heat, a substance is said to be a **liquid.**

In the liquid state, the so-called molecular forces still operate to hold the unit particles of the substance together, though it is now free to accommodate itself to the shape of its container. The molecular forces are produced by the attraction between the positively charged protons within the atomic nucleus and the negatively charged orbital electrons. There is still comparatively little space between neighbouring molecules, so that a

Fluorite

Pyrite

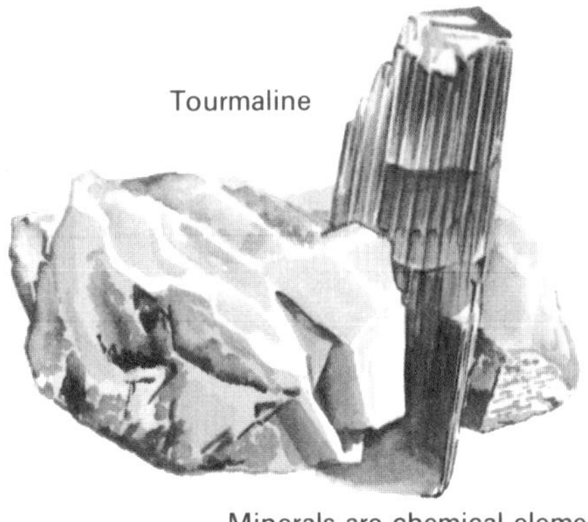
Tourmaline

Zinc-blende

Minerals are chemical elements or compounds which occur naturally in the earth. Some common forms are seen here.

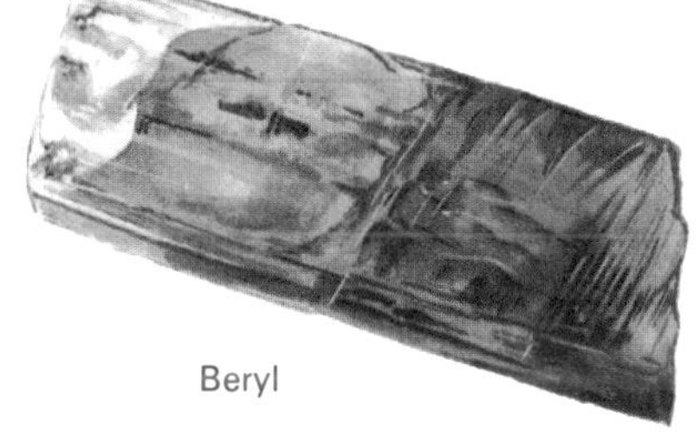
Beryl

Potassium Dichromate

All crystals belong to one of seven main shapes. They are named according to the properties of their sides and angles. From left to right are seen cubic, tetragonal, rhombic, monoclinic, triclinic, trigonal and hexagonal.

A volcano is formed by a vent in the earth through which hot gases and molten or solid rock are erupted. Icebergs are large masses broken off from glaciers or shelf ice.

liquid can be compressed only slightly.

Some of the molecules in a liquid are moving so fast that they break away from the molecular forces and escape into the atmosphere. This process is called evaporation. These faster-moving molecules contain more energy than the others, so their escape reduces the average energy of those that remain. Hence, evaporation results in a cooling of the liquid. For a particular liquid at a fixed temperature, the average number of escaping molecules is always the same. The pressure exerted by these escaping molecules is called the **vapour pressure**.

If more heat is applied to the liquid, more and more molecules escape until the surface begins to bubble violently. This is called the boiling-point. Eventually, as more heat is applied, all the molecules move at such a speed that the molecular forces holding them together are completely overcome. The liquid has 'boiled dry' and become converted into a **gas**.

Activity of Gases

In the gaseous state, molecules collide frequently, but with such speeds that the contact is very brief. They bounce off each other, continually changing direction in a random fashion with each collision. The greater the temperature, the faster the molecular movement and the greater the force and number of collisions. In a container, the molecules collide also with its walls, the speed and frequency of these collisions giving the gas the measure of its **pressure**. Because the molecules of a gas are so far apart, outside pressure can be applied to force them closer together and reduce the total volume of the gas. As this increases the frequency of collisions, so the pressure exerted by the gas on the walls of its container increases.

Whatever the chemical composition of a gas, the number of molecules in a given volume at constant temperature and pressure is always the same. At the same pressure as the atmosphere at sea-level and at a temperature of 0°C, in one cubic centimetre of any gas there will be about twenty-seven million, million, million molecules, each of which will collide with another about five thousand million times every second. The molecules of the various gases in the atmosphere are continually colliding with everything on the earth's surface, thus exerting pressure on every surface. At sea-level, this **atmospheric pressure** is about fifteen pounds per square inch.

By reducing the temperature and therefore slowing down the movement of molecules, all gases will eventually become liquids and finally solids. Steam, for instance, becomes water below 100°C and ice below 0°C. Some gases liquefy at only very low temperatures: oxygen for example at −183°C and nitrogen at −195°C. The inert gases change their physical state at even lower temperatures: neon becomes liquid at −245·9°C and solid at −248·7°C. Not all solids become liquids nor all liquids gases, however, because some compounds decompose into their separate elements or oxidise in heated air before their melting or boiling-points can be reached.

It has been said that reducing the temperature of any substance reduces the movement of the atoms or molecules of which it is composed. However, there is a limit to this. If all movement were to cease, it would mean that the atom or molecule would contain no more energy and, without energy, matter cannot exist. This would happen for all matter at the temperature of −273·15°C which is therefore called the **absolute zero of temperature**. Since matter cannot exist at this low temperature, it cannot be reached, though it has been possible to come within less than one degree of absolute zero in the laboratory.

Diamonds, like all minerals have lines of cleavage along which they break. When a diamond is cut great care is needed to follow the natural lines of the grain.

Inorganic Matter

It is convenient to divide all matter between the compounds of the element carbon with which all living things are associated, involving the study of **organic chemistry**, and the compounds of all the other elements which comprise the study of **inorganic chemistry**. Of course, atoms of carbon can be involved in non-living matter, but the differences between the organic and the inorganic will become apparent in this and the next section.

Chemical compounds often include more than two elements. Molecules of such compounds usually contain groups of atoms which maintain their identity through chemical changes that affect only the rest of the molecule. These groups of atoms are called **radicals**. A radical is most often a covalent combination between oxygen and certain other elements and is usually not capable of an independent existence. The most common radicals and their formulas are: Carbonate (CO_3), Hydroxide (OH), Nitrate (NO_3), Nitrite (NO_2), Phosphate (PO_4), Sulphate (SO_4), Sulphite (SO_3). All compounds produced by the electrovalent combination of a radical with an element, when dissolved in water, split up into the ions of the radical and the element. All such compounds are either an **acid**, a **base** or a **salt**.

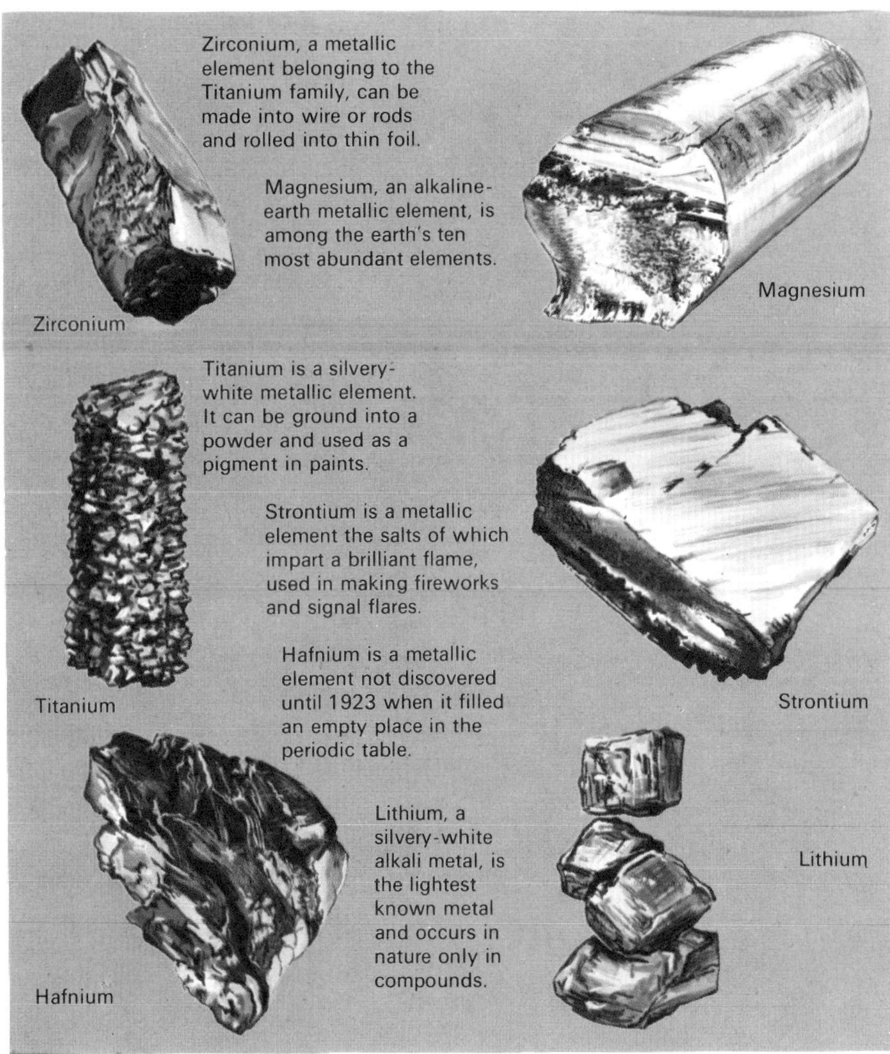

Common Acids

Acids are formed when hydrogen is electrovalently combined with almost any radical, or with atoms of some elements. The three most common acids are sulphuric (H_2SO_4), nitric (HNO_3) and hydrochloric (HCl). Dissolved in water, they form positive hydrogen ions and negative ions of the sulphate or nitrate radicals, or of the chlorine atom, respectively. Metal atoms will very easily replace the hydrogen atoms in most acids, which makes acids very corrosive of metals.

Alkali Metals

Bases are formed as **alkalis** which are electrovalent combinations of the hydroxide radical (OH) with most metals, particularly the so-called **alkali metals**: lithium (Li), sodium (Na), potassium (K), rubidium (Rb), and caesium (Ca). Typical alkalis are caustic soda (sodium hydroxide: NaOH), caustic potash (potassium hydroxide: KOH) and slaked lime (calcium hydroxide: $Ca(OH)_2$). Dissolved in water, these produce negative **hydroxyl** ions and positive ions of

Some elements were identified by alchemists. Joseph Wright, an English artist, painted a scene in 1771, on which this drawing is based, of a German alchemist who is believed to have discovered phosphorous.

the alkali metals. There are some **oxides** which are also included in the term base, which can be defined as any compound that neutralises an acid to produce a salt.

Common Salt

Salts are the electrovalent combinations formed by the neutralisation of an acid with a base. For example, sodium hydroxide (NaOH) neutralises hydrochloric acid (HCl) to produce common salt (NaCl) and water (H_2O). The equation for this chemical reaction is written like this: $NaOH+HCl = NaCl+H_2O$. Water is always produced with the formation of a salt because the negative hydroxyl ions from the base combine with the positive hydrogen ions from the acid. Thus the rule connecting acids, bases and salts can be written: **base + acid = salt + water**.

Oxygen is a very reactive element. As well as combining with certain elements to form radicals, it also combines with almost all elements to produce compounds called **oxides**. We have seen that some oxides act as bases

Two of the most important materials in the construction of aircraft and space vehicles are titanium and aluminium. On the left are capsules for Mercury and Gemini spacecraft and below samples of titanium and bauxite, a clay compound containing aluminium.

in neutralising acids to form salts. These are called **basic oxides**. They are always compounds of oxygen and metals, a fact that is used to define a metal. When dissolved in water, they form hydroxides which are alkalis. For example, sodium oxide (Na_2O) dissolved in water produces sodium hydroxide ($NaOH$).

Oxidation

Other oxides react with bases to form salts. These are called **acidic oxides**. They are compounds of oxygen and non-metals. For example, carbon dioxide (CO_2) reacts with sodium hydroxide to produce the salt sodium carbonate (Na_2CO_3).

There are some oxides of metals which can behave as both bases and acids, according to circumstances. These are called **amphoteric oxides**. An example is aluminium oxide (Al_2O_3). With hydrochloric acid it behaves as a base producing aluminium chloride ($AlCl_3$). With sodium hydroxide its behaviour is that of an acid producing sodium aluminate ($NaAlO_2$).

Chemically, the term **oxidation** is used not only when oxygen is added to a substance, but also when hydrogen is taken away from it. Conversely, the removal of oxygen or the addition of hydrogen is called **reduction**.

Chemical Properties

Each succeeding atom in the periodic table has an extra electron. This continues throughout the table of elements. Periodically, an extra electron shell is added to accommodate the increasing number of orbital electrons. The heaviest, naturally-occurring atoms have seven electron shells in all. It is the number of electrons in the **outermost** shell which determines the chemical properties of any particular element. Elements with a single electron in the outer shell are able to release it easily in electrovalent combination. This makes them into positively charged ions, so such elements are described as being strongly **electropositive**. Elements with seven electrons in the outer shell are able to accept readily an eighth to complete that shell, thus becoming negatively charged ions. Such elements are described as being strongly **electronegative**. Elements midway between these two extremes, carbon and silicon for instance, each with four electrons in their outer shells, neither release nor accept electrons readily. Such elements form covalent compounds.

The most electropositive elements,

Iron is the cheapest of all metals and occurs in pure form in nature. It was the principal material used in bridge-building in the 19th century.

those with one electron in their outer shells, are called the **alkali metals.** The most electronegative elements, those with seven electrons in their outer shells, are called the **halogens**. An alkali metal readily forms an electrovalent combination with a halogen as we have seen in the case of the alkali metal sodium (Na) and the halogen chlorine (Cl) combining to form sodium chloride or common salt (NaCl). The other alkali metals are lithium (Li), potassium (K), rubidium (Rb) and caesium (Ca). The other halogens are fluorine (F), bromine (Br), iodine (I) and astatine (At), though the last-named has no stable isotopes.

Neon is a gaseous element which, contained in a tube, produces light when an electric current is passed through it.

Progression of Elements

As the atoms get larger in the higher atomic numbers of the elements, extra electrons can be added to **inner** shells. Where this happens, they are called the **transition elements**, and all of them are metals. Those between atomic numbers 21 and 30 (scandium to zinc) all have two electrons in the outer or fourth shell, but progress from nine to eighteen electrons in their third shells. Elements between atomic numbers 39 and 48 (yttrium to cadmium) have two electrons in their outer or fifth shells and progress from nine to eighteen in the fourth shell. Elements with the atomic numbers 57 to 71 (lanthanum to lutetium) are called the **rare earths** or **lanthanides**. They all have nine electrons in their fifth shells and two in their sixth or outer shells, but progress from eighteen to 32 electrons in their fourth shells. Atomic numbers 72 to 80 (hafnium to mercury) have 32 electrons in their fourth shells and two in their sixth or outer shells, but progress from ten to eighteen in their fifth shells.

Finally, atomic numbers from 89 to 103 have nine electrons in their sixth shells have two in their seventh or outer shells, but progress from eighteen to 32 in their fifth shells. This last group is called the **actinides**. Of these, only the first six, francium to uranium, have sufficiently stable isotopes to occur in nature. The remainder, called the **transuranic elements**, can be formed only artificially by nuclear reaction and are very unstable with extremely short half-lives. The last two elements in the table, rutherfordium and hahnium (atomic numbers 104 and 105) are the recent results of fusion experiments and need not concern us here.

The actinides are important for their radioactive properties. The lanthanides are all extremely rare. All the transition metals display similar chemical properties because of the two electrons in their outer shells. Electrons can, however, move from the penultimate to the outer shell of a transition metal.

The Importance of Iron

The most important transition metal is iron (Fe), without which our modern civilisation could never have developed. With the next two transition metals in the table of elements, cobalt (Co) and nickel (Ni), iron shares the property of being magnetic. Iron is readily oxidised and therefore occurs mainly in the oxide ores haematite (Fe_2O_3) and magnetite (Fe_3O_4) from which the pure metal is obtained in blast furnaces. A small quantity of carbon converts iron into steel which is given special properties of hardness, heat resistance or anti-corrosion by the addition of other transition metals such as titanium (Ti), zirconium (Zr), vanadium (V), niobium (Nb), tantalum (Ta), chromium (Cr), molybdenum (Mo), tungsten (W) and manganese (Mn). The transition metal mercury (Hg) is unique as the only metal that is a liquid at normal temperatures and pressures. Zinc (Zn) is a metal extensively used in alloys such as brass. Copper (Cu), silver (Ag) and gold (Au) are known as the **noble** or **coinage** metals and occur in the pure form in nature, since they are not very reactive. They form compounds only when electrons from their penultimate shells migrate to the outer shell.

Of the elements that are not transition metals, we have already looked at the alkali metals. Almost as electropositive are the **alkaline earths**: magnesium (Mg), calcium (Ca), strontium (Sr), barium (Ba) and radium (Ra). They are found in nature in the combined state, magnesium and calcium being the most common. Magnesium carbonate ($MgCO_3$) is

Gold

Silver

Copper

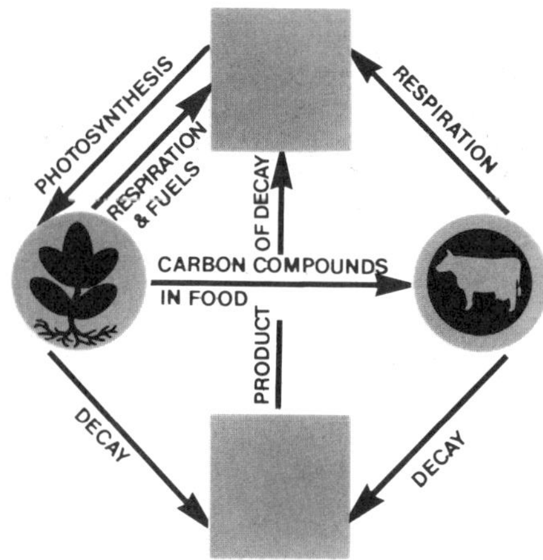

Diagram of the carbon cycle.

known as dolomite, and magnesium sulphate ($MgSO_4$) as Epsom salts. Calcium carbonate ($CaCO_3$) is widely distributed as chalk, and calcium sulphate ($CaSO_4$) occurs throughout the earth's crust. Depending upon the number of molecules of the water of crystallisation, it is known as gypsum, alabaster or plaster of Paris. Radium is important for its radioactive properties.

The elements with three electrons in their outer shells are all extremely rare except for aluminium (Al), the third most common element on earth. Being a fairly reactive metal, it occurs naturally as aluminium oxide (Al_2O_3), known as bauxite.

Forms of Carbon

Carbon is important because it combines with oxygen. This is the basis of combustion from which most of the energy on which our civilisation depends is released. Coal, oil and natural gas, the so-called **fossil fuels**, are mostly carbon. Carbon monoxide (CO) and carbon dioxide (CO_2) are the gases given off when they are burned. Upon carbon dioxide, which comprises a mere 0·03% of the earth's atmosphere, all life depends. From it, plants obtain the carbon they need by the process called **photosynthesis**. Since animals depend on plants (or upon plant-eating animals) for food, every living thing is ultimately dependent upon that small percentage of carbon dioxide in the atmosphere. It is returned to the atmosphere partly by respiration and partly by the decomposition of dead plants and animals. Over the ages, some of the decomposition has taken place underground in the absence of oxygen. This has formed the earth's store of fossil fuels which, when burned by man, return carbon dioxide to the atmosphere, thus helping to maintain the balance. Some atmospheric carbon dioxide is absorbed in sea water and converted into the shells of aquatic creatures in the form of calcium carbonate ($CaCO_3$). This **carbon cycle** is illustrated here.

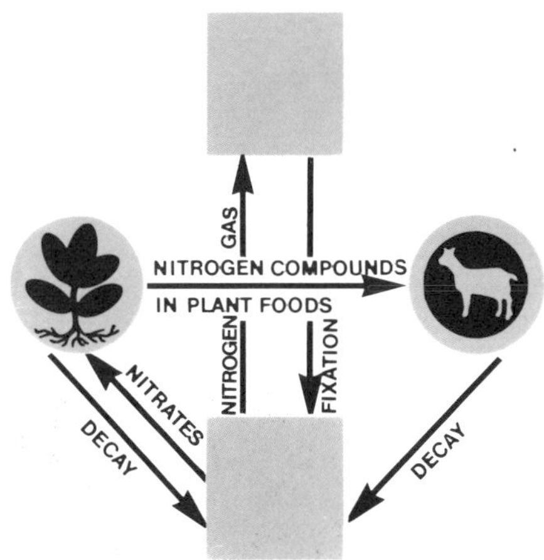

Diagram of the nitrogen cycle.

Action of Nitrogen

Nitrogen is also important to living matter. Nitrates (the radical NO_3) and salts of ammonia (NH_3) return to the soil from the excretions of animals and the decay of plant and animal bodies. Bacteria in the soil convert such waste matter into the nitrates and free nitrogen which returns to the atmosphere. Some atmospheric nitrogen is converted into ammonium nitrate (NH_4NO_3) by the action of lightning and washed back into the soil by rain. Some bacteria can convert atmospheric nitrogen into foods for the plants they live on. Ammonia is able to collect extra hydrogen ions to form the positive ammonium ions NH_4 which combine electrovalently with various radicals to form the fertilisers used by man to replenish cultivated soil. The **nitrogen cycle** is illustrated here.

Finally, oxygen has an obvious importance. The most common element on earth, it comprises nearly a quarter of the atmosphere and occurs in many compounds. Water contains about 90% by weight of oxygen; the remaining 10% being hydrogen, which is present in very many inorganic compounds and nearly all the organic ones.

Open hearth furnace changing molten iron into steel.

Organic Matter

Because carbon has a valency of four, it can combine with itself and with other elements in a continuous series to create very large molecules. Without this ability of carbon to form the basis of large molecules, life itself would not have been possible, for all living matter is made up of giant molecules. When we eat, we absorb giant protein molecules which our bodies break up and reassemble into other giant molecules to sustain the various parts of our bodies. We have learned to create giant molecules in the laboratory and in industry to substitute for the once-living matter we used in our everyday life. Thus man-made **polymers**, as the chains of molecules are called, have been created to replace such materials as silk and wool, leather and rubber, wood and vegetable fibres. These new synthetic materials are all derived from coal, oil or other fossil, animal and vegetable products so these, as well as naturally formed carbon compounds, are all contained in the study of organic chemistry.

Organic matter can be divided into two kinds: straight-chain molecules and ring-shaped molecules. Straight-chain molecules form the **aliphatic compounds**, so called from the Greek word for fat. All the aliphatic compounds are based on covalent bonds of shared electrons between the atoms but, depending on the number of bonds, there are three types.

The **paraffins** or **alkanes** have atoms linked by single covalent bonds. The simplest compound in the paraffin series is methane (CH_4), commonly called marsh gas. The structure of the molecule can be illustrated like this:

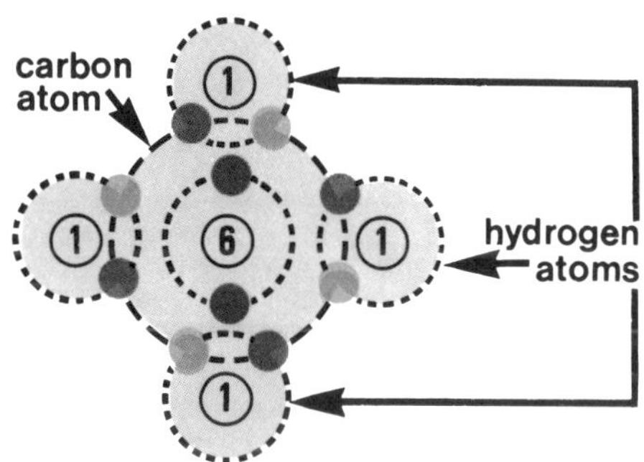

It is more usual to represent the covalent pair of shared electrons by a single short line, so the methane molecule is written like this:

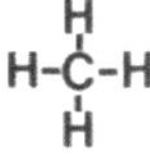

Carbon exists in several forms: in soot, diamonds and graphite (used in lead pencils). Coal and wood produce carbon as coke and charcoal.

A whole series of paraffin molecules develop from methane, each one replacing one of the hydrogen atoms with an extra carbon atom. After methane, the next in the series is called ethane (C_2H_6). Each member of the series is called a **homologue**. The third homologue, propane (C_3H_8), has three carbon atoms.

With each homologue in the series, the molecule becomes larger and heavier so that the longer chains become liquids and those larger still, solids. At normal temperatures and pressures, methane, ethane, propane and butane are gases. Pentane, hexane, heptane and octane are liquids. Hexadecane, with sixteen carbon atoms in the chain, is a solid. Natural gas, now extensively used in cookers, consists of 85% methane, the remainder being made up of ethane, propane and butane. Petrol, after refining, is mostly pentane, hexane and octane.

From the fourth homologue onwards in this series, there are other forms the molecules can take. Different forms of the same compound are called **isomers**, and such a compound is known as **isomeric**. As one would expect, homologues with larger molecules can have a greater number of possible isomers.

Paraffin Series

In the paraffin series, hydrogen atoms can often be replaced by atoms of the halogens, those elements with seven electrons in their outer shells. Chlorine can replace the hydrogen in methane, creating a new group of compounds called chloromethane, dichloromethane, chloroform and carbon tetrachloride.

The **olefins** or **alkenes** are the second type of aliphatic compounds, based on a double bond between the carbon atoms. The first homologue, called ethylene, has two carbon atoms and four hydrogen atoms. The subsequent homologues can have double bonds separated by single bonds, or by two or more single bonds. Butadiene, the basis of synthetic rubber, has the former of the two, called a **conjugated double bond**.

Olefins, like the paraffins, can substitute halogen atoms for the hydrogen atoms. If one of the hydrogen atoms is replaced by a chlorine atom in ethylene, the result is vinyl chloride. The double bond allows single molecules to be linked in a long chain, a process called **polymerisation**, resulting in this case in the **polymer** called polyvinyl chloride or PVC. Before the molecules are linked to form a polymer, the substance is called a **monomer**.

The **acetylenes** or **alkines** are the third type of aliphatic compounds. Here there is a triple bond between two carbon atoms. Acetylene is the first in the series and the only one of importance. It is a gas which burns in oxygen with a very hot flame and is used for welding metals.

Alcohols

If hydrogen atoms are replaced by the hydroxyl group, the resulting compound is called an **alcohol**. A typical alcohol, derived from propane, with three hydrogen atoms replaced by hydroxyl groups, is called glycerol, or glycerine.

If an alcohol reacts with an inorganic acid, an **inorganic ester** is produced. Glycerol reacting with nitric acid produces nitroglycerine, the explosive used in dynamite.

Under certain conditions, water can be removed with a reaction between two molecules of alcohol called a **condensation reaction**, and the result is an ether. Diethyl ether is the one commonly used as an anaesthetic.

Alcohols that are oxidised result in **fatty acids**. An olefin alcohol produces acrylic acid which is used in plastics.

A fatty acid reacting with an alcohol produces an **organic ester** such as ethyl acetate, used in industry as a solvent. Animal and vegetable fats are esters.

An alcohol with certain hydrogen atoms removed becomes an **aldehyde**. Formaldehyde is used as a disinfectant and for preserving medical specimens.

Similar to aldehydes is the series called **ketones** of which acetone, a popular solvent, is best known.

The sport of ballooning has again become popular in modern times, using colourful balloons made of light-weight nylon.

The search for new materials began at the end of the 19th century, often stimulated by chance discoveries. The vast range of man-made synthetics is represented here by just a few of the objects in everyday use.

Alcohols reacting with ammonia gas produce **amines** and water. A typical amine is methylamine used as a refrigerant.

Coal Tar Products

The main group of ring-shaped or **cyclic compounds** is composed of those called the **aromatics**. If acetylene gas is passed through a red-hot tube, a ring compound with six carbon atoms with alternate single and double bonds is formed. This is called benzene. Benzene is one of the constituents of coal tar, a by-product of the extraction of coal-gas from coal. By substituting groups of atoms for one or more of the hydrogen atoms in the benzene ring, various useful products can be created. For instance, toluene is produced by substituting a methyl group for one of the hydrogen atoms. Treated with nitric acid, toluene forms trinitrotoluene or TNT, the well-known explosive. Similarly, substituting the amine group produces aniline, the basis of dyes and drugs. Phenol, an extensively used antiseptic, is formed with the substitution of a hydroxyl group. A carboxyl group added to phenol produces salicylic acid, the basis of aspirin. Naphthalene is formed by joining two benzene rings together. Naphthalene is used in mothballs. In exactly the same way as benzene it forms many useful compounds, particularly for the dyeing industry.

From the by-products of coal-gas and oil-refining industries, synthetic resins are manufactured, the familiar and common plastics of our modern era. They are substances without a definite structure which are easily shaped in high-pressure heated moulding presses. Those that set solid under heat and never regain their plasticity are called **thermosetting resins**. Those that can be remoulded after heating again are called **thermoplastic resins**.

Synthetic Plastics

In 1907, the Belgian-American Leo Baekeland developed the first synthetic plastic which was called Bakelite. The first stage in its manufacture is the condensation of phenol and formaldehyde molecules into long chains, with the release of water. The phenol molecules are only part of what becomes a number of very long chains forming a resinous liquid. As the liquid sets into a solid, cross-linkages are formed between the chains. These linkages occur in three dimensions so that a honeycomb is built up. The chemical linkages between chains of molecules are what gives a thermosetting resin its strength and resistance to heat. Thermoplastic resins, on the other hand, are linked between chains only by molecular forces which break up under the action of heat, allowing the resin to revert to a liquid for remoulding.

Similar to the phenol-formaldehyde resins like Bakelite are the **aminoplastics** made from urea and formaldehyde, which are light-coloured and suitable for such things as plastic cups, unlike the dark-coloured phenol-formaldehydes. A recently developed group of thermosetting resins are those used for bonding glass fibres in fibreglass, in lacquers and in adhesives such as Araldite. They are called **epoxy resins** and are formed from the condensation of chloroepoxy propane with phenols and glycols.

Explosives are used in demolition of a factory chimney.

Thermoplastics

Thermoplastic resins have their chains of molecules linked only by molecular forces which break up when the substance is heated, returning it to its plastic state. The first of these to be developed was celluloid which, like more modern resins derived from it, was based on naturally occurring cellulose obtained mainly from the cotton plant. Celluloid is highly inflammable, but this disadvantage was overcome in the more modern cellulose acetate from which the form of artificial silk called rayon is made.

The polystyrenes and polyvinyls are important thermoplastic resins. Styrene can be made to polymerise to form long-chain molecules with a transparent, glass-like appearance. It is used in the radio and electrical industries. The most common vinyl resins are polyvinyl chloride (PVC) and polyvinyl acetate (PVA). Molecules of these two can be made to polymerise together into what is called a **co-polymer**.

Polyethylene, commonly called polythene, is a flexible resin used in packaging and, in a high density form, for containers and tableware. Polypropylene is somewhat tougher and is used as a substitute for jute in the manufacture of strong sacking.

Silicon is a chemical element of the carbon family from which water-repellent silicones are made for treating fabrics and paper.

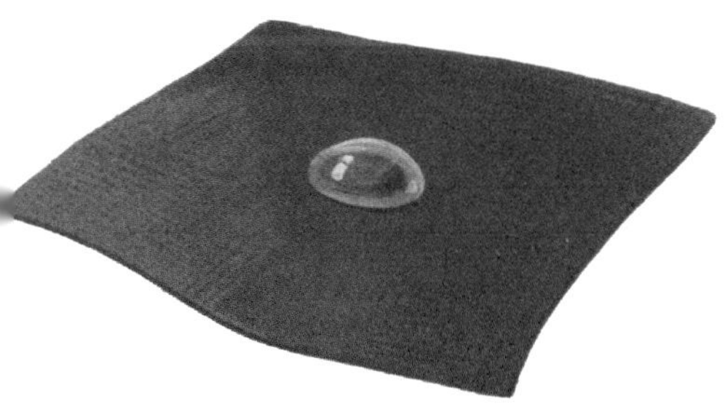

The strength of the bond between fluorine and carbon gives the very stable group known as **fluorocarbons.** Prominent among these is polytetrafluoroethylene, known commercially as Teflon. By altering the chemistry of the molecule, this thermoplastic has been made virtually thermosetting, so that it has become very resistant to heat. Thus it can be used for coating non-stick cooking vessels.

Synthetic Fibres

Other groups of thermoplastics include the acrylics, known variously as Perspex, Plexiglas, and Lucite. They have optical properties useful in the moulding of cheap lenses. The synthetic fibres known as Orlon, Acrilan and Creslan are made from polyacrylonitrile.

Fatty acids condensed with amides form a group called the **super polyamides** among which is nylon. Although produced by the same process as thermosetting resins, this group behaves like thermoplastics. Casein has properties falling between the thermosetting and the thermoplastic. Up to the stage when it is moulded into shape, it is thermoplastic. Then, by the action of formaldehyde, it is hardened into a thermosetting compound. It is used for such things as buttons and knife handles.

Lastly, there should be mentioned the group of plastics that contain no carbon, but have the element silicon in its place. Having similar properties to carbon, silicon can also form the basis of long-chain molecules. The resins formed from them are called **silicones** and are highly water repellent and heat resistant. They are commonly used in varnishes and lubricants.

Living Matter

The study of the chemical reactions involved in living matter is called **biochemistry**. In general, matter may be said to be living when it is capable of reproducing itself and when it controls its own reactions to that end. The smallest unit of living matter is called a **cell** and the total matter from which it is constructed, the **protoplasm**. Inanimate matter contains either a few atoms joined into molecules, or chains of very many atoms made into simple structures which are repeated again and again. Protoplasm, on the other hand, consists of large numbers of atoms arranged in a particular order which does not repeat itself. The simplest form of life is the single cell, endlessly reproducing itself by division. More complex forms of life, such as animals, and including humans, consist of many different kinds of cells, each constructed to perform a particular function. Growth is achieved by the multiplication of these cells.

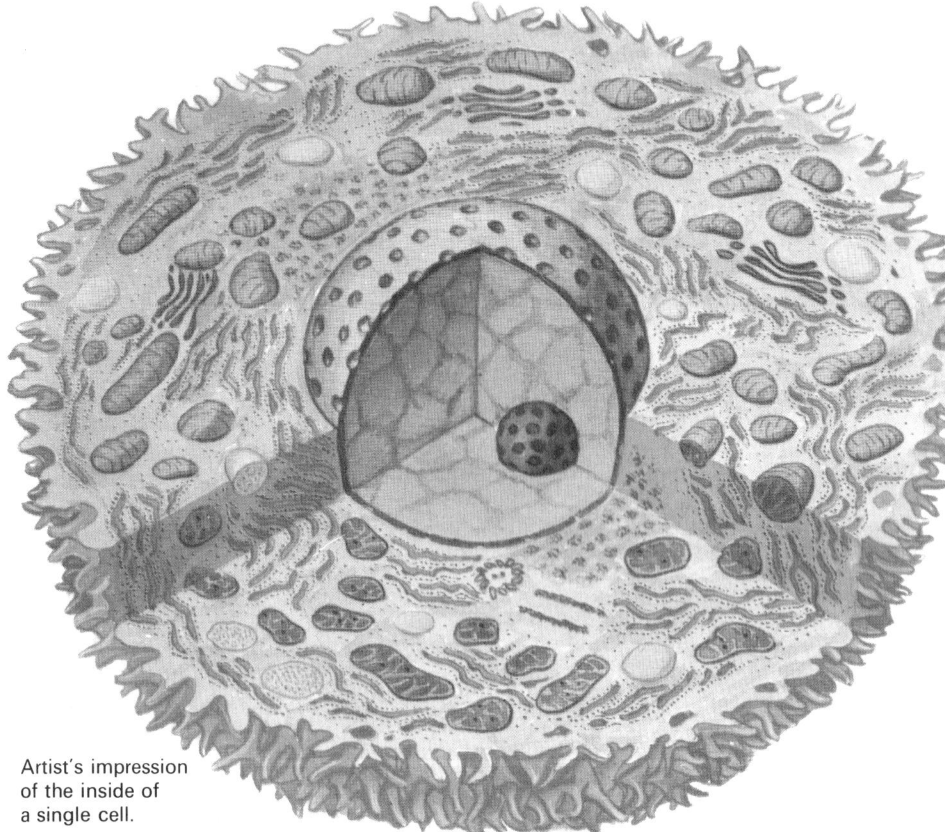

Artist's impression of the inside of a single cell.

Living Cells

A living cell consists of an outer wall containing the two distinct parts of the protoplasm, the central **nucleus** and its surrounding **cytoplasm**. When the cell is not engaged in reproducing itself, these two parts are separated by a thin skin or membrane. The nucleus of a cell must not be confused with that of an atom. The nucleus of a cell is the part that controls its reproduction. As the process begins, a number of distinct bodies called the **chromosomes** appear within the nucleus. The number of these chromosomes depends upon the species to which the cell belongs—46 in the case of human cells. Each chromosome consists of two identical filaments called **chromatids**. As the chromosomes contract and thicken, the membrane around the nucleus disappears. A spindle-like structure forms and the chromosomes arrange themselves in the middle of it. Then the chromatids of each chromosome separate and move to the opposite ends of the spindle, so that each end has an identical set. The spindle disappears, and two new membranes begin to develop, one around each set of chromatids. The cytoplasm divides into two approximately equal parts, each half surrounding one of the two new nuclei. The old cell thus divides into two new ones, the chromosomes in each nucleus fading as the cells eventually return to the resting stage.

Each separate characteristic of a particular cell is controlled by a part of the chromosome called a **gene**. By an exact replication of the genes of a chromosome in each chromatid, the characteristics of a particular cell are passed on to the two new ones. The reproduction process is called **mitosis**. During the resting stage, the cell is converting its food supply into the materials required for its construction and into the energy needed to maintain the necessary biochemical reactions. This process is called the cell's **metabolism**.

Reaction of Enzymes

Biochemical reactions taking place within a cell depend to a great extent upon **enzymes**. They cannot make a reaction take place that would not do so without them, but they speed the reactions between the other molecules, called the **substrates**. The enzymes themselves are not broken up or consumed by these reactions, but do sometimes form loose bonds with the substrates. The effect of an enzyme depends upon the shape and size of its molecule and also upon its so-called 'active centres' which come into contact with the particular substrate molecules they affect. All enzymes belong to complicated organic compounds based on nitrogen which are called **proteins**. An enzyme is always a protein, but not all proteins are enzymes.

Importance of Proteins

Proteins are made up from various combinations of **amino acids** of which some twenty different kinds are found in nature. For example, **insulin** is a protein composed of four different chains of molecules, two containing 30 amino acid molecules and two containing 21 amino acid molecules. The chains are cross-linked to each other by the sulphur atoms in one of the amino acids called **cystine**. Some protein chains are wound into a spiral pattern called a **helix**. Hair, horn and muscle have this spiral form, the turns of the helix held in position by hydrogen bonds. These bonds break when hair, for instance, is stretched and the spiral is straightened. Other

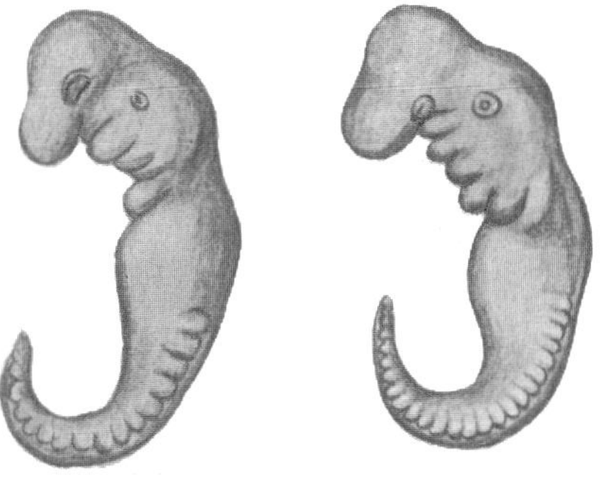

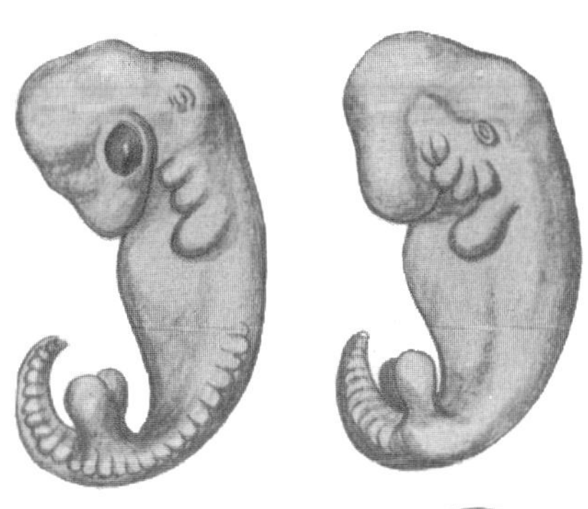

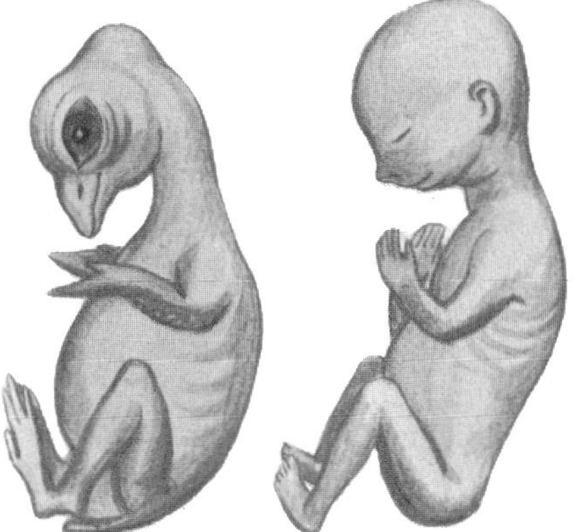

Development in the earliest stages of the embryos of a chick (left) and a human (right).

The process of mitosis, or cell division.

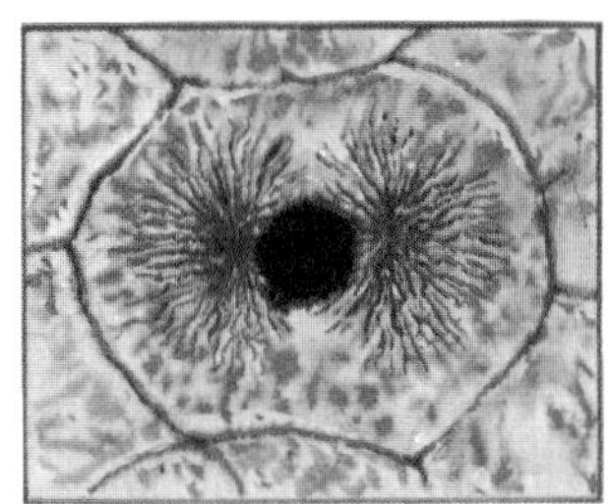

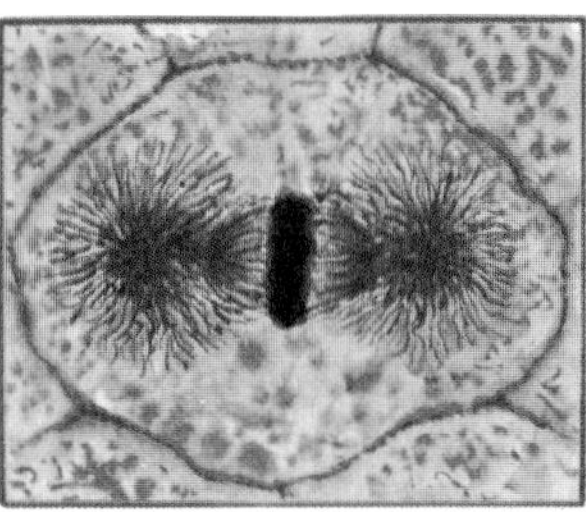

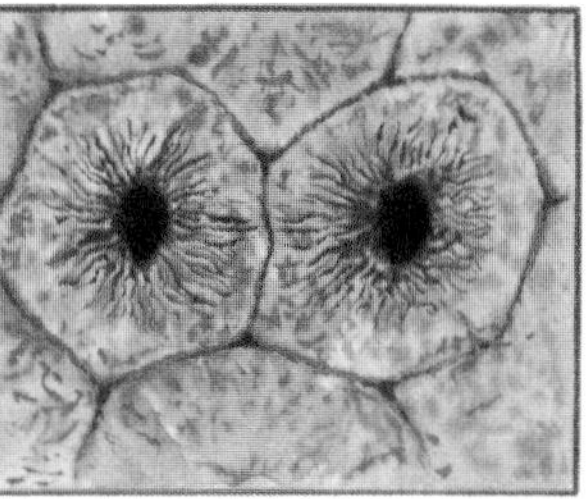

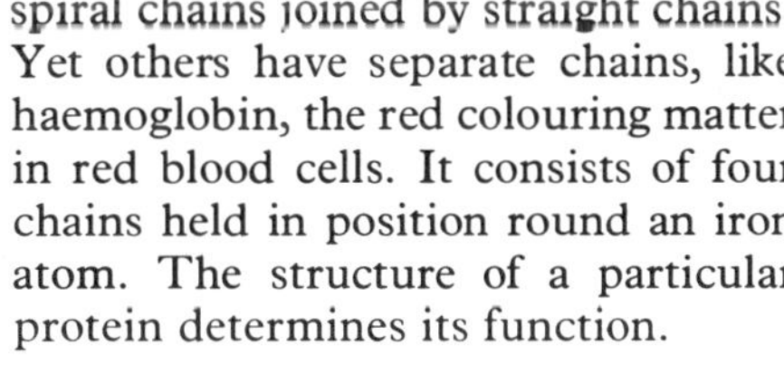

proteins, such as myoglobin, have spiral chains joined by straight chains. Yet others have separate chains, like haemoglobin, the red colouring matter in red blood cells. It consists of four chains held in position round an iron atom. The structure of a particular protein determines its function.

Cell Metabolism

Proteins are one of three types of organic compound required as foods to maintain the metabolism of a cell. The other two are **carbohydrates** and **fats**. Carbohydrates consist of the sugars such as **ribose**, **glucose** and **sucrose**, this last being the one found in sugar-cane and sugar-beet; and also of the **starches** and **cellulose**. Plants store starches in their tubers and seeds, so human beings obtain their supplies by eating such root vegetables as potato and grains such as rice.

Cellulose, to be found only in plant cells, is strongly resistant to chemical change and is used by plants as the structural material of trunks, stems and leaves. Only the sugars have molecules small enough to pass through the walls of a cell. Some cells,

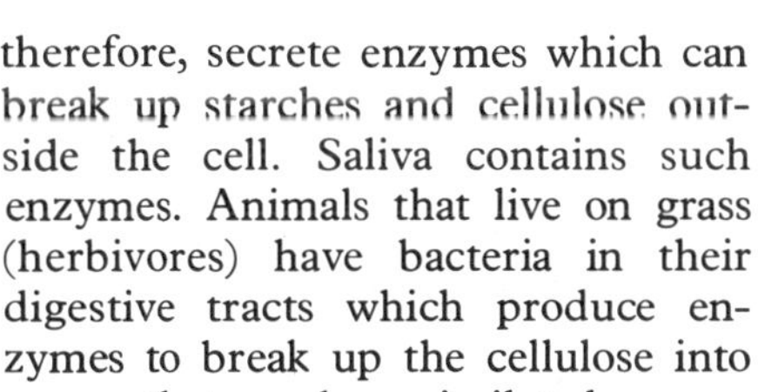

therefore, secrete enzymes which can break up starches and cellulose outside the cell. Saliva contains such enzymes. Animals that live on grass (herbivores) have bacteria in their digestive tracts which produce enzymes to break up the cellulose into sugars that can be assimilated.

Fats are part of a larger group called **lipids**. **Simple lipids** are the fats or oils (as liquid fats are called) formed by a combination of glycerol and fatty acids, or the **waxes** formed by a combination of fatty acids and alcohols other than glycerol. **Compound lipids** are made from glycerol, fatty acids, a phosphate group and a nitrogen based group. They are used by the cell to form its outer wall and the membrane surrounding the nucleus. They also occur in egg yolk and blood plasma. **Steroids** are the third type of lipid and include hormones such as the female **oestradiol** and the male **testosterone**. Fats are the most compact form in which food can be stored in a living body. The metabolism of a cell allows the fats to be converted into carbohydrates and the carbohydrates into fats.

These foods are grouped into carbohydrates (left), fats (centre) and proteins (right).

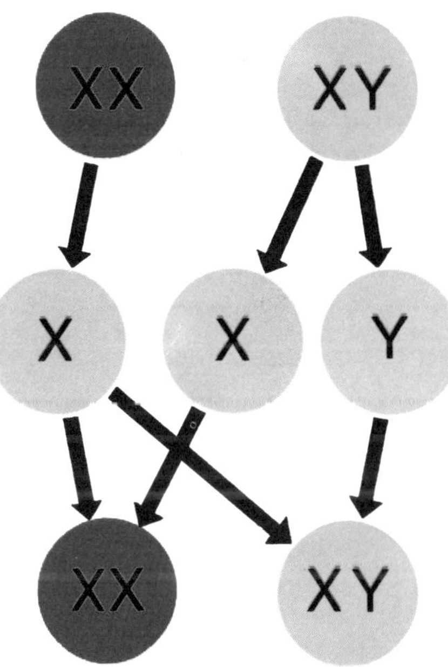

Female cells contain two X chromosomes whereas male cells contain one X and one Y chromosome. The way in which they combine determines the sex of the offspring.

Man-Made Matter

Silicones are plastics which have been used to form heat shields on spacecraft. Their effectiveness is demonstrated here as a kitten sits on a silicone sheet undisturbed by the intense heat of a gas jet beneath.

Car bodies may be made of various plastic substances, sometimes reinforced with fibre-glass.

Plastics and synthetic materials of all kinds are now so much a part of our everyday lives that it is easy to forget how recently man discovered them. The branch of chemistry which deals with polymers, or giant molecules, began only in the 1920s. Scientists then discovered something about the way in which molecules link together in orderly chains, and began to create their own.

Today, people may decry the 'plastic age' but in doing so they overlook the enormous importance of man-made materials in terms of convenience and comfort. Plastics touch every part of our lives—in homes, offices, cars, clothing—in a way which we accept and never question. Some uses of plastics and their advantages are shown here on these pages and there are many, many more. For wherever you are sitting when you read these words it is almost certain that you have only to reach out your hand to touch a familiar object that is plastic.

Indoor training for skiing enthusiasts is now possible with the invention of plastic practice slopes. The lattice work design gives a fair imitation of the surface of frozen snow and enables the learners to gain elementary skills without the expense of foreign travel. The skier's clothing and equipment are also likely to be plastic.

Plastics form a safe substitute for glass. This material is shatter-proof and has obvious advantages for use in such things as car windscreens, astronaut's helmets and shop windows. Some plastic glass can even resist penetration by a bullet fired from a gun.

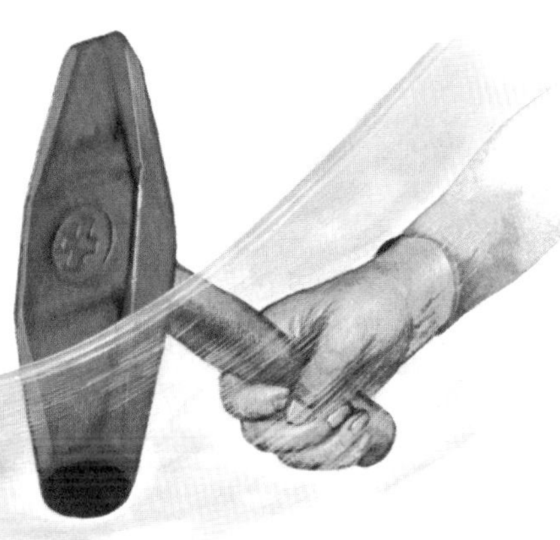

Teflon is a plastic which is best known in the kitchen where pots and pans coated with it provide a non-stick surface. Because it resists bonding and gives a surface over which other substances simply slide, it has also been used instead of ice in skating rinks.

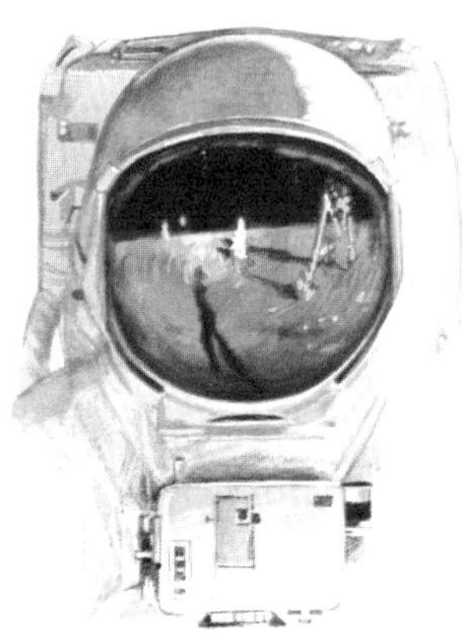

When an astronaut leaves his spacecraft he wears a protective suit which carries the earth's atmosphere around with him. His visor, covered with a thin transparent gold layer which shields him from light rays, is yet another plastic product.

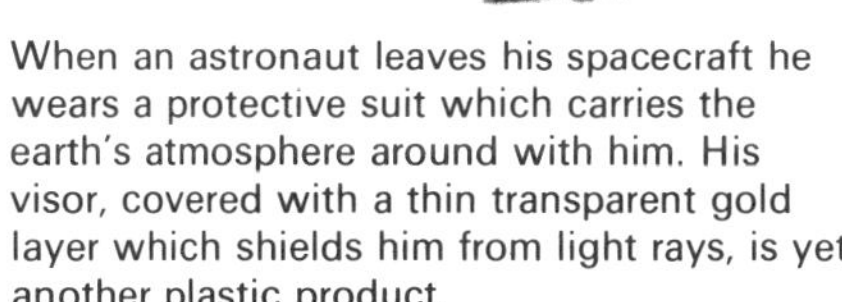

Modern plastic adhesives have spectacular powers of bonding together two surfaces so they become as one. A small quantity of adhesive will successfully join two pieces of metal which withstand separation when subjected to weights of over 450 kilograms (1,000 pounds) under test.

The all-plastic home can be a reality in modern times. Everything seen in this room, except food and drink, is plastic – even the sculpture!

In the home, not only the interiors of rooms and their fittings can be made of plastic, but the house itself may be a prefabricated plastic building. To round it off the swimming pool has a plastic lining.

Energy

When you feel yourself bursting with energy, you have a great urge to action. You want to express this in rapid or violent motion, in great physical or mental effort. This energy is given to you by the food you eat and by the air you breathe. Even while you sleep, the cells of your body are working to convert what they have absorbed into the chemical compounds that are the body's fuel. When you are awake and active, these fuels provide the energy for all your activities. As they are burned up, you need to eat more to replace them. You need periods for rest and sleep when the build-up of energy is greater than the use of it through activity.

The world we live in is alive with energy. Radiated energy from the sun warms the atmosphere. It is hotter at the equator, so the air there rises and the space is filled by colder air rushing in from the poles. With other currents set up by the rotation of the earth and by local variations of climate, this movement of the atmosphere produces the winds. They can vary between a gentle breeze and a violent hurricane.

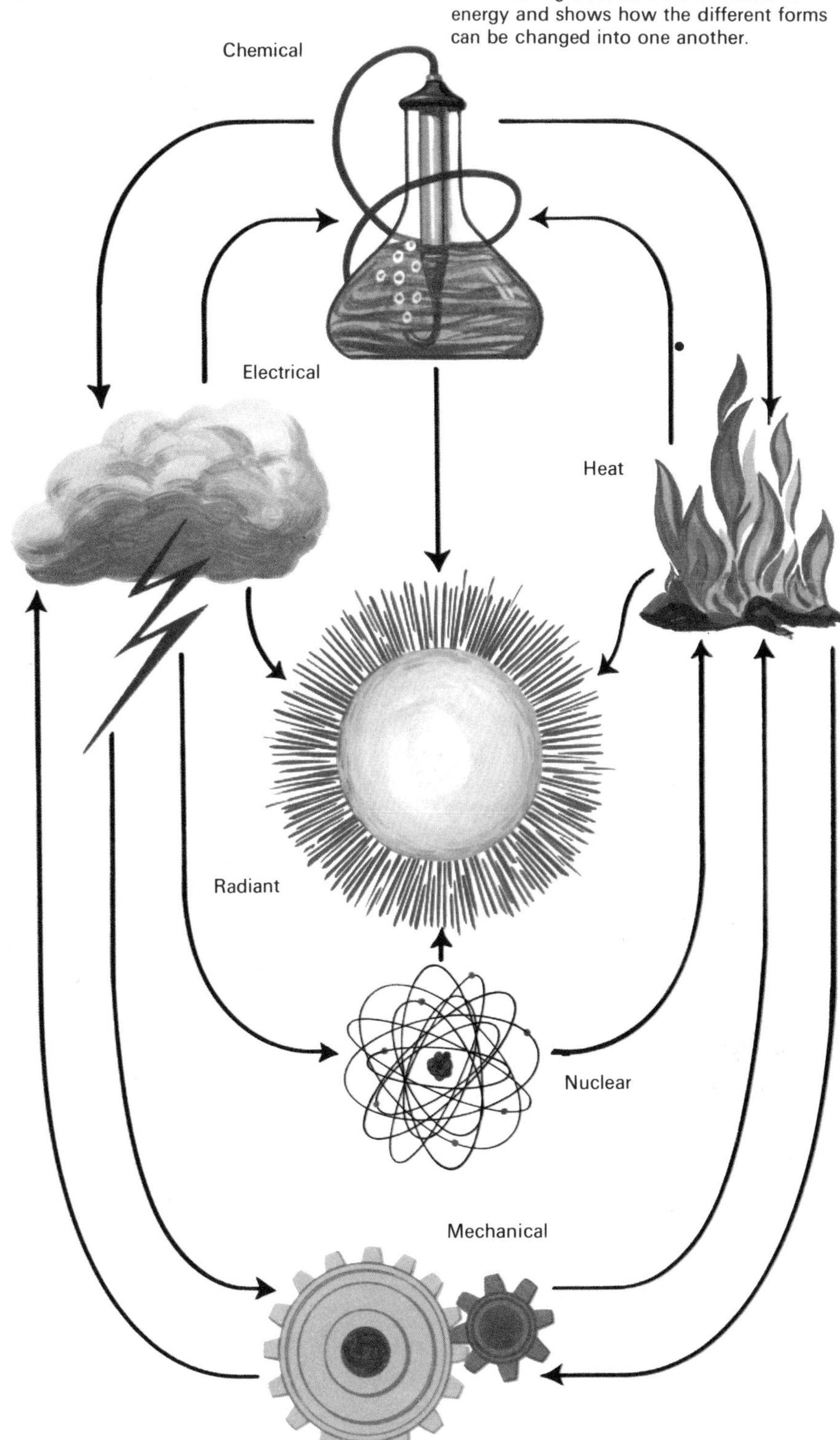

This drawing illustrates the six forms of energy and shows how the different forms can be changed into one another.

The oceans, which cover more than 70% of the earth's surface, are filled with restless energy. The winds hurl them against the shoreline to eat away at it in one place, to build up barrages of sand and pebbles in another. The gravitational pull of the moon keeps millions of gallons of water in motion in the twice-daily ebb and flow of the tides.

There is energy beneath the earth's crust. Occasionally, it breaks through the surface in earthquakes and volcanic eruptions. Its efforts in the past have shaped our present landscapes. There is energy in all living matter, used for its own growth and to feed others. In decay, it has laid down deposits of fuels such as coal and oil which can now be tapped for the energy needs of our modern civilisation.

Energy and Work

All the kinds of energy so far mentioned are obvious enough. To a scientist there are many other kinds of energy which are not immediately apparent in our daily lives. All matter, even that comprising the most solid and immobile object, is full of energy. Without energy matter cannot exist.

We use our own energy to do **work**. Even at play, we are doing work in scientific terms. When we strike a ball and make it travel through a distance, a scientist would say we have done some work. Machines do work for us. The rate at which a machine works is called the machine's **power**. When a footballer plays a game, he kicks the ball many times. The player is a machine providing the initial energy. The weight of the ball, the distances through which it is kicked, the force with which it hits the ground or another player or the net behind the goal, all add up to the work done. The time taken to do all this work is the measure of the power of the machine, in this case the footballer.

Before the footballer kicks the ball, he has a store of energy which will enable him to do so. Stored energy is called **potential energy**. After the kick, the moving ball is said to have **kinetic energy** from the Greek word for motion, *kinema*, which also gives us our word cinema for moving pictures. All matter contains both potential and kinetic energy. The electron in an atom, for instance, has the potential energy of its negative electric

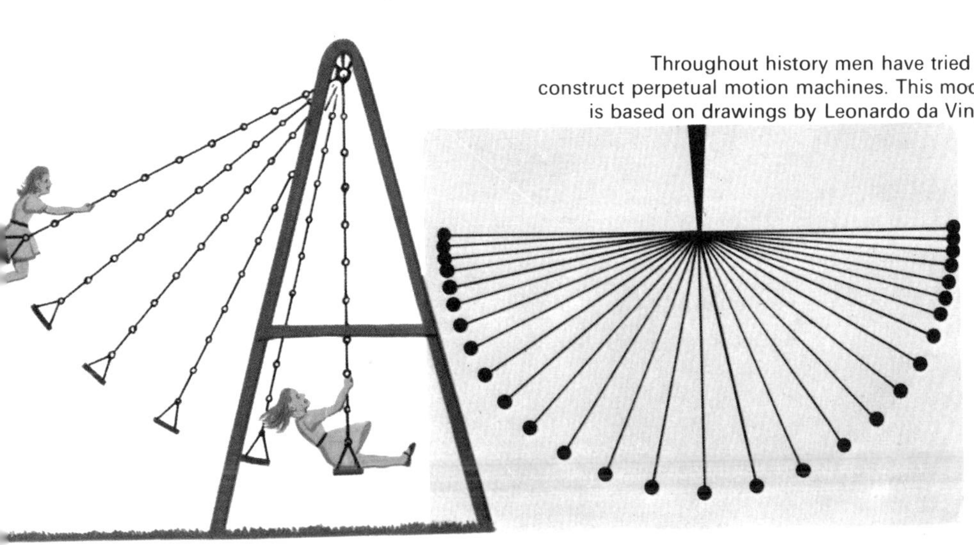

Throughout history men have tried to construct perpetual motion machines. This model is based on drawings by Leonardo da Vinci.

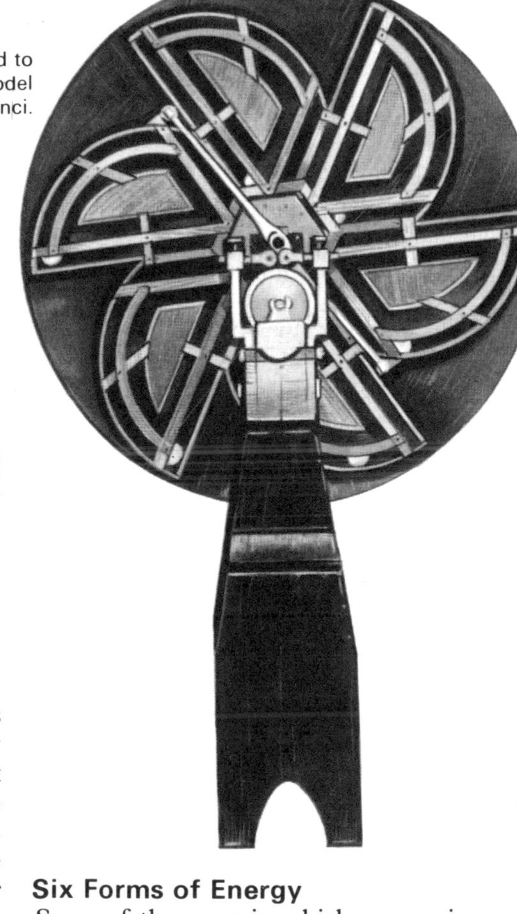

The girl on the swing achieves the point of greatest potential energy when she is at the top of her swing, and the point of greatest kinetic energy when she is level with the ground. The ball on a string swinging as a pendulum illustrates the same fact.

charge and the kinetic energy of its orbital movement around the atomic nucleus.

The potential and kinetic energy of an electron both contribute to its mass. Part of its mass comes from the electric charge and part from the energy of its movement. It is a fact that an electron moving at almost the speed of light is seven times heavier than an electron at rest. Where the energy came from to create the particles composing the first atom is a question that may never be solved. Only in one form can energy exist without matter, that is to say in empty space, and that is as radiant energy. The creation of matter involves the absorption of energy, and the release of energy involves the destruction of matter. Yet the total sum of all the energy and all the matter in the universe remains, for all practical purposes, constant.

Transformation of Energy

After the game, our footballer feels tired. He has used up a good deal of energy. Some has been used to move his body about the field of play, some to kick the ball, some has even been dissipated in the air in the form of heat generated by his exertions. All the energy he has lost has gone somewhere, perhaps transformed into different kinds of energy.

This principle of the transformation of energy is used by man in the machines he has invented. The moving parts of a machine, the pistons, shafts and wheels, like the legs of a footballer, have **mechanical energy**. The pistons are moved by the pressure of steam or the explosion of petrol vapour which contain **heat energy**. Some of the mechanical energy a machine creates is transformed back into heat energy by the friction of the moving parts, just as the footballer's body is heated by the excess energy from his rapid movements. The heat is supplied to the machine from the **chemical energy** of its fuel, perhaps coal or oil or, as in the case of the footballer, from his food and the air he breathes.

The machine might be used to drive a generator that produces **electrical energy** which in turn can be transformed into the **radiant energy** of an electric light bulb or the radiant heat from an electric fire. Finally, machines might be driven by the energy locked up in the nucleus of an atom and called **nuclear energy**. This can be transformed directly into heat energy in the form of steam, for instance, to drive the mechanical parts of an electric generator.

Fireworks show a release of chemical energy.

Six Forms of Energy

Some of the ways in which energy is converted from one form to another are illustrated in the diagram on this page. The six forms of energy: mechanical, chemical, heat, radiant, electrical and nuclear are convenient divisions for study of the subject as a whole.

The force of gravity, a coiled spring, a tautened bowstring, even a stretched rubber band, all contain potential energy which can be converted directly into mechanical energy. The fall of water from a high to a low level turns the ancient mill-wheel or the modern hydroelectric turbine. The slow release of the tension in a mainspring turns the series of cogwheels in a watch or clock. The released bowstring transfers its energy to the arrow and sends it whistling to its mark. The rubber band flicks a paper missile or the stone from a catapult.

In modern machinery, mechanical energy is more often produced by means of heat. When a gas is heated, the molecules move at great speed. A piston and cylinder is a device to use the pressure created by this rapid movement of molecules. The heated gas is contained in a sealed chamber, the cylinder, of which only one wall, the piston head, is capable of movement. The pressure within the cylinder thus moves the piston, which in turn is connected to the machine.

Heat Efficiency

Much of the heat energy used in this way is wasted, some through the friction of the moving parts (which converts mechanical energy back into heat), and some through the heating of the various parts of the machine directly from the heated gas. This heat loss is dissipated into the surrounding air. The proportion of original heat energy actually used for useful work in moving the mechanical parts of the machine is called its **efficiency**. The petrol motor in a car, for instance, is only about 20% efficient. Only 20% of the heat energy contained in a quantity of petrol is actually used to move the motor car along the road. The rest is carried away by the cooling system, by the heat of the exhaust fumes, by the friction of the engine bearings, and by the friction of the tyres on the road.

All systems involving energy suffer losses in this way. The energy lost has not disappeared. It has been converted into a form from which it cannot be easily recaptured to do useful work for us. In the case of a motor car, it has disturbed the air and moved it out of the way of the advancing vehicle. It has heated the atmosphere in the immediate neighbourhood of the moving vehicle. The lost energy cannot be put back into the engine for conversion into further mechanical energy. It can be said to have become disorganised. The extent to which energy has been disorganised in this way is called the **entropy**. In any system, regarded in isolation, the entropy increases as the available energy is used up to operate the system. If the whole of the universe can be regarded as a closed energy system, then its entropy must be increasing all the time. Eventually, there must come a time when the entropy reaches its maximum when no more energy is availabe for use. Such a state of affairs is referred to as the 'heat death of the universe'. Since we cannot be sure where the energy that first created the universe came from, however, we cannot say for certain that the universe is a closed system.

Chemical Energy

Petrol is the fuel used to power a motor car. Like all matter it contains chemical energy, due to the continual movements of its molecules and the atoms of which they are composed. In solid matter, the movement is merely a **vibration** of atoms about a fixed point within the molecule. In a liquid, to the vibration of atoms is added the movement of atoms or molecules through space, called their **translation**. In a gas, there is also a **rotation** of the whole molecule. Under certain circumstances, when different molecules collide with each other, a chemical reaction takes place. The total chemical energy content is redistributed, only the energy contained in the nuclei of the individual atoms being unaffected.

When the products of a chemical reaction contain less energy than the original atoms or molecules, the remaining energy is given out in the form of heat or radiation. The reaction is then called **exothermic**. If, on the other hand, heat has to be added to continue the reaction, it is called **endothermic**. When heat is given off by a strongly exothermic reaction which takes place very rapidly, it is called **combustion**.

The petrol in a car is first broken up into a fine spray and mixed with air in the carburettor. The resultant vapour is fed into the cylinders and combustion begun by a spark. The result is an exothermic reaction in which some of the chemical energy is converted into heat energy. In its turn, some of this heat energy is transformed into mechanical energy by the pressure of hot gases against the piston head.

In this and other similar ways, most of the energy required by our modern civilisation comes from the combustion of the so-called fossil fuels: oil, coal and natural gas. In most cases, the chemical reactions involved are started by the application of a small amount of heat, a lighted match for instance. Thereafter, enough heat is generated by the exothermic reactions to maintain combustion until all the fuel is burnt. In the case of a diesel engine, compression of the oil vapour inside the cylinder increases the number of molecular collisions until the temperature has risen enough to cause the very rapid combustion of an explosion. This process is called **spontaneous combustion**.

Measuring Temperature

The **temperature** of a given amount of matter is a measure of the average

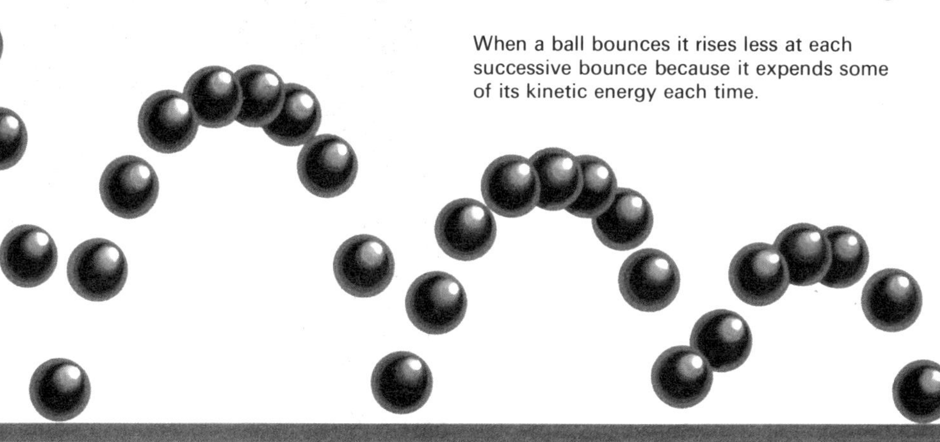

When a ball bounces it rises less at each successive bounce because it expends some of its kinetic energy each time.

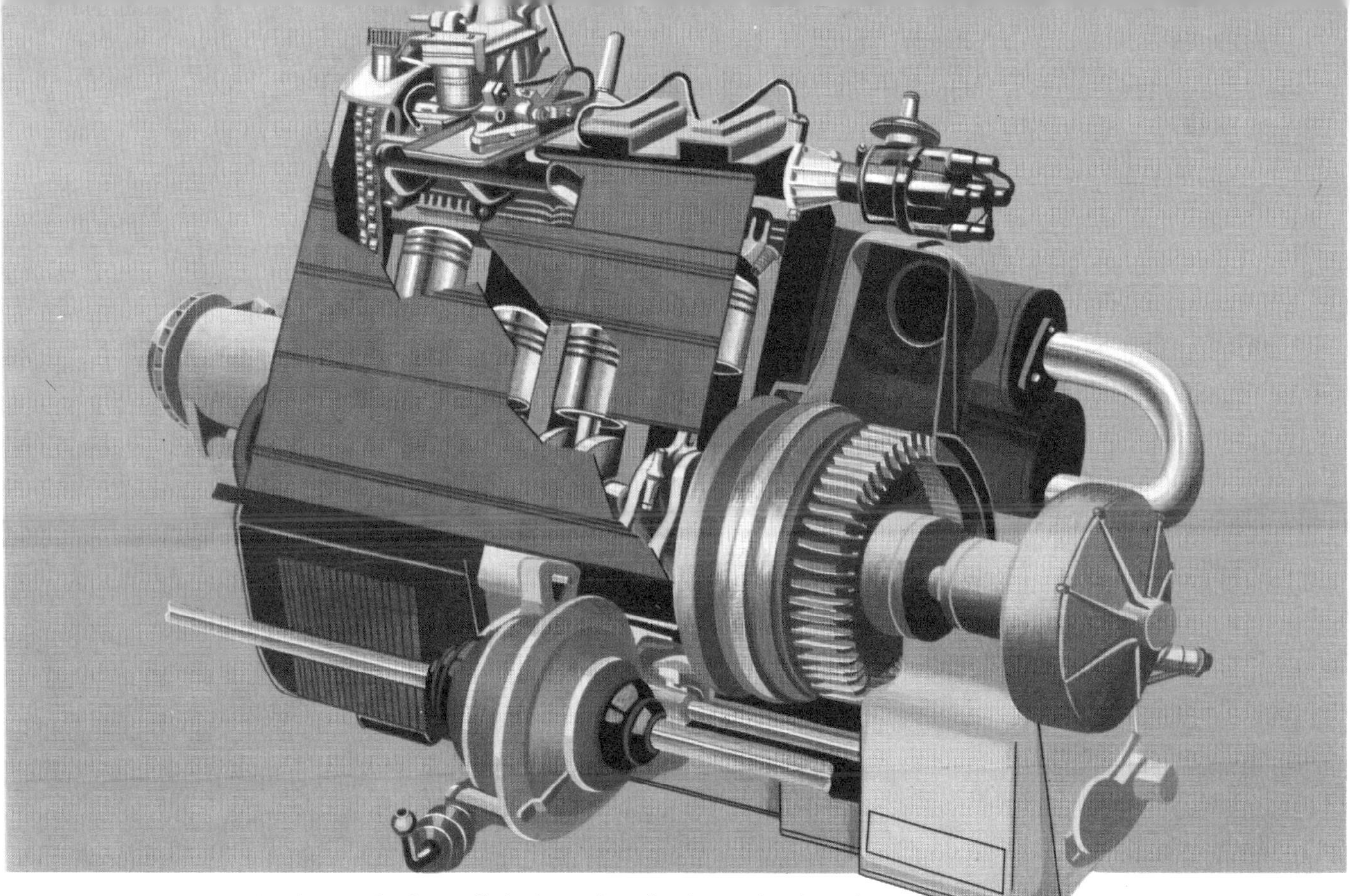

Section through an air-cooled, four-stroke, four-cylinder internal combustion engine. In such an engine chemical energy is converted to heat energy and then to mechanical energy.

Double-acting steam engine.

Gasoline jet is injected into air current and vaporises before passing to engine.

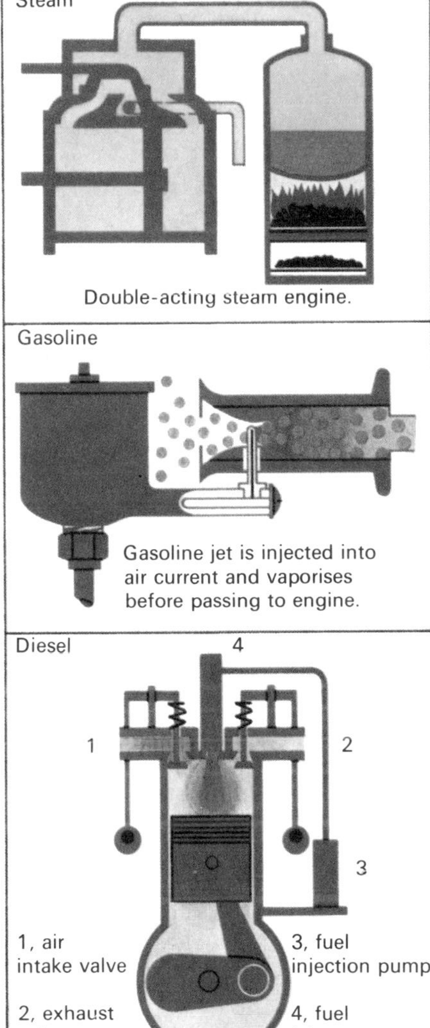

kinetic energy in the movement of its atoms or molecules. The **heat** it contains is the total of all the kinetic energy of all the atoms and molecules of which the matter is composed. Thus, a spark can have a very high temperature, yet it does not burn you when it lands on your skin because it is so small it contains very little heat energy. Conversely, the temperature of a river can be raised slightly above that of its surroundings by the hot effluent tipped into it from factories along its course. Since the river contains a large amount of water, even a slight rise of temperature represents a considerable quantity of heat. A pump can be used to extract the energy in this heat and to raise its temperature sufficiently to warm a large building.

Scientists usually measure temperature in degrees centigrade (or Celsius after Anders Celsius, 1701–44, who devised the scale). On the Celsius scale, zero degrees is the melting point of ice and 100 degrees is the boiling point of water measured at sea-level atmospheric pressure. Heat can be measured in **calories**. A calorie is the amount of heat required to raise the temperature of one gram of water by one degrees Celsius. A **Calorie** (with a captial C), used to calculate food intake, is one thousand calories (with a small c). By international agreement, the calorie has been generally replaced by the **joule** which is the amount of energy produced by a watt of electric power consumed for one second.

Thermodynamics

The study of the flow of heat or energy is called **thermodynamics**. The Laws of Thermodynamics are statistical, that is to say they apply only to quantities of matter. They do not apply to individual atoms or molecules.

The **First Law of Thermodynamics**, known also as the **Law of the Conservation of Energy**, states that energy can neither be created nor destroyed within a constant mass of matter. The energy in a closed system can change from one form to another, but the total amount remains the same.

The **Second Law of Thermodynamics** states that heat cannot be transferred, in a continuous, self-sustaining process, from a colder to a hotter body. In other words, heat always tends to flow from a high temperature mass to a low temperature mass.

The **Third Law of Thermodynamics** states that at the absolute zero of temperature, when all vibrations and movements of atoms and molecules stop, the entropy, or disorganisation of energy, is zero. Since all systems tend towards an increase of entropy, this law is a proof that the absolute zero of temperature (−273·15°C) can never be reached.

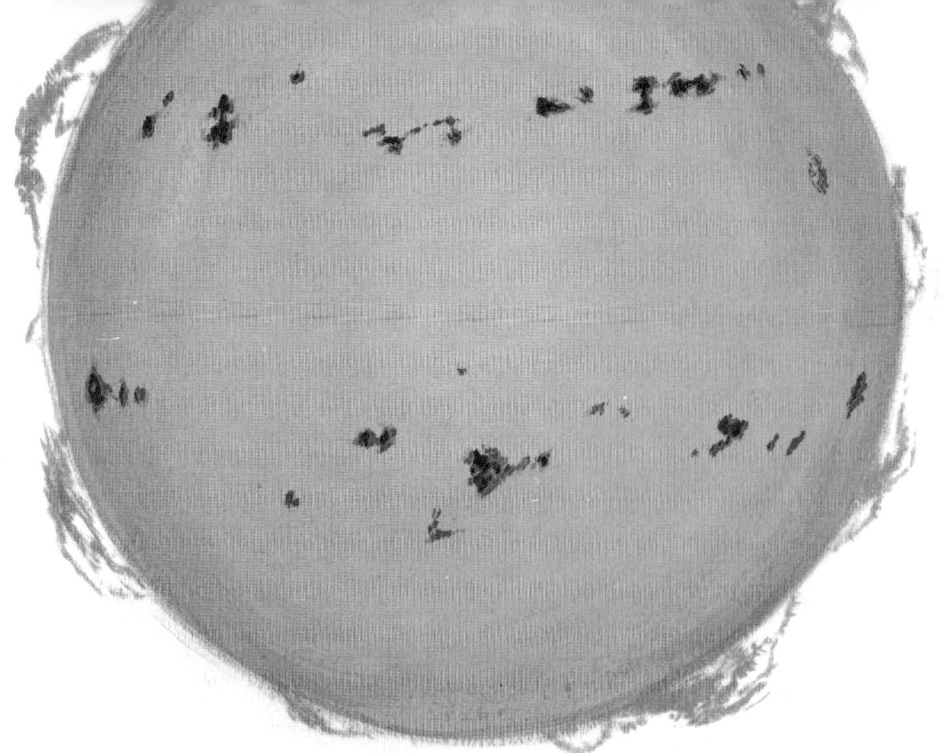

The sun is like a great nuclear reactor. Energy has poured out of it for millions of years.

Radiant Energy

The experiences of combustion common to us all are the heat and light given off by the exothermic reaction. When we sit in front of a fire, our skin feels its heat and our eyes see its glow. Some of the heat from a fire raises the temperature of the air in a room. This is a direct transmission of heat energy by exciting the molecules in the air to greater movement. The air becomes warmer and heats us.

The rest of the warmth we feel comes from heat radiation which is one of the forms of **electromagnetic radiation**. Electromagnetic radiation needs no medium, such as air, to support its movement. It travels through empty space at 300 million metres (186,000 miles) per second. This is often referred to as the speed of light, but it is common to all electromagnetic radiation, including radio waves, heat, ultraviolet radiation, X-rays, gamma rays and cosmic radiation. Through a medium such as the earth's atmosphere, this speed is slightly reduced according to the type of radiation concerned and the nature of the medium itself.

Heat Transference

To experience electromagnetic radiation, you can try a simple experiment. Take a table lamp that has been unlit for some time so that the light bulb is cold. Hold your hand close to the bulb and switch on. Immediately you feel the warmth of electromagnetic radiation. Quickly touch the bulb and it will be found to be still quite cool. It will be a few seconds before the heat of the lamp filament excites the gas molecules inside the bulb and they in turn excite the molecules of the glass so that the bulb becomes too hot to touch.

In this way, you will have experienced the two distinct forms of heat transference. One is simply the flow of heat energy from a point of high temperature—the lamp filament—through the gas to the glass of the bulb and other matter such as the surrounding air which is at a lower temperature. The other is electromagnetic radiation given off by the heated filament immediately and at tremendous speed.

The Action of Waves

There are two different ways of looking at electromagnetic radiation. The first is in terms of **waves**. When a pebble is dropped in the middle of a still pool of water, ripples spread in all directions. Individual particles of water do not travel across the pool but bob up and down at right angles to the direction of the spreading ripples. This can be shown by floating a cork on the water. It will simply bob up and down in one place. What is happening is that each bobbing particle of water affects the next one to it and so on across the pool, spreading the ripples. A similar effect takes place when the oscillations of atoms and molecules are speeded up to the point where some of the energy is radiated. The analogy with the pool of water breaks down when the medium itself is considered. The ripples in the pool are movements of the water, but

In these drawings water is carried from its source to a burning building in three ways. First each bucket is passed from hand to hand along a human chain. Second each man carries his bucket from the water source to the fire and back to the source again. Third a hose is directed upon the fire from a distance. These methods may be compared to the three ways in which heat is transmitted: by conduction, convection and radiation.

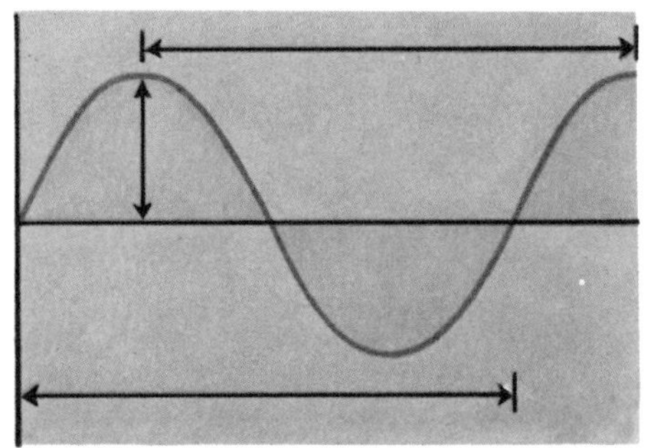

This diagram illustrates the principal characteristics of a wave. First, wavelength, the distance between adjacent peaks of a wave; second, amplitude, the rise and fall of a wave; and third, the cycle, which is one complete wave form.

electromagnetic radiation requires no medium. It can spread its 'ripples' through empty space.

Though it is difficult to visualise how this can happen, it is convenient for the study of some radiation phenomena to stick to the wave idea. A model of what is happening can then be illustrated with a graph, seen here.

The rise and fall of the wave above and below the horizontal line is the measure of the quantity of energy it contains. This amount of energy is proportional to the square of the **amplitude**. The distance between two adjacent peaks of the wave is called the **wavelength**. One complete wave form is called a **cycle**. The time taken for the wave to complete a cycle can be calculated by dividing its speed (300 million metres (186,000 miles) per second in empty space) by its wavelength. The result is known as the **frequency**. It is nowadays measured in **hertz**, one hertz equalling one cycle per second. As radiation frequencies involve very large numbers, the units used are more often thousands of hertz called **kilohertz** (kHz) or even millions of hertz called **megahertz** (MHz).

Wave Frequencies

Frequencies determine the type of radiation. Radio waves, for instance, fall between the frequencies of twenty hertz and about one million megahertz. The lowest frequencies are sometimes called audio waves because they correspond to those frequencies that can be detected by the human ear. Sound waves, however, require a medium such as air to travel through. They are not electromagnetic radiations and must not be confused with radio waves of similar frequencies.

Radio waves are produced by the oscillations of currents of electrons running through a wire. Above them in frequencies are the heat waves called **infra-red** radiation because they are below the frequency of red light. When you use a poker on a fire and then hold it close to your skin, you can feel the infra-red radiation though the poker is not yet red-hot. Infra-red radiation ranges between frequencies of about one million megahertz and more than 100 million megahertz. The inertia of solid metal in a wire is too great for oscillations at such high frequencies. Only individual atoms or molecules are sufficiently small to produce them. This brings us to the second way of looking at radiant energy.

Quantum Theory

It has been said in the section on chemical energy that one of the movements of the molecules of a gas is the rotation of the whole molecule. A certain quantity of energy is required to maintain this rotation. When energy is added to the molecule, by heating the gas for instance, the rotation does not gradually increase in speed. It changes from one speed to a higher speed in sudden jerks. It would seem that, like matter, energy has a minimum quantity. This smallest amount of energy that can exist has been called a **quantum**. The description of the phenomenon is known as the **Quantum Theory**.

Individual energy quanta are extremely small, and their effect when dealing with large quantities of matter can be ignored. At the very high frequencies associated with infra-red radiation and those above them, however, it is energy changes in individual

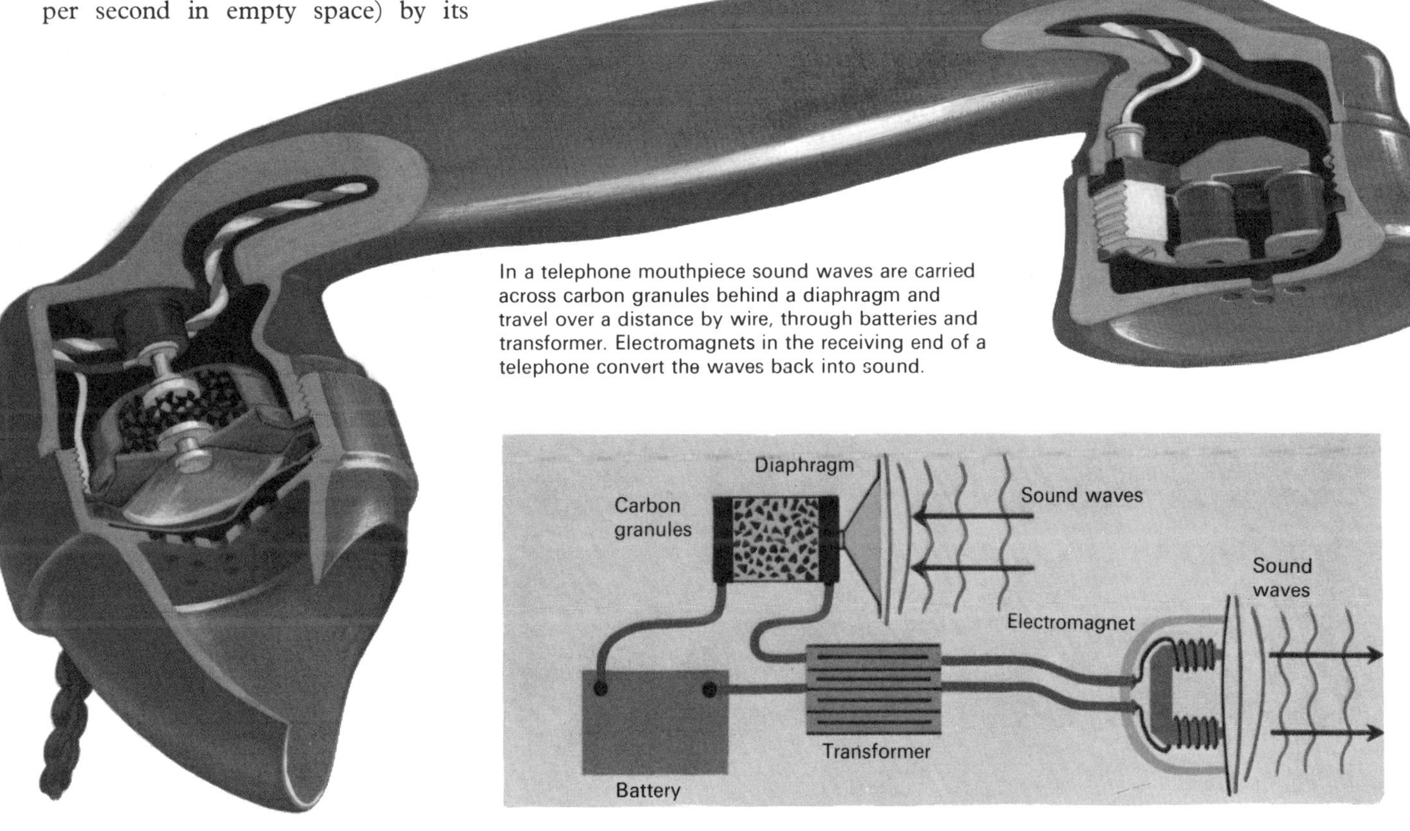

In a telephone mouthpiece sound waves are carried across carbon granules behind a diaphragm and travel over a distance by wire, through batteries and transformer. Electromagnets in the receiving end of a telephone convert the waves back into sound.

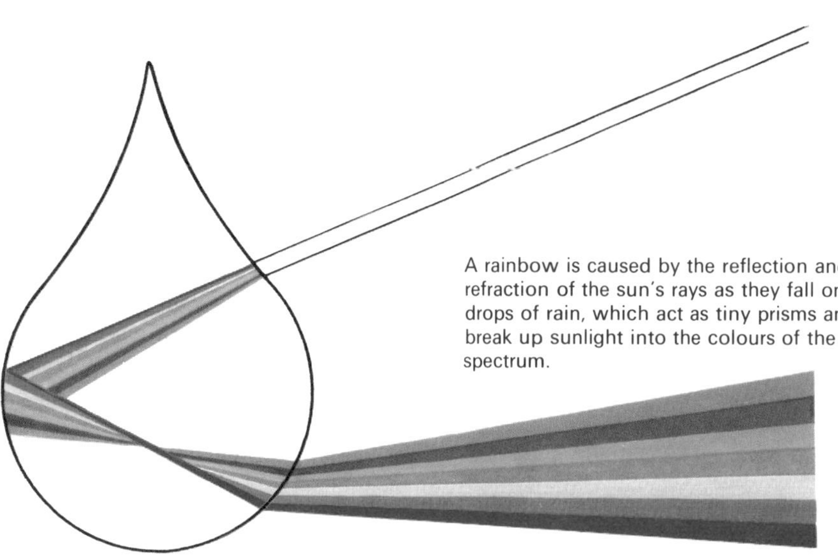

A rainbow is caused by the reflection and refraction of the sun's rays as they fall on drops of rain, which act as tiny prisms and break up sunlight into the colours of the spectrum.

atoms and molecules that are important. Radiation emission must be thought of as short bursts of energy made up of numbers of quanta. The size of an energy quantum depends upon the frequency of the radiation. It can be calculated by multiplying the frequencies with a number known as **Planck's constant** after the German physicist, Max Planck (1858–1947).

It is only by whole numbers of energy quanta that the speed of vibration and rotation of atoms and molecules can be increased or decreased. Part of a quantum cannot exist. In this respect, a quantum is similar to the smallest divisible parts of matter. Though a quantum is extremely small, at the higher frequencies of electromagnetic radiation, it begins to take on properties associated with a particle. It can be described as a tiny bundle of energy.

The refraction of light waves causes them to bend in liquid so that this spoon in a glass of water appears to be displaced.

The principal advantage of the electron microscope (right) over the ordinary optical microscope is that its power of magnification is much greater—up to 200,000 times is possible. With such magnification scientists are able to study the internal structure of matter. Instead of a mirror and light, there is an electron gun which shoots beams of electrons towards the object to be studied.

From all this it can be said that radiated energy has a dual nature. Not only does it emanate as waves, but also in short bursts measured in quanta. The study of this dual nature is called **wave mechanics**. It is a study that can be expressed only in mathematics. In words, all that can be said is that an electron or a quantum, regarded as a particle, probably exists at some point in the path of a wave. The word 'probably' is important because it is a fundamental fact that the position and speed of the smallest particles in nature cannot be determined exactly. Any instrument that might be devised to observe them or calculate their speed would itself alter their behaviour. To measure both speed and position simultaneously involves a large degree of possible error. This is known, after its discoverer, as the **Heisenberg Uncertainty Principle**.

Light Radiation

The dual nature of radiant energy as wave-particle goes some way towards explaining how it can travel through empty space, whereas the ripples of a pool require the medium of water and sound waves require the oscillations of particles of air. Further illustration of the way radiation behaves in some respects as a wave and in others as a particle can be given by a study of light radiation.

The band of radiation frequencies to which the human eye is sensitive is very narrow. Yet it is to radiations within this narrow band that all our visual experience of the world is confined. What we see are radiations emitted by or reflected from the matter around us. The infra-red radiation from a hot poker can be felt but it cannot be seen. Only when the poker is left longer in the fire does it begin to emit radiation frequencies in the light range and to glow a red colour. Further heating adds further colours until the poker is said to be white-hot. The total of all colours that make up white light is called the **visible spectrum**.

When white light is passed through a glass prism it is separated into its different colours in the well-known rainbow effect. Though all electromagnetic radiations travel at the same speed in empty space, this speed is slowed down within a medium like glass to a varying degree according to their frequencies. Those light radiations with the highest frequencies, towards the violet end of the spectrum, are slowed down most. Those with the lower frequencies, towards the red end of the spectrum, are slowed down to a lesser extent. Slowing the speed shortens the wavelength which has the effect of bending the light wave at the point where it passes from one medium to another, at one face of the prism as it enters and at the opposite face as it leaves. Thus, violet light is bent most

Good lighting is important to avoid tiring the eyes when reading. In many homes today individual lighting is directed at one point to serve one person's needs.

and red light least. The other colours are separated out in between the two extremes. This bending of light is called **refraction**. Every substance through which light passes has its own particular **refractive index**. Light is hardly slowed down at all in the air, but loses about 40% of its speed in glass.

Reflected Colours

Most of the colours we see are **reflected** from opaque objects. The paper of this book reflects most of the white light that falls upon it and thus appears white. The black type of these words absorbs most of the light and so appears black. The different pigments used in the inks that create the coloured pictures reflect some colours and absorb others. If you were sitting in red light, only red objects would look the same. Every other colour would become black, except that the white objects would look red.

At the frequencies of light radiation even an atom becomes too heavy to oscillate. At all frequencies above infra-red radiation, it is the movements of electrons that become important. At the point when our heated poker begins to give out a red glow, something has happened to some of its electrons. All the elements, if heated sufficiently in their gaseous state, will radiate at frequencies within the visible spectrum. But each element behaves in a different way.

If pure hydrogen is heated and the light emitted by it is passed through a prism, the full rainbow spectrum does not appear. Instead, there are two predominant and distinct lines of colour, one red and the other green. If the same experiment is tried with sodium vapour, there is a predominant yellow line. These effects are called the **emission line spectrum** for each element, and each element has its own distinctive arrangement of predominant frequencies. They can be likened to the 'fingerprint' of the element and can be used to identify it.

Conversely, if white light is passed through an element in its gaseous

A strange effect is created when sound is emitted from a moving source. As a car approaches an observer its sound waves are shorter and their pitch is high. As the car goes away from the observer the sound waves are longer and the pitch lower. This effect also applies to radio and light waves and is known as the Doppler effect after Christian Doppler, the physicist who discovered it.

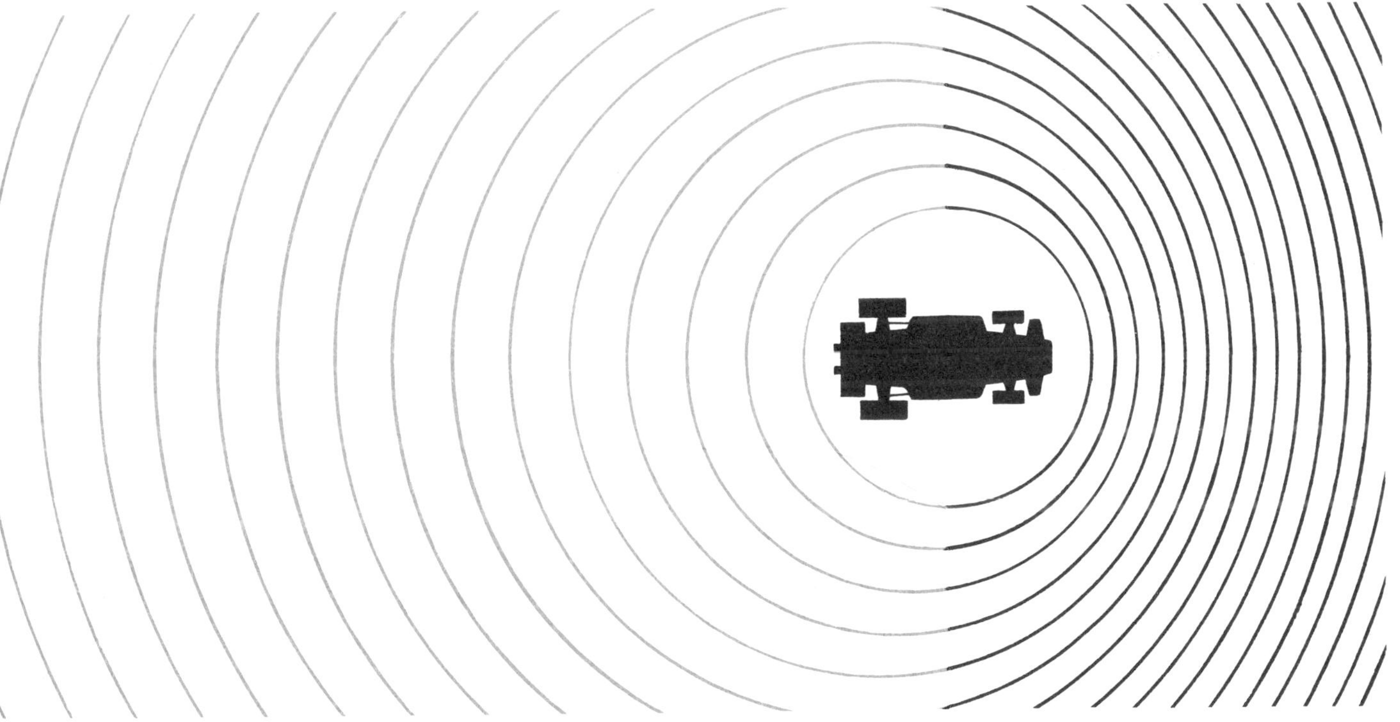

The photo-electric cell consists of a vacuum tube towards which a ray of light is directed. Some of its uses commercially are illustrated: counting in a bread factory; opening doors automatically; deciding photo finishes; and operating sound track on film.

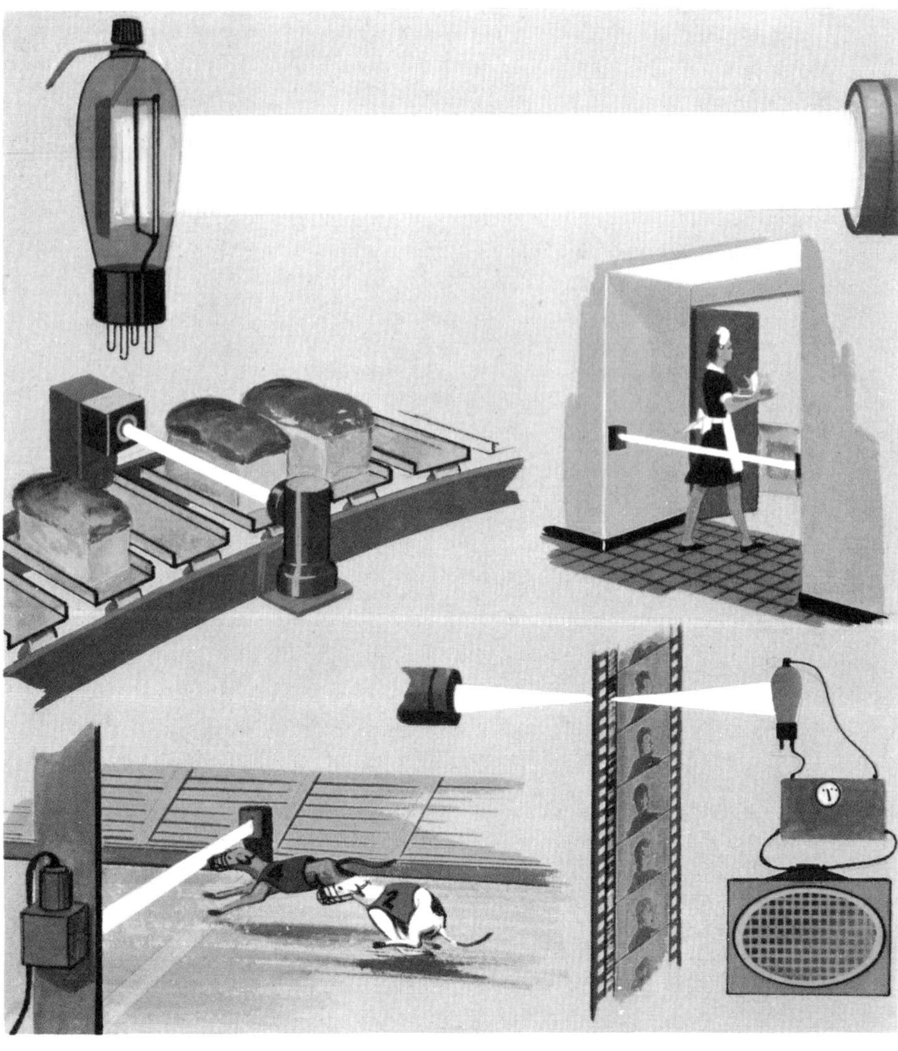

state and then through a prism, it will be found that the normal spectrum is interrupted by dark lines covering the very colours that predominate in that element's emission spectrum. The pattern of the dark lines is called an **absorption line spectrum**. In other words, a particular element absorbs radiation of the same frequencies as it emits. These phenomena take place only in the gaseous state, because in liquids and solids the atoms and molecules are too close together. Individual radiations interfere with each other and become superimposed, so that the spectrum produced is continuous. Our heated poker, which does not vaporise easily, gradually produces all the frequencies of visible radiation which add up to the emission of white light. So the poker is said to have become white-hot.

Bohr's Atom

In order to explain emission and absorption spectra, we must have a new model of an atom. It was first suggested by Niels Bohr (1885–1962), a Danish physicist, and is known as the **Bohr atom**. As we have seen, the orbital electrons in an atom are arranged in shells at varying distances from the central nucleus. Each shell can be regarded as having different depths of energy level. If an individual electron has a high energy content, it will orbit at a greater distance from the nucleus. If it loses some of its energy, it will fall back into an orbit closer to the nucleus. Both orbits are still within the particular electron's appropriate shell. In accordance with the Quantum Theory, the energy absorbed by an electron to thrust it into a higher energy orbit must come in packets of a minimal size. Thus there are only a limited number of orbits permitted to the electron within its own shell. Similarly, when an electron falls back to a lower energy orbit, it must release its energy as a quantum of an appropriate size to the frequency of the radiation. When this is a quantum of light, it is called a **photon**.

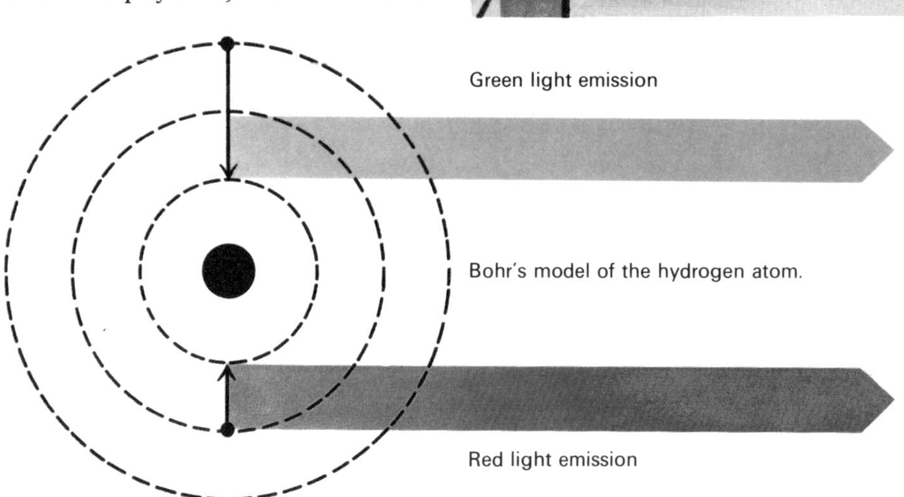

Bohr's model of the hydrogen atom.

According to Bohr's theory, the hydrogen atom could be illustrated as shown in the accompanying diagram. In this model, the hydrogen atom is depicted with its single electron having three possible orbits. When the electron falls from the outer orbit to the inner one, a photon of green light is emitted. When it falls from the middle orbit to the inner one, a photon of red light is emitted. The true situation is, of course, much more complicated than this, which takes into consideration only the predominant colours in hydrogen's emission line spectrum. It can also readily be seen that, with heavier atoms, the complications become very much greater, emissions also occur at ultraviolet and X-ray frequencies. More recently, Bohr's theory has been amplified to take into account the fact that electrons can also rotate about their own axis and that their orbits can be elliptical. Again, these complications can only be expressed mathematically.

Bohr's theory looks at light radiation from the point of view of emitted particles. That light also has a wave characteristic is proved by the **interference patterns** discovered by Thomas Young early in the 19th century. Briefly, they show that where beams of light are in phase with each other, they reinforce each other and increase the brightness where they strike a surface. But where the wave forms are out of phase, where the peak of one coincides with the trough of another, they cancel each other out and leave dark lines on the surface they strike. This could be true only of waves. It is not possible for two exactly similar particles of light or photons striking a surface to cancel each other out in this familiar interference pattern. Once again, we are faced with the mystery of the dual

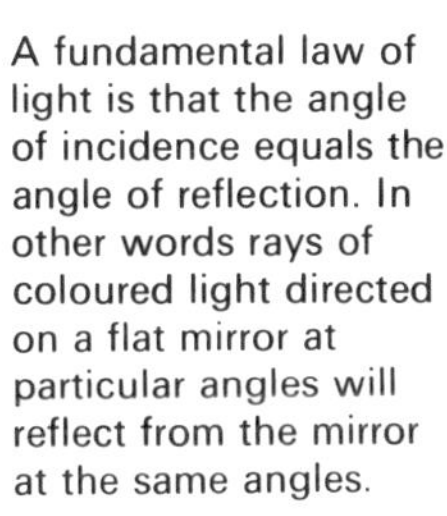
A fundamental law of light is that the angle of incidence equals the angle of reflection. In other words rays of coloured light directed on a flat mirror at particular angles will reflect from the mirror at the same angles.

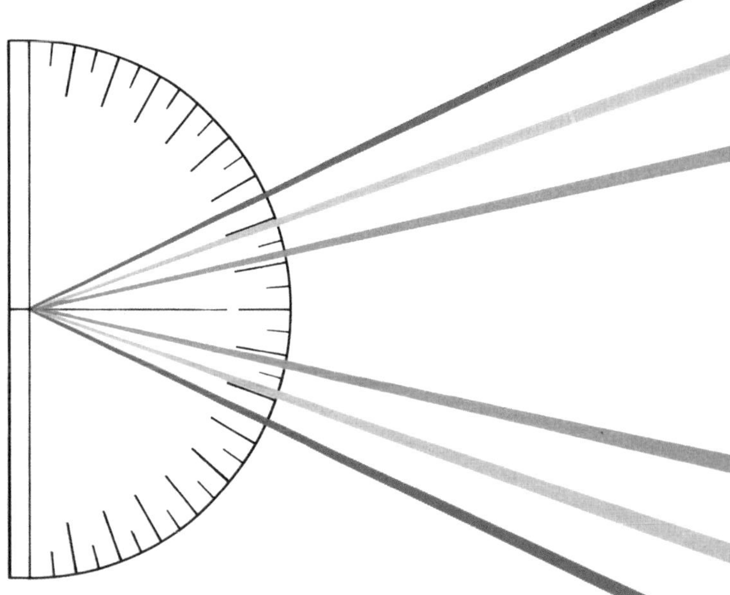

The chameleon's eyes can swivel independently of each other but when it sights its prey the eyes come together to focus so that it can operate its tongue accurately.

nature of radiation which is so difficult to visualise.

The 'Magic' Eye

Among the evidence supporting Bohr's explanation of light emission in the form of bundles of energy or photons is the **photo-electric effect.** When light falls on a clean metal surface, especially in a vacuum, the energy is absorbed by free electrons in the metal. This gives the electrons sufficient energy to escape from the metal. The number of electrons that escape depends upon the intensity of the light, in other words the number of photons that strike the metal. The speed at which the electrons fly off depends upon the frequency of the light wave. Violet light, which has a higher frequency, produces higher speed electrons than red light which has a lower frequency. Ultra-violet and X-radiations produce electrons at even higher speeds. Thus it is the quantity of energy in the photon added to the electron's original energy that determines the speed of the escaping electron. This can be explained only by regarding both electron and photon as quanta of energy that can be added together.

The effect is used in the **photo-electric cell** in which light is used to cause an emission of electrons from one terminal that can be collected from another terminal, creating a flow of electricity in a circuit. The light passing through the sound track of a film varies in intensity, thus varying the current flowing through a photo-electric cell. This variable current can be converted into sound waves by an amplifier and loudspeaker.

Laser Beams

Atoms that have electrons stimulated into the higher energy or outer orbits of the Bohr atom can be struck by light photons of the same energy content. The atom then emits a photon equal in energy to the one that struck it. The striking photon is thus doubled by the photon emitted. These two photons are doubled again by striking further stimulated atoms, and so on. All the photons released by this snowball effect have the same energy and therefore the same wavelength. This is the principle called Light Amplification by Stimulated Emission of Radiation, or the **laser beam** from its

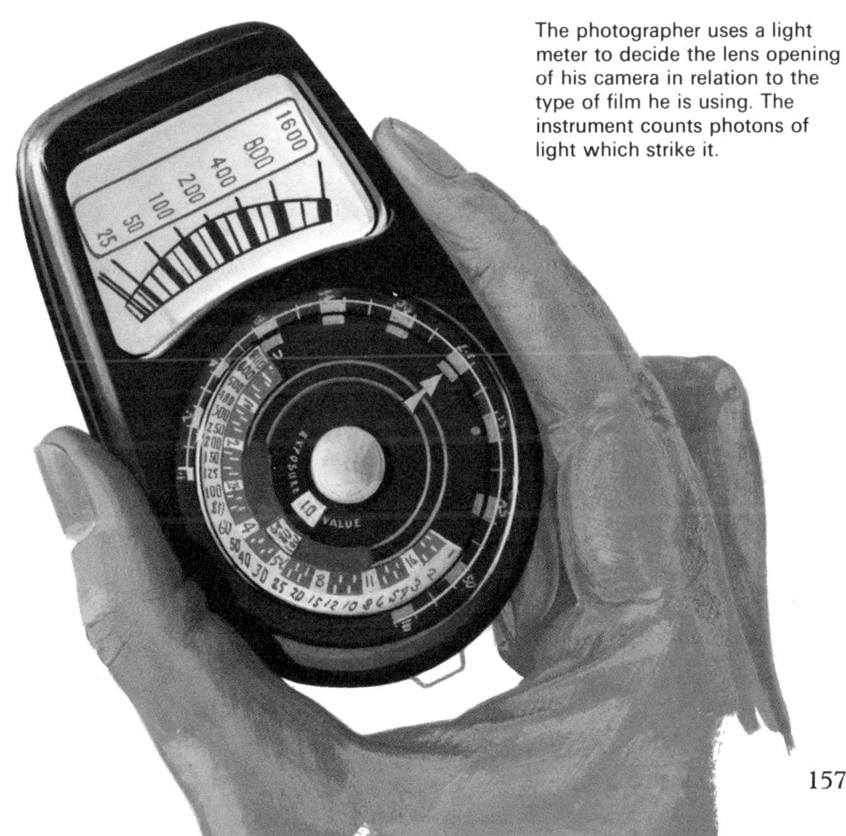

The photographer uses a light meter to decide the lens opening of his camera in relation to the type of film he is using. The instrument counts photons of light which strike it.

initial letters. The beam is composed of light of one wavelength with all the waves in phase, their peaks of energy coinciding. Such a beam diverges very little, concentrating all its energy into a small point where it strikes a surface. This energy can be used for welding or even for delicate operations like eye surgery. A laser beam can be bounced back from a reflecting surface on the moon, losing little of its energy after its long journey, thus providing a useful carrier for radio messages.

Scientists are seen here employing one of the many useful functions of the laser beam to obtain pin-point accuracy while surveying across country. The system involves a laser beam and reflector and measurements more exact than those obtained by conventional means are possible.

Light from the Sun

From the beginning of his history, man has made use of the electromagnetic radiations in the range of heat and light frequencies. Without infrared radiation and light from the sun, life itself would never have developed. Those higher frequencies beyond the range of the human eye called **ultra-violet radiations** have also had their effect upon us. They are responsible for the tanning of human skin and have therefore contributed to the appearance of the different races according to influences of climate throughout the world. They also make possible such reactions as the formation of vitamin D without which young animals and children would develop malformation of their bones known as rickets.

Radiations of even shorter wavelengths and higher frequencies are the **X-rays** and **gamma-rays**. Whereas visible and ultra-violet radiations are emitted only by electrons in the outer shell of an atom, X-rays are emitted by electrons in the inner shells. They thus contain greater energy and have greater penetrating power to pass through solid objects. They are used for exposing, on photographic plates, shadows of the internal structure of objects like the human body. More recently, their penetrating power has been used to kill the malignant cells of a cancerous growth. Gamma-rays are emitted from the nucleus of an atom.

Streams of Photons

The photo-electric effect mentioned above is produced by a stream of photons of light adding their energy to the free electrons that 'float' through the crystals of metals. Electromagnetic radiations of the upper ultra-violet frequencies, X-rays and gamma-rays, can raise the energy levels of outer orbital electrons without removing them from their atoms or molecules. The atom or molecule thus excited becomes extremely reactive. Such waves are called **ionising radiations**. Some ionising radiation that comes from beyond the earth's atmosphere, probably from the sun, is radiation of an even higher frequency than gamma-rays. It is called **cosmic radiation**.

There is too little ionising radiation penetrating the atmosphere to harm life on earth. There is, however, the possibility of nuclear explosions from modern weapons raising the level of ionising radiation to a dangerous degree. It can attack the proteins of living cells and can break chromosomes so that their characteristics are not passed on in reproduction. Such alterations of inherited characteristics

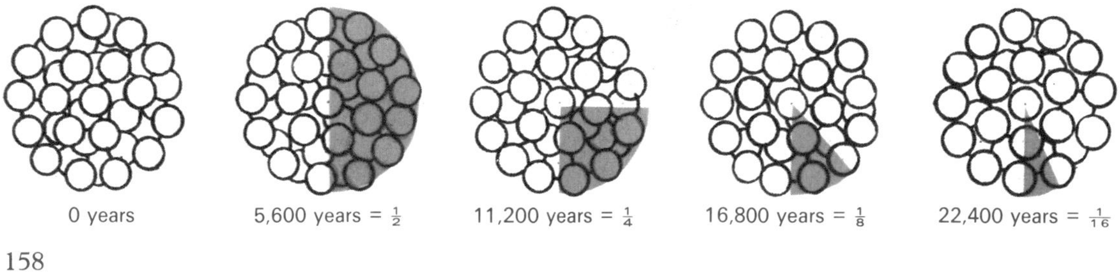

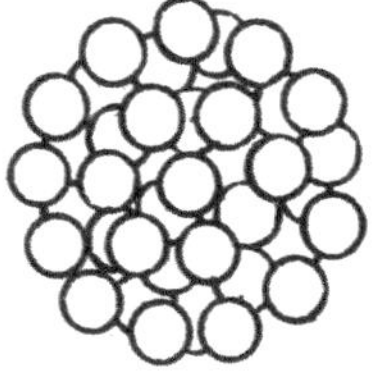

5,600 years = $\frac{1}{2}$

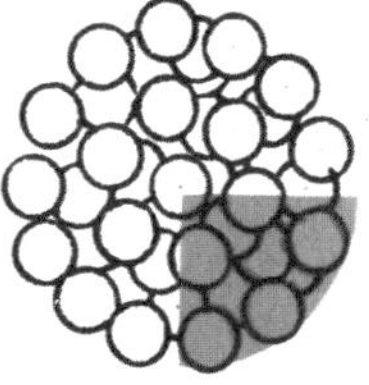

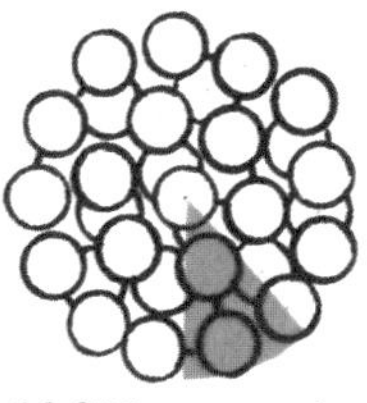

Carbon 14 is a radioactive isotope which decays at a fixed rate over thousands of years. By examining the amount of radiocarbon left in the remains of ancient life, its date can be calculated.

X-rays are used for exposing the internal structure of the human body on photographic plates which are studied by medical experts.

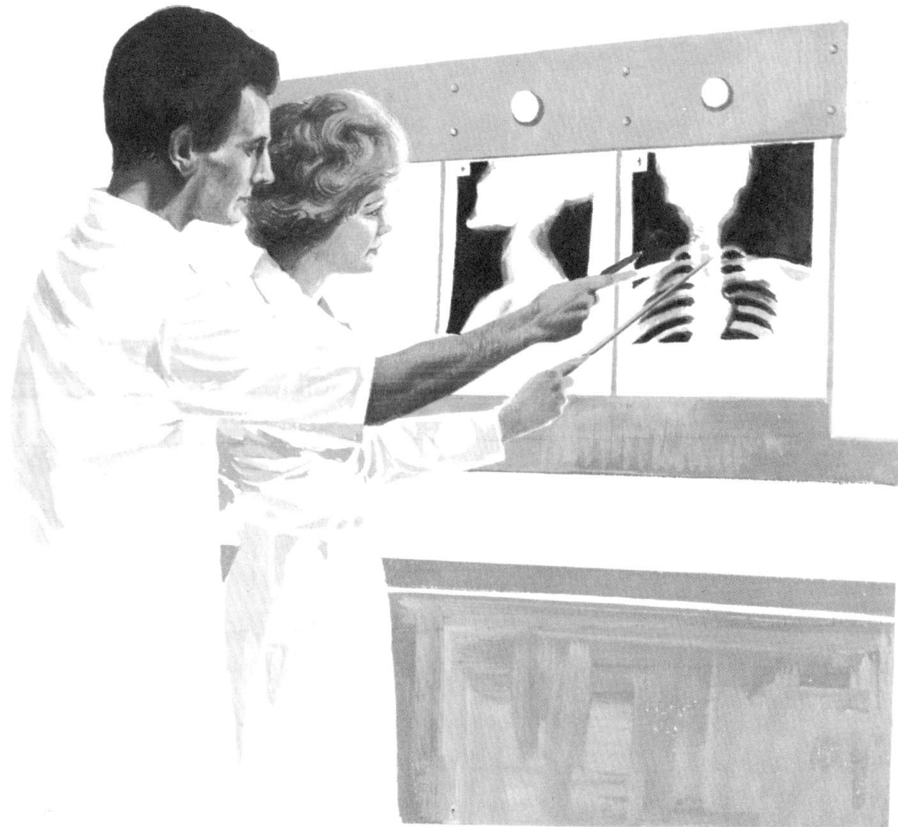

are called mutations. The progress of evolution is a history of mutations partly caused by radiation, but with a highly organised creature such as modern man, any mutation is likely to have a bad effect.

It is ionising radiation, mainly in the ultra-violet frequencies, that has excited atoms in the upper atmosphere, creating a layer called the **ionosphere**. The ionosphere lies between about 60 and 400 kilometres above the earth's surface. It makes possible the transmission of radio waves over long distances. Radio waves can be transmitted in two ways, along the ground and parallel to it or up into the sky to be reflected back again to the ground by the ionosphere. During the day when light from the sun ionises a layer of the ionosphere called the **Heaviside-Kennelly layer**, radio waves can be reflected from it. At night, the ions tend to recombine in this layer. Radio waves are then reflected by the **Appleton layer** which is at a higher altitude where the more rarefied atmosphere tends to remain ionised longer because the ions and electrons collide less frequently.

As one would suppose, radio waves travelling along the ground are weakened by the obstacles they must pass through. Only by waves reflected from the two layers of the ionosphere can long distance transmissions take place. Television frequencies are usually higher than sound radio waves and would normally pass through the ionosphere into empty space. For this reason, television transmissions have a limited range. This can be overcome by the use of satellites in stationary orbit, that is moving at the same speed as the rotation of the earth. These reflect back high frequency television waves either as **passive satellites** or, when they amplify the signal before re-transmitting it back to earth, as **active satellites**.

Electric Flow

Electromagnetic radiations in the radio frequencies are created by the oscillation to and fro of electric currents in specially designed circuits called **resonant circuits**. They consist of a **capacitor** and an **induction coil** connected within a loop of wire. A capacitor can be two metal plates separated by a non-conductor of electricity such as mica. An induction coil is a tightly-wound coil of wire. When the capacitor is charged with electricity from a battery, negatively-charged electrons collect on one of its plates, giving the other plate a positive charge. When the charged capacitor is connected to the induction coil, there is a flow of electricity through the circuit which creates a magnetic field around the induction coil. As soon as the capacitor is completely discharged, this current ceases to flow and the magnetic field around the coil disappears.

A radiosonde is an instrument, carried aloft in a balloon, used by meteorologists to measure atmospheric conditions.

It is a rule of electromagnetism, still not fully explained, but which must be accepted as a fact of nature, that any change of magnetic field will induce a momentary flow of electricity within a wire placed in that field. As the magnetic field disappears, there is an induced flow of electricity in the opposite direction, charging up the capacitor once again. Again the capacitor discharges itself through the circuit. Once again it creates a magnetic field round the coil and so on. A back and forth flow of electricity is maintained until the electrical resistance within the circuit slows it down to nothing.

Electronic Valves

This to and fro flow of electricity can be likened to the swing of a pendulum in a clock. If it is to continue to oscillate it must be provided with some

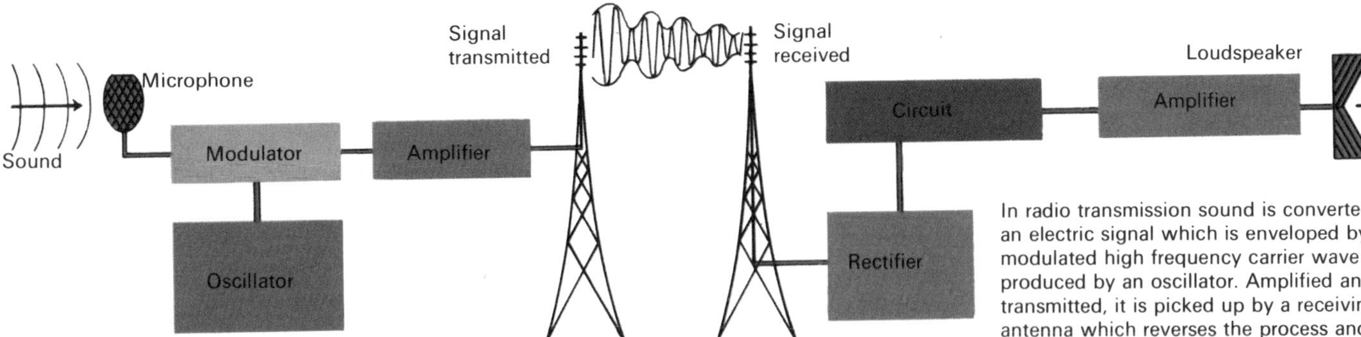

In radio transmission sound is converted into an electric signal which is enveloped by a modulated high frequency carrier wave produced by an oscillator. Amplified and transmitted, it is picked up by a receiving antenna which reverses the process and converts the carrier wave back to the original signal and so into sound.

outside power to overcome the resistance. This can be provided by an **electronic valve,** called in the United States a **tube**. A valve is a bulb of glass with air removed and fitted with two electrical terminals connected to a battery or other source of electrical power. When the terminal connected to the negative side of the battery, called the **cathode**, is heated, electrons will break free from it. The other terminal connected to the positive side of the battery and called the **anode**, will be positively charged and will attract the electrons from the cathode in a continuous flow.

If a metal gauze, called the **grid**, is placed within the path of this flow of electrons, any charge applied to it will affect the flow. A negative charge will repel the flow of negative electrons and stop the current. A positive charge, which is weaker than the positive charge of the anode, will attract the electrons and speed them on their way to the anode, increasing the energy of the current. The process can be shown in diagrammatic form.

If the low energy oscillating current from a resonant circuit is applied to the grid of an electronic valve, the output from the valve will be, an oscillating current of a higher energy but exactly the same frequency. This high energy output can be fed through another induction coil placed alongside the coil in the resonant circuit. Its continually changing magnetic field will induce in the resonant circuit coil a current sufficient to overcome its resistance and to keep it oscillating, as in a simplified radio transmitter.

In practice, several electronic valves wired in series would be used to amplify the output to a very high energy level suitable for radiation over a long distance. The resonant circuit would also be provided with a variable capacitor capable of altering the frequency of oscillations produced. It is by altering the amount of electricity stored by the capacitor, called its **capacitance**, that the resonant circuit of a radio transmitter or receiver is **tuned**.

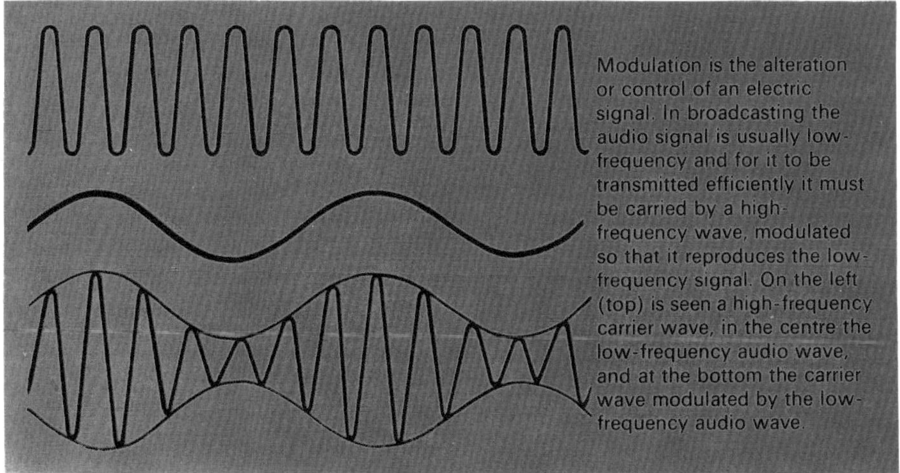

Modulation is the alteration or control of an electric signal. In broadcasting the audio signal is usually low-frequency and for it to be transmitted efficiently it must be carried by a high-frequency wave, modulated so that it reproduces the low-frequency signal. On the left (top) is seen a high-frequency carrier wave, in the centre the low-frequency audio wave, and at the bottom the carrier wave modulated by the low-frequency audio wave.

Sympathetic Vibration

It is possible to tune two wine glasses to the same pitch or frequency of sound vibrations with the addition of a little water to one or the other. Thus when one wine glass is tapped, the other will oscillate a thin strand of wire laid across it. The wine glasses are said to be in **resonance** with each other. Singers have been known to be able to pitch their voices to the resonance of a glass and shatter it by sympathetic vibration. Similarly, the resonant circuit of a radio **receiver** is tuned to accept the electromagnetic radiations of a certain frequency from a transmitter and to oscillate in sympathy with it. This received wave signal can be amplified through electronic valves in the same way as it is amplified in the transmitter.

Broadcasting

The design of a transmitting aerial can be such that it is also tuned to the frequency transmitted. In practice, electromagnetic radiations in the so-called 'audio' frequencies would require an aerial of inconveniently large dimensions. Radio broadcasting is therefore confined to somewhat higher frequencies. For long distance transmission the wavelengths are usually confined within the 2,000 metres (150 kHz, low frequency or LF) to one metre (500 MHz, very high frequency or VHF) bands. Television can be transmitted on ultra high frequencies or UHF, 300 to 3,000 MHz, with wavelengths of one metre to ten centimetres respectively.

Broadcasting frequencies are those of the **carrier wave.** To this must be added the frequencies equivalent to the speech or music to be broadcast.

The diode is a simple form of electronic valve with cathode supplying electrons and an anode which attracts them.

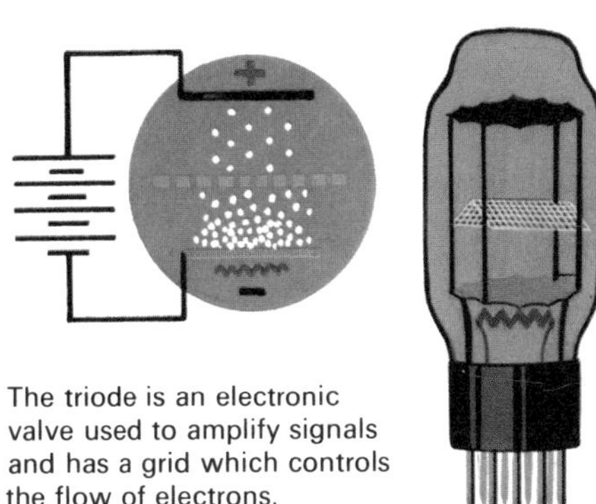

The triode is an electronic valve used to amplify signals and has a grid which controls the flow of electrons.

These frequencies are converted into electrical oscillations in a **transducer**. A typical transducer is the microphone. This can consist of a thin metal diaphragm which is vibrated by sound waves within the magnetic field of an electromagnet. The movement of this diaphragm breaking the magnetic field induces a current in the coil of the electromagnet which is equivalent to the sound frequencies causing it. A similar transducer at the receiving end uses the variations in this induced current to vary the strength of another electromagnet which in turn vibrates a diaphragm setting up sound waves equivalent to those entering the microphone. The receiving apparatus can be in the form either of an earphone or a loudspeaker.

The variable current produced by a transducer can be added to the carrier wave in either of two ways. The first of these varies the amplitude or energy content of the carrier wave and is called **amplitude modulation**.

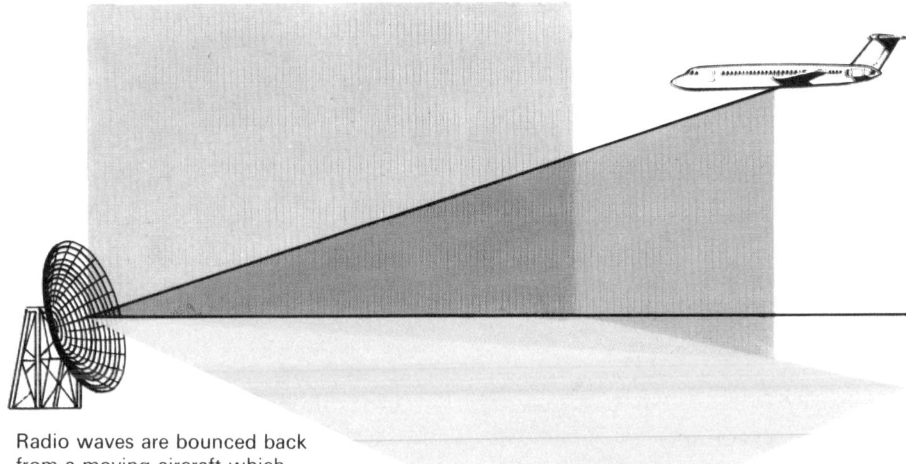

Radio waves are bounced back from a moving aircraft which enable operators on radar equipment to calculate its distance and speed.

The second method is to vary the frequency of the carrier wave by frequencies equivalent to the audio wave. This is called **frequency modulation**.

This parabolic radio telescope at Green Bank, West Virginia in the United States, is mounted on an axis which moves parallel to the equator.

Flow of Current

The audio waves can be separated from the carrier waves in the receiver by an electronic valve used as a **rectifier**. The electronic valve permits a flow of current in one direction only (hence its name). This has the effect of cutting off the bottom half of the wave forms so that variations in current amplitude or current frequency can be applied directly to the earphone or loudspeaker circuit. In such a circuit, the energy of the half-wave output increases and decreases the frequency of the audio wave modulating it, thus producing sound waves in the earphones.

Nowadays, the electronic valve has been largely replaced by **semiconductors**. These are crystals of substances like germanium and selenium which have covalent bonds between the atoms. At the impossible absolute zero of temperature, a perfect covalent crystal would have no free electrons and would therefore not pass an electric current. At normal temperatures, however, a few electrons have the energy to break free. Placed within an electric potential, from a battery for instance, these free electrons will naturally flow towards the positive terminal of the battery. Their movement will leave vacancies in the outer shells of some of the atoms. These vacancies are called **holes**, and they are repeatedly filled and vacated by passing electrons. The movement of electrons towards the positive side of the battery is called **n-type conductivity**. The holes behave like positively-charged electrons moving in the opposite direction. This is called **p-type conductivity**. Thus the total current passed by a semiconductor is the sum of its n-type and p-type conductivity.

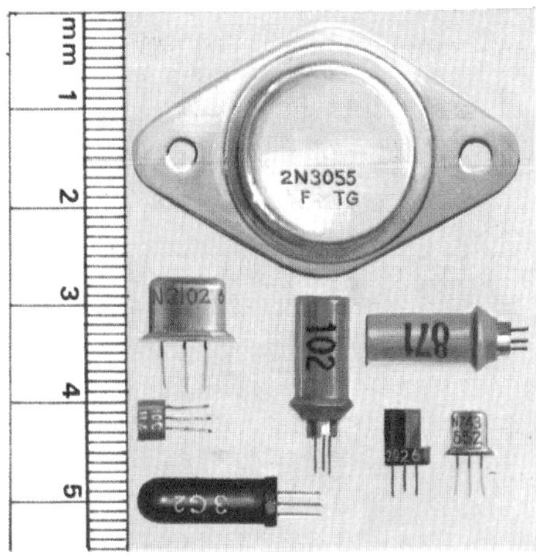

Because they require no heat to pass a current, transistors can be very small.

Changes in Conductivity

This is further increased by the addition of impurities into the crystal. Arsenic, for instance, has five electrons in its outer shell, which is one more than can pair with the four outer electrons of a neighbouring germanium atom. The remaining electron is free to add to the crystal's n-type conductivity. Indium, on the other hand, has only three electrons in its outer shell. Paired with a germanium atom, it leaves a hole to increase the p-type conductivity.

If these impurities are added to a crystal so that one end is predominantly n-type and the other end predominantly p-type, where the two meet in the middle there will be an **n-p junction**. If the p-type end is connected to the positive side of a battery, n-type electrons will move across the junction towards it. With the n-type end connected to the negative side of the battery, the holes will move across the junction in the opposite direction. Thus the flow of current through the crystal will depend only upon the voltage applied to it. If the battery connections are reversed, n-type electrons will go straight to the positive side of the battery and p-type holes to the negative, neither crossing the junction. Only the few free electrons in the p-region and the few holes in the n-region will cross the junction which will then behave like a break in the circuit, passing very little current.

Transistors

Used in this way, the crystal becomes a **semiconductor diode**, passing current in one direction only. It is thus equivalent to a rectifier valve, cutting off half the wave form of the alternating current applied to it. If two semiconductor diodes are placed back to back forming either an **npn** or a **pnp** arrangement, then they act as an amplifier. The central region, which is equivalent to the grid of an electronic valve, is called the **base**. One outside region, equivalent to the cathode of a valve, is called the **emitter**. The other outside region equivalent to the anode of a valve, is called the **collector**. Such arrangements are known as **transistors**.

The advantage of transistors is that they require no heating to pass a current and can be made extremely small. Whole circuits, called **integrated circuits**, can be built into very tiny silicon chips.

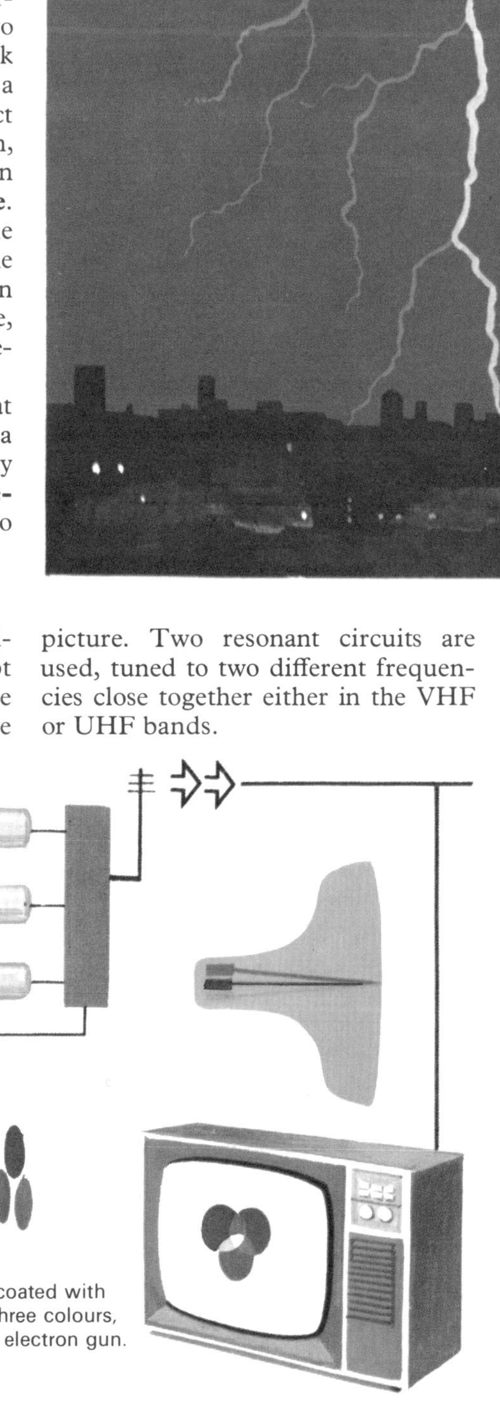

Television Transmission

Television programmes are broadcast in a similar way to radio, except that there are two carrier waves, one for sound and the other for the picture. Two resonant circuits are used, tuned to two different frequencies close together either in the VHF or UHF bands.

The colour television camera splits the image it films by means of mirror filters into three primary colours of light.

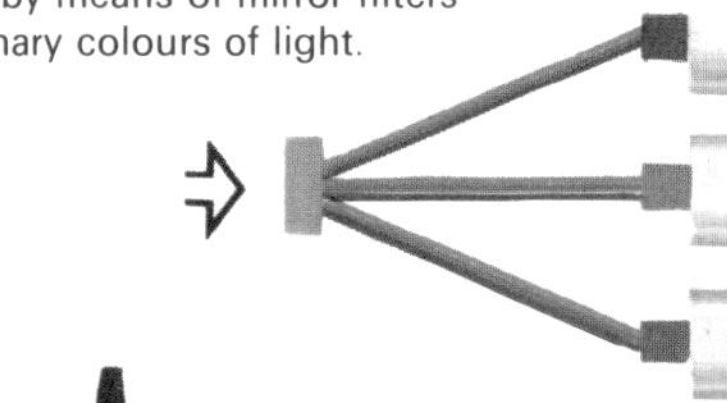

In the receiver there are three electron guns, one for red, one for blue, and one for green.

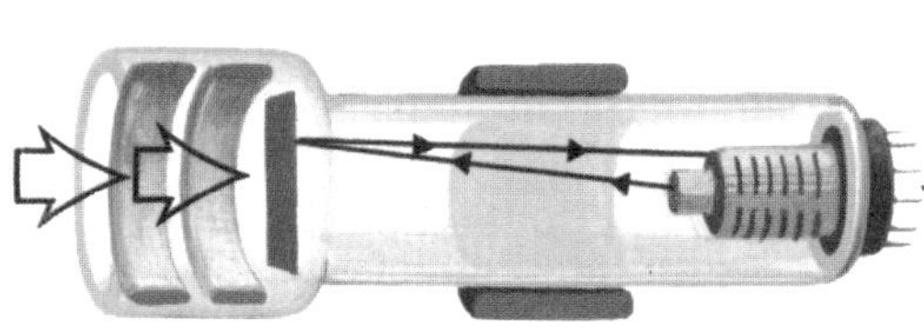

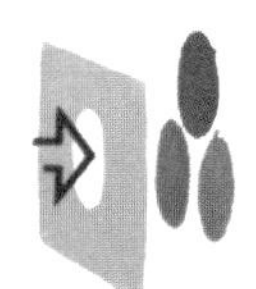

The screen of the cathode-ray tube is coated with phosphor dots in groups of the same three colours, which are activated by the appropriate electron gun.

A single flash of lightning can discharge millions of kilowatts of electricity. This drawing combines three such flashes which followed one another in rapid succession.

Electrical Energy

It has been said that an atom contains potential electrical energy. Each proton in the atomic nucleus carries a positive charge which exactly equals the negative charge carried by each orbital electron. Since the number of protons and the number of electrons are normally equal, the atom is electrically neutral. In many substances, however, some electrons are only loosely held within their orbits. They can be literally rubbed off.

If a stick of hard rubber is rubbed with fur, for instance, some electrons from the fur will settle on the surface of the rubber which then becomes negatively charged. If, on the other hand, a glass rod is rubbed with silk, some of the electrons are rubbed off on to the silk, and the glass becomes positively charged. Since unlike electrical charges attract each other, the negatively charged rubber will be attracted to the positively charged glass. Both charged substances would attract particles of dust whose atoms are neutral, because their positively charged nuclei would be attracted to the negatively charged rubber, and their negatively charged electrons would be attracted to the positively charged glass.

This is why dust is attracted to polished surfaces which all carry some static electrical charge. The study of such phenomena is called **electrostatics**. When the free electrons are moving all in one direction, as they can do in a wire for instance, then a current of electricity is said to flow along the wire. The study of the flow of electrons is called **electrodynamics**. A current of electricity is not like the current of a river. It is more like the passing of buckets of water from hand to hand by a chain of people fighting a fire. Each electron passes from atom to atom along the chain of crystals comprising the conducting material.

Volts and Amps

The direction of flow of an electric current is always from a point of high potential energy to a point of low potential energy. The force between the two points is called the **electromotive force**, and it is measured in units called **volts**. The number of electrons passing along the conductor is the measure of the amount of current flowing and the units used are called **amperes** or **amps** for short. One amp is quite a large amount of current and consists of 6,242,000,000,000,000,000 electrons moving past a particular point in a wire every second. Less than one-sixth of an amp will light a table lamp.

The amount of water firefighters can carry to a fire will depend upon their strength, their numbers and the distance involved. In a similar way, the amount of current passed by a conductor depends upon the material of which it is made, its thickness and its length. The extent to which a conductor opposes the flow of current is called its **resistance**. The higher the resistance, the less the flow of electric current. Resistance is measured in **ohms**.

Ohm's Law

The units mentioned above have been chosen so that one volt will drive a current of one amp through a resistance of one ohm. The three measurements can be related in the formula: **voltage = current × resistance**. This is called **Ohm's Law** after

The sodium used in street lights is lit by an electrical discharge.

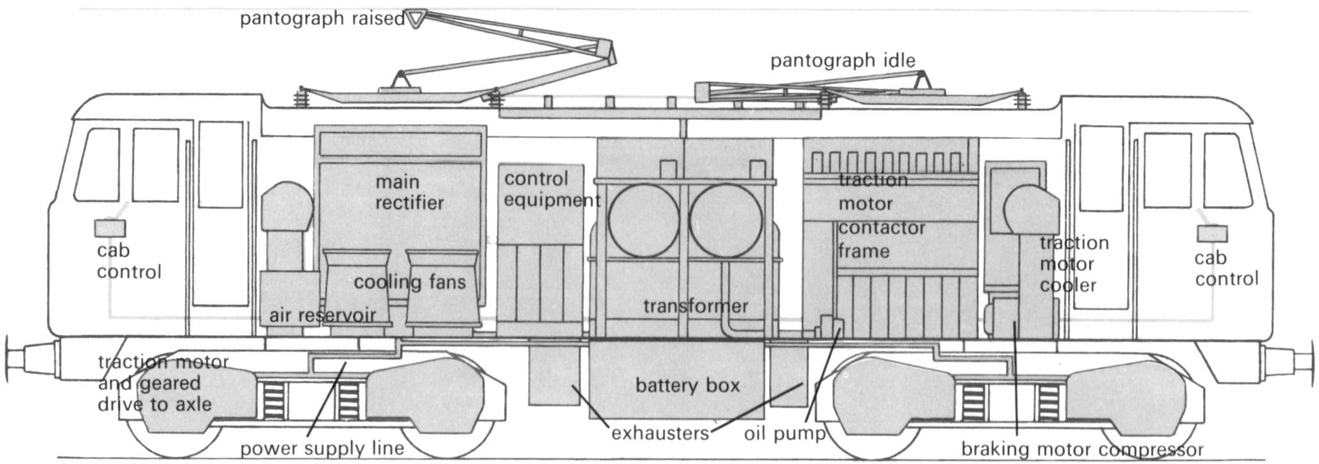

Electricity is used increasingly to power locomotives. The blue areas in the cutaway drawing above indicate transformers and rectifiers and the power circuit.

Georg Ohm (1787–1854), the German physicist who formulated it. The energy available from an electric current is the product of the current, the time for which it flows and the voltage driving it. Thus one volt driving a current of one amp represents the power of one **watt**, and one watt of electricity used in one second amounts to one **joule** of energy. As a watt-second or a joule is a very small amount of energy, electricity is usually sold in units of thousands of watts per hour or **kilowatt hours**.

An electric current can be obtained directly from chemical energy using rods of zinc and copper, called the **electrodes**. These are immersed in a bath of sulphuric acid diluted with water, called the **electrolyte**. The zinc begins to dissolve in the acid, releasing zinc ions, sulphate ions and hydrogen ions in the electrolyte solution. Electrons are left behind on the zinc rod and, if this is connected to the copper rod by a wire, an electric current will flow through the wire. This will leave extra electrons on the copper electrode which will become negatively charged. Thus it will attract the positive hydrogen ions across the electrolyte to settle around the copper electrode. There, the excess electrons from the flow of current will combine with the hydrogen ions which will be given off in the form of diatomic gas molecules. The copper electrode appears to take no part in the chemical reaction, but it is important in the sense that different metals produce different amounts of electrical energy.

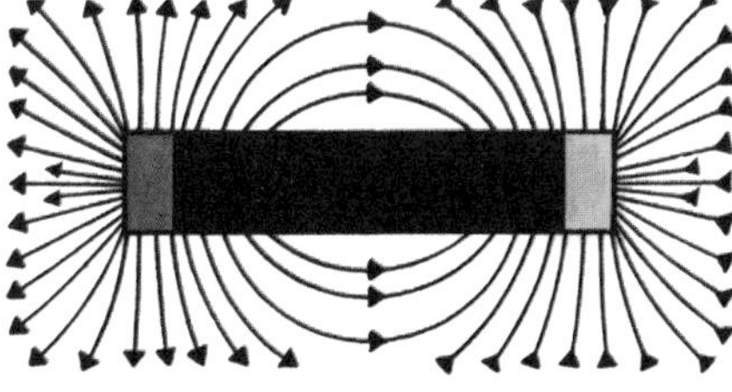

Magnetic field around a magnet.

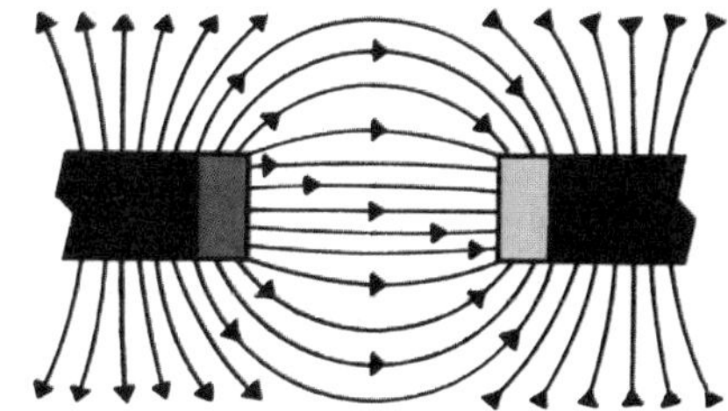

Magnetic field between unlike poles.

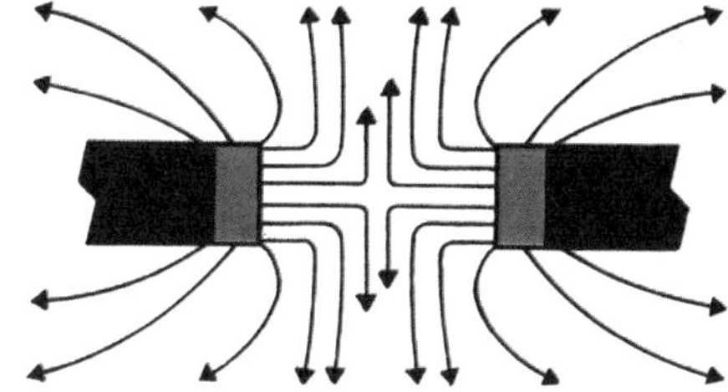

Magnetic fields between like poles.

Dry Cells

The common form of battery is the so-called 'dry' cell which has a central electrode of carbon surrounded by an electrolyte paste of ammonium chloride, manganese dioxide and carbon granules in a zinc container which acts as the other electrode. Though called a dry cell, it is essential that the electrolyte should remain moist. This sort of battery is called a **primary cell**. Cells that can be recharged, like lead accumulators used in cars, store electrical energy in the form of chemical energy and are called **secondary cells**. Almost all the chemical reactions in an electric cell can be reversed by applying electrical energy to it. This is called **electrolysis** and is used to coat cheap metals with such other metals as gold, silver, chromium and tin.

The orbital electrons in atoms spin on their axes rather as the earth spins while at the same time orbiting the sun. This and a lack of balance due to the movement of unpaired electrons in the molecule can have the effect of turning an atom into a tiny bar magnet. This means that each atomic magnet tends to line up with any outside lines of magnetic force. In most substances, this tendency is largely overcome by the normal oscillations of the atom within its molecule or crystal. Such substances are called **paramagnetic**.

In a few metals, such as iron, nickel and cobalt, the spacing within the crystal is such that groups of ions line up together magnetically in what are called domains. Each domain, being much larger than an individual atom, is not affected by the oscillations

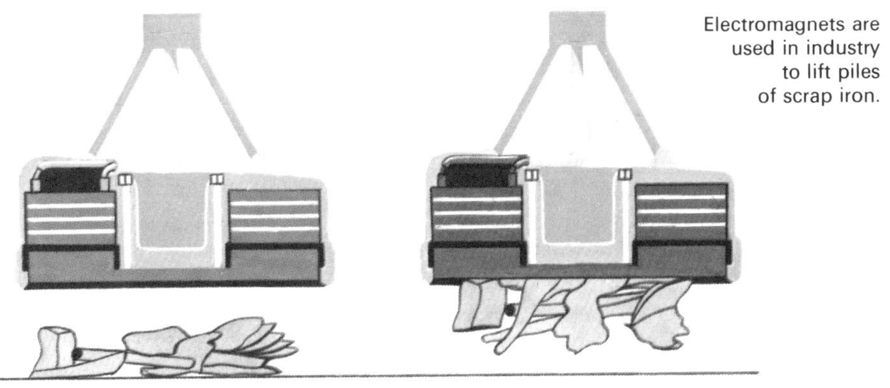

Electromagnets are used in industry to lift piles of scrap iron.

of its individual ions. When the metal is unmagnetised, its domains are arranged at random, but once they are placed within an outside magnetic field, they line up with it. Such metals are therefore easily magnetised and are known as **ferromagnetic**.

Substances such as silver or copper whose atoms do not normally behave as tiny bar magnets are affected by magnetic fields in such a way that they turn into weak magnets opposing the field that creates them. They are called **diamagnetic**, and there is some diamagnetism in all substances, though it is usually overcome by their paramagnetism or ferromagnetism.

Electromagnets

Since an electric current is a movement of free electrons in one direction and, during this movement, all the electrons spin in the same direction, it is not surprising to find than an electric current creates its own magnetic fields. This is called **electromagnetism**. It operates in concentric circles around a wire through which a current flows and disappears as soon as the current stops. If the wire is wound into a coil, the lines of electromagnetic force become similar to those of a bar magnet.

Like ferromagnetism, the force of electromagnetism operates through space. If an electromagnet is placed beside another coil of wire, the effect of its magnetism is to induce a current in the second coil, but only when the magnetic field is changing, when the electromagnet is switched on or off. Another way to produce this **induced current** is to move a wire physically across a magnetic field so that it breaks the lines of force. This is the principle of the **dynamo** which rotates a coil of wire within a magnetic field, thus producing an induced current through the coil. This is the way an **electric generator** (as a large dynamo is called) works, transforming the mechanical energy of the rotating coil into electrical energy. It is how electrical energy is supplied to the power points in our homes. The current from a battery is a **direct current** (DC) flowing in one direction. The current from a generator is usually rapidly changing direction to and fro and is called an alternating current (AC).

A simple way to obtain electric current from chemical energy is by using rods of zinc and copper connected by a wire and immersed in sulphuric acid and water (right).

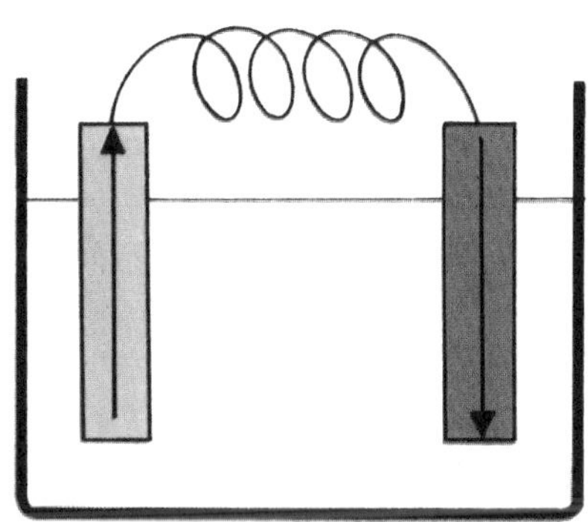

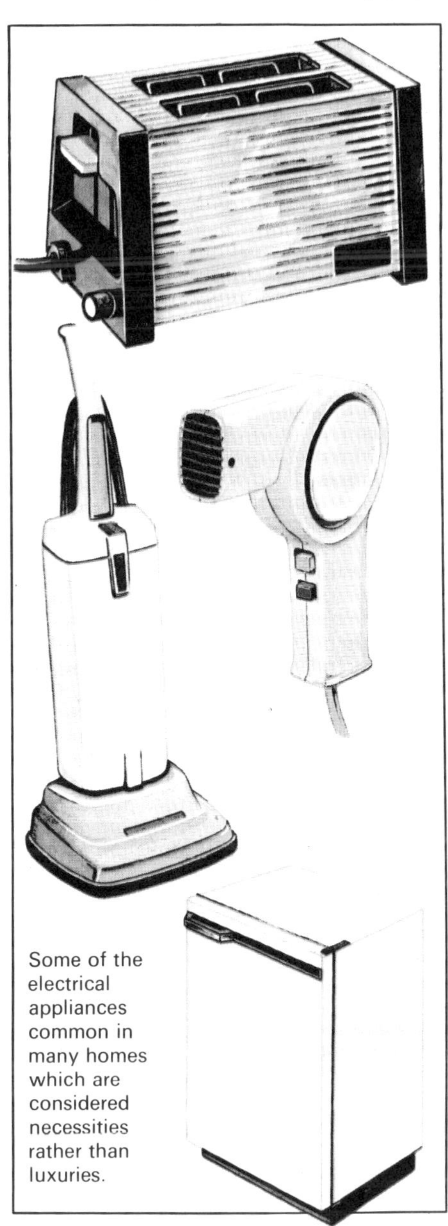

Some of the electrical appliances common in many homes which are considered necessities rather than luxuries.

Electric Motors

The electric motor is the opposite of a generator. The coil within the magnetic field is supplied with a current that is broken at intervals by an arrangement called a **commutator**. The magnetic forces rotate the coil, transforming electrical energy into mechanical energy.

An electric current does not necessarily require a conductor. The flow of electrons through an electronic valve or the cathode ray tube that provides the picture in a television set operates in a vacuum. A spark will jump across a pair of terminals where there is a high voltage. Very little current may flow in such a spark, but a voltage of 15,000 is required for every inch of leap. A single lightning stroke, on the other hand, can occur from a build-up of 100 million volts and cause a current of 160,000 amps travelling at more than 60,000 miles a second!

Electrical power can be transmitted on land or under the sea for almost any distance. The diagram below illustrates a typical land circuit for the supply of electricity from a power station to a building.

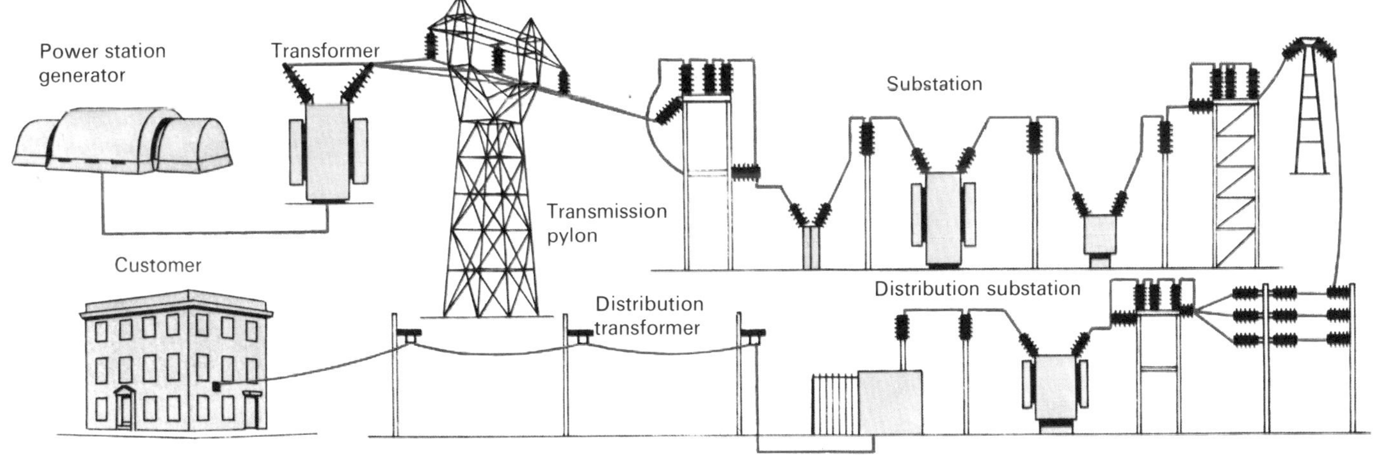

Nuclear Energy

The nucleus of an atom consists of positively charged protons and uncharged neutrons. Since like charges repel each other, it would seem that the protons should fly apart. Between them, however, there are exchanges of energy in the form of very unstable particles, existing for no more than one millionth of a second, called **mesons**. These exchanges are usually of a type called pi-mesons or **pions**. They are the nuclear equivalent of the photons that affect the energy content of electrons. They exert an attraction between the energy particles of the nucleus with what are called **exchange forces**.

The electrostatic repulsion forces between proton and proton diminish as they come closer together. Then the exchange forces, which involve a considerable amount of energy, take over. This is called the **binding energy** of the nucleus. Since protons and neutrons in an atomic nucleus are packed very close together, those in the centre are pulled from every direction, and those on the surface are pulled from the interior only. This surface effect is similar to the molecular forces that bind a drop of water together. It holds the nucleus in a spherical shape.

Natural Radioactivity

In a small nucleus with relatively few protons and neutrons, a greater proportion of the total will be at the surface, so the whole is held together more strongly. As the mass number, that is the total of protons and neutrons, gets beyond about 40, some individual protons become far enough apart for the electrostatic repulsion of like charges to have an effect. The very largest atomic nuclei become unstable. In fact, they are naturally radioactive.

In natural radioactive decay, only small parts of a nucleus, in the form of alpha and beta particles, are thrown out. For the extraction of nuclear energy that can be useful to man, a nucleus of a large mass number must be bombarded with neutrons to break the nucleus apart and release some of its binding energy. When the nucleus is split in this way, there is an increase in the energy content of the resulting pair of smaller nuclei with a corresponding loss of mass. This is called the **mass defect**.

For the lighter nuclei, up to a mass number of 40, the surface effect is more pronounced with the addition of each proton or neutron. Thus the mass defect increases with the addition of each particle and more energy is created. Beyond the mass number of 40, electrostatic repulsion begins to take effect so that a breaking up of the nucleus leads to an increase of mass defect and the production of energy. In other words, the **fusion** or joining together of light nuclei produces energy, and the **fission** or splitting of heavy nuclei produces energy.

The fusion of hydrogen nuclei to form helium gas is the process by which the sun gives off its radiant energy. Since an individual hydrogen proton must be moving at tremendous speed to overcome the electrostatic repulsion of another hydrogen proton, fusion can only take place at extremely high temperatures such as those that exist at the sun's surface. Such temperatures can be achieved by the explosion of a uranium bomb, and such a bomb surrounded by a hydrogenous substance will create a fusion reaction. This has been done in the so-called hydrogen bomb.

This mushroom cloud erupted 12·8 kilometres (8 miles) into the air after a test nuclear explosion in the Nevada desert in the United States.

Nuclear-powered submarines first appeared in 1955. They were the first nuclear craft built to operate while submerged and to stay down for long periods.

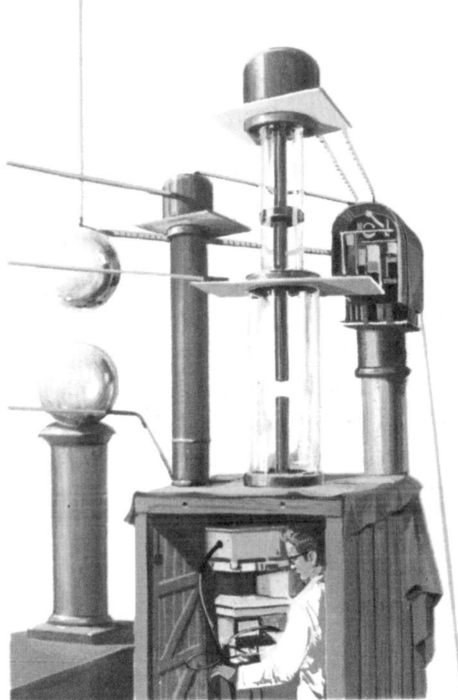

The accelerator (above left) in which the British scientists John Cockcroft and Ernest Walton first split the atom. Seen above is one of the mammoth nuclear reactors at the 3-million kilowatt plant at Brown's Ferry, Alabama in the United States.

Fusion Reaction

Obtaining a constant supply of nuclear energy from a fusion reaction would be highly desirable. Hydrogen is a very common element, every molecule of water in the oceans containing two atoms of hydrogen. Also, the fusion reaction produces no waste matter. There is no radioactive material left over which has to be safely disposed of. The problem is one of containing temperatures of millions of degrees centigrade to sustain a continuous reaction. It is a problem that has yet to be satisfactorily solved. In the meantime, nuclear energy can be obtained only by the fission of heavy nuclei such as that of uranium.

Natural uranium occurs in a mixture of three isotopes of mass numbers 234, 235 and 238 respectively. Uranium 234 is present in such tiny proportions that it can be disregarded. Uranium 235 is the important one, although it accounts for only seven in every 1,000 atoms, the other 993 atoms being the 238 isotope.

Slow-moving neutrons expelled by uranium 235 are absorbed by the uranium 238 creating a new isotope with a mass number 239. This has a half-life of only 23 minutes and decays by emitting an electron, thus gaining an extra positive charge. This transforms it into a new element called neptunium with the atomic number 93. Neptunium has a half-life of 2·3 days and also emits an electron, transforming itself into another new element called plutonium which is relatively stable with a half-life of 24,000 years.

Chain Reactions

Plutonium and uranium 235 are both readily fissioned, especially by slow-moving neutrons. Each fission produces two or three extra neutrons which are available to cause more fission. Thus a **chain reaction** is set up. In order to start this chain reaction, however, sufficient slow-moving neutrons have to be provided, slow enough to avoid absorption by the large proportion of uranium 238. This is done by bouncing them off light nuclei such as those of the pure form of carbon called graphite, or deuterium oxide known as heavy water. These substances are called the **moderators**. Of course, once the chain reaction has begun, it will build up to the explosive power of the atomic bomb unless it is controlled.

There is a minium amount of uranium 235 required before a chain reaction can begin. This quantity, called the **critical mass**, is 1·5 kilograms. Smaller quantities, with relatively high proportions of surface area, will lose too many neutrons to the atmosphere to begin the reaction. The atom bomb consists of two lumps of uranium, each below the critical mass, which are brought together by a trigger explosion.

To obtain nuclear energy for peaceful purposes, the speed of the chain reaction must be controlled. This is done by inserting rods of a material, such as the metal cadmium, which has the property of absorbing neutrons. These rods can be raised if the fission reaction shows signs of slowing down. If the chain reaction begins to speed up to a dangerous degree the rods are lowered into the fissionable material, thus reducing the number of neutrons available for fission.

In a heavy water reactor (HWR), the liquid deuterium oxide is used as a coolant by transferring the heat energy to ordinary water, producing steam to drive a turbine. This turbine can in turn be used to operate a generator to produce electrical power.

Two diagrams showing nuclear fission (right) and nuclear fusion (far right). The latter explosion is regarded as 'clean' since it does not leave radioactive waste material to be safely disposed of.

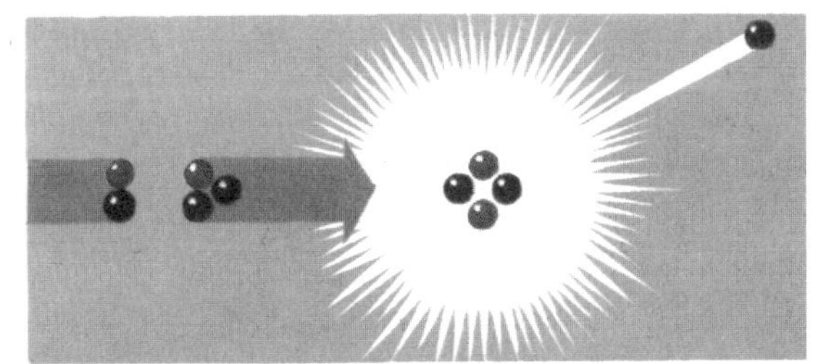

Energy from the Earth

A turbine is a wheel turned by the natural force of water, steam or gas. The potential energy of a fluid such as water can be simply converted into rotary kinetic energy by means of a turbine. One of the first turbine engines to be proposed was the device of Hero of Alexandria who lived in the 2nd century A.D. His simple machine turned a sphere by means of the thrust of steam escaping from two outlets. Apart from Hero's toy, the steam turbine did not come into effective use until modern times, less than a hundred years ago. Turbines using fluids directly, as in a water-wheel, are much more ancient, and windmills were invented probably in the 7th century A.D. The gigantic steam turbines of today use blades made with great precision from the finest quality steel.

Niagara Falls provide the greatest single natural source of water power in North America. They consist of two great cascades separated by Goat Island along the borders of Canada and the United States, one fall in each country. The Great Horseshoe Falls on the Canadian side are more than twice the width of those in the United States, although the latter are slightly taller. The potential power of the falls began to be harnessed in the 1850s and the first electricity produced by their turbines was directed into the village of Niagara in 1881. Today, the falls serve New York, Pennsylvania and Ontario.

People of the ancient world made great use of the power of water, particularly the Romans, whose engineering skills developed the water-wheel into a machine capable of really heavy work. They used three different types of water-wheel, seen here. The undershot (left) is driven by the flow of a stream beneath the wheel. The breast wheel (centre) catches water at a midway point in the drop of a stream. The overshot wheel has water flowing over it and gains much extra power from the force of falling water.

There are various forms of nuclear reactor. The fast breeder reactor is a type which is economical in its use of fuel and can produce large quantities of heat from a comparatively small plant. On the right is seen the first reactor at Dounreay in Scotland which, when it was completed in 1963, was the most powerful operating in the world.

Most electrical power today is provided by thermal power stations which convert the heat energy of a fuel—coal, oil or gas—into electrical energy. The fuel is burned in order to heat water in a boiler until it becomes steam. At a very high pressure and temperature the steam is directed on to the blades of a turbine, which in turn is connected to a generator. When the steam has done its work it is condensed and the water returns to the boiler to continue the process in a continuing cycle of energy conversion. The condensation of the steam requires the large cooling towers which are characteristic of thermal power stations.

The Technological Revolution

Power

Film sent back by astronauts travelling to the moon showed the earth dwindling behind them. More than at any other time in history, the 20th century has made the world we inhabit seem smaller. From the beginning of the century, scientists have been drawing more and more accurate maps of the universe in which our own environment is such a tiny speck. Sophisticated instruments now search beyond our universe. Astronomers measure distances in thousands of light years and count stars in their billions of billions in a limitless universe.

Amidst all this universal matter and energy, the matter and energy which comprise our spaceship earth seems insignificant indeed. If all the conventional fuel on earth were gathered in one place and burned at the same rate as the energy output of the sun, it would last no longer than four days Yet it can be calculated that the complete destruction of just one gram of matter would produce about $1\frac{1}{2}$ million horsepower for 24 hours.

This is the paradox of energy. Nature needs immense amounts of it to perform the simplest task. Great quantities of energy are locked in a single atom just to hold it together and make it react with other atoms. Yet 20th-century man is beginning to talk about the Energy Crisis. It has taken millions of years to lay down deposits of the fossil fuels such as coal and oil. Our technological revolution has increased their consumption to such an extent that their complete exhaustion can be counted in decades rather than centuries.

Modern man has set out along a road from which there is no turning back. He has altered the face of the land to serve him. The earth has become a machine working for the benefit of the human consumer. The power

The Kariba dam on the river Zambesi between Rhodesia and Zambia provides electricity for both countries and irrigates the Zambesi Valley.

to operate it and the materials to maintain it must continue to be provided if it is not to run down. It is this that makes the scientist so important and, indeed, makes scientists of us all.

Basic Needs

Man's basic needs are much as they ever were. He cannot do without food and clothing, a place to sleep and a means of warming it. In tomorrow's world, his food will have to be more and more 'invented' in the laboratory. Plants can already be multiplied without recourse to the flowering and seeding cycle. Entirely new ones will be created with built-in fertilisers and resistance to disease. Much of our protein, though still looking like meat and cheese, will be made in factories without the involvement of animals. The textile industry is already experimenting in this field, just as it has largely replaced the use of natural fibres from plants and animals with man-made materials. Our homes are already becoming mini-factories for the provision of our comfort. Distribution of our needs and communication with our fellows is becoming almost impossible without machines and the fuels to power them. Every single individual in an advanced society must become a machine operator from early childhood.

Science has brought many benefits to mankind, but anxieties follow in their wake. A growing population produces a growing demand. Resources must be marshalled to meet it. Ingenuity is needed to direct those resources to the best advantage. We are now well into the 20th century, and there are no signs that the ingenuity of man is flagging.

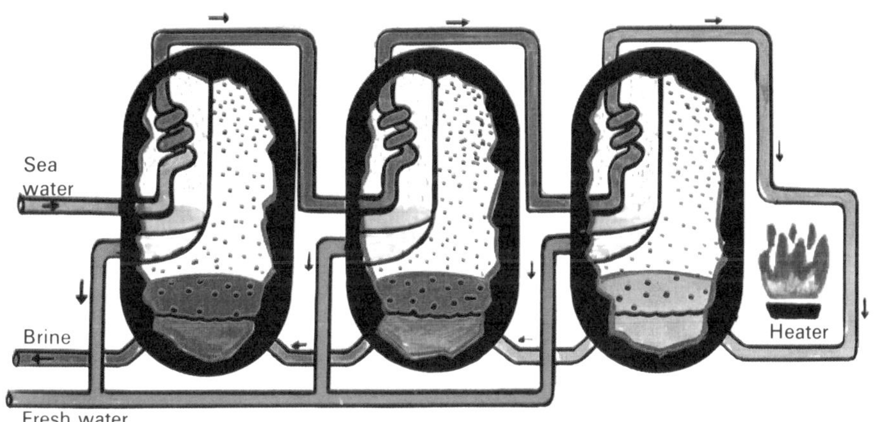

Flash distillation plant and diagram illustrating the process whereby brine is removed from sea water to give fresh water.

The Energy of Water

When man first appeared on this planet, there were approximately 1,350 million cubic kilometres (326 million cubic miles) of water. Today, in spite of the continually increasing use of water and the never-ending search for new sources of supply, there is still the same amount of it. Water is one of the most stable compounds on earth. It is unique as a source of life and power in that it can be used over and over again. Somewhere in the world today, someone may be drinking a glass of the very same water in which, in ancient times, Archimedes took his famous bath. The mechanical energy of a waterfall can turn a waterwheel. The water flows on to the sea. There it evaporates and falls as rain on the high ground above the waterfall. The process goes on endlessly.

Control of Water

The problem of water is not one of shortage but of having it in the right place at the right time. Man's earliest engineering feats were concerned with the control and use of water. Of all fresh water 97 per cent is under the ground. Even such a dry region as the Sahara desert is estimated to be underlain by vast amounts of water spread over a great area. The problem is to find the places where it is close enough to the surface to make the sinking of wells practicable. Some underground water is heated by volcanic action. It can emerge naturally in the form of a steam geyser. At Lardarello in Italy, there is a man-made steam well. The heat energy extracted from it operates turbo-generators, transforming the heat into electrical energy. The steam is then condensed and valuable chemicals obtained from the water.

In some parts of the world, there is too much water on the surface. Rivers flood and destroy crops and homes. Their passing carries away topsoil, eroding the countryside and decreasing the agricultural value of the land. One such area was the vast Tennessee River system in the United States. The Tennessee Valley Authority was set up in 1933 to improve the situation. Five existing dams were taken over and 21 new ones built. At first, they supplied hydroelectric power to an area of over 200,000 square kilometres (80,000 square miles). About 70 per cent of the water power has now been turned over to steam generating from the atomic energy plants set up in the TVA area.

The Kariba dam on the river Zambesi between Zambia and Rhodesia in East Africa is another modern scheme. It generates electricity for both countries bordering the river and supplies water for irrigation of 80,000 hectares (200,000 acres) of the Zambesi valley. At the mouth of the river

Rance near St Malo in France, tides rise and fall by as much as 13·5 metres (44 feet). There the first dam of its kind has been erected, making use of both the ebb and the flow of the tides through it to generate electricity. The turbines can also be electrically driven to push water into the upper reservoir when the tide is slack. Every month, somewhere in the world, another dam project is completed.

Heavy work is done increasingly by machines. This giant grab is used in open cast mining. Compare its size with the truck alongside.

Industry's Needs

Industry's thirst for water is unquenchable. To produce the steel for a single motor car 77,000 litres (17,000 gallons) of water are needed. Another 36,000 litres (8,000 gallons) are used in the car's assembly. Many more thousands of gallons are used in the production of the plastics, glass, fabrics and other materials used in its parts. Even 4½ litres (one gallon) of petrol requires 270 litres (60 gallons) of water in the refining process. There is scarcely a manufactured article that does not need water on a similar scale.

Most of the water used in industry eventually finds its way back into a plumbing system of a modern household. Much of the rain that falls on fertilised fields drains eventually into some waterway. All this water can carry with it organic or inorganic compounds that pollute the rivers and even the oceans. The vast use of water has presented mankind with the modern problem of purification. The very stability of the water molecule is an aid in this process. Cleansing methods make it possible to rid even sewage of poisons and impurities so that the water content can be recycled back to our taps.

Coal has regained its position as an essential fuel in modern times. In contrast to the age-old method of pick and shovel, this conveyor belt system is extracting surface coal entirely by an automatic process operated by remote control.

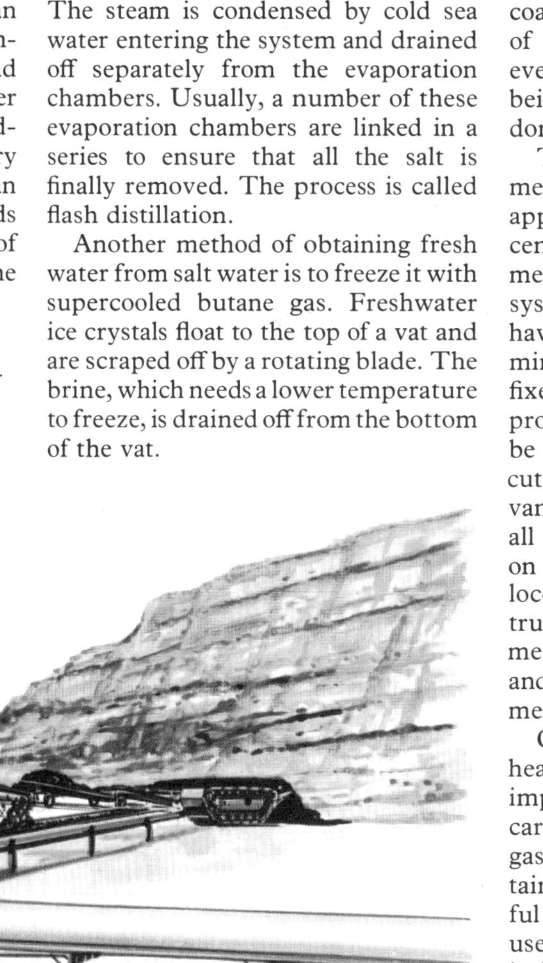

In the search for fresh water, even the mighty reservoirs of the oceans have not been ignored. Sea water can be superheated to a temperature of 120°C and pumped into evaporating chambers where it flashes into steam. The steam is condensed by cold sea water entering the system and drained off separately from the evaporation chambers. Usually, a number of these evaporation chambers are linked in a series to ensure that all the salt is finally removed. The process is called flash distillation.

Another method of obtaining fresh water from salt water is to freeze it with supercooled butane gas. Freshwater ice crystals float to the top of a vat and are scraped off by a rotating blade. The brine, which needs a lower temperature to freeze, is drained off from the bottom of the vat.

Coal Reserves

If the problems of water utilisation are those of recyling and distribution, those of coal have become problems of dwindling supply. It has been estimated that there are less than ten million million tons of reserves left in the ground throughout the world. Yet coal is still one of our principal sources of energy. It is being used up at an ever-increasing rate. Seams of coal are being worked out and mines abandoned every year.

The age-old hand-pick and shovel method of extracting coal began to disappear towards the end of the 19th century with the introduction of mechanical cutters and conveyor-belt systems. The most modern mines now have remote control machinery with miners sitting at consoles at certain fixed control points. Even hydraulic props with cantilevered roof bars can be advanced by remote control as the cutting and extracting equipment advances. Coal can sometimes be brought all the way to the bottom of the shaft on conveyor-belts. Diesel and electric locomotives are also used to draw coal trucks and to transport equipment and men. Sometimes monorails are used and even overhead ropeways to carry men on the ski-lift principle.

Once mined solely as a source of heat energy, coal is now perhaps more important for its by-products. The carbonisation of coal produces coal gas, coke and coal tar, the latter containing around 400 different and useful chemicals. Coal gas is, of course, used for household cookery and in industrial furnaces. Coke is a useful smokeless fuel. The various constituents of coal tar are used in dyestuffs, pharmaceuticals, explosives and plastics. These account for only about 10 to 15 per cent of the products of the distillation of coal tar. The remainder consist of pitch and creosote which are used for tarring roads, preserving wood, protecting steel and concrete from corrosion or weathering, as disinfectants and even as a fuel oil. Substitutes for all the coal tar products will have to be found as coal resources dwindle.

Electrical Energy

Electrical energy, as a fact of nature, need never be in short supply. All that is required is some source of mechanical energy to turn a generator. The consumption of electrical energy in the western world doubles every twelve years. The use of traditional fuels, diminishing in supply, to generate electricity will ultimately raise the cost. Countries with swift-flowing rivers are turning more and more to water power. Others are developing their capabilities for the production of nuclear power.

The grid systems that have been set up in most advanced countries for the distribution of electrical energy can have certain disadvantages. There are peak hours when the power is being used and the generators are replacing it at their peak output. At other times, generators are idle. The answer is to extend the grid systems so that the hours of darkness and daylight vary throughout the whole system. A national grid is planned for Russia so that the time difference between east and west spreads the peak periods. Western Europe already has such a system, and a cross-channel link with Britain has recently extended it.

A grid system is an interlinking mesh of high voltage transmission cables, usually at 275 or 380 thousand volts and even higher, with sub-stations within the network for passing on the voltage or transforming it to a lower voltage for distribution in the immediate neighbourhood. For safety the cables are usually carried high above the ground and supported by pylons at intervals. In some cases, the cables have been buried underground, but this is expensive where any great distance is involved. Most high tension cables carry alternating current, but for long distances, and submarine

No city is more dependent on the power of electricity than New York, whose night skyline displays millions of lighted windows.

Typical oil rig on land.

1 Drilling tower
2 Mud hose
3 Motor and pump
4 Mud outlet
5 Mud pit
6 Drilling bit

cables such as the link between Britain and France, direct current is used.

The electric motor is one of the most efficient of all energy converters. It transforms more than 90 per cent of the electrical energy fed to it into useful work. Already it has replaced much of the world's steam locomotion and is likely to have an important place in all land transport. The problem is to make storage batteries small enough to fit into private motor cars and still provide long continuous working periods without recharging. Perhaps the solution will be a combination of different motors such as the diesel-electric railway locomotive. This has a diesel-oil engine which charges the batteries that power an electric motor. Or perhaps the tiny power cells that are used in hearing aids and small electronic calculators will be developed for work requiring a high power output.

The Oil Boom

Certainly, oil will become more and more scarce and expensive for use as a fuel by the individual motorist. It is one of the most important fuels in the development of the technological revolution, and its history is likely to be the shortest. The oil boom began as recently as 1859 when Edwin L. Drake sank the first commercial well near Titusville, Pennsylvania in the United States. His well was barely 21 metres (70 feet) deep and, at first, produced a mere 35 litres (eight gallons) a day. Within a year, there were 74 wells in the district and four years later, the yield was a daily 6,000 barrels.

Drilling for oil is an expensive business. The average cost of a new well is very high. One well in Texas was drilled eight kilometres (five miles) deep at a cost of a million pounds and no oil was found. The oil industry throughout the world spends great sums of money every year just looking for it. The search has spread from the land to the shallower areas of the oceans. Sometimes the pressure in a well is so low the oil has to be pumped out. Sometimes it is so high there is a blow-out, even a fire that can ruin the oilfield and leave vast quantities of oil stranded in the earth.

Once the oil has been obtained, it must go through a complicated refining process to extract every valuable chemical compound it contains. Most modern refineries are nowadays so automated they need only a few men to operate them. A large one can process 150,000 barrels a day.

The process begins by heating the crude oil to a temperature of about 370°C in a distillation tower where the lighter vapours condense at a high level and the heavier ones at lower levels. This is a process called fractional distillation. The oils of different densities are collected on trays at different levels. Some of the lightest oils are carried away to the polymerisation plant where they are converted into the giant molecules that form the basis for detergents, plastics, synthetic fibres and synthetic rubber.

Oil Products

Some heavier oils go through the catalytic reformer which uses chemical catalysts to rearrange the molecules into high-octane petrol. Others go through the catalytic cracker which breaks down heavy molecules to produce lighter oils that burn more

Oil-drilling rig at sea.

A modern oil refinery at night where the complicated work of processing crude oil continues 24 hours every day. These great plants are automated to a high degree and their smooth operation depends on a small number of key workers.

efficiently in motor-car engines. Petrols produced by the reformer and the cracker are then blended together in huge tanks. By-products such as lubricants, furnace oil, diesel fuel and cooking gas are all drawn off at various stages.

Over the years, improvements in refining methods have not only produced new by-products, but have increased the percentage yield of petrols from the crude oil. Another bonus to the oil companies has been the discovery of vast reservoirs of natural gas which is now often piped directly to consumers who live within reasonable distance of the original drilling operation.

The oil boom has been a romantic story. The oil prospector can be regarded as the last of the great geographical pioneers. His search has taken him into the remotest parts of the world. He has dug his wells in the jungles of South America, in the burning desert sands of the Middle East, in the frozen wastes of Alaska and beneath the storm-tossed waters of the North Sea. It is the very remoteness of its sources that has made oil the most unreliable of fuels. States rich in oil can use it as a political and economic weapon, threatening to cut off supplies when agreements with less-endowed nations break down.

Atomic Power

The most hopeful source of almost boundless energy for the future must be in atomic power. It was on the 2nd December 1942 that Dr Enrico Fermi, an Italian-born physicist, set off the first self-sustaining chain reaction in a squash court at the University of Chicago. He did it with a so-called 'atomic pile'. It consisted of a quantity of radioactive uranium embedded in a large mass of graphite with cadmium rods inserted into it. Bouncing off the graphite slowed the free neutrons to just the right speed to split the nuclei of the uranium atoms and thus release more neutrons to split more nuclei and so on. By absorbing some of the neutrons, the cadmium rods prevented the chain reaction from reaching explosive intensity.

Further research was at first turned into the production of an atomic bomb. But once the Second World War was over, the delicate balance that Fermi had achieved was developed in the building of the first nuclear fission reactor to create energy for peaceful purposes. Early problems were concerned with obtaining enough uranium 235. Fermi had used six tons of uranium in his atomic pile which had achieved a comparatively slow chain reaction. Natural uranium is not a common element, and the search for it took on the proportions of a goldrush.

Since then, the spread of atomic power has not been as rapid as was at first expected. There are certain disadvantages to it. It produces a great deal of radioactive waste matter which has to be disposed of. It takes a hundred years or more for the waste to lose its dangerous radioactivity, and meanwhile it must be stored somewhere. The only answer at the moment seems to be to bury it. Doing this in a way that ensures no escape of dangerous radiation is expensive and becomes more of a problem as more reactors are built. Building in the necessary safety factors with each new reactor also adds quite considerably to their cost. Nuclear power has not produced the generous supply of cheap energy that was expected of it when its potential was first considered.

One useful by-product of nuclear fission which is proving more and more versatile is the ease with which radioactive isotopes of a great many substances can be prepared. These are used as 'labellers' which are easily detected in the flow of liquids, for instance through the human body or through plants, for the estimation of speeds of flow, faults in systems and so on.

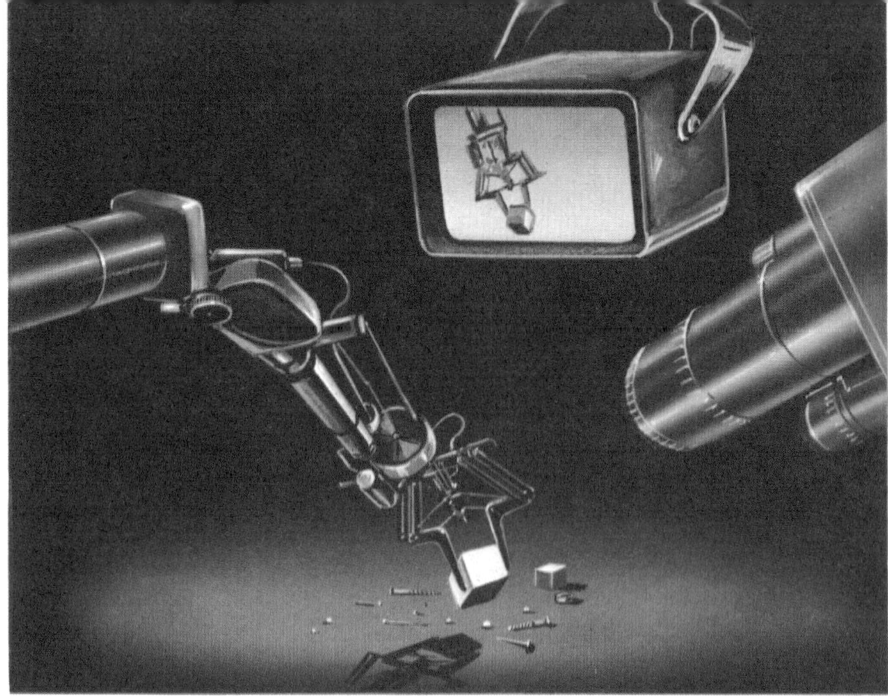

Automatic handling system linked to a TV set and computer which is 'taught' to manipulate.

Nuclear Fusion

The disadvantages that apply to fission reactions, the splitting of heavy nuclei, do not apply to fusion reactions which bring together the nuclei of light atoms with a similar evolution of energy. Fusion results in no dangerous waste products. It is a fusion reaction of hydrogen nuclei to form helium atoms that gives the sun its enormous energy output. For hydrogen nuclei to fuse requires them to be travelling at a speed which causes temperatures of millions of degrees centigrade. Such fusions are called thermonuclear reactions. The high temperatures required have been achieved only in the laboratory for very brief periods of fractions of a second, and they have to be kept away from any container by the use of magnetic fields. There is also a problem of making use of the energy evolved. It might be done by surrounding the core in which the reaction takes place with a jacket cooled by liquid lithium which could then be passed to a heat exchanger to raise steam for the generation of electricity.

Sooner or later, fusion reactors must come. They will probably use as raw material the isotope of hydrogen called deuterium. Since hydrogen is one of the most common elements on earth, they will offer an almost boundless source of energy at reasonable cost. Nor will the siting of fusion reactors be subject to any geographical limits. Nations will become independent of imports for their energy requirements.

Space-age design for an atomic power station near Munich in Germany.

New Sources of Power

The need for new sources of power is urgent. The demands of increasing technology and the population growth are expected to quadruple our energy requirements by the year 2000. By then, we shall probably not be able to afford the burning of traditional fuels. We shall need them for the raw materials of our manufacturing industries. By then, we shall be looking even more strenuously at the possibilities of using natural energy, of which the winds, the tides, and the light and heat of the sun represent a largely untapped reservoir.

Power is the key to man's future. He can no longer return to the simple life, each family tilling its own plot of land. He has created too complex a society, every part of it interdependent on every other. The failure of even a small part can spread ripples of disaster far and wide. For better or worse, we are all crew members of a single spaceship. To maintain it, even at its present state of efficiency, we must tend the machinery. We must replace what we use up and repair the parts that wear out. Technology is the tool we have been given to help us.

Machinery

The history of machines follows man's efforts to lessen his workload, to harness powers greater than his own muscles or those of other animals. The technological revolution began by making manpower a part of the machine by the use of new techniques of mass-production. Mass-production goes back to ancient times. The Chinese bronze founders of the first millenium B.C. made moulds so that articles could be reproduced over and over again in exact replicas of each other. But these were articles produced by one man and perhaps a handful of assistants. Modern mass-production methods involve the speeding up of the whole manufacturing process by the carefully planned use of manpower and machinery.

Automation

The process can be divided into five parts. First, there is the division of labour whereby each man or woman is given a separate task which, because of its repetitive nature, can be easily and rapidly performed. Machines can be devised to speed up this one task even further. Second, the parts of the finished product are standardised so that they are interchangeable both within a particular article and from one finished article to another, perhaps even a different article altogether. Third, machines are designed to produce a part with exact precision so that all the parts fit together without the chance of having to discard any because of mistakes or inaccuracies in manufacture. Fourth, the parts are fitted together to produce the finished article on an assembly line where each part of sub-assembly of parts is added by an individual worker practised in the fitting of that particular part. Finally, mass-production aims at reducing the unit selling price. Alongside this, a mass demand must be created for the article by efficient distribution and advertising.

Mass-production methods of this kind were tried out by Christopher Polhem who set up a factory at Stjernsund in Sweden in 1700. He recruited about 200 workers, some with special skills but mostly people he had to train himself to operate particular machines. These machines were driven by water power. Seven water-wheels in one building drove hammers, cutters and rollers. Polhem himself devised methods to speed production. For instance, iron dishes were made on a production line where one large hammer roughly shaped the white-hot metal blank, three smaller hammers shaped the edge and two others the interior. By such methods, he produced all kinds of containers, cutlery and hand-tools, sheet-iron roofing and gutters, nails, screws and bolts, even locks and clocks. When he died in 1751 at the age of 90, his factory fell into disuse.

It took war production to stimulate similar efforts elsewhere. In revolutionary France at the end of the 18th century musket locks were designed to consist of 50 interchangeable parts which could be assembled rapidly on a production line. The process was introduced into America where Eli

A basic principle of an efficient assembly line is to take the job to the workers rather than the workers to the job. The American automobile engineer Henry Ford was one of the first to put the principle into practice at his Highland Park car factory in 1913 (seen below). A forerunner of modern mass production techniques, his assembly line ended outside the factory where the bodies for the immortal Model T Fords (right) were slid down a ramp to join each completed chassis.

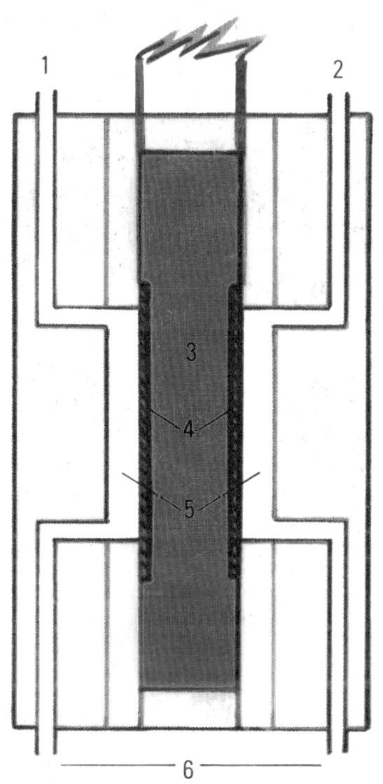

The hydrogen/oxygen fuel cell produces electrical power without machinery. 1 hydrogen intake, 2 oxygen intake, 3 electrolyte, 4 electrodes, 5 gas chambers, 6 pure water exhaust.

Whitney, the inventor of the cotton gin, set up a factory with machines designed to produce all the parts of the famous Charleville musket. Employing largely unskilled labour, by 1803 he was able to turn out 1,000 muskets a year, three times as many as the government gunsmiths could produce by hand. Whitney's neighbour, Eli Terry, set up in 1807 a similar factory for producing clocks which he could sell at four dollars each.

Meanwhile, the American meat-packing industry had developed production line techniques. In Cincinnati, known throughout the country as 'Porkopolis', pigs were slaughtered, scalded, scraped, then hung on travelling overhead conveyors to be split open, disembowelled, cleaned and inspected before being carried off to cold-storage. The canning industry followed similar methods. By 1890, tinned food, once the delicacy of the rich man's table, became cheaper than fresh food.

Time and Motion

As industry continued to investigate the possibilities of the production line, a new science appeared in America, the study of time and motion. Frederick Taylor, for instance, used a stop watch to work out that a coal-shoveller produced his best effort with a shovel containing 9·5 kilograms (21 pounds) of coal at a time. Shovels were designed to hold just this amount. Frank and Lillian Gilbreth, the husband and wife time and motion experts, attached lights to workers' hands and took photographs of their movements. These were analysed, and workers were trained to use the most economical movements. The worker had become part of the machine.

The man above all others who set the production line humming was the American car manufacturer, Henry Ford. He followed the principle that the work should be brought to the worker. No worker should need to take more than one step or to stoop down to pick up a part or a tool. The assembly of a car magneto took one man 20 minutes. Broken up into 29 different operations, it took a line of men thirteen minutes and ten seconds. Raising the assembly line to bring everything within convenient reach reduced the time to seven minutes. Finally, speeding up the line achieved an assembly time of only five minutes.

Assembling the chassis of a motor car with a team of workers gathered round it and carrying the parts to a central point had taken twelve hours and 28 minutes. By raising the chassis to waist height and moving it along past 45 assembly points at a speed of 1·8 metres (six feet) per minute, the whole job could be done in one hour and 35 minutes. The principle behind the assembly was that the man who positioned the part left it to the next man along to fasten it. One man inserted a bolt, the next man attached a nut and a third man tightened it.

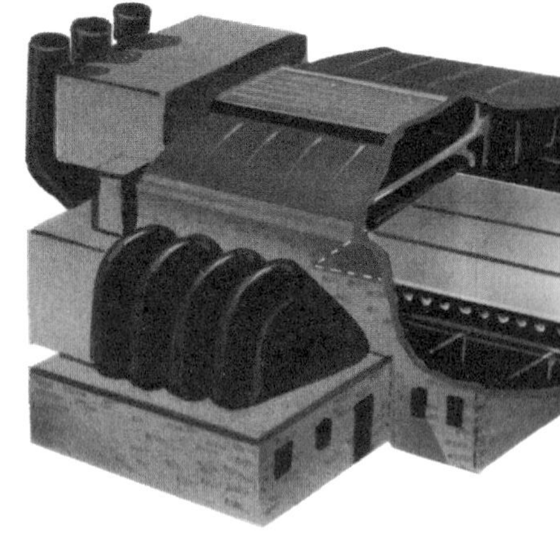

One operator controls the output of this section of a steel factory from a control booth. In modern terms, automation seeks even to do away with this key figure and replace him with a programmed computer.

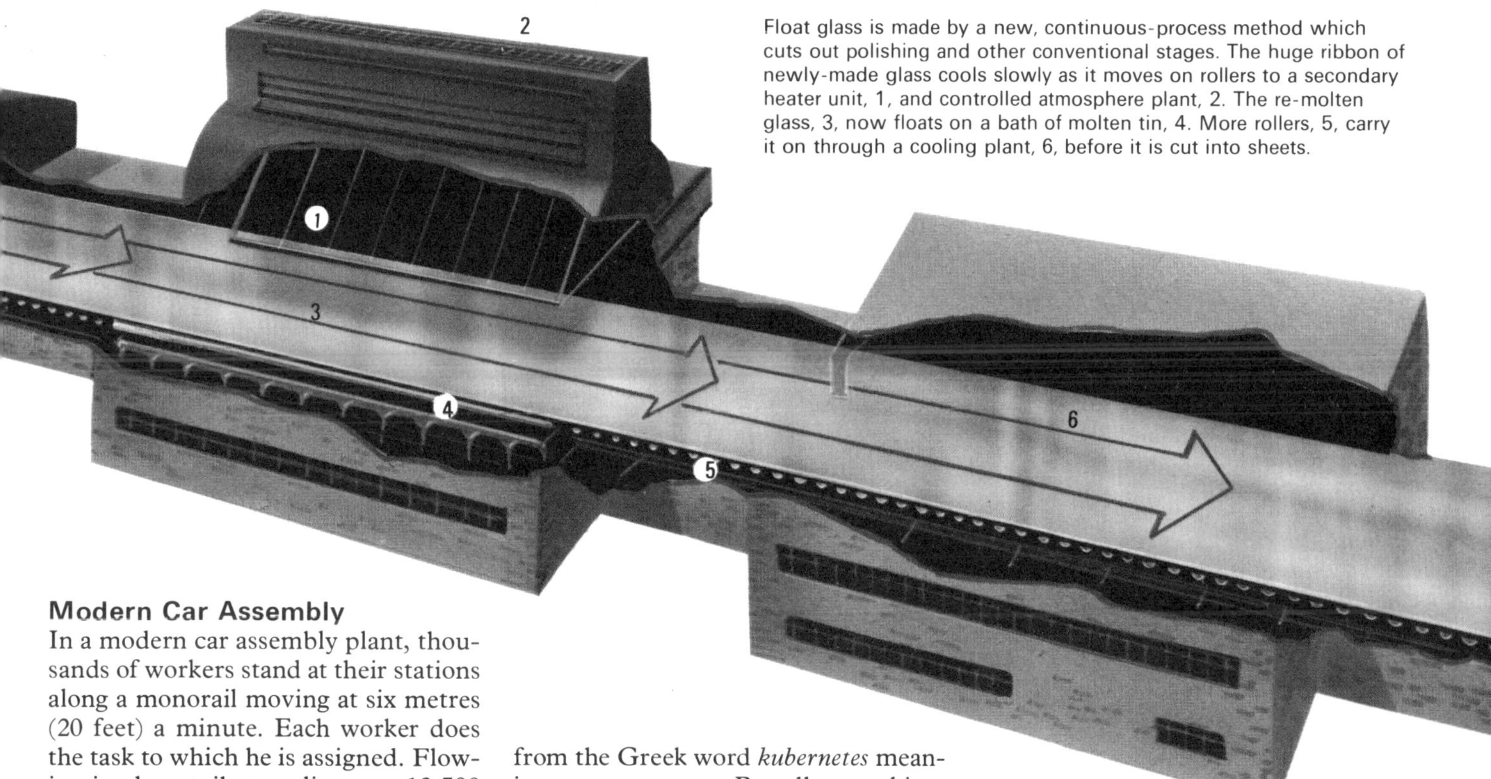

Float glass is made by a new, continuous-process method which cuts out polishing and other conventional stages. The huge ribbon of newly-made glass cools slowly as it moves on rollers to a secondary heater unit, 1, and controlled atmosphere plant, 2. The re-molten glass, 3, now floats on a bath of molten tin, 4. More rollers, 5, carry it on through a cooling plant, 6, before it is cut into sheets.

Modern Car Assembly

In a modern car assembly plant, thousands of workers stand at their stations along a monorail moving at six metres (20 feet) a minute. Each worker does the task to which he is assigned. Flowing in along tributary lines are 13,500 parts, some fitted together in subassembly lines of their own. Automatic welding guns make 45 welds in 60 seconds. Springs are fitted to all four wheels in 60 seconds. Wheelnuts are tightened in one go by an electrically operated machine suspended from the roof where the power supply lines are strung. Finished cars can roll off at the rate of one a minute. Similar methods can be adapted to the production and assembly of almost any article. They can be used in the packing of consumer goods. They can even be applied to food production and the husbandry of animals.

Increased production enabled the employer to pay his workers more money. This, in turn, allowed the worker to buy more cheap mass-produced articles. To a certain extent, the system fed upon itself. But the skilled craftsman began to disappear. His product could never compete in selling price with a mass-produced article. More and more people were forced into the factories to do unrewarding, monotonous work, often in an appallingly noisy and unhealthy atmosphere. Over the years, both pay and conditions in factories have improved, but the jobs too often remain unsatisfying. Workers feel themselves to be mere extensions of the machines that dominate most of their waking hours.

Cybernetics

To solve this problem, a new science has emerged. It is called cybernetics, from the Greek word *kubernetes* meaning a steersman. Broadly speaking, cybernetics is the study of methods of communicating with machines so that they can perform the tasks without the aid of human operators. The idea is to relieve the worker of the boring, repetitive jobs that have become so much a part of many people's lives. Wherever possible and desirable, cybernetics aims at achieving automation.

Communication with machines began in the textile industry. In France in 1725, Basile Bouchon constructed a weaving loom that could be set to obey a coded list of instructions in order to weave a pattern into a silk material. The code message was in the form of a paper with holes punched into it. When this was pressed against a set of needles, those opposite the holes remained in position and those where there were no holes were pushed forward. The needles controlled the raising of certain warps when the shuttle passed, thus weaving the precoded pattern. At first, the punched paper operated only a single row of needles. Later improvements involved punched cards strung on a long roll which could be advanced as the pattern progressed, operating several rows of needles. About 1804, Joseph-Marie Jacquard perfected an even more complex system which presented a punched card to as many as 1,200 needles with every passage of the shuttle. His system remains basically unchanged to this day.

The punched card system was adopted by the American Dr Herman Hollerith. He was a statistician who had been given the job of tabulating the 1890 United States census of population. The previous census had taken seven years to tabulate a population of 50 million. The new population count was over 63 million. Hollerith solved the problem by providing a punched card for every person in the census return. The punched holes were positioned to represent age, sex and other details about the individual concerned. The cards were placed over tiny cups filled with mercury in a machine with needles that passed through the holes and completed an electric circuit that registered the count on dials. Tabulation of the entire population was completed by this method in just over two years.

Storage on Tape

Hollerith went on to manufacture his invention through a company that eventually became one parent of the giant International Business Machines Corporation, known familiarly as IBM. Punched cards are still used for storing information. Very sophisticated reading machines convert the presence of a hole into an electric impulse. The holes can be in separate cards or punched into rolls of tape. Card-reading speeds can reach 1,000 per minute. Tape can be read at 500 perforations a second. Magnetic tape is also used to communicate with machines. It is similar to the tape used in recorders except that it is

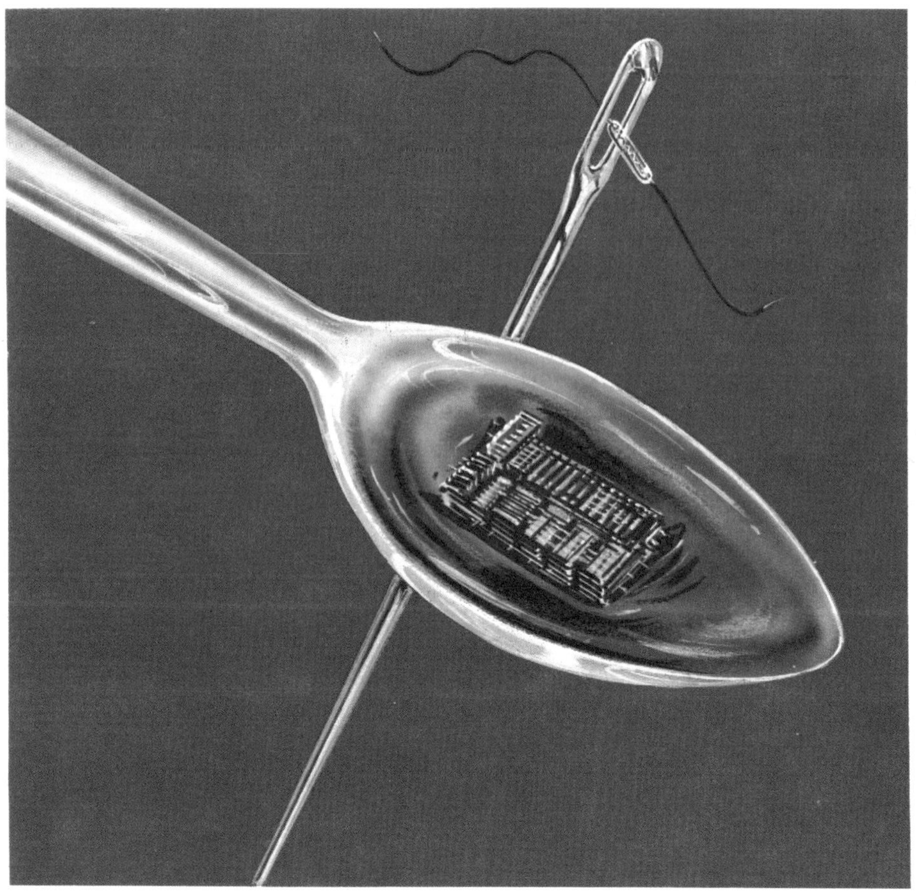

Two triumphs of miniaturisation: a light bulb small enough to go through a needle's eye and a radio set using a molecular structure in a teaspoon. Below is a picture phone which can transmit images as well as sound to a viewer.

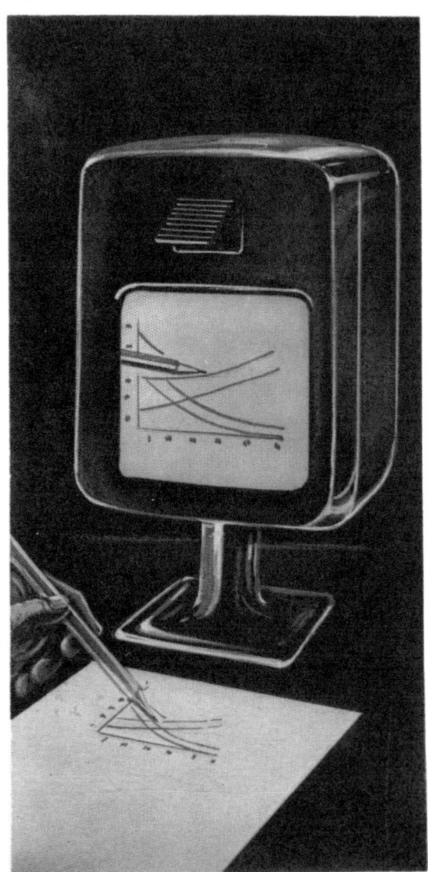

usually twice the width and carries seven channels. Instead of holes, it has magnetised spots which can be read off at rates reaching 630,000 spots a second.

Computer History

Punched or magnetic tape must communicate with machines using a language of only two words which can be taken to mean, yes and no, on and off or 0 and 1. The machine must be programmed to ask questions which can be answered on a simple yes or no basis, the so-called binary system. Though the programming might take a long time, the instructions can thereafter be passed on at the speed of an electric current. Instructions can be changed or modified at the same rapid speed. This is the basic principle behind every computer.

The first all-electric computer was designed by Presper Eckert, an electronics engineer, and Dr John Mauchly, a mathematician. It went into service in 1946. The electric pulses fed into it were amplified by electronic valves of which there were 18,000 altogether. The whole machine weighed 30 tons and covered a floor space of 1500 square feet. It was known as ENIAC and could do 20 man-hours of calculations in 30 seconds.

Since then, old-fashioned wiring has been replaced by printed circuits, and the electronic valve has been superseded by the transistor. Modern computers can be quite small and can do many times the calculations of which ENIAC was capable. They come in two kinds. The analogue or proportional computer provides answers in physical rather than numerical terms. It gives voltages, speeds, angles of rotation and that sort of thing. A digital computer is a calculator, giving its answers in numbers.

Modern Computers

The modern computer can be divided into five main compartments. The input devices receive the information fed into them. The control represents the rules by which the calculation is to be made. Storage contains the answers to intermediate steps in the calculation. Processing is the actual step by step calculation. Output devices give us the final answers on a print-out or a dial. Computers can keep millions of individual items of information in their memory banks. Retrieval systems can find and print out any one of these items in seconds. Calculations can be made faster than half a million people working with hand-operated electronic calculators.

A machine can nowadays be designed to accept a programme of work in one or two ways or in a combination of both. The first is known as open-loop control. It puts a machine through a pattern of behaviour, going step by step through a series of operations to a final completion. Such a control is that built into an automatic washing machine, an automatic record changer or a slot-machine that pours out a cup of coffee.

Feed-back Control

The second type of control is called a closed-loop or feed-back. James Watt fitted a feed-back control to his steam-engines in the form of a governor. This was two heavy weights that spun round with the engine. If the engine went too fast, the weights were flung outwards by centrifugal force and this movement closed the throttle and slowed down the engine. An electric thermostat is a modern type of feed-back mechanism. It takes the temperature of a room or a boiler and, when it rises too high, shuts off the heater until the temperature falls again below the level required, when it switches the heater on again.

When such controls as these are

Modern computer installation

linked to information stored and passed on by a computer, a whole range of very sophisticated operations is possible for a machine, without human intervention. Repetitive drudgery can be taken out of much of our work. Quality and quantity control can be set and maintained. Machines can be re-programmed with the minimum delay to the production line.

Automated Systems

Automated systems are now in use for almost everything the modern consumer uses. In food production, ingredients are automatically weighed and mixed, cooking temperatures are controlled, the size and quality of the finished product regulated and the food packed for distribution. The processes through which this book has gone before it reaches you are very largely automated, from the production of the paper to the printing and binding of the pages. The telephone in your home is attached to an exchange capable of processing the number you dial and ringing a bell in the home of a friend perhaps thousands of miles away in another country. Automatic telephone exchanges handle total numbers of calls that would take the entire female population of a country to put through by the outdated operator methods.

In industry, machines are now designed to take coded instructions which can be so simply fed in that a single human operator can be responsible for the variable output of several of them. Computers can be used to check and regulate the output of a huge oil refinery. They may be used to control the products of a steel mill or the output of generators to an electric grid system. They can be used to control and monitor every detail of the transportation of a crew of astronauts to the moon and back to a safe splash-down in the sea close to a predetermined chart reference. They can be fitted into a missile to guide it through a journey of thousands of miles and to seek out its target at the end. They can even be used to estimate the outcome of a battle before a single platoon of soldiers is committed to the actual conflict.

There is a flood-tide of new machinery designed to do without people, to eliminate human error and the fatigue and boredom of work. The eyes that watch the process are photo-electric cells, metal hands guide it and feedback mechanisms check the results. Computers direct the distribution of the finished article, do the stocktaking in the individual shop and order fresh supplies of goods to keep the shelves filled.

Correct delivery through a complex conveyor system. 1, operator sets code by push button; 2, belt under parcel is invisibly coded; 3, memory unit is informed by 4, reader; 5, code eraser at end of belt; 6, new belt picks up code from memory unit; 7, reads code and operates diverter, 8.

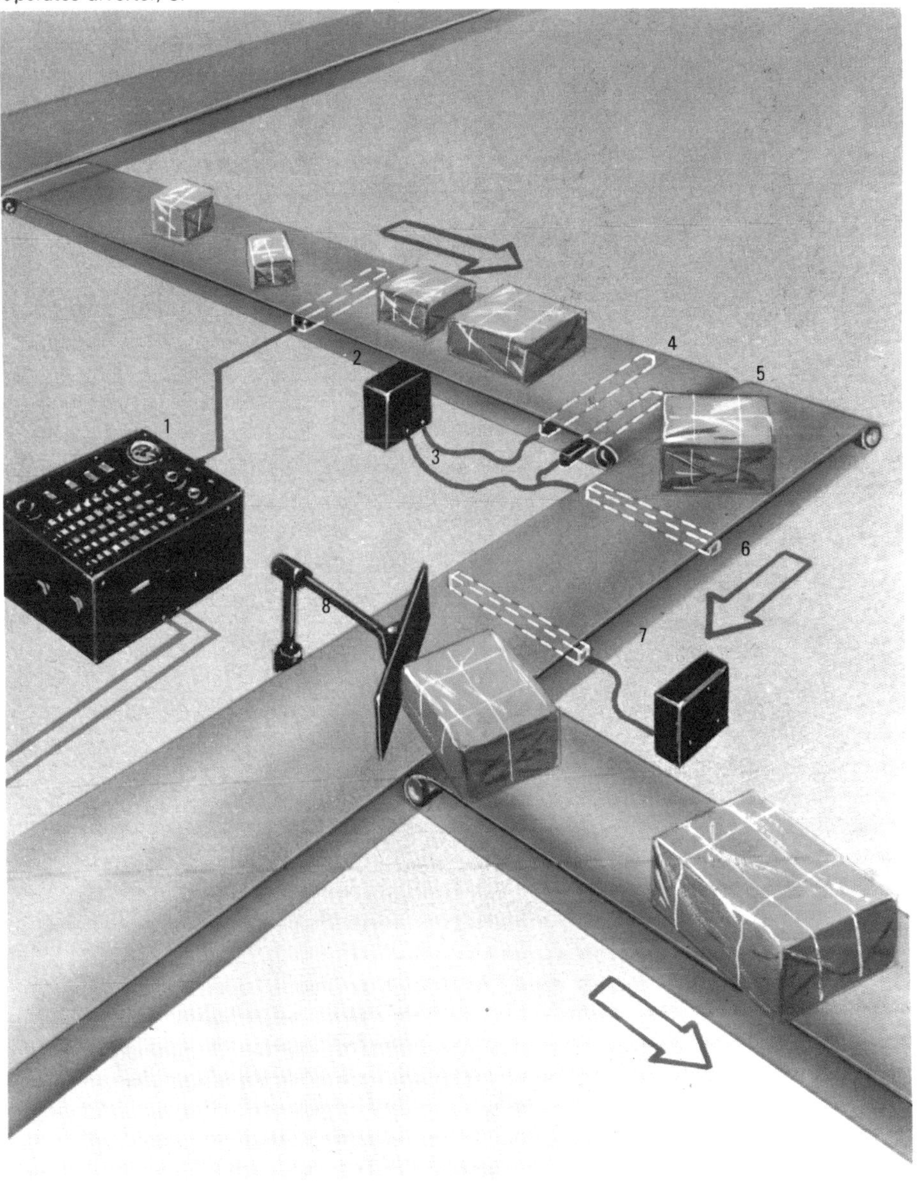

The robots of early science fiction have become a reality. Some of the machines which man has constructed to work for him are built in his own image. Seen here are two experimental models, on the left a robot firefighter, programmed to combat nuclear fires; and on the right an American walking machine which has many possible uses in military operations or the exploration of difficult country.

There are undoubtedly more wonders to come. Computers are being taught to learn from their mistakes. One IBM scientist programmed a computer to play draughts. He built in an ability to avoid making the same mistake twice. In the end, the computer could beat him in every game.

Biological Computers

There are attempts to design what are called biological computers that can do more than just calculate and assess information. Using the light-sensitivity of photo-electric cells, they have been taught to recognise patterns. Computers have been used to recognise spoken words and to react with appropriate answers. They have been designed to translate from one language to another. They have been programmed to produce musical compositions according to the rules of harmony.

All this is still very experimental, but as the capacities of computers increase, the possibilities multiply. Computers are in use, not only to design machines but also better computers than themselves. Though they may never be able to rival the abilities of the human brain, they may be able to free that brain from much of the wasteful anxieties that beset it.

The machine may yet free mankind from the machine itself. A return to work on a human scale for human beings may become possible. The human mind may be able to return to a concern for environment and constructive leisure. The contemplation of man may become centred on the understanding of man himself, on the pursuit of health and happiness.

Aristotle's Vision

As long ago as the 4th century B.C., Aristotle said that, if every instrument could accomplish its own work, obeying or anticipating the will of others, if the shuttle could weave and the plectrum touch the lyre without a hand to guide them, foremen would not need workers nor masters slaves. If our present generation makes the right choices and pursues the right paths, perhaps Aristotle's vision will be realised. Perhaps we will emerge from the technological revolution to a new era of adventure and delight.

Transport

After almost a hundred years of popularity, the end is in sight for the internal combustion reciprocating engine, so called because it burns fuel in a closed cylinder to move a piston up and down by gas pressure. The two types are the Otto engine which uses a spark to ignite the fuel and the Diesel in which the fuel is fired spontaneously by compression of the air intake, raising its temperature to about 900°C. About 99 per cent of all powered road vehicles throughout the world use one or other of these two engines. Objections to them are that they use the rapidly diminishing fossil fuel, oil; that they are inefficient because no more than 20 per cent of the fuel's heat energy is transformed into mechanical energy; and that they pollute the environment with noise and dangerous chemicals

Rotary Engines

Recently, rotating combustion engines have been produced. An example of these is the Wankel which has a rotary piston, almost triangular in shape, mounted eccentrically on the output shaft. The cylinder is a near-oval, and the corners of the piston rub against the inside of it as they rotate, creating alternately large and small spaces in which the fuel is compressed. Since no parts move up and down, the output

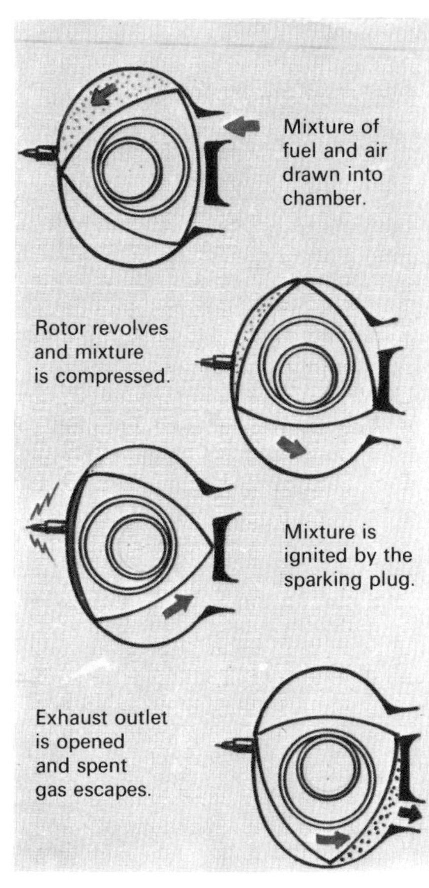

The rotary action of the Wankel engine.

is smoother and faster running than with reciprocating engines. Difficulties have arisen from the need to provide an effective seal with long-wearing properties at the corners of the piston. Also, the Wankel and other rotary engines still use the dwindling supplies of fuel oil.

This last objection also applies to the gas-turbine which is coming into use for heavy road vehicles. This is also a rotary engine which has been developed particularly for use in aircraft. In aero-engines, the air intake is compressed to between 20 and 30 times atmospheric pressure. Smaller road vehicles can use a heat exchanger to feed back exhaust temperatures to the incoming air so that a pressure of only three times that of the atmosphere is required. The turbine may turn the blades of the compressor at speeds as high as 70,000 revolutions per minute. Engineering problems are therefore connected with maintaining clearances around such moving parts at constantly changing speeds and temperatures. Turbine engines need neither clutch nor gearbox and can be sealed within sound-proofed boxes. Noise and vibration are all but eliminated and exhaust fumes reduced to almost nothing. There is very little maintenance, a low fuel consumption and a wide choice of cheap fuels. It is not so easy, however, to make smaller gas-turbines for use in the lower-powered vehicles such as family cars. Here, the problems centre round the mass-production of a heat exchanger which must withstand temperature changes from white-hot gas to cold air without leaking.

The electric motor car offers many advantages for city use.

Electric Motor

The electric motor is almost silent, emits no pollution and is about 90 per cent efficient. It would be the answer to all land transport problems if batteries storing sufficient energy, yet small enough for a family car, could be devised. Milk floats and city delivery vans with electric motors have ordinary lead and acid batteries of the sort used for the electrical circuits of cars. But in their case, speed and distance are not important. High-energy nickel and cadmium or silver and zinc aircraft batteries are expensive. Lithium and chlorine would be ideal but for the dangers of the high temperatures reached by such materials. At the moment, the electric car can really be only a city runabout. Political action or the shortage and rise in price of fuel oils would be necessary to force people to give up their larger petrol-driven cars.

Vehicle Control

An increasing objection to present-day road transport is the danger of allowing everybody to have control of their own vehicles. In 1972, there were 90,000 road deaths in Western Europe alone and the figures are rising. Experiments are going forward to devise metal strips built into roadways which would take some of the control from the driver, by slowing him down, for instance, when he approaches the vehicle in front too closely. Perhaps the motorways of the future will include aluminium strips providing the forward thrust for linear electric motors in the vehicles themselves. With controlled speeds and built-in safety checks, vehicles could travel closer together, allowing greater numbers per mile, thus relieving congestion. Control would be removed entirely from the driver who would take over only when leaving the motorway.

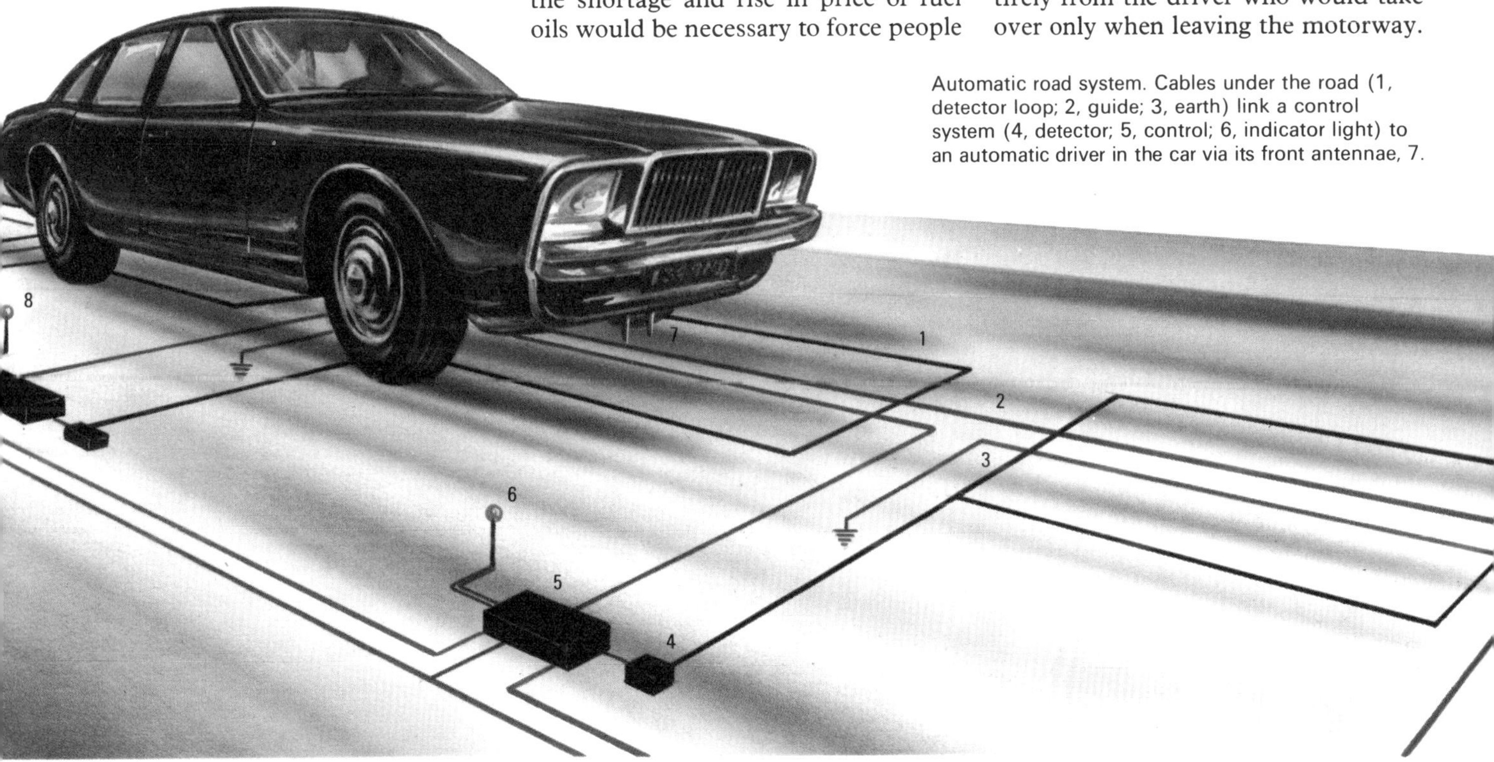

Automatic road system. Cables under the road (1, detector loop; 2, guide; 3, earth) link a control system (4, detector; 5, control; 6, indicator light) to an automatic driver in the car via its front antennae, 7.

On long journeys, he could amuse himself watching television.

No method has yet been conceived for making the adhesion between tyres and road surfaces absolutely safe in all weathers. Much of the inefficiency of road transport comes from the wasted energy used to distort the tyres as the vehicle moves along. The part of the tyre in contact with the road is squashed flat and this is what provides the adhesion. With metal wheels on metal rails, the distortion is very much less, and much less energy is wasted in moving the vehicle forward. This makes the railway still the most efficient means of transport. Work is going on, particularly in Britain, France, Japan and the United States, to provide faster and more comfortable trains.

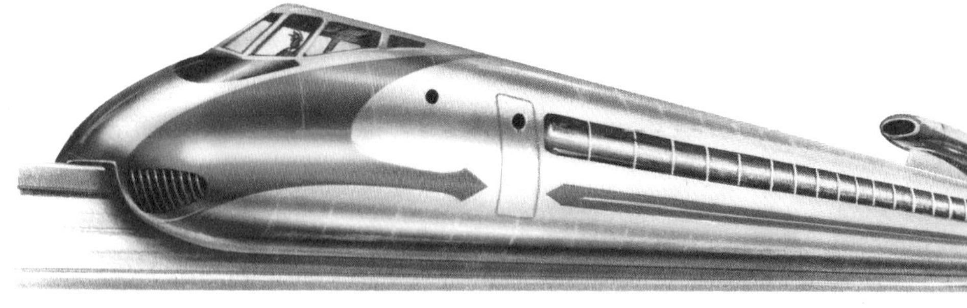

Like many other countries France is experimenting with transport systems and is considering the hover method as used in hovercraft. Speeds of over 400 kilometres (250 miles) per hour are the aim.

The roller road, proposed by United States engineers. Flat-bottomed carriers, moving on rubber rollers, would carry people and their cars at speeds up to 280 kilometres (175 miles) per hour.

Railway Development

Most advanced countries have now abandoned the steam train. With coal as the fuel, there are difficulties in supplying it to the furnace fast enough to maintain a constantly high pressure in the boilers for long periods, even with mechanical firing systems. Also, even modern locomotives were only about nine per cent efficient in their use of the heat energy in the fuel. Nowadays, locomotives are powered by oil-burning diesel engines which are coupled to generators supplying power to electric motors which turn the driving wheels. Alternatively, electric power at voltages as high as 25,000 is picked up from overhead cables to drive the electric motors directly. The Tokaido line between Tokyo and Osaka in Japan uses the latter system. Trains hold a steady speed of 190–210 kilometres per hour (120–130 mph), and the average speed for the whole 515-kilometre (320-mile) journey, including intermediate stops, is never less than 160 kilometres per hour (100 mph). Britain has a similar line between Euston in London and Glasgow in Scotland for which a complete new railway was built on top of the old one. British Rail, however, has concentrated research on high-speed trains that can run at 240 kilometres per hour (150 mph) on existing track. Their Advanced Passenger Train promises to maintain schedules of 3·2 kilometres (two miles) per minute throughout the mainline system by the early 1980s.

Monorail systems have been in existence since the 19th century, though none has proved as efficient as the twin-track system. The invention of air-cushioned transport in recent times may adapt successfully to monorail working, and there are even experiments in suspending trains by magnetic forces. With such systems, the linear motor seems a promising locomotive force. It consists of electrified coils within the vehicle itself which react magnetically against aluminium strip in the track, impelling the vehicle forward. Monorails are most likely to be built where entirely new rail links are required, as for instance between a new airport and a city centre. There

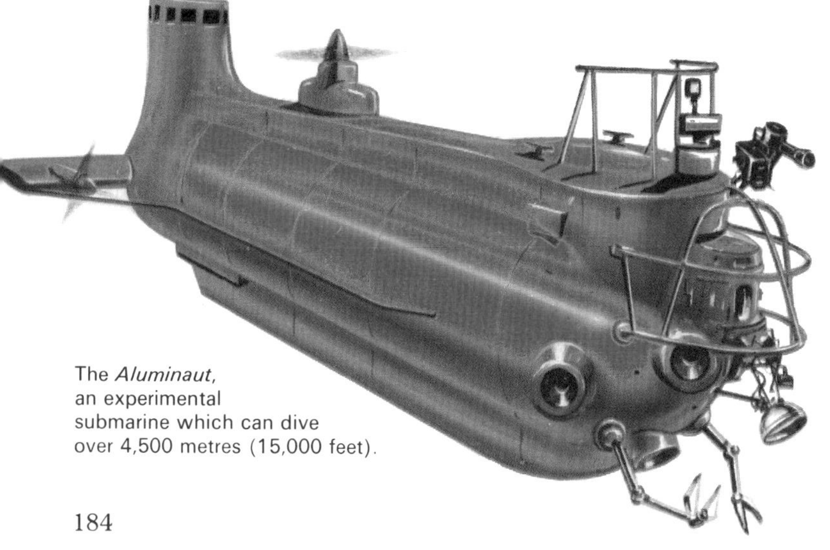

The *Aluminaut*, an experimental submarine which can dive over 4,500 metres (15,000 feet).

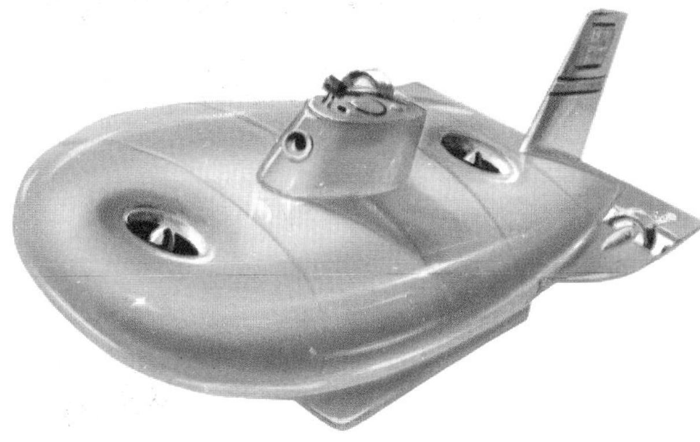

Another of the many unusual-looking craft used by man to explore 'inner space'—under the sea.

A revolutionary system designed for fast city-suburb, and city centre, passenger transport. Cars would be computer controlled, without a driver, and would travel at 40-second intervals, carrying four or five passengers.

are also schemes for city monorail systems built high above street level, like the one planned to replace the tramway system in Munich, West Germany. A British Cabtrack visualises four-seater vehicles in which the destination is selected on a dial and the cab automatically carried there by the quickest route under computer control. The French Urba system involves 30-seater trains slung under the monorail and held clear of the track by vacuum suspension. Such systems would radically alter the appearance of our cities. Long distance monorails for very high speed trains would also be built high above the land surface so that they could be accurately aligned, ignoring undulations in the countryside. Trains could then be impelled more like projectiles, travelling at speeds in excess of 480 kilometres per hour (300 mph).

Tunnelling

Advances in tunnelling techniques suggest an increase in underground railways which may even have vehicles held magnetically clear of the tunnel walls or fitting like a piston in a cylinder and propelled by vacuum or air pressure. One rather bizarre suggestion is to tunnel in a straight line, ignoring the curvature of the earth's surface, from one point on that surface to another. Trains would then be helped on their way for the first half of the journey by the increasing force of gravity as they travelled nearer to the centre of the earth. By the mid-point, sufficient speed would be reached to enable the vehicle to coast on to the exit point with the use of very little power. A Japanese suggestion would have the rails fixed to the underside of the train which would travel over wheels mounted on posts.

Modern ACVs, or air cushion vehicles, are a development of the original Hovercraft built in the 1950s. They are used extensively for ferry services although the problems of operation in rough weather remain.

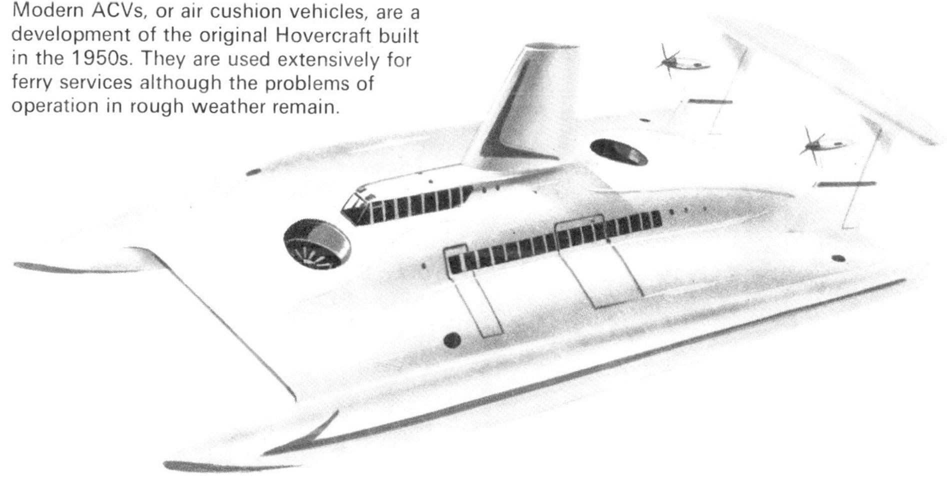

Water Transport

The development of water transport has recently speeded up with the aid of new technology. Hovercraft and hydroplanes have concentrated on lifting the hull above water level to reduce drag and increase speed with a given power output. The largest ships still use steam, though in some cases this is generated by nuclear power. By far the greater majority of shipping nowadays, however, uses diesel engines. Nuclear power is a late development that is certain to continue. The fuel takes up so much less room than traditional oil or coal, so the vessel's range is much greater. The USS *Savannah* can cruise at 20 knots for 300,000 nautical miles without refuelling. Nuclear power has a particular application to submarines, because its use does not require oxygen, and a submarine is working at its greatest efficiency only when submerged to a depth several times the diameter of its hull. Huge cargo-carrying submarines may become a feature of certain routes, under the polar ice, for instance. Certainly all shipping, particularly bulk-carrying tankers, is becoming larger, and containerisation is speeding the turnaround in port.

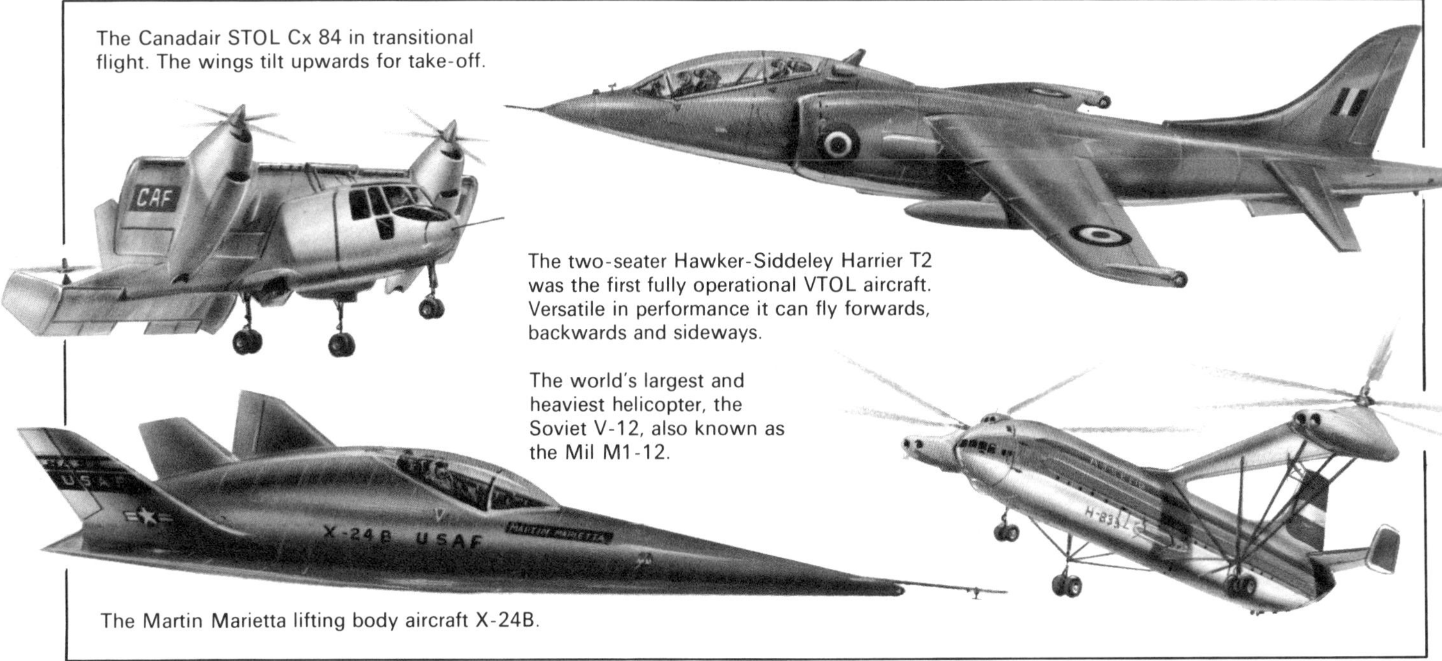

The Canadair STOL Cx 84 in transitional flight. The wings tilt upwards for take-off.

The two-seater Hawker-Siddeley Harrier T2 was the first fully operational VTOL aircraft. Versatile in performance it can fly forwards, backwards and sideways.

The world's largest and heaviest helicopter, the Soviet V-12, also known as the Mil M1-12.

The Martin Marietta lifting body aircraft X-24B.

Air Transport

No other form of transport has involved so much advanced technology as air travel, and its development has been dramatic. The great breakthrough was the invention of the jet engine which doubled the speed compared with ordinary piston engines. It was at first thought to have only a military application, but the appearance of the de Havilland Comet changed that. No piston-engined propellor aircraft could compete with it for speed and comfort. The Comet ended tragically when two crashes showed that its pressurised cabin cracked because of metal fatigue, but the concept of jet travel for passengers had been born. A new generation of long-range turbojet aircraft with high payloads followed.

The key to these was the Pratt and Whitney engines which had two separate rotating assemblies, the first to begin the build up of pressure in the air intake, the second to increase it to a high pressure. The next stage was to replace the first compressor with a large diameter fan which provided a greater air intake to be transformed into higher thrust by the high pressure compressor. Today, the turbofan jet engines have replaced the turbojets in all the wide-body aircraft such as the jumbo jets. They are economical in fuel consumption and quieter in operation than old-style jets.

The next advance belongs to the supersonic aircraft such as the Anglo-French Concorde and the Russian Tupolev Tu-144. There is also a good deal of research going into short take-off and landing (STOL) and vertical take-off and landing (VTOL) aircraft. A long-established VTOL aircraft is, of course, the helicopter, but its rotating blades cannot match conventional airframes for speed and overall efficiency. Planes that have special lifting jets or engines that swivel downwards to provide lift and then straighten up for level flight seem to be the answer. For quiet take-off from short landing strips, development is likely to take place in the design of wing shapes and high-ratio turbofan propulsion.

Hinged wings that move forward for maximum lift at take-off and sweep back for fast level flight are one suggested solution.

Airport Control

A good deal of modern technology has gone into airline control and landing systems. It is now possible for the landing of an aircraft to be taken over from the pilot by ground control. For this, automatic systems have been devised which have the advantage of making a landing safe in adverse conditions when the pilot cannot see. Much of the pilotage of aircraft throughout their journeys is nowadays aided by fully-automated systems. In this respect, the future of rocket-propulsion may become involved with earth transport. Rockets that carried men to the moon were abandoned after their job was done. Now, the establishment of manned earth satellites is leading to the development of shuttle rockets capable of landing back on earth. These may be entirely automated and remote-controlled from land bases. We may yet see intercontinental cargo-carrying rockets operating without any crew. This will be the fastest transport of the future. Among the slowest may be a revival of the airship for carrying heavy loads like huge electric transformers for short distances direct from factory to site.

The housewife of the future may do her shopping by computer link with shops.

Science and the Future

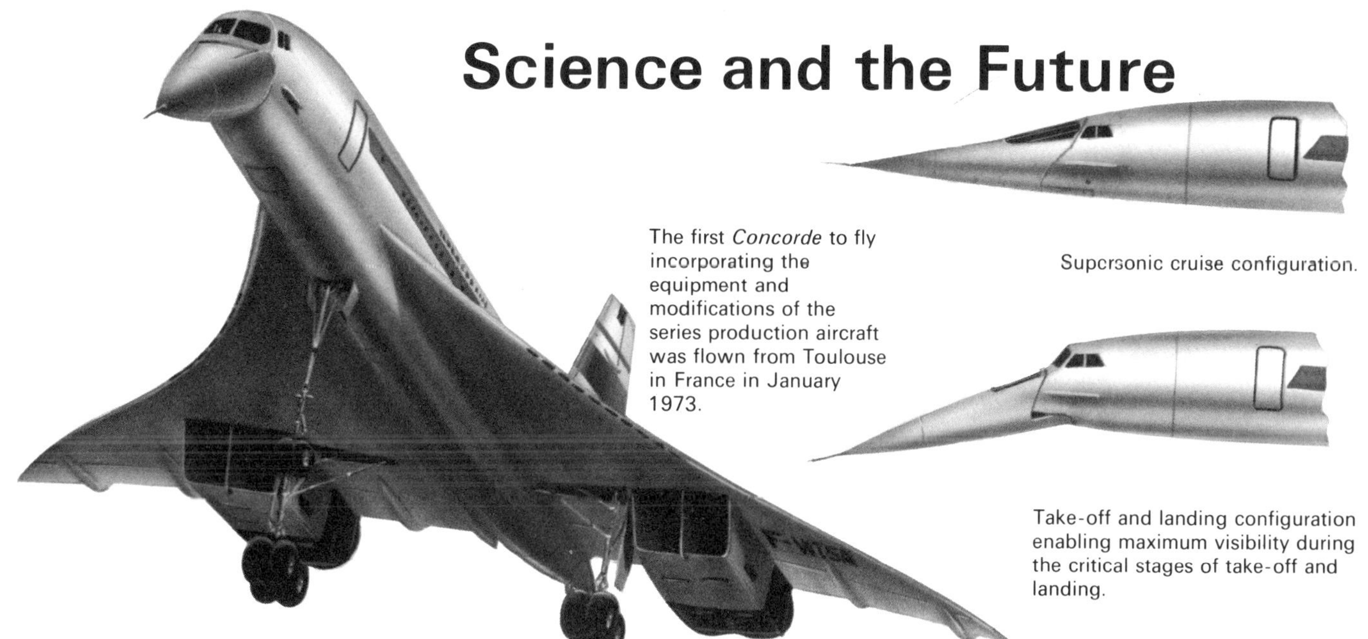

The first *Concorde* to fly incorporating the equipment and modifications of the series production aircraft was flown from Toulouse in France in January 1973.

Supersonic cruise configuration.

Take-off and landing configuration enabling maximum visibility during the critical stages of take-off and landing.

Power, machinery, transport—these are the keys to the good life in a modern technological society. Meanwhile, we continue to ask the questions man has asked from the beginning. How was the universe created? How did our earth evolve within it and bring forth life? Was all matter, all the stars in all the galaxies, packed closely together until, about ten thousand million years ago, there was a mighty explosion that sent it all whirling outwards into empty space? This is the Superdense or Big Bang Theory. Or does space itself have the property of creating matter? As the stars rush apart, are more stars created to take their place and maintain a balanced universe? This is the Steady State Theory.

What is a quasar, a star that, by all known methods of calculation, should be an immense distance away from us and yet appears so bright? Is it the bebinning of a new galaxy, giving off gigantic quantities of energy? What is a pulsar, a star that emits regular pulses of electromagnetic radiation? Is it a star at the end of its life composed almost entirely of neutrons bound closely by nuclear forces? Such a dense mass would spin at tremendous speed. Any activity at its surface would appear to send out pulses like the flashes from the rotating beam of a lighthouse.

Temperatures within a star like our sun are high enough for thermonuclear reaction to fuse the nuclei of hydrogen to form helium, but not to create the heavier elements. Yet space contains clouds of hydrogen mixed with the dust particles of heavier, non-gaseous elements. They are thought to have come from the kind of star called a supernova which can emit a thousand million times as much energy as the sun. A star runs out of hydrogen and shrinks. Internal pressure and temperature rise, fusing nuclei to form the heavier elements. Energy is absorbed, temperature falls and the star collapses. It spins faster and faster until this heavy material is flung off, exposing the hot interior and increasing the star's brilliance. When it has lost most of its matter, the small, bright, highly dense star remaining is called a white dwarf. Perhaps our sun had a companion star that became a supernova. The dust particles flung off it could have been trapped by the sun's gravity into a great whirling disc of heavy elements which, as they cooled, would be drawn together to form the planets in our solar system.

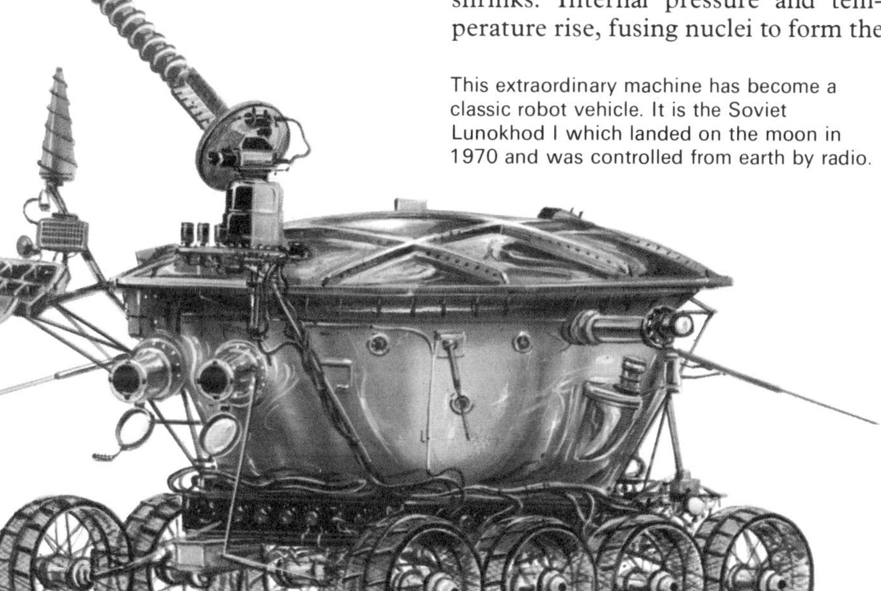

This extraordinary machine has become a classic robot vehicle. It is the Soviet Lunokhod I which landed on the moon in 1970 and was controlled from earth by radio.

The Creation of Life

The sun's ultraviolet radiation can build simple molecules like water, methane and ammonia into amino acids. This happened on the young earth. Amino acids were built up into proteins. The property of self-duplication turned some proteins into virus-like molecules from which living cells evolved. How did this happen and can it be duplicated in the laboratory? Will scientists soon be able to create life?

Like the ancients, the modern scientist looks outward to the stars to solve the riddles of the universe. He looks inward into the very heart of the atom whose secrets have not yet all been revealed. We have studied the relationship between matter and energy, but we have given only an interim report on our findings. As our story has shown, the study of science is open-ended. As scientists have done in the past, old concepts must be abandoned as new ones bring us closer to some ultimate truth. There is a challenge in this that has been nobly met in the past and gives promise of an even more exciting future.

Index